Text and Intertext in Medieval Arthurian Literature

Garland Reference Library of the Humanities
Volume 1997

Text and Intertext in Medieval Arthurian Literature

Edited by
Norris J. Lacy

Garland Publishing, Inc.
New York and London
1996

Library of Congress Cataloging-in-Publication Data

Text and intertext in medieval Arthurian literature / edited by Norris J. Lacy.
         p.   cm. — (Garland reference library of the humanities ; v. 1997)
      Papers presented at the triennial Congress of the International Arthurian
Society, which was held 1993 Bonn, Ger.
      Includes bibliographical references.
      ISBN 0-8153-2385-9 (alk. paper)
      1. Arthurian romances—History and criticism—Congresses.   2. Litera-
ture, Medieval—History and criticism—Congresses.   3. Intertextuality—
Congresses.   I. Lacy, Norris J.   II. International Arthurian Congress
(17th : 1993 : Bonn, Germany)   III. Series: Garland reference library of the
humanities ; vol. 1997.
PN685.T49   1996
809.1'3—dc20   96–2392
                                                                   CIP

Printed on acid-free, 250-year-life paper
Manufactured in the United States of America

Contents

Preface

The term "intertextuality" is still comparatively recent. Intertextuality the phenomenon, however, is as old as literature itself. And to medievalists in particular, it was a critical commonplace long before the term was coined: we have routinely recognized that, during the Middle Ages, texts consistently borrowed from one another and from the traditions they all shared. Those borrowings can take the form of thematic echoes, of the appropriation of characters and situations, and even of direct citation.

Former generations of medievalists recognized that phenomenon as readily as we and perhaps more so. However, it was too often the case that intertextual relationships were formerly taken as a sign of creative sterility, of a poverty of literary imagination, as if authors conveniently drew from a literary tradition and from a body of stock conventions because they lacked the ability to create "original" themes and structures. It is only in recent decades that we have properly understood what now seems so obvious: intertextual borrowing—the more accurate word would be "sharing"—is the inevitable and positive consequence of an esthetic that defined literary values in terms of participation in a tradition rather than idiosyncratic departure from it.

Arthurian romance is not unlike other genres or types in these regards, but the intertextual links among works are even more elaborate and pervasive than in most other literary forms. Arthurian characters, themes, and motifs are no respecters of textual boundaries, and thus each work connects with another and yet another, until it can reasonably be argued that Arthurian literature constitutes an enormous, overarching cycle, each part of which is intended to be read against a background of all others.

In 1993 the Triennial Congress of the International Arthurian Society (meeting in Bonn, Germany) had as one of its announced themes the intertextual dimensions of Arthurian literature. The treatment of intertextuality, however, was defined in a particular way: one of the emphases was to be "generic intertextuality," a term that (as Donald Maddox comments in his essay) retains a fundamental ambiguity, inviting us to discuss textual sharing either with other Arthurian compositions or between an Arthurian romance and a work belonging to another genre. The latter, which might be more accurately defined as "intergeneric intertextuality," was doubtless the intent of the conference organizers, but the ambiguity proved extraordinarily productive. The result was a remarkable variety of presentations, having as their common dimension a concern with the processes of intertextual composition—sometimes a matter of influence, always a question of sharing.

At one end of the spectrum, a good number of papers treated the specifically intergeneric links among works, and we offer several of those here, including two of the plenary addresses, a theoretical essay by Donald Maddox and a detailed consideration by Elspeth Kennedy of intergeneric relations among the *Lancelot-Grail* and other compositions. We also include essays on subjects as diverse as the possible Arthurian connections with a non-Arthurian Middle Dutch play, discussed by Bart Besamusca; a study of Dante and the Prose *Lancelot*, by Daniela Delcorno Branca; Edward D. Kennedy's evaluation of influences (Boccaccio and others) on the *Alliterative Morte Arthure;* and essays by Frank Brandsma and Thea Summerfield on the relationships between chronicles and romances.

A second group includes studies that concentrate on particular texts and consider their authors' use of material drawn from other genres and works. Barbara Sargent-Baur treats Geoffrey and Wace, identifying the ways the writers drew on generic distinctions and the ways readers responded to them. Michael Twomey defends the centrality of Morgain in *Sir Gawain and the Green Knight* by examining the narrative resources available to that author. Sara Sturm-Maddox explores the uses of eating scenes through a number of Arthurian texts; Anne Berthelot deals with the way several later texts react to (or, rather, *against*) Chrétien's presentation of the Grail; and Janina Traxler discusses the effects achieved by the Prose *Tristan* author through the juxtaposition of borrowed and invented material.

Finally, we offer several papers that are more restricted in scope. Katalin Halász studies the representation of time in the Prose *Tristan* (including the use of inter- or intratextual images to crystallize earlier sequences and juxtapose them with later ones). And Mary B. Speer focuses on the intertextual dimensions of a single work, examining the relationship of two manuscripts of the same text (*La Mort Artu*) in order to illustrate the processes of "abbreviation as rewriting."

"Intertextuality" is by now a heavily overworked term, perhaps to the point of being as irksome to some readers as it is accurate, helpful, and even indispensable. Whatever we think of the term—and I am not fond of it—the phenomenon is such a crucial element in medieval literary creation that we cannot neglect it without obscuring the very character of the literary artifact in the Middle Ages.

Yet, even if medievalists now recognize intertextual influences as the most fundamental of compositional procedures, we still have a great deal of work to do before we understand fully the bases and effects of textual sharing and appropriation. Until we do so entirely, if indeed that can ever be possible, studies such as those included in this volume will address a continuing and pressing need. We therefore trust that the variety and quality of these fourteen essays—both theoretical and practical, studies of both text and intertext—will assist medievalists in general and Arthurians in particular in elucidating some crucial elements of literary composition.

Norris J. Lacy
Washington University

Text and Intertext in Medieval Arthurian Literature

Generic Intertextuality in Arthurian Literature

The Specular Encounter

Donald Maddox

In dealing with the question of generic intertextuality in medieval literature, there is constant tension between works created according to the poetic canons of a remote age and the critical concepts one may bring to them from one's own era.[1] Medieval poets obviously did not adhere to a concept of genre like those entertained in the scholarly discussions of today, and of course they were totally free of any necessity to come to terms with the word "intertextuality." We should not view these tensions with suspicion or dismay, however, for they are not only inevitable but also vital to renewal of the potential for discovery. Thus it is that, here in the democratic republic of *Rezeptionsästhetik,* I acknowledge as a given the irreducible alterity of the Middle Ages, and it is with pleasure and after my own fashion that I broach the question of generic intertextuality, obviously without being able to explore here the full implications of so vast a notion.[2]

To begin, let us note that—at least in my view—this concept nurtures within itself a fundamental ambiguity: by "generic intertextuality," do we designate the intertextual relations within one genre or among several?[3] This conceptual indeterminacy will in fact allow me to address both possibilities: initially I will examine the profile of a motif that, by virtue of its frequent appearances in Arthurian romance, constitutes a powerful *generic intertextuality*. Then, the fact that this same motif also figures in a wide variety of non-Arthurian narrative texts will allow me to identify it as a type of *intergeneric textuality*. By situating the Arthurian intertextuality of the motif in relation to the intergeneric domain of its occurrences, I hope to reveal gradually some of its principal properties, to indicate the nature of its functions in the narrative economy, and to explore a few of its cultural and ideological implications.[4]

What, then, is this kind of intertextuality that, in my estimation, is at once generic and intergeneric? Among the salient properties of twelfth- and thirteenth-century French Arthurian literature, in verse as well as in prose, one that has always fascinated me most, by both the frequency and the variety of its occurrences, is the way in which a given protagonist—whether King Arthur himself or one of the illustrious knights in his entourage—suddenly becomes acutely aware of aspects of his own identity or his own past that are for him both extremely meaningful and exceedingly obscure. It is certainly not a question of an omniscient character, for whom the past holds no mystery, one who already knows from the outset virtually all that he will ever need to know concerning himself and his origins. On the contrary, the Arthurian hero about whom I am thinking is a profound enigma unto himself, and much of the fascination his subsequent development will hold for us revolves around the consequences of the liquidation within him of this cognitive deficit, of this lack of crucial knowledge.

Typically, the protagonist's illumination occurs when he meets another character through whom elements of this personal history are revealed. In most cases these are details of which he himself had been ignorant or which he had misunderstood. In certain cases, instead of meeting an interlocutor, the protagonist discovers a document, an inscription, or an iconic representation of the message that concerns him. Whatever the means by which the message may be transmitted, the basic comprehensive format of this type of encounter remains stable enough, although its discursive embellishments exhibit an astonishing variety.

For my part, it seems that these moments are all amplifications of one and the same motif. Since it is basically a question of the discovery of the self in the discourse or in the representation of the other, I propose to call this kind of phenomenon the motif of the specular encounter.[5]

Let us first examine one of the most arresting and dramatic amplifications of this motif in the entire medieval Arthurian corpus, the one concerning, at the very beginning of his reign, the young King Arthur, where he at last discovers his true identity in the revelations of Merlin. It will be recalled that, according to the Prose *Merlin,* Arthur grows up totally unaware of the identity of both his father and his mother. The marvel of his election to the vacant paternal throne comes about through the manifest will of the eternal Father, yet even at the moment of his coronation near the end of the romance, Arthur still does not know the name of his earthly father. To fill this lacuna, the Estense manuscript E39 of Modena and manuscript 4166 of Paris, Bibliothèque Nationale, each in its own way, supply a passage in which Arthur finally learns the identity of his parents and thus, at long last, his own.[6] Following the coronation Merlin reveals before the assembled barons that this new king is Arthur and that because he is the son of the late King Uther and of Ygerne, he is in fact the legitimate heir to the throne. Then, in a private conversation with Arthur, Merlin explains that the Round Table is symbolically associated both with the table of the Last Supper and with the Grail table, and he sums up the latter's long and eventful odyssey into the West, emphasizing that the future of the kingdom, as well as that of the Grail, will depend on the exaltation of the Round Table by a knight of surpassing merit.

We can see that this episode contributes to the material and cyclic unity of the pseudo-Robert de Boron prose trilogy: it marks the intersection of the story of Arthur's coming to power with the story of the Grail, creating a link from the *Joseph d'Arimathie* to the *Merlin* on the one hand, and to the Prose *Perceval* on the other, thus between the Arthurian kingdom's protohistory and its future. It is quite remarkable that the *conjointure* of the Grail's westward itinerary intersects in this manner with the Arthurian polity precisely at the moment of the latter's foundation. Merlin's disclosure is in fact a story with multiple layers: first there is a testimony to the legitimacy of king and kingdom, as prophesied two hundred years before; this is linked in turn with the origin, in an even more remote past, of the founding ethic of a spiritual kind of chivalry; finally, the allegory of the three tables unveils the profound link between earthly, temporal order and the universal *ordo*. But what is most notable here is that Merlin causes the new monarch to experience the passage from ignorance to knowledge, a "reflexive" recognition if you will, without the king himself being in any way the agent of this discovery. Before a mute and passive monarch, that which dissipates darkness, boldly laying bare the identity of the new ruler and the transhistorical dimension of his kingdom, is the revelation spoken by an omniscient interlocutor. As a specular encounter, Merlin's words place the young monarch before a mirror in which he finds himself situated at the crossroads of two courses, that of the kingdom and that of the holy vessel; as yet still a beautiful and promising effulgence, his own image rises up before him, projected against a cosmic background.

Instead of evoking that part of the principal intrigue that has already been recounted, reflexivity here creates a much deeper temporal palimpsest, identifying the self not only in relation to biological and genealogical contexts but also locating the reign of Arthur in relation to a much longer span of time, measured symbolically and temporally by the three tables. This first example of specular encounter makes of the motif a veritable keystone of

Arthurian intertextuality and demonstrates its capacity for uniting the most varied material. But it illustrates only a single type of usage, one in which the very *identity* of the addressee is at issue.

In a second variety of usage, already evident in the twelfth century, the identity of the main character is already well known, and the revelation instead highlights certain troubling elements of his recent past, a fate common to heroes in Chrétien de Troyes's romances. We know that Chrétien tends to organize the two major parts of his narrative around an intervening crisis,[7] thereby creating a highly significant relation between an unsatisfying initial development and a compensatory continuation. In Chrétien's works this comprehensive format, which I have discussed elsewhere as a textuality of crisis,[8] displays one salient characteristic that has not been noticed heretofore: the crisis that develops in the middle of the format is always organized around the motif of specular encounter. To fill the deficit of knowledge that occasions the protagonist's crisis, the narrative momentum pauses for a moment of illumination, constructing around an intersubjective core an encounter that dilates the hero's consciousness with indispensable information.

In three of the romances, Chrétien exploits the autoreflexive possibilities of the motif by confronting the protagonist with a retrospective devaluation of his previous behavior. In *Erec et Enide* the desperate monologue of Enide inadvertently ushers in Erec's crisis, holding up to him the mirror image of his own *recreantise* and thereby initiating a quest that will ultimately result in the couple's assumption of exemplary roles on behalf of a feudal world destabilized from within by social tensions.[9] In the *Chevalier au lion,* when Laudine's messenger informs Yvain that his wife has repudiated him for his failure to return to her by the appointed deadline, he sinks into madness and despair through a long crisis that brings him to the threshold of a new series of adventures leading to expiation and a higher order of achievement.[10] In the *Conte del Graal* Chrétien twice employs this motif to initiate a crisis: first, in the scene where the Hideous Damsel castigates Perceval at great length for his failures at the grail castle; then, when Guiromelant reveals to Gauvain that the inhabitants of the castle at the Roche de Canguin belong to his own lineage, thus imposing upon him a familial obligation of which he had previously been unaware.[11] In these romances the specularization of the hero causes him to take a decisive turn in his development, thus defining what might be termed a biographical specular encounter, a segment that leads to the establishment of a corrective relation between the future and the past of the message's addressee. It is through an analytical flashback that the devalued personal past reveals the negative situation occasioned by the hero's transgression or ignorance. During the crisis or ensuing from it, the realization of failure gradually gives way to the conceptualization of a compensatory course.[12]

Whereas in those three romances the motif serves to indicate the hero's negligence or error, its use in the *Chevalier de la charrete,* as in *Cligés,* is instead ludic, and in both cases it ultimately serves to exculpate the couple. In the *Charrete* the first of the two major segments of the romance is brought to completion by Lancelot's combat with Meleagant and his night of love with the Queen. The crisis erupts the next day when, in the presence of Lancelot, Meleagant presents his interpretation of the bloodstains on the Queen's bed. But this specular encounter is totally specious, for Meleagant, in accusing Keu and the Queen of adultery, communicates to the hero a completely erroneous version of the preceding night and thus ends up obscuring the truth of Lancelot's passion for Guinevere.[13] In *Cligés* the numerical center of the romance is punctuated by the oneiric specular encounter, not of the hero but of his paternal uncle and adversary, Alis, whom an illusory dream dupes into believing that he has actually consummated his marriage.[14] Thus, as in the *Charrete,* the motif provides the means to conceal the scandal concerning the couple and, thereby, to launch the second major segment of the plot.

Chrétien proves himself to be very skillful in exploiting the circumstantial virtualities that the motif holds without ever reducing it to a simple narrative peripeteia. Moreover, in his last romance, Chrétien sets the stage for the motif's use to disclose identity. Like the King Arthur of the prose *Merlin,* the young *naïf* who grows up in the Gaste Forest had never known his true identity or the name of his father. Perceval's cognitive awakening is in fact a gradual process, as he passes through a whole series of specular encounters: from his mother's *chastoiement* he learns the chivalric identity of his father and of his two older brothers, all victims of feudal conflicts (ll. 407–88); later, upon meeting his cousin, he discovers that he belongs to the lineage of the Fisher King (ll. 3422–690); finally, long after the Hideous Damsel's execrations, which mark both his crisis and the midpoint of his journey, the hermit, Perceval's uncle, finishes his initiation with a specular discourse, a mirror in which the hero can perceive himself in a genealogical as well as a theological context (ll. 6392–433). In thus combining the motif with explicitly lineal preoccupations, Chrétien gives special prominence to a formula that will prove to be a boon to many of his successors.

Thus, Renaut de Beaujeu develops *le Bel Inconnu* in accordance with the maximal dimensions of a textuality of crisis.[15] Moreover, he makes the numerical center of the poem the locus of a specular encounter. At that juncture the hero puts an end to the enchantments at the Gaste Cité by succeeding in the principal test, the serpent's kiss, or "Fier Baiser," whereupon he learns from an ethereal voice that his name is Guinglain and that he was borne by a fairy-mother, Blancemal, and fathered by Gauvain (ll. 3216–42).[16] This speculum places him at the confluence of a bifurcated genealogy, Arthurian on the agnatic side and matrilineally supernatural, as well as at the crossroads of otherworldly and feudal concerns that will, each in turn, leave him torn between the imperatives of love and duty.[17] The conflict resonates in the rest of the romance through two other specular encounters, first with Blonde Esmeree, the daughter of the King of Wales whom he had unwittingly liberated from her captivity in serpentine form by submitting to the kiss and whose discourse (ll. 3304–400) prefigures their marriage. The second involves the fairy-guardian who is in love with him, the Pucele aux Blances Mains: she tells him at length of how she had always manipulated circumstances to ensure his success and enjoins him to remain with her lest he lose her forever (ll. 4915–5016). This reiteration of the motif thus intensifies Guinglain's dilemma, clearly highlighting the conflict between the alluring attractions of the supernatural imaginary realm and the more sober exigencies of the feudal symbolic order.

We see then that Chrétien is not alone among his contemporaries in bringing the motif to the fore. As for the Tristanian heritage in verse, the female characters are more often in the role of receiver of the revelation. In the Oxford *Folie Tristan*,[18] for example, the motif is treated in a subtly ludic manner and undergoes a singular amplification: in this text of modest dimensions (966 lines), Iseut, a very skeptical narratee in the presence of a Tristan disguised as a madman, listens to her lover's long narration, as he recalls through successive episodic evocations all their past clandestine encounters.[19] While the specular encounter thus pervades virtually the entire text, the loquacious "madman's" nostalgic reminiscences effect a double *mise en abyme*: captured *en abyme,* the couple find themselves in Tristan's recollections of their previous encounters, while these reminiscences encapsulate, again *en abyme,* a substantial portion of the very romance that provides the inspiration for the *Folie Tristan*.[20]

In the thirteenth century the fortunes of the motif remain undiminished with the advent of the great prose romances. In the Prose *Lancelot,* for example, although Lancelot's adventurous itinerary is strewn with extraordinary encounters, our motif functions as a specular index of identity.[21] This occurs in quite systematic fashion, in a series of episodes set before a tomb—the site of reflexive revelations par excellence, be it through voices, visions, or inscriptions.[22] The first of these scenes that are both spectral and specular occurs at the cemetery of the Dolorous Guard where, in an episode modeled on the well-known analogue in Chrétien's *Charrete*, Lancelot raises the stone slab covering the tomb long ago reserved for him and discovers therein both the name of his father and his own (XXIVa, 32).[23] Later, at the Saint Cimetiere, he opens the tomb of his ancestor Galaad and thereby learns that he is a descendant of the guardians of the Grail (XXXVII, 32). However, this exaltation of the eponymous hero is followed by a relativization of his status, again by recourse to the motif: because he is not free of carnal sinfulness, Lancelot is informed that he must fail to open the tomb of Symeu, the nephew of Joseph of Arimathea, an exploit reserved exclusively for his son Galaad (XXXVII, 37–40). The question of his sinfulness is once again brought to his attention at the tomb of his ancestor Lancelot, and again by contrast to the exceptional purity of his prefigured son (XCIII, 1–23). On the other hand, having previously opened the tomb of Galehaut, Lancelot had attempted to venerate their deep chivalric bond by transferring his friend's remains to his own tomb at the Dolorous Guard (XLIX, 5–24).[24] This event in fact prepares an eventual confirmation of cyclic coherence: at the very end of *La Mort le roi Artu,* in the episode depicting Lancelot's burial in the tomb he will forever share with Galehaut, an archbishop recounts "the life of Lancelot and his end."[25] Thus, in the final episode of the cycle, which culminates in the symbolic immortalization of a chivalric bond, the late hero's entire *vita* becomes specularized, his own entombment giving rise to a mirroring of the cycle's center. Far from being confined to the Prose *Lancelot,* then, sepulchral specularity associated with the itinerary of the Queen's lover is a component of cyclic unity that extends to the conclusion of the entire *Lancelot-Graal* cycle.

Another theme often developed through a specular account in prose romance is that of the birth or childhood of the hero, as for example in two episodes of the *Roman de Perlesvaus.*[26] In one, Arthur arrives at Tintagel without realizing that it is the very place of his conception. When he asks the reason for the cave-in of the land around the castle, a priest explains that this occurred because it was here that King Arthur was conceived in sin, the adulterous father having murdered his rival before marrying the latter's widow (Branch IX, XXXII). After the fashion of Merlin's tale, this story, while attributing a royal and therefore legitimate origin to the king, nonetheless emphasizes a paternal transgression heretofore unknown to Arthur; this is one of several hints in the romance that are suggestive of the waning of his realm's brilliance against the background of a superior spiritual order. Later it is Gauvain who unknowingly arrives at the castle where he was born, and once again it is a priest who assumes the explanatory role, this time by interpreting wall paintings. From his detailed account Gauvain learns that his mother had sent him away following his birth in the hope that he might die and thus spare her the shame of a child conceived out of wedlock. Rescued by a benevolent knight who provided him with gold, silver, and a sealed letter attesting to his royal lineage, he was raised by a peasant; eventually he had reached Rome, where, thanks to the letter, the pope had recognized and nurtured him. He was eventually chosen to be emperor of Rome but had refused because of persistent murmurings about his origins, the truth of which had been withheld from him. In due course he had left Rome and become a world-renowned knight. Provided with this concise narration of his own biography, Gauvain, like Arthur, learns that he was born in sin, but this synopsis of his origins ultimately serves to exalt his image by affirming his doubly royal lineage, his Christian education, and the eventual marriage of his parents (Branch X, XXXIV). Here the motif satisfies an impulse apparent in the cyclicity of certain late *chansons de geste:* recounting the youth of a hero whose mature exploits are already well known.

These two instances highlight a detail that appears often in Arthurian occurrences of the motif in the thirteenth century: the purveyor of the revelation is an ecclesiastic. This figure frequently appears as an informant in *La Queste del saint Graal,*[27] where time and again the symbolism of objects and events and the covert meanings of adventures that befall knights-errant remain totally obscure—to the reader as well as to the knight who has just experienced them—until a venerable *preudomme* garbed in white arrives to elucidate them.[28] This proliferation of segments of internal gloss scattered intermittently throughout the romance creates reflexive relations between the literal details of an adventure and the ensuing explication of their significance in terms of a universe of religious allegory—a kind of typological diptych, as it were.[29] Thus, at the root of fundamental moral oppositions, such as that between Synagoga and Ecclesia, the Old Law and the New, we find that the order of events is juxtaposed with an explanation to the hero of their allegorical meanings, so that the fiction's literal, descriptive integument serves as vehicle for an incremental paratextuality whose substance is grounded in a perspective that is essentially theological. Recourse to this type of "exegetical" specular encounter in certain Arthurian texts of the thirteenth century would seem to attest to an awareness of the weakening of a sense of the transcendental signified and therefore to a desire to render it all the more explicit through reconfiguration of events in an allegorical mode. Such metadiscursive usage of the motif thus betrays an effort to reaffirm the efficacy, at once contemporaneous and transhistorical, of the Beyond.

In another usage of the motif, which is less frequent but equally significant, the monarch is obliged to confront unsettling political circumstances in his realm. In the Prose *Roman de Tristan,* for example, King March, unrecognized, questions his shepherds and not only hears the unfavorable opinions that are widely held about him, but especially becomes aware of the widespread admiration of Tristan.[30] In the Prose *Lancelot,* a *preudomme* upbraids Arthur in front of the court for his shameful failure to avenge the death of King Ban, his vassal.[31] Like the didactic *chastoiement,* earlier in the same work, of a youthful Lancelot by the Dame du Lac concerning the meaning of chivalry (XXIa, 7–19), the elucidations and chastisements addressed to the monarch and other major personages exploit the specular encounter's potential as a vehicle for explanation, commentary, and critique of political policies and institutions.

Many other examples of this motif could be cited from Arthurian texts, but this necessarily limited sampling already allows us to observe that in the context of twelfth- and thirteenth-century Arthurian romance, the specular encounter is a narrative component that serves numerous important functions. Among the instances considered thus far, we can recognize at least four spheres that are enriched by information provided by the specular encounter. The most limited of these is the biographical sphere, which concerns the protagonist's situation, his status, his previous behavior, and, in some instances, his very identity, especially in relation to a distinguished lineage. Next there is the political sphere, concerning in particular the kingdom of Arthur, its origins, and the successive stages of Arthurian civilization. A larger historical sphere extends back to the time of Christ and includes the story of the Grail, from Joseph of Arimathea to Galaad. Finally the motif evinces an ability to evoke the maximal temporal dimension, the eschatological sphere, which subsumes all of the preceding spheres. We can thus see that the chivalric and courtly instances of the motif are ultimately related to a mythico-theological function. In the course of the successive recyclings of the Arthurian matter, it is precisely through the perspective of the specular encounter that its most illustrious personages are eventually contextualized within the vast canvas of universal history.

THE INTERGENERIC DIMENSION

Although the preceding overview allows us to affirm that, in the generic *mouvance* of Arthurian romance, the specular encounter is indeed part of a dense network of intertextual relations lying within a varied typology of usages, we should not overlook the fact that medieval intertextuality does not always respect the separate categories into which we tend to classify medieval narrative genres. Arthurian texts share the same properties with other varieties of narrative literature and often draw upon the same spheres of feudal and courtly culture. In order to avoid any artificial and unjustified cloistering of Arthurian literature, the motif requires scrutiny in relation to what I propose to call "intergeneric textuality."[32]

Only a handful of examples can be evoked rapidly here in order to provide some idea of the motif's intergeneric profile.[33] Consider first an occurrence from a hagiographic text: the numerous Old French versions of the *Vie de Saint Eustache* depict the dramatic conversion of Placidas, the leader of the Emperor Trajan's armies; while hunting, he encounters a stag speaking in the voice of Christ. The hunter finds himself in the proleptic discourse of his "prey," which in prescribing the way to saintliness places him in the eschatological context of universal history.[34] The specular encounter combines with the motif of the speaking animal in other texts, a notable example from brief narrative being Marie de France's *Guigemar*.[35] In this instance a hind curses the hunter who has mortally wounded it (ll. 106–22), specifying that Guigemar, heretofore indifferent to amorous involvement, must suffer until he finds a woman who will reciprocate his love and thus heal him; this injunction ushers in his voyage to a countervailing domain where he will find his feminine, reflexive counterpart. Still in the context of Celtic matter, in the anonymous lay *Tydorel* the motif undergoes a remarkable amplification. Like Perceval, Tydorel learns the identity of his father from the meticulous explanation of the past given him by his mother, whose account comprises nearly 20 percent of the entire poem.[36] Among prominent instances of the motif in the *chansons de geste*, in the Oxford version of the *Chanson de Roland* it is used systematically as an oneiric element: Charlemagne's four proleptic dreams encapsulate *en abyme* the four principal segments of the entire poem and also allow the audience to foresee the course of future events.[37] In *Ami et Amile*[38] an angel in the role of divine emissary threatens Ami with the scourge of leprosy should he perjure himself to save his friend and alter-ego, Amile. In the second half of the poem, his transgression will eventually be redeemed by Amile, whose sacrifice brings about the miraculous healing of his friend. Situated in the center of the poem (ll. 1812–20), the specular encounter with the angel conjoins the two major segments of the story, creating a symmetrical diptych of exemplary self-denial and friendship as an absolute reciprocity.[39] In another type of usage that has many antecedents in antiquity, the motif serves as the nucleus of an episode of recognition resulting in the reunion of family members separated long before, as in *Guillaume d'Angleterre* and *La Fille du comte de Pontieu,* the latter being among the numerous texts to present a specular encounter involving a female protagonist.[40]

The motif also prospered in other medieval literatures, one of the most remarkable examples being Dante's use of it in the *Commedia,* a text in which the specular encounter once again appears at the center of a cosmic panorama within a vast textuality of crisis. From the start the poem unfolds as a pilgrimage engaged by the poet-persona in the very midst of life ("Nel mezzo del cammin di nostra vita / mi ritrovai per una selva oscura," *Inferno* I, 1–2).[41] Thus begins a pseudoautobiographical odyssey organized in bipartite fashion around a central crisis. The entire cosmos is represented in this visionary journey, the investment of the eschatological scheme being divided into three parts, each containing thirty-three cantos. The symbolic and ethical disjunction between the *Inferno* and the *Paradiso* is mediated by the *Purgatorio,*[42] whose seven central cantos (XIV–XX, the center both of the *Purgatorio* and of the *Commedia* as a whole) emphasize, according to Charles S. Singleton, a "conversion" of orientation away from the material and the worldly.[43] The poet's illumination with regard to a reality of a higher order is crystallized by his specular encounter with the spirit of Beatrice, who during her lifetime was the object of Dante's love. Precisely at this highly significant turning point, Beatrice replaces Virgil and the classical poets as Dante's guide: "Io mi rivolsi'n dietro allora tutto / a' miei poeti . . . poi a la bella donna torna' il viso" (*Purgatorio,* XXVIII, 145–46; 148).[44] In recalling for the poet certain moments of his past, Beatrice relativizes human desire in relation to a sublime, ethereal love, which the remainder of their journey together will emphasize. Here the motif, the pivotal point of the entire poem, helps to orient the couple's imminent ascension toward *Paradiso.*[45]

POETIC AND CULTURAL CONSIDERATIONS

Examples of what we have identified here as the motif of specular encounter could be adduced from a wide variety of narratives from other periods. It is the frequency with which the motif appears in the foreground of many medieval texts that leads to inquiry concerning possible reasons why it so often came to prominence in these works. The role of revelation, which is the principal narrative function of the motif in almost all of its instances, would seem to be of considerable importance in this regard, in view of the fact that during the many centuries in which a theological conceptualization of universal history was predominant, revelation enjoyed considerable prestige as a reliable cognitive modality. The respect accorded revelation in medieval texts is clearly of long duration and in some cases harks back to archaic origins, a case in point being the faunal figuration of Christ in the *Vie de Saint Eustache,* which likely emanates from an eighth-century anti-iconoclastic prototype.[46] More generally, in countless biblical and hagiographic stories, revelation is the keystone of a major turning point centered in a protagonist, whereas numerous instances of the specular motif in epic and romance make angelic voices, prophecies, miracles, and eremetic commentaries the vehicles of the revelation, thus communicating a strong connotation of the absolute veracity of a transcendentally ordained message.

Indeed, in its most characteristic occurrences, the motif is crucial to the operations of a veridictory modality, veridiction being the process by which the cognitive dimension of discourse constructs and signifies the "true" as a discourse-intrinsic condition.[47] An early theoretician of this phenomenon was Aristotle, whose concept of *anagnorisis* in the *Poetics*—that moment of tragic recognition in which truth imposes its ineluctability on the consciousness of the tragic character—is certainly akin to the concept of specular encounter in that both involve a punctual and decisive illumination of the protagonist. The principal *anagnorisis* in Sophocles's *Oedipus Rex* clearly has affinities with our motif. This rapprochement nonetheless neglects certain poetic and cultural particularities in important medieval instances of specular encounter: in addition to serving as an instrument of veridiction concerning the truth of a particular situation or set of circumstances, medieval incarnations of the motif not uncommonly serve also to discriminate between the two extremities of a bipolar disjunction. Like early French epic texts that highlight the polemical confrontation between two religious ideologies, many hagiographic narratives, religious plays, and secular romances informed by religious allegory also display a disjunctive polemicity (e.g., heaven/hell; Christian/pagan; Synagoga/Ecclesia; virtues/vices).[48]

Elsewhere, in many courtly romances and brief narratives for example, the terms of the disjunction are far less clear-cut and often involve an opposition of a negatively valorized course of action or subjective state and its positive counterpart. Whatever the nature and degree of the opposition, however, in medieval occurrences of the specular motif the content of the revelation is of relatively little consequence to the auditor/reader, to whom it is in most (though certainly not all) instances already well known. The full weight of the revelation's modification of the cognitive dimension is brought to bear through internal focalization, within the subjective world of the addressee of the message, while the remainder of the story emphasizes the profound consequences brought about by this subjective modification. Moreover, unlike the tragic, dysphoric finality of *anagnorisis,* medieval specular veridiction consistently occurs at an intermediary juncture, where it serves as the catalyst of a new narrative process that typically corrects or compensates for some earlier insufficiency and thus moves toward a euphoric culmination.[49] In sum, to the extent that the motif characteristi-

cally serves in medieval narratives as a primary locus for coordinating revelation, conversion, and the adumbration of meliorative processes, the
specular encounter suggests its cultural affinities with specifically medieval
modes of conceptualization and depiction of exemplary intrigues, whereby
a crisis bringing new cognitive awareness is located in the midst of representations of subjective experience. While the dominance of such modes may
indeed be traced back to influential ecclesiastical implementations, the usages of our motif in vernacular literature attest to the adaptability of persistent formal modes to a remarkably wide variety of content.

As for the purveyors of truths, or informants, this role may be invested
with a whole gamut of characters, though one also finds some synecdoches—
such as the sepulchral voice in the Prose *Lancelot* (XXXVII, 37–40)—or even
simply, on the margins of the motif, certain anonymous messages. As we have
seen, Lancelot manages to reconstitute an entire familial and lineal heritage
from the miraculous voices and funerary inscriptions that punctuate his adventures. Elsewhere the specular message works in conjunction with anthro-
pomorphic iconographic representations such as the murals in *Perlesvaus* and
La Mort le roi Artu, or the ancestral statue containing its own biographical
gloss in the *Roman de Mélusine.*[50] Whatever the medium, the message always creates a complex game of mirrors within the fiction. While the flashback, or analepsis, often revolves around the narratee's lineage and may refer back to a very remote past, the prolepsis anticipates the fiction's futurity,
particularly as it concerns the narratee, whose image, as it takes shape before him, is projected onto a temporal horizon of unsuspected proportions.

While these tendencies remain apparent into the later French Middle
Ages, the specular encounter is also sometimes implemented in a different
spirit, beginning with Chrétien, who manifests this attitude already in *Cligés*
and again in our example taken from the *Charrete.* While keeping the reve-
latory function, this transgressive or ludic modality follows the precarious
itinerary of reasoning. In contrast with the relative prestige enjoyed by revelation and intuition in medieval literature, reasoning is accorded an ambivalent status: man's rational faculty exalts him above all other creatures but
also leaves him vulnerable to error. Yet this presents the possibility, occasionally exploited to ironic or humorous ends, for investing the specular
encounter with reasoning that proves to be specious and speakers who,
like Meleagant (*Charrete,* ll. 4737 ff.), become entangled in their own
paralogisms. Thus, in a famous episode in Béroul's *Roman de Tristan,* after
King Mark has visited the sleeping lovers in their forest bower, Iseut listens
to Tristan's long—and utterly erroneous—analysis of why Mark left without waking them.[51] This play with epistemic and veridictory modalities be-

gins in the twelfth century shortly after the reconstitution of the full *Organon* of Aristotle and is sometimes especially suggestive of the last of these treatises, the *Sophistical Refutations*, which takes up varieties of defective reasoning in ways prefigurative of certain episodes in verse romances.[52] To the extent that the Aristotelian *Logica Nova* prompted narrative poets to amplify dialectical topics and to construct fictional cases similar to those more formally analyzed in logical treatises, the specular encounter provided them a propitious locus for the elaboration of such material.

SPECULARITY AND IDENTITY

This quite general distinction between two ways in which the motif is used, one for affirmative revelations, the other for transgressive play with the conventions of revelation, demonstrates the motif's remarkable elasticity and adaptability, which is no doubt also what accounts for its longevity as a prominent component in a wide range of medieval narratives. However, given the considerable variety of ways in which the specular motif is used in medieval texts, a full treatment of the question of cultural values evident in such instances will require the dimensions of the longer study in preparation. To conclude let me therefore offer only a few observations concerning the most frequently used variety in the context of Arthurian literature, which I shall call the identitary type—borrowing a term from the realm of culture studies—since it captures the motif's use as a device for the disclosure or for the clarification of the addressee's identity.

In this type of usage, the motif frequently serves ends reminiscent of those fulfilled by what Freud called "family romance," whereby the subject, whether a child or the analyst's client, nurtures the fantasy of an exalted parent or family in order to compensate for what is felt to be the inadequacy of real-world counterparts.[53] Identitary usage of the motif anchors a fiction that would fulfill the kind of wish harbored in such a fantasy: the protagonist, heretofore unaware of his true identity, learns from an informant that he is the offspring of a distinguished personage, or that he belongs to a venerable and prestigious lineage or is related to an illustrious, even supernatural ascendant. The hero thus gains access to a family history that had until then eluded him, and this discovery invariably modifies his subsequent orientation and conduct, often enhancing his power and esteem or affirming a positive correlation between degree of nobility and longevity of a lineage. In some cases the revelation concerns a deceased father or an ancestor whose example redefines the hero's mission. For example in *Tydorel, Le Bel Inconnu,* and the previously cited examples from the Prose *Lancelot,* the disclosure concerns the father or an agnatic line, ascending on the paternal side; in others, a notable matrilineal background is at issue, as in the *Conte del Graal*. In the *Roman de Mélusine* there are in fact two principal identitary specular encounters, one agnatic, in which Mélusine narrates to her husband Raymondin the legendary exploits of his father, Hervé de Léon; the other matrilineal, in which Geoffrey, the son of Mélusine and Raymondin, discovers both the tomb of Mélusine's father, Elinas d'Albanie, and a written account of the latter's marriage to the fairy Présine.[54] Together these two episodes reconstruct the entire protohistory of the main intrigue and depict the origins of the bilateral chronicle, both feudal and *féerique,* of the Lusignan dynasty.

It was a cultural anthropologist who, some thirty years ago, came close to identifying the mechanism of the identitary specular encounter in his study of the medieval romances of the Grail. Claude Lévi-Strauss posited a "Percevalian myth," based on the theme of "interrupted communication,"[55] asserting that in certain Grail romances from Chrétien's *Conte del Graal* onward, the Grail hero's genealogical background long remains an enigma to him, until the moment he finally succeeds in reestablishing communication with his forbears, the guardians of the Grail.[56] Lévi-Strauss did not suggest, however, that the questions that the Percevalian hero must ask are precisely those destined to provoke a specular narrative revealing the familial connection between the hero and the Grail family. Moreover, he did not take account of the fact that this type of motif far exceeds the limits of Grail literature, moving extensively into the much larger context of feudal and courtly narrative in general, from which a few examples have been discussed here.[57]

Yet can we assume that the Percevalian specular encounter in Chrétien's unfinished romance was the principal model for all subsequent "identitary" specular encounters in later Arthurian romances, or that it was what provided the primary impetus for similar episodes in a wide range of later non-Grail romances? Such an assumption seems quite unlikely in view of the fact that similar episodes in brief narratives based on Celtic matter, such as *Tyolet* and *Tydorel,* remind us that the motif's own genealogy is a long and venerable one. It also feeds back into widely divergent traditions: Chrétien's last work is not the first major Old French verse romance to use the specular encounter to construct a genealogical infratext. In an equally seminal non-Arthurian work that predates the *Conte del Graal* by several years, a hero discovers, thanks to his specular encounter with his long-dead father, that he is destined to fulfill a lineally ordained mission of the highest collective significance. I refer, of course, to the *Roman d'Énéas,* where the eponymous hero, confronted by the paternal shade of his father Anchises, learns of his future role as founder of a Latin empire, successor to the venerable House of Troy.[58] Aeneas's catabasis in Book Six of Virgil's *Aeneid* thus provides, rather early in the development of medieval courtly narrative literature, a fully mature model of the identitary specular encounter in service to genealogical and dynastic designs.

For more than two centuries, then, between the *Roman d'Énéas* and the *Roman de Mélusine* (1393), there developed a sizable corpus of courtly texts that gave special prominence to the specular encounter as a means for the disclosure of matters pertaining to identity, lineage, and genealogy. Whether it addressed matters of concern to nobility or monarchy, this particular usage of the motif would seem to be well suited to express the crisis of consciousness in the feudal world, which, by the end of the twelfth century, was caught up in an accelerated and disquieting state of transition. Georges Duby has examined important examples of how, even before the beginning of the twelfth century, the feudal nobility, experiencing considerable growth and proliferation as well as an emergent sense of self-consciousness as a class, shows signs of a desire to flaunt a distinguished genealogy, in some cases constructing a line tracing back to an illustrious, albeit wholly fictitious, founder.[59] Something other than mere antiquarian curiosity or family pride was at the root of such retrospective fictionalization; it was a matter of putting the past into the service of the present, by revealing one's identity within the context of a long and venerable lineage whose antiquity would theoretically help to provide a positive sanction for juridical prerogatives. The past might thus become capable of conditioning and guaranteeing the future of a class that was in fact to become increasingly vulnerable to marginalization and financial insolvency. As regards the motif's reflexive representation of the feudal monarch, one finds a similar emphasis on maintaining a sense of genealogical continuity, as in Merlin's revelation of Arthur's identity, or on providing guidance for the reconsolidation of political power in harmony with a retrospective view of institutional stability, as in various instances in the Prose *Lancelot*.

It seems significant that in many occurrences—far more, in fact, than in those few associated with "interrupted communication" in Grail narratives—the identitary use of the motif serves to restore an awareness of lineage previously obscured by some type of social calamity that had apparently occasioned a total break in consciousness of links between one or more generations. For Lancelot and Raymondin, just as for Énéas and Perceval, loss of contact with an antecedent order is due to turbulent events born of a political struggle. If we may view this specialized use of the motif as a literary, imaginary means of supplementing what were sensed or experienced as harsh deficits in the sociocultural sphere, its repeated occurrences to mend temporal discontinuities in noble families as well as in feudal institutions suggests that the perennial vulnerability of memory and a lack of contact with a lineal or a political heritage handed down from a venerable past were not uncommonly felt with particular acuity, either potentially or in fact. If this was indeed the case, then the longevity of this particular usage of the motif might be a symptom of sporadic and intermittent collective anxieties concerning genealogical memory and continuity in the most ambitious, yet also the most fragile, social sectors. Since the pertinent observations of the late Erich Köhler,[60] others have discussed ways in which the political and economic marginalization of feudal nobility remains palpable in literary and historiographic works, whether in representations of the nefarious effects of this marginalization or in the elaboration of compensatory fictions designed to strengthen power and privilege.[61] The microfictional supplement provided by the specular encounter as a bearer—whether from afar, long ago, or even from the beyond—of concise oral archives of empowerment clearly bears scrutiny along those lines of inquiry.

In these intensely revealing segments, the recovery of knowledge concerning forebears is seldom an end in itself, however. To echo Braudel, if the past might serve to explain the present, the present may at times also elucidate or redeem the past.[62] Closely associated with the disclosure or reaffirmation of the self's ties to a significant past is an implicit mandate for individual initiative toward some type of social reanimation or renewal. Having limned the traits of the absent father or the exemplary ancestor, the specular message seldom prescribes the addressee's mere emulation of an antecedent model, but instead points the way toward his eventual creation of unique and optimal circumstances, often superior to those antecedent to an interruption of genealogical awareness or to those evoked in terms of the deeds of an illustrious forebear. Accordingly, the protagonist who heeds the specular message typically comes, in due course, to a higher order of achievement, one more positively valorized than any of those revealed as part of the legacy of an ascendant.[63] This makes the specular encounter with aspects of identity a crucial accessory to the meliorative design of the host narrative and thus would invite consideration of the motif's role as a component of a fiction with distinctly utopian tendencies.

Thus what I have here briefly studied as the motif of specular encounter would eventually sustain rapprochement with many contemporaneous sociocultural tendencies, both among the numerous mentalities that grapple with the diversifications and disaggregations taking place within late feudal culture, and in literary works through which these tensions and conflicts come into full prominence. From the middle of the twelfth century onward, the specular encounter used as a purveyor of matters relating to identity would seem to provide one fundamental paradigm of feudal and courtly fiction, particularly within the *mouvance* of Arthurian romance. As the anchor of fictions with potential heuristic value within the context of their initial reception, the motif allowed amplifications predicated on its format to probe sensitive issues harboring collective anxieties and, if only on an imaginary scale, to mediate deep-seated conflicts arising therefrom, so that the perception of selfhood in the mirror of the past might provide reliable guidance for engaging the troubling uncertainties of an indeterminate future.

NOTES

1. This essay was translated from the French by David S. King.

2. Be it noted that generic intertextuality is not a notion of my own devising. It was apparently conceived by the central committee of the International Arthurian Society, and subsequently ratified at a general assembly of the Society, as one of the topics of the Society's Seventeenth International Congress, held in Bonn in July, 1993. In my plenary paper, of which this is a revised translation from the French original, I was addressing the topic "sur commande," so to speak.

3. The intertextual properties of medieval French Arthurian literature are explored by Matilda Tomaryn Bruckner, "Intertextuality," in *The Legacy of Chrétien de Troyes,* ed. Norris J. Lacy, Douglas Kelly, and Keith Busby, 2 vols. (Amsterdam: Rodopi, 1987–88), I, 224–65. See also Paul Zumthor, "Intertextualité et mouvance," *Littérature,* 41 (1981), 8–16, and the essays in *Romance: Generic Transformation from Chrétien de Troyes to Cervantes,* ed. Kevin Brownlee and Marina Scordilis Brownlee (Hanover, New Hampshire: University Press of New England, 1985).

4. Only one aspect of the motif's medieval literary fortunes can be profiled briefly in this essay. A study currently in preparation—one that goes well beyond the sphere of Arthurian literature—will examine these issues more fully and with regard to a much larger corpus of medieval narrative texts.

5. This element's properties as a motif will be taken up in the aforementioned study (see n. 4).

6. For both versions of this episode, see the appendix to Robert de Boron, *Merlin, roman du XIIIe siècle,* ed. Alexandre Micha (Geneva: Droz, 1979), pp. 292–302, and, idem, *Étude sur le Merlin de Robert de Boron* (Geneva: Droz, 1980).

7. William W. Ryding, *Structure in Medieval Narrative* (The Hague: Mouton, 1971); Donald Maddox, "Trois sur deux: Théories de bipartition et de tripartition des œuvres de Chrétien," *Œuvres et critiques,* 5 (1981), 91–102.

8. Donald Maddox, *The Arthurian Romances of Chrétien de Troyes: Once and Future Fictions* (Cambridge, Massachusetts: Cambridge University Press, 1991), pp. 16–18 and passim; idem, "Medieval Textualities and Intergeneric Form," *L'Esprit Créateur,* 33 (1993), 40–50.

9. Chrétien de Troyes, *Erec et Enide,* ed. Mario Roques (Paris: Champion, 1963), ll. 2492–571.

10. Chrétien de Troyes, *Le Chevalier au lion (Yvain),* ed. Mario Roques (Paris: Champion, 1965), ll. 2707–75.

11. Chrétien de Troyes, *Le Roman de Perceval, ou le conte du Graal,* ed. William Roach (Geneva: Droz, 1959), Perceval: ll. 4646–83; Gauvain: ll. 8560–614.

12. See also Donald Maddox, "The Awakening, a Key Motif in Chrétien's Romances," in *The Sower and His Seed: Essays on Chrétien de Troyes,* ed. Rupert T. Pickens (Lexington: French Forum, 1983), pp. 33–51.

13. Chrétien de Troyes, *Le Chevalier de la charrete,* ed. Mario Roques (Paris: Champion, 1970), ll. 4737–984.

14. Chrétien de Troyes, *Cligés*, ed. Alexandre Micha (Paris: Champion, 1957), ll. 3309–30.

15. The episodes on either side of the crisis create a quasi-chiastic configuration. See Jeanne Lods, "'Le Baiser de la reine et le cri de la fée': Étude structurale du *Bel Inconnu* de Renaut de Beaujeu," in *Mélanges de langue et littérature françaises du Moyen Age, offerts à Pierre Jonin* (Aix-en-Provence: CUERMA, 1979), pp. 413–26. On reminiscences of Chrétien's works, see William H. Schofield, *Studies on "Li beaus Desconus"* (Cambridge, Massachusetts: Harvard University Press, 1895).

16. Renaut de Beaujeu, *Le Bel Inconnu, roman d'aventures* (Paris: Champion, 1929). At the midpoint, l. 3133, "Hom ne vit onques sa parelle" ["Nothing like it was ever seen"], the hero is confronted by the redoubtable *wivre*, the monster to whom he administers the requisite embrace, the "Fier Baisier" (l. 3186), thus ending the castle's enchantment.

17. See Laurence Harf-Lancner, *Les Fées au moyen âge: Morgane et Mélusine; La naissance des fées* (Paris: Champion, 1984), pp. 331–38.

18. *La Folie Tristan d'Oxford*, ed. Ernest Hoepffner (Strasbourg: University of Strasbourg, 1943).

19. I addressed this matter in "Etiologies and Genealogies: The Quest for the Specular Story," an unpublished paper presented at the Fifth Congress of the International Courtly Literature Society, Dalfsen, The Netherlands, August 11, 1986, and subsequently in a graduate seminar at the University of Massachusetts, Amherst, in 1992.

20. On reflexivity in this text, see also Jacqueline T. Schaefer, "Specularity in the Mediaeval *Folie Tristan* Poems, or Madness as Metadiscourse," *Neophilologus*, 77 (1993), 355–68; and Matilda Tomaryn Bruckner, *Shaping Romance: Interpretation, Truth, and Closure in Twelfth-Century French Fictions* (Philadelphia: University of Pennsylvania Press, 1993), p. 28.

21. On the question of the identity theme in the prose *Lancelot* and other contemporaneous texts, see Elspeth Kennedy, *Lancelot and the Grail: A Study of the Prose Lancelot* (Oxford: Clarendon, 1986), pp. 10–48.

22. See also Daniel Poirion, "La Douloureuse Garde," in *Approches du Lancelot en prose*, ed. Jean Dufournet (Paris: Larousse, 1984), pp. 25–48; and Charles Méla, *La Reine et le graal: La conjointure dans les romans du graal, de Chrétien de Troyes au Livre de Lancelot* (Paris: Seuil, 1984), pp. 385–86.

23. *Lancelot, roman en prose du XIIIe siècle*, ed. Alexandre Micha, 9 vols. (Geneva: Droz, 1978–83). References in parentheses are to this edition; roman numerals indicate chapters; arabic numerals designate numbered divisions within chapters.

24. Cf. Christiane Marchello-Nizia, "Amour courtois, société masculine, et figures du pouvoir," *Annales: Économies, Sociétés, Civilisations*, 36 (1981), pp. 969–82, esp. 974–77.

25. *La Mort le roi Artu, roman du XIIIe siècle*, ed. Jean Frappier (Geneva: Droz, 1964), p. 263.

26. *Le Haut Livre du graal: Perlesvaus*, ed. William A. Nitze and T. Atkinson Jenkins, 2 vols. (Chicago: University of Chicago Press, 1932–37).

27. *La Queste del saint Graal*, ed. Albert Pauphilet (Paris: Champion, 1923).

28. This aspect of the text is frequently discussed by scholars. See, for example, Jean Frappier, "Le Graal et la chevalerie," *Romania*, 75 (1954), 165–201; Tzvetan Todorov, "La Quête du récit: le graal," in *Poétique de la prose* (Paris: Seuil, 1971), pp. 129–50; Emmanuèle Baumgartner, *L'Arbre et le pain: Essai sur la Queste del saint graal* (Paris: SEDES, 1981); Nancy Regalado, "'La Chevalerie celestiel': Spiritual Transformations of Secular Romance in *La Queste del saint graal*," in Brownlee and Brownlee, eds., *Romance*, pp. 91–113. On reflexivity: Laurence N. de Looze, "A Story of Interpretations: The *Queste del saint graal* as Metaliterature," *Romanic Review*, 76 (1985), 129–47.

29. See for example the succession of episodes in which Perceval learns that in what has just befallen him his spiritual mettle was being tested, pp. 91–115; these explanations after the fact together comprise an initiatory itinerary.

30. *Le Roman de Tristan en prose,* ed. Philippe Ménard (Geneva: Droz, 1987), I, 269–72.

31. *Lancelot do lac: The Non-Cyclic Old French Prose Romance,* ed. Elspeth Kennedy (Oxford: Clarendon, 1980), p. 54, ll. 11–34. See also, after the episode of the false Guinevere, the hermit's castigation of Arthur: "tu es li plus viels foimentie del monde et li plus viels pechieres et foimentie et escommuniés et traîtres. La fus tu desloials ou tu guerpesis ta feme espose par une autre que tu tiens contre Dieu et contre raison, et de ce fus tu foimentie que tu li fausas la foi que tu li avoies creanté en Sainte Iglise, quant tu la feis jugier a destruire; et por ce que tu t'en partis desloialment sans le congié de Sainte Iglise es tu escommuniés, ne biens ne te porroit pas avenir tant com tu soies en tel point" ("you are the world's master perjurer, sinner, excommunicant, and traitor, who unlawfully left your spouse for another, whom you hold against the will of God and unreasonably; for this are you a perjurer, for you betrayed the faith of your betrothal in Holy Church when you ordered her execution. And because you made this severance without the sanction of Holy Church you are excommunicated and nothing of any good will befall you as long as you remain in this state," Micha edition, IX, 3).

32. See also the recent collection of articles in *Intergenres: Intergeneric Perspectives on Medieval French Literature,* ed. Sara Sturm-Maddox and Donald Maddox, *L'Esprit Créateur,* 33 (1993), comprised of the papers from a colloquium on the intergeneric in medieval French literature, held at the University of Massachusetts, Amherst, in November 1990.

33. Fuller treatment will be given this issue in the separate study now in preparation, as it obviously exceeds the scope of this article.

34. *La Vie de saint Eustace, version en prose française du XIIIe siècle,* ed. Jessie Murray (Paris: Champion, 1929), pp. 6–8; 10–13.

35. Marie de France, *Lais,* ed. Jean Rychner (Paris: Champion, 1971), ll. 76–122.

36. Prudence Mary O'Hara Tobin, *Les Lais anonymes des XIIe et XIIIe siècles* (Geneva: Droz, 1976), *Tydorel,* pp. 207–26.

37. See laisses 56, 57, 185, 186.

38. *Ami et Amile, chanson de geste,* ed. Peter F. Dembowski (Paris: Champion, 1987).

39. On reflexive aspects of this work, see also Cesare Segre, "Due casi di 'gemelli' per amicizia: Contributo alla definizione del *motivo,*" in *Notizie dalla crisi: Dove va la critica letteraria?* (Torino: Einaudi, 1993), pp. 227–37; and Donald Maddox, "Medieval Textualities," pp. 42–43.

40. Chrétien de Troyes, *Guillaume d'Angleterre,* ed. Maurice Wilmotte (Paris: Champion, 1962), ll. 2636–3281; *La Fille du comte de Pontieu,* ed. Clovis Brunel (Paris: Champion, 1926), pp. 25–34. Feminine addressees of specular messages will be considered in the longer study.

41. Dante Alighieri, *The Divine Comedy,* ed. C.S. Singleton (Princeton: Princeton University Press), Vol. I, *Inferno* (1970); Vol. II, *Purgatorio* (1973).

42. From the twelfth century, Purgatory was conceptualized as a segment of crisis and axiological transition between two radically opposed orders. See Jacques Le Goff, *La Naissance du purgatoire* (Paris: Gallimard, 1981).

43. Charles S. Singleton, "The Poet's Number at the Center," in *Essays in Numerical Criticism of Medieval Literature,* ed. Caroline Eckhardt (Lewisburg, Pennsylvania: Bucknell University Press, 1980), pp. 79–90.

44. On this passage, see Teodolinda Barolini, *The Undivine Comedy, Dethe-ologizing Dante* (Princeton: Princeton University Press, 1992) p. 102: "The spiral of conversion that moves away from the noble temporal goods for which the soul feels a backward-turning love in the direction of their eternal counterparts is paradigmatically rendered in the concluding verses of *Purgatorio* 28, where the pilgrim 'lapses' toward his classical poets and converts to Beatrice."

45. See Sara Sturm-Maddox, "The *Rime petrose* and the Purgatorial Palinode," *Studies in Philology,* 84 (1987), 119–33.

46. Thomas J. Heffernan, "An Analysis of the Narrative Motifs in the Legend of St. Eustache," *Medievalia et Humanistica,* 6 (1975), 63–89.

47. A.J. Greimas, "Le Contrat de veridiction," *Man and World,* 13 (1980), pp. 345–55; Donald Maddox, "Veridiction, Verification, Verifactions: Reflections on Methodology," *New Literary History,* 20 (1989), 661–77.

48. On this, see Larry S. Crist, "Roland, héros du vouloir: Contribution à l'analyse structurale de la *Chanson de Roland,*" in *Mélanges de philologie et de littérature romanes offerts à Madame Jeanne Wathelet-Willem* (Liège: Marche Romane, 1978), pp. 77–101.

49. See also Donald Maddox, "Rewriting Recognition in Medieval Veridictory Drama," in *Continuations: Essays on Medieval French Literature in Honor of John L. Grigsby,* ed. Norris J. Lacy and Gloria Torrini-Roblin (Birmingham, Alabama: Summa, 1989), pp. 277–95.

50. Jean d'Arras, *Le Roman de Mélusine,* ed. Louis Stouff (Dijon: Bernigaud and Privat, 1932, rpt. Geneva: Slatkine, 1974), pp. 265–66.

51. Béroul, *Le Roman de Tristan,* ed. Muret-Defourques (Paris: Champion, 1982), ll. 1981ff.

52. On the consequences of the *Organon*'s recovery for twelfth-century literature, see Tony Hunt, "Aristotle, Dialectic, and Courtly Literature," *Viator,* 10 (1979), 96–102, and Eugene Vance, *From Topic to Tale: Logic and Narrative in the Middle Ages* (Minneapolis: University of Minnesota Press, 1987). On the *Sophistical Refutations* in Chrétien and Béroul, see Donald Maddox, "Opérations cognitives et scandales romanesques: Méléagant et le roi Marc," in *Farai chansoneta novele: Essais sur la liberté créatrice au Moyen Age, en hommage à Jean-Charles Payen,* ed. Huguette Legros et al. (Caen: University of Caen, 1989), pp. 239–51.

53. See Sigmund Freud, "Family Romances" (1909), *Standard Edition of the Complete Psychological Works* (London: Hogarth, 1959), Vol. 9. See also Donald Maddox, "Specular Stories, Family Romance, and the Fictions of Courtly Culture," *Exemplaria,* 3, No. 2 (1991), 299–326.

54. *Mélusine,* pp. 48–51; 265–66.

55. Claude Lévi-Strauss, "De Chrétien de Troyes à Richard Wagner," in *Parsifal, Programmheft der bayreuther Festspiele,* I (1975), 1–6; 60–65; slightly expanded in Lévi-Strauss, *Le Regard éloigné* (Paris: Plon, 1983), pp. 301–24. See also Lévi-Strauss, *Paroles données* (Paris: Plon, 1984), pp. 129–40.

56. See also the articles by Charles Méla, "Perceval," *Yale French Studies,* 55/56 (1971), 374–440; Jean-Guy Gouttebroze, "L'Arrière-plan psychologique et mythique de l'itinéraire de Perceval dans le *Conte du graal,*" in *Voyage, quête, pèlerinage dans la littérature et la civilisation médiévales* (Aix-en-Provence: CUERMA, 1976), pp. 340–52; Sara Sturm-Maddox, "Lévi-Strauss in the Waste Forest," *L'Esprit Créateur,* 18 (1978), 82–94.

57. See also Donald Maddox, "Lévi-Strauss in Camelot" in *Culture and the King,* ed. Martin Shichtman and James Carley (Syracuse, New York: Syracuse University Press, 1994), pp. 30–43.

58. *Roman d'Énéas,* ed. J.-J. Salverda de Grave, 2 vols. (Paris: Champion, 1964–68), I, ll. 2161–218; 2839–996.

59. Georges Duby, "Remarques sur la littérature généalogique en France aux XIe et XIIe siècle," in *Hommes et structures du Moyen Age* (The Hague: Mouton, 1973), pp. 287–98. See also Léopold Génicot, *Les Généalogies* (Turnhout: Brépohls, 1975); R. Howard Bloch, *Etymologies and Genealogies: A Literary Anthropology of the French Middle Ages* (Chicago: University of Chicago Press, 1983), pp. 79–87; 203–17; and Gabrielle M. Spiegel, "Genealogy: Form and Function in Medieval Historical Narrative," *History and Theory,* 22 (1983), 43–53.

60. Erich Köhler, *Ideal und Wirklichkeit in der höfischen Epik* (Tübingen: Niemeyer, 1956).

61. For an extensive recent investigation in the historiographic domain, see Gabrielle M. Spiegel, *Romancing the Past: The Rise of Vernacular Prose Historiography in Thirteenth-Century France* (Berkeley: University of California Press, 1993). For a recent appraisal of literary sensitivity to such issues, see Judith Kellogg, *Medieval Artistry and Exchange: Economic Institutions, Society, and Literary Form in Old French Narrative* (New York: Lang, 1989). See also R. Howard Bloch, *Medieval French Literature and Law* (Berkeley: University of California Press, 1977); idem, *Etymologies and Genealogies;* Denyse Delcourt, *L'Éthique du changement dans le roman du XIIe siècle* (Geneva: Droz, 1990).

62. Fernand Braudel, *Écrits sur l'histoire* (Paris: Flammarion, 1969), pp. 239–314.

63. The atypical case in this regard is the hero of the Prose *Lancelot,* some of whose later encounters with the past relativize the significance of his own deeds. Yet even these are viewed as vital accessories to the foretold achievements of his long-anticipated son, Galaad.

Veraces historiae aut fallaces fabulae?

Barbara N. Sargent-Baur

It is generally agreed that Arthurian literature, as a written phenomenon with more or less datable texts, begins with Geoffrey of Monmouth and stems from his *Historia regum Britanniae*. At its inception, then, it is a genre associated not with storytelling but with what purports to be the faithful recording of real events preserved in reliable sources by writers who can be considered as trustworthy, as authorities. Although Geoffrey mentions oral tradition in his Dedication, the main prop of his own enterprise and of his own claim to respectability is an alleged written source provided by an unimpeachable agent, Archdeacon Walter of Oxford, who is credited with furnishing him "a very old book in British."[1] Furthermore, the early-British material in Geoffrey's own book is anchored in time through plentiful references to events in the Old Testament and also to such solidly historical personages as Julius Caesar and Constantine the Great. Such matters reassuringly serve as prelude to the conception, birth, career, conquests, and disappearance of Arthur and the passage of dominion[2] to later British rulers. If much of this is spurious, some of it looked sufficiently historical for Geoffrey's contemporaries, and successive generations of medieval readers (aside from a few tough-minded skeptics), to take it as historical. They mentally classified it in a familiar genre, that of historiography.

To us the question of how much of the *Historia* text derives from legend, how much from folklore and dimly-remembered Celtic myth, and how much from sheer invention on Geoffrey's part, remains open, and its chances of remaining so appear to be excellent.[3] What I mean to suggest here is that Geoffrey's habitual blurring of the distinction between fact and fable, the old and the new, historiography and what we moderns would term romance, marked from the outset the production of writing on Arthurian subjects. It fostered on the one hand a long line of derivative and hybrid accounts of events in sub-Roman Britain; on the other hand Geoffrey's reiterated insistence on authority, on veracity, on folk memory, but above all on old and credible written sources would for a long time be a stock-in-trade of practitioners of the new genre of vernacular narrative fiction composed for a cultivated and well-paying courtly audience. Whether the readers or hearers of narrative accounts in the twelfth century were aware of such ambiguities and enjoyed them is not easy to establish. The most literate among them were school-trained, their minds sharpened by years of familiarity with the standard authors; they not only knew the classical theory and practice of genre but were bringing an increasingly refined technique to the task of literary analysis of both secular and sacred texts, as A.J. Minnis has recently shown.[4]

What I propose to explore in this essay are the distinctions drawn in principle by some medieval thinkers between the fabulous and the historical, between the invented (and hence unreliable) and the authentic or "true." Perhaps it would not be too anachronistic even to use the modern opposition between fiction and nonfiction (which is not unproblematical either). Writers in the twelfth century, following their predecessors, had a good deal to say concerning such distinctions and appeared confident of their ability to make them, both in the abstract and with reference to this or that particular author. I shall look first at a few theoretical statements on genre made by authors working in Latin and also in French. Then I shall take up the case of some individual works, either specifically cited by medieval critics or imitated and adapted by other practicing writers, to see how well the theoretical categories worked in application to real texts. Here my focus will be on the reception of Geoffrey's *Historia* and Wace's *Roman de Brut*. In doing this, I hope to clarify somewhat the way that medieval readers, or at least certain ones among them, understood generic differences and made them in practice, and how some medieval writers, while seeming to respect these differences, in fact played refined and complicated games with them.

We might begin with a glance at the classical bases of medieval composition and literary-critical theory, the Roman theorists whose works were preserved and much studied in the monastic and episcopal schools of the West. The dominant figures were Cicero (in *De oratore* and *De inventione*), Quintilian (in the *Institutio oratoria*), and the author of the *Rhetorica ad Herennium*. Composers of such prescriptive manuals had in mind the primary function of eloquence in their day, the art of persuasion; yet the application to uses other than political oratory and forensic pleading of the devices of rhetoric was a reality under Republic and Empire, just as it was to remain in the Middle Ages. These three authorities on rhetoric pay attention to *narratio,* among other matters, with the acknowledgment that one kind of narration is appropriate for judicial pleading and another for other purposes; for these last, they make subdivisions according to degrees of truth. They propose (as do many minor writers on the topic as well) the categories of *fabula, argumentum,* and *historia*. A *fabula* is a tale not only invented but containing impossible or highly improbable elements: talking animals, for instance, or humans metamorphosed into flora and fauna. *Argumentum* is also invented but neither impossible nor improbable; and *historia* is the relation of actual events. The literary genres deriving from these types of *narratio* are: tragedy or *carmina* from *fabula,* comedy from *argumentum,* and from *historia* history, the setting forth of the fact, of *res gesta,* the thing done.[5]

Between the classical theorists and the writers and producers and consumers of narrative of the High Middle Ages stands a cultural middleman, Isidore of Seville. In his *Etymologiae* he conferred upon antique views on language and literature an incomparable cachet through his reputation for orthodoxy and saintliness as well as learning. Of this encyclopedic work the first book, the *Grammatica,* was especially potent in shaping the ways in which later generations thought about generic distinctions, for it was preserved in some one thousand manuscripts and consulted throughout the medieval period.[6] Like the *auctores* he followed, Isidore used the notion of "truth" in its varying degrees as a criterion in classifying written compositions. We find him (after mentioning *argumentum* in passing), erecting a high wall between *historia* and *fabula,* between *res factae* and *res fictae* (I, xl, l).[7] Here *historia* is the *narratio rei gestae* (I, xli, l), and more specifically the report of deeds "worthy of memory,"[8] deeds that have actually been observed, for eyewitness accounts, being produced *sine mendacio,* have a unique claim to being authentic. *Fabula* by contrast is made-up, contrived, merely verbal, unreal, as in the tales of Æsop. Hence *narrationes* of whatever kind, not derived from the testimony of witnesses who recorded what they had witnessed, are cast into the category of *fabula*. The distinction, for Isidore, was not one of compositional techniques (prose as against verse, for example), nor was it one of language (since only one was in use for written composition in the West in the seventh century). It was purely one of "truth," that is, factual accuracy guaranteed by a reliable source.

When we move from the seventh century to the twelfth we have the impression that, at least among the growing ranks of historiographers, a willingness to contemplate three levels of "truth" is not widespread.[9] With regard to the Arthurian materials, those writers who have anything of an analytical nature to say about them seem to know just what they are dealing with and show no hesitation in labeling it in an either/or manner. Thus William of Malmesbury, writing his *De rebus gestis regum Anglorum* about

1125, uncompromisingly sets up the polarity *fallaces fabulae / veraces historiae* that supplies the title of my essay.[10] There is no middle ground for him between true histories and fallacious tales; his brisk establishment of two and only two categories shows his own conviction in this regard, and his impatient tone suggests that his contempories cannot help seeing what is involved. For all its brevity, William's excursus deserves a close look. It is a bit of editorializing inserted into what looks like a straightforward account of the post-Vortigern resistance to the Saxons led by Ambrosius with the assistance of the warlike Arthur. This is Arthur's first entry into *De rebus gestis,* and it provides William with the chance to spurn the still-flourishing *nugae Britonum* at the same time that he asserts Arthur's deserving of better things, namely not having wild yarns spun about him but being proclaimed in true histories. This leads into a highly condensed narration of Arthur's military accomplishments. The inference is unavoidable: the true accounts that Arthur richly earned must include the account William is at the moment presenting. Well and good; but a line or so later Arthur's entitlement to serious consideration is shored up by his performance at the battle of Badon where he single-handedly threw down nine hundred of the enemy. One can only wonder what were the *nugae Britonum* that William so brusquely dismissed if he gave credence to an exploit that certainly appears to be a tall tale, a *nuga* if ever there was one.

Popular tales about Arthur are cited dismissively by other twelfth-century writers as well. The account by Hermann of Tournai (or Laon) of the squabble in the church at Bodmin in 1113 over the belief in Arthur's survival is too well known to excuse the retelling of it;[11] and we are familiar with Wace's 1155 allusion to the "Roünde Table / Dunt Bretun dient mainte fable" ("the Round Table, of which the Bretons tell many a fable").[12] Toward the end of the century Peter of Blois mentions *histriones* who related *fabulosa* about Arthur, Gawain, and Tristan.[13] This was the normal attitude of *clerici* toward the uneducated. But it is fascinating to see what they made of such material when they met it in what purported to be a work of historiography, the *Historia regum Britanniae.* Here was a book composed by an educated man, a Latin-writing man, a quoter of Gildas and Bede—one of their own number, in fact. As it happens, Geoffrey's venture was a spectacular success. It gave rise to few negative comments—these came later—but those few it did call forth in the next decades reflect a sharp polarity with regard to written narrative. Either a writer tells the truth or he is a tale-teller, a liar.[14] This is implied by Gerald of Wales, who at first touches Geoffrey's account lightly: in *Iterarium Cambriae*[15] he establishes an opposition between the demon-repelling powers of the *Historia* and of the Gospel of St. John, the premise being that demons hate truth and love lies, and he records a clear victory for John (the demons find Geoffrey's book irresistible).[16] In a more serious vein, Gerald in the *Descriptio Cambriae* aims at Geoffrey a passing but stinging blow; not only is the *Historia* inaccurate on a particular etymological point, but it lies (*mentitur*); and Geoffrey's account is blackened globally by the juxtaposition of two terms usually kept separate; his history is a "fabulosa . . . historia."[17] Gerald leaves it there, and well he might, since these books of his own really belong to the "travel" rather than "history" category. More wounding in the long run would be criticism of the sort leveled by William of Newburgh, for this was a man who himself wrote history and had pronounced and strict views as to what history was and was not. In his *Historia rerum anglicarum* he attacks Geoffrey using the antonyms fable/history, true/false, veracity/lying. Geoffrey was on the wrong side of the wall, "For he who does not declare the truth of things done, indiscriminately admits the vanity of fables." Even worse, Geoffrey told lies wantonly and impudently, so that only a person ignorant of ancient history could be taken in by his book, and he cloaked his *fabulas* with the honest name of history through the superimposed color of the Latin language. Furthermore he caused his mendacious account to be commonly known ("spreading disinformation" would be the modern equivalent); and at this point William is so incensed that in place of his victim's name he repeatedly uses "homo ille" ("that man"), and he rounds out his invective thus: "let that fable-monger with his fables be promptly spewed out by everyone."[18]

Yet William of Newburgh seemingly raised a lone voice among historians of the twelfth century. Far more typical was the reaction of Henry of Huntingdon, whose excited letter to Warinus is well known (he wrote it after seeing a copy of the *Historia* at Le Bec as early as January 1139). The large number of *Historia* copies made throughout the rest of the 1100s in monastic scriptoria and kept in monastic as well as secular libraries attest to the respect this work quickly and widely gained.[19] Alfred of Beverley expressed reservations, but drew on the *Historia* anyway.[20] Geoffrey's many twelfth-century admirers and his few detractors appear to have agreed that his account was indeed history, although the latter thought it bad history. It exploited the familiar conventions, it used sources perceived as factual, it asserted not novelty but antiquity, and it was composed in Latin.[21]

The case of the *Roman de Brut* may throw even more light on the limits of twelfth-century generic distinctions when it came to their practical application. The diverse treatment accorded the *Historia* and the *Brut* is enlightening; as Douglas Kelly has put it, "one writer's truth may be another's lie."[22] One thing that influenced the reception of a work was the language its writer chose to use. Wace, undertaking to translate Geoffrey, did so in

Norman French, and called the result a *romanz* (l. 14,866), a designation whose nuances are not purely linguistic. A writer of *romanz,* even if treating the same materials as historians and in similar fashion, was unhesitatingly placed by his contemporaries in a segregated area reserved for nonhistorians. Why should this be? Wace after all, like "proper" historians, reaches back to the classical past, as had done not only Geoffrey but also Gildas and Bede; like not only Geoffrey but "Nennius" he traces the British to their postulated Trojan origin; like "proper" historians he draws on multiple sources while feeling free to abridge, correct, explain, and expand.[23] Perhaps more important, he displays a critical historical sense along with an appreciation of the need to convince his readers that his account is reliable, is on the side of the wall marked "truth." Sometimes he acknowledges the separation of truth and fable positively: "If anyone wishes to hear . . . who were those who first held England and where they came from, what kings there were in succession . . . Master Wace who gives a true account has translated it."[24] He takes account of it negatively in the passage where, amplifying Geoffrey's brief statement of the twelve-year Arthurian peace, he shrugs off the fables of the *Bretun* about the Round Table. *They* tell tales about it; by contrast the following development seems offered as trustworthy information from someone who *knows*—the King really did have his noble barons seated as equals, foreign noblemen did flock to his court, and so on. The continuation of this again slips and slides on the ground of reliability. "In this great peace . . . were tested the marvels and encountered the adventures that are told so much about Arthur that they are turned into fables, neither lie nor truth, neither foolishness nor wisdom. The storytellers have told so much and the fable-makers have fabled so much to embellish their tales that they have made everything seem like a fable."[25] Yet these strange doings really happened; both Wace and the anonymous *fableürs* are reporters of true events. The difference between them is not so much one of subject matter as of treatment; the techniques of the professional storytellers have cast doubt on the veracity of the entire body of Arthuriana or at least that part of it situated in the halcyon period of the *pax arthuriana*.[26] Yet there is no reason to suspect Wace himself of not endeavoring to present a true account based closely but not slavishly[27] on a work that had been widely and admiringly received as history. (We may think of it as pseudohistory, or historical fiction; but we should remember that the veracity of Geoffrey's *Historia* would not become a *casus belli* until much later.[28])

Like other writers of his time, Wace wanted to be respected but also to be read; like them, he knew the value of a picturesque touch and a good story to please his readers. As between Geoffrey and Wace one might even argue for Wace as having better historiographical credentials, at least by modern standards. William Leckie has made such a case, affirming that "Wace serves as a reminder that a twelfth-century translator could be a historian in his own right, one whose familiarity with conventions and standard authorities rivaled that of many of his contemporaries."[29] One of his most engaging traits is his honesty, which goes with an enquiring and critical spirit, as J.S.P. Tatlock observed.[30] Charles Foulon warmly commended Wace's desire for accuracy, his skepticism, and his common sense.[31] The omission of the *Prophetiae Merlini* from his translation attests to these qualities. Wace's hardheaded and empirical cast of mind is perhaps best on display in the passage (in the *Rou,* not the *Brut*) where he returns to the *Bretun* and their yarning, this time about the forest of Broceliande and its fountain. He was intrigued by the accounts of magical rain-making, sightings of fairies, and other remarkable things, "se li Breton nos dient veir" ("if the Bretons tell us the truth"),[32] enough to make a special trip and try an experiment. "There I went to seek for marvels; I saw the forest and the land. Marvels I sought, but found none. A fool I returned, a fool I went, a fool I went, a fool I returned. It was folly I sought, a fool I think myself."[33] The repetitions suggest not only disappointment but self-condemnation for having done these idle reports the honor of testing and refuting them, of having thought even for a moment that there might be something in them. We must remember that if Wace was a chronicler when writing the *Rou,* he brought a chronicler's mind to bear on the *Brut,* which was an adaptation of a very recent book that widely passed as historiography.[34]

With Wace, perhaps more than with Geoffrey, we find ourselves at the heart of the matter. Generic intertextuality is widespread in Francophone Europe in the second half of the twelfth century; historiography in Latin, history or pseudohistory in Latin or French, romance in French—all proliferated at the time, were encouraged by some of the same patrons, read by the same readers, copied by the same scribes, produced by writers whose cultural baggage and formal training were the same, who had learned their trade by reading the same *auctores*. As Per Nykrog puts it, "it was the scholarly writer who groped his way toward fiction, not the oral story-teller who simply resorted to writing."[35] I should not want to propose that resemblances among narratives of that period were inevitable; but they are certainly not surprising. Those of us who come to the reading of these texts are perhaps not troubled by the blurred frontiers between them, nor perhaps particularly by generic questions at all, or by the fact that when Geoffrey and Wace and Béroul and Chrétien were busy, "les frontières entre le roman et l'histoire étaient on ne peut plus floues" ("the boundaries between romance and history could not be more blurred"), as Guy Raynaud de Lage has remarked.[36] We may be quite content to take individual works on what seem, for various reasons, to be their individual merits; perhaps we shall wish to classify all more-or-less historical narrative of the twelfth-century Francophone West as "serious entertainments" (in Nancy Partner's phrase[37]) and let it go at that.

Contemporary producers, consumers, and critics, though, were in principle *not* willing to let it go at that. We have seen what the grammarians and the literary theorists had to say, in a prescriptive way, and what some historians and some men who wanted to be taken as historians offered by way of distinctions concerning bodies of material,[38] professionalism generally, and the competence of certain practitioners. Not only did they hold generic categories to be important, they were confident of their ability to identify different kinds of narrative and to assign this work or that to the appropriate classification. Do such advertised discriminations hold up in practice? Here the examination of manuscripts, more specifically collective codices, can be highly instructive. The texts with which a particular work associates can tell us much—*qui se ressemble s'assemble* ("birds of a feather flock together"); at least we can postulate this as a working principle of medieval patrons and collectors.[39] Now, the *Brut* of Wace, preserved in some twenty-two manuscripts, none earlier than the first half of the thirteenth century, does not associate at all with his *Rou* (of which only four manuscripts give the complete text anyway). Nor does it associate with Geoffrey's *Historia*.[40] The company it keeps includes a few Latin regnal lists and some histories and chronicles composed in French; but it comprises primarily what is now termed *romans d'antiquité* and Arthurian romance. This is the case, for example, with the celebrated copy of Guiot, Paris B.N. fr. 794: here we encounter Chrétien's first four romances, then the Oriental romance *Athis et Prophilias,* then the *Roman de Troie* of Benoît de Sainte-Maure, the *Brut* of Wace, a list of Roman emperors by Calendre, Chrétien's *Perceval,* and parts of the *First* and *Second Continuations.* Even more interesting are the associations in Paris B.N. fr. 1450 (the manuscript that inserts all five of Chrétien's romances into the *Brut* at the passage where Wace mentions the adventures punctuating the Arthurian peace). The codex begins with the narrative reaching the farthest back in time, Benoît's *Roman de Troie,* follows it with the *Roman d'Enéas* (Æneas's story forming a sort of sequel to the fall of Troy), and then presents what Wace calls "la geste des Bretuns" (14,859), which travels with the descendants of Æneas from Italy to Britain and tells of Brutus and *his* posterity through the reign of Arthur and beyond. The last text contained in the codex is an incomplete *Dolopathos.* As Keith Busby has pointed out in his edition of Chrétien's *Perceval,* the manuscript "a été conçu comme un tout, puisqu'aucun des ouvrages ne commence sur un nouveau cahier" ("was conceived as a whole, since none of the works begins on a new quire").[41] In fact, in copying *Troies, Enéas,* and *Brut* (and other texts as well), the scribe has thriftily filled his page with the end of one work and the start of the next. In three other manuscripts also, *Enéas* precedes *Brut.*[42] Therefore we can postulate, among thirteenth- and fourteenth-century collectors interested in the *Brut,* a tacit generic classification the labeling of which is for us moderns a delicate matter.

Whatever it may be, it differs from the typing implied by the manuscripts preserving the *Historia regum.* Unlike Wace's translation, Geoffrey's original associates with *no* Arthurian romance, and with very few vernacular texts at all. It keeps company exclusively with didactic and what were taken for historical works: for example, Bede's *Historia ecclesiastica,* Robert of Torigny's *Chronica,* the *Pseudo-Turpin,* and even with the *Historiae* of William of Malmesbury in one manuscript.[43] It is also neighbor to the *Historia de excidio Troie* of pseudo-Dares the Phrygian in twenty-seven manuscripts, the highest number of associations. Particularly intriguing is the proximity to Geoffrey's text, in five manuscripts, of the 1287 *Historia destructionis Troiae* of Guido delle Colonne, a jurist of Messina. In four of the five manuscripts Guido's text precedes Geoffrey's, in three of them immediately so, making a Trojan-British sequence. Guido's *Historia* has in common with Geoffrey's the fact of being a highly successful fraud (215 manuscripts for Geoffrey, some 150 for Guido). It claims to spurn the fictions of Homer, Virgil's adaptation of them, and the abridgment made by Cornelius Nepos, in favor of the two "original" and authoritative sources, Dares the Phrygian and Dictys the Greek. Guido warns his readers that certain persons, treating the Troy story poetically, have made true matters (*vera*) seem fictitious (*fabulosa*),[44] a sentiment echoing one of Wace on the Breton *fableürs* quoted earlier.[45] In fact Guido's *Historia* is part paraphrase, part translation into Latin of a rhymed French original, the *Roman de Troie* of Benoît de Sainte-Maure,[46] a debt nowhere acknowledged by Guido. I should point out that, unlike Guido, Benoît does not associate in manuscripts with Geoffrey; his *Roman de Troie* turns up with other rhymed vernacular treatments of antique materials. We can infer that the Latin texts of Guido and Geoffrey, neighbors in five codices, were akin in the minds of readers: these texts were true, were authentic, were the pre-eminent sources of information in their respective areas. Their authors were considered historians, unlike the composers of *romans d'antiquité* (to say nothing of such as Chrétien de Troyes).[47] The two groups of narrative writers were segregated by the great barrier, generally thought in the twelfth century to be unbreachable: *historia* here, *fabula* there.[48]

Quite understandably the rising generation of *romanciers* took their cue from the historians: they borrowed not only their patron-pleasing materials but also their techniques of authentification, so as to appear serious in matter but more accessible in treatment. Citations of nonspecified books (by implication, ancient and hence respectable) in ecclesiastical libraries or private collections turn up in Chrétien and many other vernacular writers. Chrétien's allusions to *livres* are familiar to us.[49] On the other side of the wall, and perhaps less well known, is the case of Walter Map. His connections with Arthuriana were certainly not intended by him, but they deserve a look in the context of literary authenticity. The author of the *Queste del saint Graal* avers in his epilogue that *aventures* reported in the preceding prose narrative were told by Bors, a participant and eyewitness, to King Arthur, who in turn ordered their setting-down (in Latin) by *clers;* and they were then kept in the library of Salisbury, whence Walter Map withdrew them to make his book about the Holy Grail, translating the *estoire* from Latin to French out of love for his lord King Henry. This epilogue is followed in the Vulgate Cycle by the prologue of the *Mort le roi Artu,* a romance also ascribed to Walter. We know that, by the time of the *Queste* and the *Mort Artu,* Walter Map had been dead for some years, and perhaps we may frivolously indulge in the notion of him turning in his grave at such an attribution. This is the same writer who in his lifetime was denied paternity regarding something he really did father, the antimarriage tract *Dissuasio Valerii ad Rufinum,* acknowledged as his by him in his *De nugis curalium.*[50] Some of his contemporaries thought that the true author of *De nugis* was not Walter but rather that Valerius Maximus named in the title; a work of such quality, meeting the essential criteria of veracity and sagacity,[51] had perforce to belong to an *auctor.* Intrinsic worth and seeming authenticity implied a respectable age; it could not be modern, nor *a fortiori* could the writer still be alive. Walter Map predicted, correctly as it happens, that appreciation of his work would come only much later. "My only offence is that I am alive; it is, however, one which I have no intention of correcting by dying."[52]

Walter Map's reply to contemporary experts in literary matters was of course a *boutade,* but it illustrates the very real problem of authenticity—of trustworthiness in written narrative—that I have been exploring here. For a secular narrative to be welcomed into the genre of historiography—to be respected, taken as authoritative—it had to be attributed to a known *auctor* or at the very least to a reliable transmitter of eyewitness testimony to certain major happenings of general significance, "deeds worthy of memory." That the report should appropriately be in Latin was taken for granted. It also helped if the *auctor* had lived a long time ago. If these conditions obtained, well and good; otherwise the narrative was looked on as perhaps entertaining, perhaps even instructive, but still unreliable, unsubstantiated, fabulous, mendacious, "vain et plaisant" (as Jean Bodel labeled the *matière de Bretagne*).[53]

On the one hand, then, educated North-Western Europeans in the twelfth century took generic distinctions seriously, both in theory and in confronting particular texts. On the other, they could be wildly mistaken in classifying this work or that, or even deliberately misled by professional writers who also knew the current generic critera and turned them to their own advantage.

It is not at all my intention to imply that twelfth-century readers of texts, whether in Latin or in French, were simple and unsophisticated souls easily taken in by any clever and ambitious writer who had mastered the tricks of his trade. It would be rash to conclude that they were any more gullible than educated readers of any other age including our own. We ourselves respond to a new book partly because of prior expectations: author's reputation if known, publisher's blurb, reviews in scholarly journals or the *Times Literary Supplement,* recommendations from respected colleagues, and so forth. If we judge or prejudge a work to be "literature," we read it in one way; in another, if we have mentally filed it as "historical account" or "biography." The minority of the medieval population who were literate constituted, by and large, the intellectual elite. What I should like to propose, as a working hypothesis, is that these readers were very far from being naive, but were, if anything, overeducated, overprepared to deal with some of the kinds of verbal composition being produced in bewildering and innovative abundance by their contemporaries. The old generic guides inherited from classical Rome, distinguishing the fictional from the factual and classifying genres and individual works by "truth" and reliability, had become unreliable in their turn. They were simply inadequate in a situation in which the distance between the familiar categories was shrinking, when there was more than one language available for serious communication in writing, and when the field of narrative was being invaded by a new and hybrid genre, historical fiction or romance history.

NOTES

1. ". . . optulit Walterus Oxinefordensis archidiaconus, uir in oratoria arte atque in exoticis historiis eruditus, quendam Britannici sermonis librum uetustissimum qui a Bruto primo rege Britonum usque ad Cadualadrum filium Caduallonis actus omnium continue et ex ordine perpulcris orationibus proponebat" ("Walter, Archdeacon of Oxford, a man learned in the art of discourse and also in foreign histories, offered [me] a certain very old book in the British language, which set forth the acts of all [those kings], from Brutus the first king of the Britons to Cadwallader son of

Cadwallo, consecutively and in order, in the finest discourse," Geoffrey of Monmouth, *The Historia regum Britannie* I: Bern, Burgerbibliothek, MS. 568, ed. Neil Wright [Cambridge: Brewer, 1984], chap. 2 [same numbering in Edmond Faral, *La Légende arthurienne*, Paris, 1929]; p. 1 in Wright. See also Wright, ed., chap. 177 [pp. 129–30] and chap. 208 [p. 147]).

2. The phrase "passage of dominion" is borrowed from R. William Leckie, Jr.: *The Passage of Dominion: Geoffrey of Monmouth and the Periodization of Insular History to the Twelfth Century* (Toronto: University of Toronto Press, 1981).

3. A modern historian of English historiography, Antonia Gransden, has summed up Geoffrey neatly: "Geoffrey was a romance writer masquerading as a historian"; *Historical Writing in England* (Ithaca: Cornell University Press, 1974), p. 202. She calls his work "romance history" (201). For a view more favorable to Geoffrey, see Julia C. Crick, *The Historia regum Britanniae of Geoffrey of Monmouth*, IV: *Dissemination and Reception in the Later Middle Ages* (Cambridge: Brewer, 1991), pp. 224–26.

4. A[listair]. J. Minnis, *Medieval Theory of Authorship: Scholastic Literary Attitudes in the Later Middle Ages* (London: Scolar, 1984), especially chap. 1.

5. "Fabula est, quae neque veras, neque veri similes continet res, ut hae, quae in tragoediis traditae sunt. Historia est res gesta, sed ab aetatis nostrae memoria remota. Argumentum est ficta res quae tamen fieri potuit" ("A fable is that which contains things neither true nor probable, such as those that are consigned to tragedies. A history is a thing done, but remote from the memory of our age. An argument is an invented thing that nevertheless might happen," *Ad Herennium* I, 8, 13). Similarly in Quintilian, *Institutio* II, iv, 2. See also some minor rhetoricians, e.g. Victorinus, Martianus Capella, and Priscianus, in Carolus [Karl Felix von] Halm, *Rhetores latini minores* (Leipzig: Tübner, 1863), pp. 202, 486, 551–52. For the survival of these distinctions into the later Middle Ages, see Paul Strohm, "Some Generic Distinctions in the *Canterbury Tales*," *Modern Philology*, 68 (1970–71), 312–32, and Stanley J. Kahrl, "Allegory in Practice: A Study of Narrative Styles in Medieval Exempla," *Modern Philology*, 63 (1965–66), 103–10. For history writing as a branch of rhetoric, hence literature, see R.W. Southern, "Aspects of the European Tradition of Historical Writing, I: The Classical Tradition from Einhard to Geoffrey of Monmouth," *Transactions of the Royal Historical Society*, 5th Series, 20 (London: R.H.S., 1970), pp. 173–96, esp. pp. 177–83.

6. Ernst Robert Curtius speaks of its "binding authority," in *European Literature and the Latin Middle Ages*, trans. W.R. Trask (New York: Pantheon, 1953), p. 455.

7. ". . . inter historiam et argumentum et fabulam interesse. Nam historiae sunt res verae quae factae sunt; argumenta sunt quae etsi facta non sunt, fieri tamen possunt; fabulae vero sunt quae nec factae sunt nec fieri possunt, quia contra naturam sunt" ("there are differences among history and argument and fable. For histories are real things that were done; arguments are those that, although not done, yet might be done; but fables are those that neither have been done nor could be done, for they are against nature," I, xliv, 5).

8. Deeds worthy of memory, and hence of being committed to writing, constitute in their written form part of grammar. Isidore here follows Augustine, *De officiis*, in *P.L.* vol. 32, p. 1012.

9. We should note, however, that the three categories do turn up again in the *Metalogicon* (ca. 1159), John of Salisbury's defense of the trivium, Book I, Chap. 24, ll. 27ff.

10. William of Malmesbury, *De gestis regum Anglorum libri quinque: Historiae novellae libri tres*, ed. William Stubbs, 2 vols. (London: Longman, 1887–88), I, 8.

11. Hermann of Tournai, *De miraculis*, in P.L. 156, 983; text E.K. Chambers, *Arthur of Britain*, (Cambridge: Speculum Historiale / New York: Barnes and Noble, 1927, rpt. 1964), p. 249.

12. Wace, *Le Roman de Brut*, ed. Ivor Arnold, 2 vols. S.A.T.F. (Paris: Picard, 1938–40), ll. 9751–52.

13. Peter of Blois, *De confessione,* in P.L. 207, 1088. Text in Chambers, p. 267. Walter Map also contrasts *historia* and *fabula,* while acknowledging that both may be edifying; see *De nugis curialium/Courtiers' Trifles,* ed. and trans. M.R. James (Oxford: Clarendon, 1914), rev. ed. C.N.L. Brooke and R.A.B. Mynors (Oxford: Clarendon, 1993), I, 31, p. 128.

14. The implied though unexpressed assumption is that anyone with a grain of sense ought to be able to distinguish between truth and falsehood in a historical narrative.

15. *Opera* vi. 7, in Chambers, pp. 268–69.

16. The inclusion of this anecdote in a work purporting to be true, because it is largely an eyewitness report, is in itself problematical, the more so that Gerald borrowed freely from Geoffrey in many a passage.

17. Gerald, *Descriptio Cambriae, Opera,* I. 7, in Chambers, p. 271.

18. "Nam qui rerum gestarum veritatem non didicit, fabularum vanitatem indiscrete admittit." ". . . fabulator ille cum suis fabulis incunctanter ab omnibus respuatur." William of Newburgh, *Historia* I, ii, in Chambers, p. 275, 276. One may smile at this degree of heat; but for William of Newburgh the communication of truth and the allegiance to the truth were what made a historian worthy of his readers' attention. There was also the fact that a book that he viewed dimly had rapidly become famous in elevated circles. Anyone in the 1990s who has read or, a fortiori, reviewed a book of doubtful scholarship published by a prestigious academic press, praised in print, and awarded a prize, can well sympathize with William of Newburgh. Nancy Partner comments that William "seems to be arguing with some other body of opinion"; see *Serious Entertainments: The Writing of History in Twelfth-Century England* (Chicago: University of Chicago Press, 1977), p. 62; see also Leckie, pp. 95–97.

19. For the manuscript evidence see Crick, *Historia* IV, especially chap. IX and X, and also Dumville, "An Early Text of Geoffrey of Monmouth's *Historia regum Britanniae* and the Circulation of Some Latin Histories in Twelfth-Century Normandy," in *Arthurian Literature,* 4 (Woodbridge, Suffolk: Boydell and Brewer; Totowa, New Jersey: Rowman and Littlefield, 1985), 1–36.

20. See Leckie, *Passage,* pp. 45–46.

21. See Nancy Partner, "Making Up Lost Time: Writing on the Writing of History," *Speculum,* 61 (1986), 102–3.

22. Kelly, *The Art of Medieval French Romance* (Madison: University of Wisconsin Press, 1992), p. 220; and the whole section "Truth of Narrative Matters," 208–26.

23. See Charles Foulon, "Wace," in *Arthurian Literature in the Middle Ages: A Collaborative History* [hereafter cited as *ALMA*], ed. Roger Sherman Loomis (Oxford: Clarendon, 1959, rpt. 1961, 1967, 1971), pp. 94–103.

24. "Ki vult oïr e vult saveir / De rei en rei e d'eir en eir / Ki cil furent e dunt il vindrent / Ki Engleterre primes tindrent, / Quels reis i ad en ordre eü, / Ki anceis e ki puis i fu, / Maistre Wace l'ad translaté / Ki en conte la verité" (*Brut,* 1–8).

25. "En cele grant pais ke jo di, / Ne sai si vus l'avez oï, / Furent les merveilles pruvees / E les aventures truvees / Ki d'Artur sunt tant recuntees / Ke a fable sunt aturnees. / Ne tut mençunge, ne tut veir, / Tut folie ne tut saveir. / Tant unt li cunteür cunté / E li fableür tant flablé / Pur lur cuntes enbeleter, / Que tut unt fait fable sembler" (*Brut,* 9787–98).

26. As if to demonstrate the activities of fable-mongers, the unique copyist of Paris B.N. fr. 1450 interrupted the *Brut* at this spot to insert all five of the romances of Chrétien de Troyes plus part of the *First Continuation* of the *Perceval.* He also supplied a brief transition beginning at 1. 9795: "Tant ont li conteor conté / Et par la terre tant fablé / Pour faire contes delitables / Que de verité ont fait fables / Mais ce que Crestiens tesmogne / Porés ci oïr sans alongne" ("The storytellers have told so much, and fabled so much throughout the land to make delightful stories, that they have made the truth into fables; but what Chrétien affirms you can hear without de-

lay"). See Alexandre Micha, *La Tradition manuscrite des romans de Chrétien de Troyes* (Geneva: Droz, 1939, rpt. 1966), p. 37.

27. Wace appears to have used both the Vulgate and the First Variant of the *Historia*; see Robert A. Caldwell, "Wace's *Roman de Brut* and the Variant Version of Geoffrey of Monmouth's *Historia regum Britanniae*," *Speculum*, 31 (1956), 675–82, and Wright, *Historia regum Britanniae* I, lv–ixiii.

28. See James Carley, "Polydore Vergil and John Leland on King Arthur: The Battle of the Books," in *Arthurian Interpretations*, 15 (1984), 86–100.

29. Leckie, *Passage*, p. 23.

30. J.S.P. Tatlock, The *Legendary History of Britain: Geoffrey of Monmouth's Historia Regum Britannae and Its Early Vernacular Versions* (Berkeley: University of California Press, 1950), p. 465.

31. Foulon, "Wace," in *ALMA*, p. 98.

32. Wace, *Le Roman de Rou*, ed. A.J. Holden, 3 vols. (Paris: Picard, 1970–73), l. 6399.

33. "La alai jo merveilles querre, / vi la forest et vi la terre, / merveilles quis, mais nes trovai, / fol m'en revinc, fol i alai; / fol i alai, fol m'en revinc, / folie quis, pour fol me tinc" (6393–98).

34. Curiously Antonia Gransden, author of a generally excellent overview of history writing in England to 1307, gives the *Brut* two lines (p. 210) and a half-dozen to the *Rou*, which she labels a "verse romance" (*Historical Writing*, p. 219).

35. Per Nykrog, "The Rise of Literary Fiction," in *Renaissance and Renewal in the Twelfth Century*, ed. R.L. Benson and G. Constable (Cambridge: Harvard University Press, 1982), p. 594.

36. Guy Raynaud de Lage, "Le Roman de Troie," in *Grundriss der Romanischen Literaturen des Mittelalters* (Heidelberg: Winter, 1978), IV, 178. Robert Marichal traces all modern *romans* to the *romans d'antiquité* and the *Brut*, but not to Geoffrey's *Historia*; see "Naissance du roman," in *Entretiens sur la renaissance du 12ᵉ siecle*, ed. M. de Gandillac et E. Jeauneau (Paris: Mouton, 1968), p. 451.

37. Partner, *Serious Entertainments*. On the intellectual significance of the renewed interest in historiography in the twelfth century, see M.D. Chenu, "Theology and the New Awareness of History." in *Nature, Man, and Society in the Twelfth Century*, trans. J. Taylor and L.K. Little (Chicago: University of Chicago Press, 1968).

38. E.g., the jongleur Jean Bodel, purveyor of popular history in epic form:

Ne sont que trois materes a nul home entendant:
De France et de Bretaigne et de Rome la Grant;
Et de ces trois materes n'i a nule semblant.
Li conte de Bretaigne sont si vain et plaisant.
Cil de Rome sont sage et de sens aprendant.
Cil de France sont voir chascun jour aparant.

["There are but three subject matters for anyone of understanding: of France and of the Celtic world and of great Rome; and among these three matters there is no resemblance. The Celtic tales are so idle and entertaining. Those of Rome are wise and instructive. Those of France are true, as is manifest every day."] *Saxenlied* (*Chanson des Saisnes*), ed. F. Menzel and E. Stangel, 2 vols. (Marburg: Elwert, 1906–09), ll. 6–11.

39. Regrettably the manuscript evidence does not tell us anything about reception of Wace in the twelfth century. For the *Brut* manuscripts see the Arnold edition, I, vii–xiv; the information on the other contents of the codices given there is extremely sketchy. For the *Rou*, see the Holden edition, III, 19–24, where the full contents of each codex, with folio numbers, are supplied.

40. For Geoffrey, see Associated Contents in Crick, *Historia* IV, 19–77. (Note that Crick's analysis is limited to works associating with the *Historia* in two or more manuscripts.) The *Historia* does associate with the *Rou* in one manuscript, from the beginning of the thirteenth century: London, B.L. Royal 4 c xi. See Holden, ed., *Rou* III, 19–20.

41. Keith Busby, ed., *Le Roman de Perceval ou Le Conte du Graal* (Tübingen: Niemeyer, 1993), p. xxvii.

42. These codices are Paris B.N. fr. 1416, B.N. fr. 12603, and Montpellier Bib. de l'Ecole de Médecine 251.

43. How annoyed William would have been! To make matters worse, a thirteenth-century Glastonbury scribe had the audacity to inflate William's history of the abbey with material taken from a "book of the deeds of the famous King Arthur," i.e., from some Arthurian romances; see Felicity Riddy, "Reading for England: Arthurian Literature and National Consciousness," *Bibliographical Bulletin of the International Arthurian Society,* 43 (1991), 329.

44. Guido de Columnis, *Historia destructionis Troiae,* ed. Nathaniel Edward Griffin (Cambridge, Massachusetts: Medieval Academy of America, 1936), pp. 3–4.

45. See above, p. 30 and n. 25.

46. I am much obliged to my colleague Mary Elizabeth Meek for bringing this to my attention. Guido's debt to Benoît was noted, independently, by Herman Dunger and Aristide Joly in 1869 and 1870; see *Historia destructionis Troiae,* trans. Mary Elizabeth Meek (Bloomington: Indiana University Press, 1974), pp. xxx–xxxi.

47. As Felicity Riddy puts it, "The historians are a particularly significant group in the development of the Arthur legend in England because it is they who confirm Arthur's status as a text and what is more, as a Latin text. They treat Geoffrey as an *auctor* and his *Historia* becomes an *auctoritas* in the process of the English conceptualization of the past" (p. 320).

48. Translators into French tried to circumvent the association of verse presentation with inauthenticity by using vernacular prose, beginning in the late twelfth century and in Flanders. As one translator of the (putatively historical) *Pseudo-Turpin* put it in his prologue, "nus contes rimés n'est verais" ("no rhymed tale is true"). His rendering of the Latin into French, dated 1195–1205, was requested by the Lord of Senlis, Baudouin VIII, Count of Flanders; the use of prose was the choice of the Count's sister Yolande, Countess of Saint Pol. The (diplomatic) text is in Gabrielle M. Spiegel, *Romancing the Past: The Rise of Vernacular Prose Historiography in Thirteenth-Century France* (Berkeley: University of California Press, 1993), p. 55. Another translator of the *Pseudo-Turpin,* "Jehan," working in 1206 for Count Renaut de Bologne, wrote similarly, "Et por ce que rime se velt afeitier de moz conqueilliz hors de l'estoire, voust li cuens que cist livres fust sans rime selonc le latin de l'estoire que Torpins l'arcevesque de Reins traita et escrist si com il le vit et oï . . ." ("And because rhyme wants to arrange itself with words taken from outside the account, the Count desired that this book be without rhyme according to the Latin of the account that Turpin, Archbishop of Rheims, treated and wrote just as he saw it and heard it"); prologue of *The Old French Johannes Translation of the Pseudo-Turpin,* ed. Ronald N. Walpole (Berkeley: University of California Press, 1976), p. 130. See also Diana B. Tyson, "Patronage of French Vernacular History Writers in the Twelfth and Thirteenth Centuries," *Romania,* 100 (1979), 186–89; and also Jeffrey Kittay and Wlad Godzich, *The Emergence of Prose: An Essay in Prosaics* (Minneapolis: University of Minnesota Press, 1987), pp. xii–xv.

49. See Chrétien, *Cligés,* ll. 18–27, and *Perceval,* ll. 61–67.

50. Walter Map, *De nugis,* Dist. iv, c. 3 (p. 288) and Dist. iv, c. 5 (p. 312).

51. Minnis, p. 10.

52. Map, *De nugis,* Dist. iv, c. 5 (p. 312).

53. See above, n. 38. The Latin Arthurian romances *De ortu Walwanii* and *Historia Meriadoci,* written by an unidentified author sometime from the last quarter of the twelfth century to the second quarter of the thirteenth, and showing close verbal parallels to Geoffrey's text, present a special case; see Neil Wright, "The Influence of Geoffrey of Monmouth on the Latin Prose Romances *De ortu Walwanii* and *Historia Meriadoci,*" in *Arturus Rex: Acta Conventus Lovaniensis 1987* (Leuven: Leuven University Press, 1991), II, 320–99.

GENERIC INTERTEXTUALITY IN THE ENGLISH
ALLITERATIVE MORTE ARTHURE
THE ITALIAN CONNECTION

Edward Donald Kennedy

The early fifteenth-century English *Alliterative Morte Arthure*, based primarily upon English chronicles that tell of Arthur's war against the Romans, does not fit neatly into modern conceptions of genre. Although it has been described as chronicle, romance, epic, *chanson de geste*, exemplum, a mirror for magistrates, a tragedy, and a "non-tragedy," most scholars who have recently written on it have not attempted to classify it.[1] This is sensible, since the author probably did not have the interest in genre that postmedieval readers have had. He appears instead to have been primarily concerned with presenting a new version of the events leading to Arthur's death, and in order to do so, he drew upon Arthurian and non-Arthurian material of various types. As W.R.J. Barron has observed, this work "is so highly individual that its sources remain uncertain: rooted in some version of the chronicle tradition, . . . it shows an eclectic familiarity with other romance matters, the list of possible sources growing as research progresses" (p. 138). Sources that scholars have so far suggested include four chronicles (Geoffrey of Monmouth's *Historia*, Wace's *Roman de Brut*, Laȝamon's English alliterative *Brut*, and Robert Mannyng's metrical *Story of England*), the French Alexander-romance *Li Fuerres de Gadres*, the Middle English Charlemagne-romance *Sir Ferumbras*, the Middle English *Parlement of the Thre Ages*, the Anglo-French *Voeux du heron*, the Middle English *Siege of Jerusalem*, the Insular French version of Mandeville's *Travels*, the Vulgate *Mort Artu*, and possibly the French *Les Voeux du paon*.[2] Like most other Arthurian writers, the author would have assumed that his audience was familiar with Arthurian works outside his own text;[3] and the extent to which his work would have seemed orthodox or not would have varied with the background of the individuals who read or heard his work.

Unlike chronicle accounts of Arthur's reign, the *Alliterative Morte Arthure* begins not with Arthur's birth but, like many romances, with a challenge: Roman ambassadors arrive at Arthur's court and demand tribute. Arthur refuses to pay and responds by invading the continent, defeating the Romans, and conquering much of Europe. Then, as in the chronicles, as Arthur prepares to march to Rome to be crowned emperor, he hears of Mordred's rebellion, returns home, and dies in his final battle against the forces of Mordred.

Although the *Alliterative Morte Arthure* drew upon Arthurian chronicles, it differs from English chronicle tradition in its suggestion that Arthur is punished for his sins. This difference has some authority, however, in a work that has intertextual affinities with the *Alliterative Morte* and that could have influenced it: Boccaccio's account of Arthur in his series of tragedies *De Casibus Virorum Illustrium.* Many of those listening to or reading the *Alliterative Morte* would have certainly recognized its intertextual relation with this Italian work.

Arthurian material is, as Derek Brewer observed in a discussion of Malory's *Morte Darthur*, "a big traditional story" that constitutes "a set of 'facts' coming from the past."[4] An author who writes such a story is not bound to follow earlier accounts closely but is free to add much that distinguishes his work from that of his predecessors. Brewer, in another essay, observes that one important feature of a traditional tale is "rationalisation" or the desire of the author "to make his version as effective as possible." An author, Brewer writes, will "introduce or suppress elements in his verbal realisation that will at least superficially account for, will 'rationalise,' the events. A favourite device is to sketch in a character study which seems to the teller to accord with the action."[5] Although the *Alliterative Morte Arthure* is in many ways different from the type of traditional tale that Brewer was discussing, some of the changes that its author makes in his presentation of Arthur are of this type; Arthur is considerably different from the Arthur of the English chronicles, but the author of the *Alliterative Morte* must have believed that his changes helped explain Arthur's fall and made it seem less capricious.

Among the passages in the *Alliterative Morte* that have attracted most attention are battle scenes that have suggested to some that the work was written as a protest against the brutality of unjust war. Although Arthur is presented at the outset as a great king and although his campaign begins as a just one in answer to the Roman demand for tribute, after Arthur kills the Roman leader Lucius and achieves the original purpose of his campaign, the war becomes, in the words of William Matthews, a "manifestation of mounting cruelty, covetousness, and imperialistic ambition" (Matthews, 128). Of particular note are lines that the author added describing the brutality of

Arthur's campaigns in Metz, Combe, and Milan, lines that depict Arthur as a king dominated by vicious and foolish pride (see Göller, "Arthurian Chivalry," 60). In Metz,

> Mynsteris and masondewes they malle to þe erthe,
> Chirches and chapells chalke-whitte blawnchede—
> Stone [s]tepells full styffe in þe strete ligges
> Chawmbyrs with chymnés and many cheefe inns—
> Paysede and pelid down playsterede walles;
> The pyne of þe pople was peté for to here! (ll. 3038–43)

> [Holy buildings and hospitals they hammered to the ground,
> Churches and chapels painted chalk-white;
> Very strong stone steeples were strewn in the streets,
> Also many fine inns and houses with chimneys,
> And they battered and broke to bits plastered walls.
> To hear the inhabitants' anguish was pitiful.][6]

Then the author describes Arthur's advance into Tuscany:

> Into Tuskane he tournez, when þus wele tymede,
> Takes townnes full tyte with towrres full heghe;
> Walles he welte down, wondyd knyghtez,
> Towrres he turnes and turmentez þe pople;
> Wroghte wedewes full wlonke, wrotherayle synges,
> Ofte wery and wepe and wryngen theire handis,
> And all he wastys with werre thare he awaye rydez—
> Thaire welthes and theire wonny[n]ges wandrethe he wroghte!
> Thus they spryngen and sprede and sparis bot lyttill,
> Spoylles dispetouslye and spillis theire vynes,
> Spendis vnsparely þat sparede was lange;
> Spedes them to Spolett with speris inew.
> Fro Spayne into Spruyslande, the worde of hym sprynges
> And spekynngs of his spencis— disspite es full hugge! (ll. 3150–63)

> [Arthur turned into Tuscany when the time seemed ripe,
> And tumultuously took its high-towered towns,
> Welting down walls, wounding knights,
> Overturning towers and tormenting the people.
> Worshipful widows he made wail in woe,

Cursing and crying and clasping their hands.
Wherever he went he laid waste with war
Their wealth and their dwellings, working misery.
They spread their surging assaults, sparing few,
Pitilessly plundering and despoiling their vines,
Consuming without stint what had been saved with care,
Then sped on to Spoleto with spears in plenty.
From Spain to Prussia word spread about him,
With talk of his extravagance; and terrible was the bitterness
(Stone, 131–32)]

This attack on one of the papal states, Spoleto, Mary Hamel writes, appears to be a "deliberate violation" of an earlier promise Arthur had made to "gyffe . . . protteccione   to all þe Pope landez" ("proffer . . .   protection to all Papal domains," l. 2410; Stone, 109). With this action, Hamel observes, "Arthur has now committed the ultimate chivalric sin of breaking his word" (Hamel, 357, n. to l. 3161).

Another significant innovation in this story of the destruction of Arthur's kingdom is the 178-line account of a dream in which Arthur, as one of the Nine Worthies, is seated at the top of the Wheel of Fortune and cast down. Karl Josef Höltgen, William Matthews, and Mary Hamel have emphasized the importance of this scene in understanding the author's major thematic concerns.[7] When Arthur asks his counselors to interpret his dream for him, one tells him that it foreshadows the destruction of his realm. Fortune, the counselor says, has become Arthur's foe because he has "schedde myche blode, and schalkes distroyede, / Sakeles, in cirquytrie,   in sere kynges landis" ("destroyed sinless men and spilled much blood / In vainglory in . . . victories in various kings' lands," ll. 3398–99; Stone, 139). Thus, according to the counselor, Arthur will fall not simply because of the whims of capricious Fortune but because of punishment for sin; desire for more land and the resulting unnecessary bloodshed will lead to his ruin. As Peter Korrel writes, "pride or hubris will prove to be Arthur's undoing. . . . his fate is self-inflicted, and Modred is a mere instrument used by Fortune to scourge Arthur for his vaulting ambition."[8]

Although the author of the *Alliterative Morte* condemns Arthur for unnecessary bloodshed and unjust conquests, in the final part of the work he once again presents Arthur sympathetically: when he must return to fight Mordred, Arthur's campaign changes from unjust to just. He becomes a champion of God fighting a usurper who has an army supported by many "Ethyns of Argayle   and Irische kynges / . . . Peghttes and paynymes   with perilous wapyns" ("heathens from Argyll and Irish kings. . . Picts and pagans with perilous weapons," ll. 4123–24; Stone, 161); through "myghttis of Criste" (the "might of Christ," l. 4070; Stone, 160), Arthur's eighteen hundred men are able to overcome Mordred's army of sixty thousand. Nevertheless, as in the chronicles, in his final combat against Mordred Arthur is mortally wounded, and in this work he is buried at Glastonbury, which was frequently identified as Avalon in the Middle Ages.

The author of the *Alliterative Morte Arthure* thus presents a pattern of a king who begins fighting a just war, but who errs through brutal and unjustifiable conquests and is punished for it; then in fighting a final just war against a usurper supported by heathen armies, Arthur once again deserves sympathy.

The suggestion that Arthur's fall is a punishment for sin occurs earlier in Arthurian literature. In fact, the author of the *Alliterative Morte Arthure* based his account of the dream of the Wheel of Fortune on an episode in the thirteenth-century French Vulgate *Mort Artu*: in that work Arthur has a dream in which the goddess Fortuna, a lady, who is "la plus bele qu'il eüst onques mes veüe el monde" ("the most beautiful he had ever seen in the world"), tells Arthur, before casting him from her wheel, that earthly pride ("orgueil terrien") is such that anyone who has climbed so high can not help but fall.[9] Although Jean Frappier interpreted this as a general statement about the vicissitudes of earthly existence,[10] Fortune's reference to pride, combined with a picture of her as a beautiful lady that bears more resemblance to the rational guides of dream visions than to the often blindfolded and grotesque figure common to portraits of Fortune,[11] suggests that the author may have wished to portray Fortune as an agent who punished Arthur for his pride. Arthur is also punished for sin in the thirteenth-century Post-Vulgate *Roman du Graal*; in this work, although the author presents a sympathetic portrait of Arthur, he nevertheless presents an Arthur who is punished for unwittingly committing the sin of incest with his half-sister.[12]

Arthur's being punished for sin was, however, unusual in a work based upon the chronicles. Although one could read into the chronicle accounts of Arthur's fall the workings of a capricious Fortune, in most of them, such as those of Geoffrey of Monmouth and Wace and the popular English prose *Brut*, Fortune is not mentioned. The fall is due simply to what Eugène Vinaver, commenting upon the accounts in Geoffrey of Monmouth, Wace, and Laȝamon, described as "a military disaster for which the chances of war were alone to blame."[13] The mid-fifteenth-century English chronicler John Hardyng mentions the mutability and caprice of Fortune but does not suggest that the fall was a punishment for sin.[14]

Although the author of the *Alliterative Morte Arthure* could have derived the suggestion for the fall as punishment directly from the Vulgate *Mort Artu,* he may have found a closer model in Boccaccio's *De Casibus Virorum Illustrium,* a work that the author of the *Alliterative Morte* could have known either through Boccaccio's original Latin version or through a French adaptation by Laurent de Premierfait.

Boccaccio's account of Arthur in the *De Casibus* is, like the *Alliterative Morte Arthure,* basically the chronicle story of Arthur's war against Rome, to which some details from romance have been added.[15] However, unlike most English chroniclers who had accepted the story of Arthur as historically true, Boccaccio is skeptical about Arthur's conquest of the Romans: he describes Arthur as having been known through "Britonum celebris fabula" ("the celebrated English fables"), and he announces at the outset, "cuius magnitudinem atque casum, etsi ex fide digna testimonio non noscamus" ("We do not recognize the evidence of his greatness and his fate as worthy of credence").[16] He nevertheless wants to relate the story since it is one known to the whole world.

Boccaccio expresses admiration for Arthur, but he nevertheless makes the story into a moral exemplum by giving a negative bias to the account of his conquests and by adding passages that give Arthur considerable responsibility for his fall. As Janet L. Smarr observes, "Boccaccio's treatment of Arthurian materials seems remarkably negative. The famous king and his . . . knights offer moral examples of what to avoid, not what to imitate."[17] Boccaccio's Arthur is a great king, but his conquests result from his pride. When Arthur became king of the Britons, Boccaccio writes, "videretque eo venisse rem publicam romanam ut quantum quisque surripuisset eidem, tantum possideret impune" ("he realized that the power of the Romans was gone from the country, and that any man could take and keep what he wished of it without reprisal"); consequently, "non contentus relicti a patre imperii" ("not content with the power left him by his father," §1, p. 728; Hall, 215), he increased it by conquering Ireland, the Orkneys, Dacia, Norway, the land of the Goths, and many other provinces. Then, satisfied that his kingdom and his reputation were great enough,[18] he stopped his warfare and, as in some of the romances, with the advice of Merlin established his Round Table; because of this table, his military alliances, and his great deeds Arthur gained a reputation that Fortune could never diminish.[19] Boccaccio also lists ideals of the Round Table that are later echoed in English works of Lydgate, Hardyng, and Malory.[20]

After the establishment of the Round Table, however, Boccaccio's account again becomes less positive. Although, in the chronicles that follow

Geoffrey of Monmouth, the Romans demanded unjust tribute from Arthur, in Boccaccio Arthur had less justification for the war: he refused the Romans what Boccaccio calls their "solitum vectigal" ("customary tribute," §5, p. 730; Hall, 216) and "copiis in Galliam deportatis, signis collatis, aduersus Lucium consulem illud armis poscentem descendit in aciem" ("with the banners of his army flying, [he] invaded Gaul, fighting against the consul, Lucius," §5, p. 730; Hall, 216). After Arthur defeated Lucius, as in the *Alliterative Morte Arthure*, he set out to conquer more territory: "Et cum illi cessisset victoria, in omissum desiderium recidens, occupaturus ampliora processit" ("his earlier desires for conquest [were] reawakened" and he "enlarged his attack"). Consequently, Boccaccio observes, Arthur's pride led to his death: "Sed elato iam parabatur occasus" ("But now his pride paved the way for his death," §5–6, p. 730; Hall, 216).

While Arthur "armis interiora infestaret Gallie" ("pillaged the interior of Gaul"), he left his son Mordred to defend his kingdom during his absence. Mordred, motivated by desire for power, looked upon the king's absence as a chance offered him by Fortune. He incited the "pressos" ("oppressed") to fight for liberty (§6, p. 730; Hall, 216). Boccaccio then tells of Arthur's returning to fight Mordred, and here, as in the *Alliterative Morte Arthure*, the readers' sympathies are expected to shift back to Arthur as he fights a usurper: Mordred "tanteque fuit obstinate perfidie ut non vereretur adversus patrem in pugnam descendere" ("was of such obstinate faithlessness that he was not ashamed to fight against his father," §8, p. 732; Hall, 217). Arthur's forces were so strong, however, that the rebels soon became aware of the crime of attacking an established ruler. There was, however, great slaughter on both sides. Mordred and Arthur killed one another in combat. When Arthur realized that he had been mortally wounded, he ordered that he be taken to Avalon, where he died.

Although Boccaccio blames Mordred for the destruction of Arthur's kingdom,[21] he concludes his account by reminding his readers of the importance of humility: "Gloria ingens regis et claritas desolatione in ignominiam et obscuritatem deleta est adeo ut possint, si velint, mortales advertere nil in orbe preter humilia posse consistere" ("The triumphant glory of King Arthur and his brilliant renown gave way to shame and obscurity by this rebellion and destruction. From this example people can learn, if they wish, that in this world only the humble things endure," §16, p. 734; Hall, 218).

H.A. Kelly has observed that although "Boccaccio's stated intention at the beginning of the *De casibus* is to give examples of great men who . . . fell as a consequence of their wickedness," he believes that Arthur "is one of the blameless ones" ("Non-Tragedy," 106–7). This interpretation, however, is questionable. Although Boccaccio expresses admiration for Arthur, his final reference to the importance of humility and his earlier allusions to Arthur's pride and desire for conquest imply that Arthur is to some extent responsible for the destruction of his kingdom. In Boccaccio's account, the pattern is similar to that of the *Alliterative Morte Arthure*: Arthur is a great king, but his pride leads to unjustifiable conquests. The reader is nevertheless expected to sympathize with him when he returns to fight the usurper Mordred.

In addition to Arthurian chronicles, Boccaccio drew upon the Vulgate *Mort Artu*. His having Mordred forge letters claiming that Arthur was dead and his telling of the ray of sunlight that pierces Mordred's wound when Arthur withdraws his lance from it point to this source. Moreover, in Boccaccio's version, Mordred is not Arthur's nephew, as in the chronicles, but his son, as in the *Mort Artu*. However, Boccaccio's account and the *Mort Artu* are significantly different on this point. In *Mort Artu*, when Mordred is described as Arthur's son, the author was expecting his readers to recall the reference in the earlier Vulgate *Lancelot* to Mordred's being the child of the incestuous union of Arthur and his half-sister; thus, in that work he is both son and nephew. Boccaccio omits the incest: he writes that Mordred is Arthur's son by a concubine ("eius ex concubina filius," §6, p. 730) Although there is some question as to whether the story of the incest was widely known in Italy,[22] Daniela Delcorno Branca points to an allusion to the incest in one of the Italian versions of the prose *Tristan*, *La Tavola Ritonda*, and her suggestion that Boccaccio, in describing Mordred simply as Arthur's son by a concubine, wished to omit a sin that might have greatly diminished Arthur's stature as a great king is plausible.[23] Nevertheless, Boccaccio may also have not wished to refer to incest if he wanted to present Arthur's fall resulting from his pride; otherwise his fall could have been interpreted as a punishment for incest.[24]

Familiarity with the Vulgate *Mort Artu* and Fortune's allusion in that work to "orgueil terrien" ("worldly pride") could have suggested to Boccaccio his presentation of Arthur's fall as being to a considerable extent due to pride and desire for conquest. Thus Boccaccio presents an account of Arthur's Roman war in which Arthur has responsibility for his fall not found in the chronicles.

Boccaccio's *De Casibus Virorum Illustrium* was translated into French twice in the early fifteenth century by Laurent de Premierfait. The first version, completed in 1400 and known as *De la Ruyne des nobles hommes et femmes*, is a close translation of the Latin; the second, completed in 1409 with the title *Du Cas des nobles hommes et femmes*, is a freer translation that circulated more widely.[25] Like Boccaccio, Laurent is, in the words of

Florence A. Smith, "to say the least chilly in his treatment of Arthur."[26] Although Laurent, like Boccaccio, praises Arthur as a great king, he retains in his account such negative elements as the references to Arthur's early desires for conquest; his not being content with the lands left him by his father; his desire, after defeating Lucius, for further conquests; his pride leading to his downfall; and the final warning that only humble things endure.

Although Boccaccio's Latin *De Casibus*, the first version of which was completed about 1360 (Ricci and Zaccaria, xv), was widely read on the Continent, it does not appear to have been well known in England. Most of the surviving manuscripts that can be proven to have been in England in the Middle Ages date from the mid- to the late fifteenth century, and, A.S.G. Edwards has argued, they apparently had a "limited academic circulation"; many of the English references to Boccaccio in the fifteenth century are, in fact, references to Lydgate's English translation, *The Fall of Princes* (completed ca. 1438).[27]

Some English writers, however, knew the Latin version. Chaucer's *Monk's Tale*, for example, appears to have been indebted to it: although some have suggested that Chaucer's knowledge of the *De Casibus* was derived from other works, others believe that he used it as a primary source for at least some of his tragedies.[28] Since Chaucer visited Italy on at least two occasions, he could have read it there, but he might also have read it in England. Chaucer's contemporary John Gower may also have used it in his *Confessio Amantis*.[29]

The best evidence for Boccaccio's Latin version being known in England by the late fourteenth century, however, appears in a manuscript of an unpublished Latin chronicle of English history from its legendary beginnings until the reign of Richard I (*Chronicon de Origine et Rebus Gestis Britanniae et Angliae*), found in Magdalen College, Oxford, Lat. 72. In his catalogue of the manuscripts in the colleges at Oxford, H.O. Coxe describes the chronicle as dating from the late fourteenth or early fifteenth century and notes that it is drawn from Geoffrey of Monmouth, Bede, Florence of Worcester, Henry of Huntingdon, Richard of Devizes, Ailred Rievaulx, and Ranulf Higden, "with a few additions, chiefly fabulous, of little importance." In his study of Arthurian chronicles Robert Huntington Fletcher noted some of the peculiarities of this chronicle version of the Arthurian story, particularly its reference to Merlin's advising Arthur to establish the Round Table and to Mordred's being Arthur's son by a concubine.[30] Daniela Delcorno Branca points out, however, that almost all of the Arthurian section of this chronicle is taken from Boccaccio's *De Casibus*.[31] Although there is no proof that this manuscript was in England in the Middle Ages,[32] it seems likely that a chronicle drawn from so many other English chronicles would have been produced in England for English readers, and the manuscript thus offers evidence that Boccaccio's Latin version was available in England by the late fourteenth century.

The author of the *Alliterative Morte Arthure* might also have read Laurent's version of Boccaccio. Since the *Alliterative Morte Arthure* appears to have been written between 1399 and 1402,[33] its author could not have read the 1409 version of Laurent's translation. Laurent's first version, however, completed in November 1400, would have been contemporary with the *Alliterative Morte Arthure*. Over one hundred manuscripts of the two versions of Laurent's work survive, at least twelve of which are in Britain.[34] Of the twelve, two—B.L. Additional 11,696 and Harley 621—represent the early version, although it is not certain that these were in England in the Middle Ages.[35]

The Latin and early French versions would, of course, have been available on the Continent, and the author of the *Alliterative Morte Arthure* might have read either of them there. Several scholars have argued that the text of the *Alliterative Morte Arthure* offers evidence that its author had traveled on the Continent, particularly in Italy. The author's interest in northern Italy is shown in part by the many place names that he introduces into his account and that are not derived from known chronicles: Pietrasanta, Lombardy, Tuscany, Pisa, Pontremoli, Piacenza, Como, Pavia, Milan, Venice. He also had some accurate information about contemporary Italian politics as indicated by allusions, for example, to the Sire of Milan's control of much of northern Italy and his control of Pisa, which did not occur until 1399.[36] Hamel writes that the poet's description of the capture of Como, which is without precedent in the chronicles, is so visual that it "seems to reflect observed or reported contemporary experience." She also suggests that the *Alliterative Morte* shows the influence of the *Divine Comedy*, a work generally unknown at first hand to Middle English writers, except to Chaucer, who had been to Italy.[37] Thus, even if the works of Boccaccio and Laurent were not widely read in England by 1400, an author who traveled on the Continent could have read either of them there, and either of these works could have suggested to him a version of Arthur's war against Lucius quite different from those he had read in English chronicles; it was a version in which there was a rational reason for Arthur's fall.

Florence A. Smith, discussing Laurent's influence in England on works like *Fall of Princes* and *Mirror for Magistrates*, comments on the development in England of a tradition of narrative tragedies of Fortune in verse which linked on the one hand with the chronicle histories and on the other with an increasing understanding of genuine tragic themes, till the writers of history ceased to be moralists and the conception of tragedy became that of internal conflict, conditioned by external happening, but not dependent on the irresponsible turnings of Fortune's wheel. (p. 526)

The story of Arthur in both Boccaccio and Laurent offers a good example of the inspiration for this development: there the fall is caused not by a capricious and irrational Fortune, but by the sins of Arthur and Mordred, both of whom wished to have more power. Arthur's pride, as Boccaccio wrote, paved the way for his death.

That such an interpretation might have been objectionable to some English readers accustomed to the heroic accounts of Arthur in the chronicles is evidenced by English adaptations of Boccaccio. Daniela Delcorno Branca observes, for example, that the author who incorporated Boccaccio's account of Arthur into Magdalen College Lat. 72 added to it the well-known chronicle references to Arthur's devotion to the Virgin Mary and omitted references to Fortuna and to Arthur's hubris ("De Arturo," p. 179, n. 63). Thus, missing are Boccaccio's "elato iam parabatur occasus" and the moralization about humble things enduring. The author, although retaining the portrayal of Mordred as Arthur's son by a concubine, tried to make Arthur somewhat consistent with the Arthur of the chronicles.[38]

John Lydgate's adaptation of Laurent's 1409 version for *Fall of Princes* shows similar concern. Since Lydgate believed that tragedy resulted from "vicious lyuyng" rather than from the caprice of Fortune,[39] the Boccaccio/Laurent interpretation of the Arthurian story would have been compatible with his own views of tragedy; but Lydgate, having read several of the English Arthurian chronicles,[40] admired Arthur too much to make him in any way responsible for his downfall. As the studies of Professors Höltgen, Göller, Dwyer, and Withrington have made clear, Lydgate's portrait of Arthur is one of the most enthusiastic in English literature.[41] He did not have Arthur fall, like many others in *Fall of Princes*, because of his own mistakes; Arthur's tragedy resulted from the "double goddesse" Fortune, who "envied at his glorie,"[42] and from Mordred, who treacherously rebelled against him. Lydgate omits the statement in his source that Mordred was Arthur's son and describes him only as his "cosyn" (l. 3000), which in Middle English could mean "nephew" and is therefore consistent with the chronicles. Lydgate omits his source's implicit condemnation of Arthur's conquests: instead of not being content with the power left him by his father, Arthur's earlier wars are fought in Lydgate's version for self-defense ("He droof Saxones out of his contre," l. 2721) or for other good reasons ("Wrouht bi counsail, and bi the ordynaunce / Of prudent Merlyn," ll. 2726–27). Arthur does not refuse the Romans their customary tribute, as in the source; instead, the Roman demand is "froward & outraious" (ll. 2876). Like the author of the account in the Magdalen College manuscript, Lydgate omits the reference to Arthur's pride leading to his death, and instead enhances Arthur's reputation by describing him as the "wisest prince & the beste kniht" (l. 2667), "curteis, large, and manly of dispence, / Merour . . . off liberalite" (ll. 2717–18), "a briht sonne set amyd the sterris" (l. 2795). At the end Arthur is "crownid in the heuenly mansioun" as the most honored of the Nine Worthies (ll. 3106–8). Lydgate omits the moral that only humble things endure and instead warns his readers to beware of treasonous kinsmen (ll. 3130–36).

Although the allusion to Arthur's pride in the accounts of Boccaccio and Laurent did not appeal to the author of the account in the Magdalen manuscript or to Lydgate, it could have suggested to the author of the *Alliterative Morte Arthure* an interpretation of the Arthurian chronicle story that had not previously been attempted in English. Even though the vision of Fortune's wheel and the suggestion of punishment for the sin of pride were present in the Vulgate *Mort Artu*, Boccaccio's innovative portrayal of an Arthur who, although a great king, was nevertheless intent on unjustifiable conquests during his war against Rome and whose pride led to the killing of innocent people and to his downfall probably seemed appropriate to an Italian living in the country that Arthur had supposedly conquered. Such details of characterization, not found in the Vulgate *Mort Artu* or earlier chronicles, also probably seemed appropriate to the author of the *Alliterative Morte Arthure*, an English moralist concerned more with condemning the unnecessary brutality of aggressive warfare than with repeating the standard account found in the chronicles.

Although scholars have been unable to classify the *Alliterative Morte Arthure* according to modern conceptions of genre, they have agreed that its author was well-read and have commented upon the *Alliterative Morte*'s intertextual affinities with such works as Arthurian chronicles, travel literature, the Vulgate *Mort Artu*, and other romances. The *Alliterative Morte* also appears to have affinities with Boccaccio's account of Arthur in *De Casibus Virorum Illustrium*, a work also related to the chronicles but considerably different from them in its interpretation of the tragedy. Matilda Tomaryn Bruckner observes, with reference to Chrétien de Troyes, that readers today are often unfamiliar with many of the traditions available to a medieval writer: "there are bound to be moments when we are unsure about . . . intertextual play: 'is this a reference to Chrétien or to the common tradition?' . . . not all resemblances indicate direct contact" (pp. 224, 233). The reader could similarly ask if the author of the *Alliterative Morte* was alluding to Boccaccio and expecting some of his readers to recognize this or if he simply conceived by coincidence an account of Arthur's fall that has similarities to the account in this work. In my opinion it was in all likelihood a source for the author. But even if the similarities were coincidental, in the later fifteenth century, when the works of Boccaccio and Laurent had circulated more widely, many of those listening to or reading this work would have recognized its affinities with an Italian interpretation of the Arthurian story.

NOTES

1. On some attempts at classification, see Karl Heinz Göller, "A Summary of Research," and "Reality Versus Romance: A Reassessment of the *Alliterative Morte Arthure*," in *The Alliterative Morte Arthure: A Reassessment of the Poem*, ed. Karl Heinz Göller (Cambridge: Brewer, 1981), pp. 7–29, and his "Arthurian Chivalry and War in the Fourteenth and Fifteenth Centuries: History and Fiction," *Spätmittelalterliche Artusliteratur*, ed. Karl Heinz Göller (Paderhorn: Schöningh, 1984), p. 65; John Finlayson, ed., *Morte Arthure* (Evanston: Northwestern University Press, 1967), p. 11; W.R.J. Barron, *English Medieval Romance* (London: Longman, 1987), pp. 138–42; Hanspeter Schelp, *Exemplarische Romanzen im Mittelenglischen*, Palaestra 246 (Göttingen: Vandenhoeck and Ruprecht, 1967), pp. 171–78; William Matthews, *The Tragedy of Arthur: A Study of the Alliterative "Morte Arthure"* (Berkeley: University of California Press, 1960); H.A. Kelly, "The Non-Tragedy of Arthur," *Medieval English Religious and Ethical Literature: Essays in Honor of G.H. Russell*, ed. Gregory Kratzmann and James Simpson (Cambridge: Brewer, 1986), pp. 92–114.

2. See Mary Hamel, ed., *Morte Arthure: A Critical Edition* (New York: Garland, 1984), pp. 34–53. Quotations from the *Morte Arthure* are from this edition.

3. On intertextuality in Arthurian romance, see, for example, Matilda Tomaryn Bruckner, "Intertextuality," in *The Legacy of Chrétien de Troyes*, ed. Norris J. Lacy, Douglas Kelly, and Keith Busby, 2 vols. (Amsterdam: Rodopi, 1987–88), I, 223–65; Douglas Kelly, *The Art of Medieval French Romance* (Madison: University of Wisconsin Press, 1992), pp. 311–13; Elspeth Kennedy, "The Re-Writing and Re-Reading of a Text: The Evolution of the *Prose Lancelot*," in *The Changing Face of Arthurian Romance*, ed. Alison Adams, Armel H. Diverres, Karen Stern, and Kenneth Varty (Cambridge: Boydell and Brewer, 1986), p. 2.

4. Derek Brewer, "Malory: The Traditional Writer and the Archaic Mind," *Arthurian Literature*, 1 (1981), 95.

5. Derek Brewer, *Symbolic Stories: Traditional Narratives of the Family Drama in English Literature* (Cambridge: Brewer, 1980), p. 4.

6. *King Arthur's Death*, trans. Brian Stone, Penguin Classics (London: Penguin, 1988), p. 128. Unless otherwise noted, translated passages are from this edition.

7. Höltgen, "König Arthur und Fortuna," *Anglia*, 75 (1957), 35–54; trans. as "King Arthur and Fortuna" in *King Arthur*, ed. Edward Donald Kennedy (New York: Garland, 1996) pp. 121–37; Matthews, 115–50; Hamel, 42–44.

8. Peter Korrel, *An Arthurian Triangle: A Study of the Origin, Development and Characterization of Arthur, Guinevere and Modred* (Leiden: Brill, 1984), pp. 211–12; also see Göller, "Chivalry," 65.

9. "Mes tel sont li orgueil terrien qu'il n'i a nul si haut assiz qu'il ne le coviegne cheoir de la poesté del monde," *La Mort le Roi Artu,* ed. Jean Frappier, 3rd ed. (Geneva: Droz, 1964), §176, pp. 226–27 ("But such is earthly pride that no one is seated so high that he can avoid having to fall from power in the world," *The Death of King Arthur,* trans. James Cable [Harmondsworth: Penguin, 1971], p. 205.)

10. Jean Frappier, *Étude sur La Mort le Roi Artu,* 3rd ed. (Geneva: Droz, 1972), pp. 255–56.

11. See Howard R. Patch, *The Goddess Fortuna in Mediaeval Literature* (Cambridge, Massachusetts: Harvard University Press, 1927; rpt. New York: Octagon, 1967), pp. 42–49.

12. See Fanni Bogdanow, *The Romance of the Grail: A Study of the Structure and Genesis of a Thirteenth-Century Arthurian Prose Romance* (Manchester: Manchester University Press, 1966), pp. 141–45. Also see her "La Chute du royaume d'Arthur: Évolution du thème," *Romania,* 107 (1986), 504–19, trans. as "The Evolution of the Theme of the Fall of Arthur's Kingdom," in my *King Arthur,* pp. 91–103, and Helen Adolf, "The Concept of Original Sin as Reflected in Arthurian Romance," *Studies in Language and Literature in Honour of Margaret Schlauch,* ed. Mieczyslaw Brahmer, Stanislaw Helsztynski, and Julian Krzyzanowski (Warsaw: Polish Scientific Publishers, 1966), pp. 21–29.

13. *The Rise of Romance* (Oxford: Clarendon, 1971), pp. 129–30.

14. Hardyng, in emphasizing the capriciousness of Fortune, was probably influenced by Lydgate's *Fall of Princes.* See the discussion of Lydgate below.

15. For recent discussions of Boccaccio's sources of the Arthurian story, see Daniela Delcorno Branca, "'De Arturo Britonum rege': Boccaccio fra storiografia e romanzo," *Studi sul Boccaccio,* 19 (1990), 151–90, and her *Boccaccio e le storie di re Artù* (Bologna: Mulino, 1991), pp. 69–112.

16. Boccaccio, "De Arturo Britonum rege," *De Casibus Virorum Illustrium,* ed. Pier Giorgio Ricci and Vittorio Zaccaria, in *Tutte le opere di Giovanni Boccaccio,* gen. ed. Vittore Branca (Milan: Mondadori, 1983), IX, 726–27; translation from *The Fates of Illustrious Men,* trans. Lewis Brewer Hall (New York: Ungar, 1965), p. 214. Quotations are from these editions. All of the other Latin quotations are from chapter xix, rather than xviii, of Book VIII of the Ricci and Zaccaria edition.

17. *The New Arthurian Encyclopedia,* ed. Norris J. Lacy et al. (New York: Garland, 1991), p. 43.

18. "Porro cum satis visum foret regni terminos et nominis gloriam ampliasse" ("He then felt that his kingdom was large enough and his reputation ample," §2, p. 728; Hall, 215).

19. "Regium nomen in tam splendidam gloriam delatum est ut nec Fortuna seviens nec annosa vetustas agere potuerit" (". . . gave such brilliance to King Arthur's name that neither the ravages of Fortune nor the history of the ancients were able to affect it," §4, p. 730; Hall, 216).

20. For a suggestion concerning the possible relation of Lydgate's work to that of Hardyng and Malory, see John Withrington, "The Arthurian Epitaph in Malory's *Morte Darthur,*" *Arthurian Literature,* 7 (1987), 131, n. 82.

21. "Quo ergo unius nepharii hominis ausu parvissimo temporis tractu ampliatum Arturi regnum diminutum est cum vita subtractum" ("Arthur's huge kingdom was shrunk and his own life lost through the temerity of one evil man," §15, p. 734; Hall, 218).

22. Edmund G. Gardner believes that few of the commentators on Dante were aware of the story. See his *The Arthurian Legend in Italian Literature* (London: Dent, 1930; rpt. New York: Octagon, 1971), p. 235.

23. "De Arturo," 172; *Boccaccio,* 81. On the incorporation of the incest story into the French prose romances, see James Douglas Bruce, "Mordred's Incestuous Birth," *Medieval Studies in Memory of Gertrude Schoepperle Loomis* (Paris: Champion, 1927), pp. 197–208; Frappier, *Étude,* 32–37, 429 (under "Additions et corrections"), and his

edition, *Mort Artu*, pp. xvi–xvii. On difficulties medieval writers may have had with incorporating this story into the story of Arthur, see Elizabeth Archibald, "Arthur and Mordred: Variations on an Incest Theme," *Arthurian Literature*, 8 (1989), 1–27. Incest was a topic some writers clearly chose to avoid: the closest Chaucer came to writing of incest, for example, was the story of Tereus's love for his sister-in-law ("The Legend of Philomela" in *The Legend of Good Women*), and, in fact, he alludes with apparent disapproval to his friend Gower's inclusion of the stories of Canace and Apollonius of Tyre in the *Confessio Amantis*. See Chaucer, "Introduction to the Man of Law's Tale," ll. 77–89 in The *Riverside Chaucer*, 3rd ed., gen. ed. Larry D. Benson (Boston: Houghton Mifflin, 1987), p. 88 and the note to these lines, p. 856. Whether the author of the *Alliterative Morte Arthure* knew the story of incest has been a matter of debate: he does not refer specifically to it, but Gawain's lament about Mordred's treason ("Of siche a[n] engendure full littyll joye happyns" [l. 3743]; "From such an engendering little joy follows"—trans. E.D.K.) and the allusion to Mordred as a "churles chekyn" ("churl's chicken," l. 4181) have led some to speculate that the author was referring to the incest. Hamel does not believe that the author intended to allude to it (see her comments, with references to earlier scholarship on the subject, pp. 53, 93 n. 146, 377 n. to l. 3743, 391 n. to l. 4181). Those listening to or reading the romance may have seen an allusion to the incest if they, like modern readers, were aware of the story; if they were not, they may have seen in these allusions a suggestion that Mordred was a bastard, a suggestion that also departs from the chronicle tradition where Mordred is the legitimate son of Arthur's sister Anna and her husband King Loth. If the author wished to suggest that Mordred was a bastard, he may have derived the idea from Boccaccio's description of him as Arthur's son by a concubine.

24. Arthur's fall is seen as punishment for his unwittingly committing the sin of incest in the Post-Vulgate *Roman du Graal*. See n. 12 above.

25. See Patricia M. Gathercole, "Two Old French Translations of Boccaccio's *De Casibus Virorum Illustrium*," *Modern Language Quarterly*, 17 (1956), 304. Laurent's first version was published at Bruges in 1476 and at Lyons in 1483. An edition of the later version appears in Wilhelm Perzl, *Die Arthur-Legende in Lydgate's Fall of Princes: Kritische Neu-Ausgabe mit Quellenforschung* (Munich: Wolff, 1911) and was reprinted in Henry Bergen, ed., *Lydgate's Fall of Princes*, Pt. IV, Early English Text Society Extra Series No. 124 (1924), pp. 329–36. Also see Emil Koeppel, *Laurent de Premierfait und John Lydgate's Bearbeitungen von Boccaccios De Casibus Virorum Illustrium* (Munich: Oldenbourg, 1885).

26. "Laurent de Premierfait's French Version of the *De Casibus Virorum Illustrium* with Some Notes on Its Influence in France," *Revue de Littérature Comparée*, 14 (1934), 521.

27. See A.S.G. Edwards, "The Influence of Lydgate's *Fall of Princes* c. 1440–1559: A Survey," *Mediaeval Studies*, 39 (1977), 425–28.

28. For doubts about Chaucer's knowledge of the work, see Edwards, p. 426 and his references to earlier scholarship; also see Edmund Reiss, "Boccaccio in English Culture of the Fourteenth and Fifteenth Centuries," *Il Boccaccio nella Cultura Inglese e Anglo-Americana*, ed. Giuseppe Galigani (Florence: Olschki, 1974), pp. 19–20. Reiss observes that Chaucer may have used the *De Casibus* but that the evidence is questionable. For the possibility that Chaucer had used Boccaccio for some of his tragedies, however, see the notes to the *Monk's Tale* by Susah H. Cavanaugh in Benson, ed., *Riverside Chaucer*, pp. 929–30.

29. See Charles Lionel Regan, "John Gower and the Fall of Babylon: *Confessio Amantis*, Prol. ll. 670–686," *English Language Notes*, 7 (1969–70), 85–92.

30. See Coxe, *Catalogus Codicum Manuscriptorum Qui in Collegiis Aulisque Oxoniensibus Hodie Adservantur* (Oxford: e Typographeo Academico, 1852), Pt. 2.2: *S. Mariae Magdalenae*, pp. 41–42; Fletcher, *The Arthurian Material in the Chronicles*, Harvard Studies and Notes in Philology and Literature, 10 (1906), 2d ed. Roger Sherman Loomis (New York: Burt Franklin, 1966), pp. 176, 187–88.

31. "De Arturo," p. 179, n. 63. I am indebted to Professor Delcorno Branca for pointing this manuscript out to me and for giving me a copy of her article before I read my paper at the Congress of the International Arthurian Society in Bonn in 1993. Three mid-fifteenth- and sixteenth-century English manuscripts also incorporate brief selections from the *De Casibus* (Edwards, 426–27). Scribes often treated Lydgate's *Fall of Princes* in the same way; see Derek Pearsall, *John Lydgate* (London: Routledge and Kegan Paul, 1970), pp. 250–51.

32. It is not included among the manuscripts, known to have been in medieval English libraries, listed in N.R. Ker, *Medieval Libraries of Great Britain: A List of Surviving Books*, 2nd ed. (London: Royal Historical Society, 1964), or in *Supplement to the Second Edition*, ed. Andrew G. Watson (London: Royal Historical Society, 1987).

33. Hamel, 53–58. Also see Larry D. Benson, "The Date of the Alliterative *Morte Arthure*," *Medieval Studies Presented to Lillian Herlands Hornstein*, ed. Jess B. Bessinger, Jr., and Robert K. Raymo (New York: New York University Press, 1976), pp. 19–40.

34. In *John Lydgate*, published in 1970, Pearsall writes that there are over one hundred manuscripts of Laurent's translations (p. 232). Patricia M. Gathercole had estimated there were sixty-five ("The Manuscripts of Laurent de Premierfait's 'Du Cas des Nobles' [Boccaccio's 'De Casibus Virorum Illustrium']," *Italica*, 32 [1955], 14–21.) Gathercole writes that twelve manuscripts are in Britain, but more may have been discovered since then.

35. Neither Kerr nor Watson, in his supplement to Kerr, lists these two manuscripts among those they know were in medieval English libraries. Cyril Ernest Wright was able to trace Harley 621 back only to the library of Sir Simonds D'Ewes (1602–50). See Wright, *Fontes Harleiani: A Study of the Sources of the Harleian Collection of Manuscripts* (London: Trustees of the British Museum, 1972), pp. 131–37.

36. See Benson, "Date," 24–28; Hamel, 62. Also George B. Parks, "King Arthur and the Roads to Rome," *JEGP*, 45 (1946), 164–70.

37. Hamel, 37, 42–43; also Hamel, "The Dream of the King: The *Alliterative Morte Arthure* and Dante," *Chaucer Review*, 14 (1980), 298–312.

38. The story of Arthur appears on ff. 23v–25r of the manuscript. There is a microfilm of this manuscript in Davis Library at the University of North Carolina at Chapel Hill.

39. See Lydgate's *Fall of Princes*, ed. Henry Bergen, Part I, Early English Text Society, Extra Series 121 (1924), Bk. 2, l. 46.

40. According to Bergen, Lydgate supplemented Laurent's text with "memories of what he had heard or read of the Arthur story in Layamon, Geoffrey of Monmouth, Wace's *Brut*, Robert of Gloucester and the prose 'Brut of England'" (*Princes*, Pt. IV, p. 326). Perzl suggests that Lydgate knew the works of Geoffrey of Monmouth and other chroniclers, but he cites specific borrowings only from the Prose *Brut* and Robert of Gloucester (pp. 80–91).

41. Karl Josef Höltgen, "König Arthur und Fortuna," pp. 53–54; Göller, *König Arthur in den englischen Literatur des späten Mittelalters*, Palaestra, 238 (Göttingen: Vandenhoeck and Ruprecht, 1963), pp. 131–36, and "Arthurs Aufstieg zum Heiligen," *Artusrittertum im späten Mittelalter*, ed. F. Wolfzettel, Beiträge zur deutschen Philologie, 57 (Giessen: Schmitz, 1984), 93–94; R.A. Dwyer, "Arthur's Stellification in the *Fall of Princes*," *Philological Quarterly*, 57 (1978), 155–71; Withrington, 124–38.

42. *Princes*, Pt. III, Early English Text Society, Extra Series No. 123 (1924), Bk. VIII, l. 2868. Other references to Lydgate's story of Arthur are from this volume and appear within parentheses in the text.

THE EYEWITNESS NARRATOR IN VERNACULAR PROSE CHRONICLES AND PROSE ROMANCES*

Frank Brandsma

An encyclopedia in the vernacular for the general reader: that seems to have been what the Antwerp townsclerk Jan van Boendale had in mind when, in 1330, he wrote *Der Leken Spiegel*, "the laymen's mirror of the world." In four books Boendale discusses Creation; the life of Christ; the world's history from the beginnings down to Charlemagne; Heaven, Hell, etc. In Book Three, which is dedicated to moral precepts, there is a small chapter called "How writers should write and what they should pay attention to," which is one of the first medieval poetic treatises in the vernacular.[1] In the first paragraph of the text Boendale states that a genuine poet should be thoroughly schooled in Latin grammar, that he should be truthful, and that he should lead an honorable life. In the three hundred lines that follow, Boendale elaborates on each of these three requirements. The moral requirements for being a writer are the author's main concern, but he also dwells on a number of more strictly poetic issues. Special attention is paid to the question of veracity in historical texts and to the truthfulness of their authors.

Boendale stresses the vital importance of the writer's truthfulness in historical and religious matters. With regard to the latter, he considers it unacceptable that a writer would tell lies about Christ, his Church, and its Saints. The divine nature of this kind of text warrants their truth. In secular historical writing, however, an additional assurance guaranteeing its veracity is deemed necessary. Boendale adheres to the traditional opinion that a poet should have been eyewitness to the events he describes in order to provide this additional assurance. As an example he mentions Dares the Phrygian's eyewitness account of the Trojan War, which we now know to be a falsification. Boendale says in ll. 67–90,

> Twee dinghen sijn onder dandre al
> Daer men niet in lieghen en sal.

Hystorien dat sijn deene;
Want om saken en ghene
En salmen daer in lieghen een haer;
Want wilen in doude jaer
En moeste dichten nieman
Dan hi diese scouwede an,
Alse Darijs Troyen dede:
Hi sach selve die waerhede
Vanden orloghe altemale,
Dat hi screef scone ende wale
Also hijt sach mitten oghen;
Want en hadde niement moghen
Bescriven dan hi diet sach;
Wantmens doe ghemeenlijc plach,
Ende noch met rechte soude,
Waert datmen trecht doen woude.
Daer omme heet ment hystoria:
Hystoria, alsic versta,
Coomt van *hysteron*, ic hout in dien:
Dats Griecsch ende luudt also vele als *zien*,
Om datmens niemene betrouwe
Dan den ghenen diet aen scouwe.

[There are two things, among all others, about which one should certainly never lie. The first of these is the description of historical events, for on no account should one tolerate even the smallest falsehood in this. Formerly, in classical antiquity, no one was allowed to chronicle events unless he had witnessed them, as Dares did the Trojan war. He himself saw the true course of the entire war, which he described elegantly and accurately, just as he saw it with his eyes—for no one would have been able to describe it but he who saw it. For that is how it used to be done—and actually still should, if one were to proceed correctly. That is why it is called "hystoria." *Hystoria*, as I understand, derives from *hysteron*; as far as I know this is Greek and means so much as "to see," because in this matter no one was trusted but he who observed it.]

The word "historia" Boendale explains as coming from Greek "hysteron," meaning "to see," therefore only an eyewitness is able to compose a true historical account. Nowadays the general opinion is that "historia" is derived from Greek "historia," that is "research, especially historical research." Boendale's etymological explanation, however, was quite common in the Middle Ages: according to Jeanette Beer, it goes back to Isidore of Seville's *Etymologiae*, and so does the idea of the eyewitness as the most truthful narrator. In her book on *Narrative Conventions of Truth in the Middle Ages*, Beer states, "Isidore's definition of history contained also the bold and influential non-sequitur that the eye-witnessing of events was the best guarantee not only of the accuracy of the historical information but also of its presentation. Truth came from the eye-witness."[2] Boendale's statements thus seem to reflect the traditional medieval view on the status and authority of the eyewitness narrator, a view that was eagerly exploited in both prose chronicles and prose romances.

Two very early examples of eyewitness narrators may have been at least as influential as Isidore's words. The prime example is, of course, the Vulgate Gospels according to Matthew, Mark, Luke, and John. As each of the Evangelists was an eyewitness to and narrator of the words and deeds of Christ, each presents a narrative with its own accents, highlights, and omissions.[3] The second example is Virgil's *Aeneid*, "the principal secular book of the Western world," read and admired throughout the Middle Ages.[4] In books II and III, Aeneas is welcomed by Dido to Carthago, and at the banquet he gives a long and dramatic firsthand account of the sack of Troy and of his travels. These two examples prompt three preliminary remarks.

In the first place, the Gospels and the *Aeneid* confirm Boendale's assumption that a religious text would more easily be accepted as undeniable truth in the Middle Ages than would a secular one. The divine subject of the Gospels will have put them above doubt, even if they had not been written down by eyewitnesses, but Aeneas's account may have been more susceptible to disbelief.[5] In fact, the acceptance of the truth claim by the medieval audience is hard—and often impossible—to assess, and for this essay it forms a tight spot. I hope to squeeze out of that spot by focusing not on the possible acceptance of the truth claim or on its validity in real life, but on its presentation, on the narrative technique used to suggest veracity.

My second remark concerns another difference between the two texts: the narrator Aeneas was the protagonist, or one of the protagonists, of the events he describes, whereas the apostles were witnesses to the deeds of Christ.[6] In modern terms they were true eyewitnesses to a series of events, not its actual perpetrators. Aeneas, however, describes his own deeds and decisions and therefore is more strongly committed in his narrative. This distinction between "I-as-protagonist" and "I-as-witness," which does not seem to impair the suggestion of veracity, will turn up again in the discussion of prose romances and chronicles.

The position of Aeneas's account within the larger epic calls for the third preliminary remark: embedded accounts like his will be considered here as eyewitness narratives in their own right, even if they are incorporated in texts with an overall, external personal or impersonal narrator. As far as I know, the internal first-person narrator is found only in this kind of embedded episode in texts from the late twelfth and early thirteenth centuries.

In fact, the first eyewitness narrative to be discussed here is an embedded one: Calogrenant's story in Chrétien's *Chevalier au lion ou Yvain*, a relatively short but detailed eyewitness account, which also has the "I-as-protagonist" narration in common with the *Aeneid*.[7] Almost dragged into telling his "conte de honte" ("tale of shame"), Calogrenant stresses the truthfulness of his account:

> "Et qui or me voldra entandre,
> cuer et oroilles me doit randre,
> car ne vuel pas parler de songe,
> ne de fable, ne de mançonge,
> dont maint autre vos ont servi,
> ains conterai ce que je vi."[8]

["So he who now would hear me, must surrender heart and ears to me, for I do not wish to speak of a dream, nor a fable, nor a lie, which many others have served you; instead I'll tell what I saw."]

Calogrenant will speak of the adventure he saw and experienced himself.[9] In his report he mentions the fact that he is describing his failure as an additional guarantee for its veracity, stating: "Parmi le voir, ce sachiez bien, m'an vois por ma honte covrir" ("I'm telling you the truth, you understand, so as to explain the cause of my shame.")[10] Within the narrative world of *Yvain*, the truth of Calogrenant's account is confirmed in detail when Yvain follows up on it and sees everything his cousin saw.[11] He finds the described narrow path, stays with the kind vavassor, whose daughter's beauty even surpasses Calogrenant's description, meets the bulls and the ugly giant herdsman, and finally comes to the fountain, where he beholds all that he had come to see.[12] The victory over the defender of the fountain then gives Yvain's story a different turn and eventually a more happy outcome, but his experiences up to this point confirm both Calogrenant's report and his reliability as eyewitness narrator.

In *Yvain*, Calogrenant's account is embedded in the romance narrated by a first-person narrator, who, quoting the character, passes the tale on to the audience. In the prose version of Robert de Boron's *Merlin*, a similar transference of eyewitness information is presented in a more explicit way through the introduction of the scribe Blaise. The Merlin character is equipped with two qualities that assure the audience of his veracity. On the one hand, as a devil's child he has the demonic knowledge of the past, which is balanced or even surpassed by the knowledge of the future God provided him with through his pious mother.[13] On the other hand, he is eyewitness to many of the events in the story of Vortigern, Uther, and Arthur. In short, the divine and secular guarantees for truth that Boendale mentioned are combined in the omniscient and omnipresent Merlin, who at regular intervals reports everything he has seen and done and all he knows of past, present, and future events to the faithful "scriptor" Blaise, who writes it all down in a book. Merlin's visits to Blaise are described, for instance, as follows: "Einsi s'en ala Merlins a Blaise et li dist ces choses, ce qu'il sot que a avenir en estoit, et par ce qu'il dist a Blaise en savons nos ce que nos en savons"[14] ("Thus Merlin went to Blaise and told him of these things what he knew was going to happen, and because he told Blaise we know what we know about these things"). Because Blaise has written everything down, we know what we know. The scriptor's book is the alleged source for Robert's verse romance, its prose version, and the *Estoire de Merlin* in the Vulgate Cycle. The authority of Blaise's work comes from the eyewitness Merlin, as he himself explains to his scribe:

> "et toz jorz mais sera ta poine et ton livre retrait et volentiers oïz en toz leus. Mais il ne sera pas en auctorité, por ce que tu n'ies pas ne ne puez estre des apostoles, car li apostole ne mistrent riens en escrit de Nostre Seingnor qu'il n'eussent veu ne oï et tu n'i mez rien que tu en aies veu ne oï, se ce non que je te retrai."[15]

> ["And always your work and your book will be mentioned and gladly heard everywhere. But it will not have authority, because you are not, nor could be like the disciples, because the disciples wrote nothing down about Our Lord which they had not seen or heard, and you don't write anything down that you have seen or heard, but only what I tell you."]

Alexandre Leupin discusses these phrases in his *Le Graal et la littérature* and says:

Est ce à dire que le mage renonce à fonder l'authenticité de ce qui est devenu sa propriété narrative? Pas le moins du monde: simplement l'*auctoritas* n'est pas localisé au niveau du sténographe qu'est Blaise: elle réside tout entière dans la parole même de Merlin, qui, lui, est témoin *de visu* des événements de la fiction.[16]

[Is this to say that the magician declines to provide a basis for the authority of what has become his proper narrative? Not at all: it is just that the au[c]thority is not located on the level of the stenographer Blaise: it resides completely in the words of Merlin, who, himself, is an eyewitness of the events of the fiction.]

The authority comes from the eyewitness—in this respect Merlin considers himself equal to the evangelists—but the truth of the *Merlin* is of a different nature from that of the Gospel, where the divine status of the story precludes any doubts of its veracity. Leupin is right in describing the events in the *Merlin* as fiction. We have entered the realm of the prose romance. Yet what matters most here is that in both cases the presentation of the material as "true" is founded on the same basis: the alleged reliability of the eyewitness narrator.

Apart from these "fictions of authority," as Jane Burns has called them (p. 35), the prose versions of the *Merlin* texts suggest trustworthiness through the use of prose instead of verse. After 1200, rhymed stories tend to be condemned as lies, whereas prose narratives are considered true, as among others Erich Köhler and Walter Haug have shown.[17] In this context the eyewitness status of the "source" occasionally forms an additional argument for the veracity of a prose text. The Old French Johannes Translation of the *Pseudo-Turpin* chronicle, made for count Renaut de Beaujeu in 1206, states, "Et por ce que rime se velt afeitier de moz conqueilliz hors de l'estoire, voust li cuens que cist livres fust sanz rime selonc le latin de l'estoire que Torpins l'arcevesque de Reis, traita et escrist si com il le vit et oï"[18] ("And because rhyme tends to embellish itself with words taken outside the narrative, the count wished this book to be made without rhyme according to the Latin history which Turpin, the archbishop of Reims, described and wrote down as he had seen and heard it.") According to Ronald Walpole, the success of the Latin *Pseudo-Turpin* chronicle and its French prose translations and their acceptance as true accounts depended largely on the alleged presence of the narrator Turpin at the scene of the battle, on its "I-as-witness" narration (Walpole, xi–xvi). The fact that other Charlemagne chronicles did not describe the events could be easily explained away by the argument that their authors, such as Einhard, were not there, did not see what happened (Walpole, xiv–xvi). I would, just for the sake of the argument, like to continue this line of thought toward the Oxford *Chanson de Roland* and its account of the same events and even of the very bishop Turpin's death. Seen in this light the Oxford version might have been the less believable one of the two conflicting presentations, because it describes in great detail events that knew no French survivors. Not one Frank of the rearguard was left alive to tell the tale of its glorious demise. Turpin's eyewitness account, on the other hand, was, in Walpole's words, "generally esteemed throughout the Middle Ages as no less authentic than Einhard's *Vita Karoli Magni*." [19] The credit given to this kind of prose chronicle must have been beneficial to the credibility of prose texts in general.

The suggestion of truth thus came from the eyewitness, notwithstanding the fact that the actual Turpin story was as fictitious as the Oxford *Roland* or the prose *Merlin*. Yet there were real eyewitnesses to real events as well. The Fourth Crusade was described by two such eyewitness narrators: Robert de Clari and Geoffroy de Villehardouin. They have different points of view according to their social positions. Villehardouin was one of the leaders of the campaign and well-informed on every plan and policy, whereas Robert de Clari was just a minor knight. Each of the two knights-narrators testifies what he saw, heard, and remembers in a prose account, which both called *La Conquête de Constantinople*. In his epilogue Robert explicitly proclaims his veracity:

> Ore avés oï le verité, confaitement Coustantinoble fu conquise . . . que chis qui i fu et qui le vit et qui l'oï le tesmongne, Robers de Clari, li chevaliers, et a fait metre en escrit le verité, si comme ele fu conquise; et ja soit chou que il ne l'ait si belement contee le conqueste, comme maint boin diteur l'eussent contee, si en a il toutes eures le droite verité contee, et assés de verités en a teutes qu'il ne puet mie toutes ramembrer. [20]

> [Now you have heard the truth of how Constantinople was conquered [. . .], as he who was there and who saw it and who heard it describes it, Robert of Clari, the knight. He has had the truth put into writing, of how she was taken, and if perhaps he has not so well described the conquest as many good narrators would have done, he has at all accounts told the straightforward truth, and he has left out a lot of true things because he cannot remember them all.]

The sincerity of this eyewitness, so humbly and therefore convincingly put forward here, has not been doubted. Clari could be considered an "I-as-witness" narrator. Villehardouin, however, is of the Aeneas-like "I-as-protagonist" type. This results, as again Jeanette Beer has argued, in a slightly biased account, meant to persuade the homefront that Villehardouin and his companions did the right thing when they went to Contantinople instead of to the Holy Land.[21] Both Crusade chronicles derive their alleged truthfulness from their eyewitness narrators.

The Prose *Lancelot*, the final text to be discussed here, is in fact a fictitious romance, but it claims to be a complete and true chronicle of Arthur's reign. In order to support this claim, the author or authors of the text have used narrative techniques that are found in the contemporary prose chronicles and often also throughout Arthurian romance. Thus it is written in prose like the Crusade chronicles mentioned above, the *Pseudo-Turpin* translations, and the prose version of Robert's *Merlin*. The application of the narrative technique of interlace in the *Lancelot* shows the influence of Chrétien's *Yvain* and his *Conte del Graal*, but also that of the interlace in Villehardouin's text. As far as the narrative technique is concerned, the *Lancelot*, in my opinion, also combines the generic characteristics of the prose chronicle and Arthurian romance when it comes to the figure of the eyewitness narrator.

Calogrenant, Robert de Clari, Turpin, and Geoffroy de Villehardouin in the two genres represent the knight-narrator, the eyewitness narrator who is also to be discovered in the *Lancelot*. The text claims to be based upon the writings of Arthur's clerks, who recorded the accounts the knights gave when they returned from their adventures. It is even said that these recording sessions were already standard procedure in the days of Uther Pendragon.[22] The most elaborate remark on the clerks and their function states:

> Chelui jor furent assis li .III. chevalier [Gauvain, Hector, Lancelot] en la Table Roonde et furent mandé li clerc qui metoient en escript les proeches des compaignons de la maison le roy Artu. Si en y avoit .IIII., si en ot non li uns Arodiens de Coloigne et li secons Tantalides de Vergeaus et li tiers Thumas de Toulete et li quars Sapiens de Baudas. Cil quatre metoient en escript tout chou que li compaignon le roy Artu faisoient d'armes, *ne ja lor grant feit ne fusent autrement seu*; si mistrent en escript les aventures monsieur Gauvain tout avant. . . .[23]

> [On All Saints' Day the three knights were seated at the Round Table, and the scribes who recorded the deeds of the companions of King Arthur's household were summoned. There were four of them: the

first was named Arodian of Cologne, the second Tantalides of Vercelli, the third Thomas of Toledo, and the fourth Sapient of Baghdad. These four wrote down all the feats of arms of King Arthur's companions and otherwise their great deeds would never have been known. First of all they wrote down the adventures of Sir Gawain. . . .]

The phrase "ne ja lor grant feit ne fusent autrement seu" closely resembles the statement "et par ce qu'il dist a Blaise en savons nos ce que nos en savons" ("and because he told Blaise, we know what we know about these things") in the Prose *Merlin*.[24] The function of the four clerks is the same as that of Blaise: they are the "scriptores," taking down the words of the "I-as-protagonist" eyewitness that each knight-narrator is. The larger number of narrators—Blaise had only Merlin to listen to—and scribes makes no difference here, but at first glance the status of the knights-narrators does, as the knights lack Merlin's divine omniscience. However, because they do not foretell the future or describe things they have not witnessed themselves, this does not endanger the suggestion of truthfulness, which their status as eyewitnesses provides to the narrative. Here, as in the *Merlin*, the authority lies in the speaker(s), rather than in the scribe.

In fact, the veracity of the knights-narrators is stressed time and again, as the knights on departure are sworn to give a full and true report of whatever adventures they will encounter:

> Et li saint furent aporté, si com il estoit a costume, que nus chevaliers ne movoit de la maison lo roi por aventure querre qui avant ne jurast sor sainz que il verité diroit au revenir de totes les choses qui li avandroient a son escient. Et se il au movoir nel juroit, il lo jureroit au revenir, ainz que il fust creüz de nule rien.[25]

> [Holy relics were brought, as was customary, for no knight would set off from the royal court in search of adventure without first swearing on holy relics that on his return he would tell the truth, to the best of his knowledge, about everything which befell him. Or, if he did not swear it when he set off, he would swear it on his return, before he was believed about anything.]

Even though the actual interlaced romance features "li contes" as its impersonal narrator and has not been given the narrative form of a series of "I-as-protagonist" reports, the prose *Lancelot* makes use of the suggestion of truth that the eyewitnesses provide. In the *Queste del saint Graal* and the *Mort Artu* a sole survivor of the essential events is provided in order to testify truthfully what happened to Galahad, Perceval, and the Grail, in Bohort's case, and to Arthur and Mordred in Bedivere's case. With regard to Bohort's account the text states explicitly that he describes the adventures of the Grail "com il les avoit *veues*" ["as he had seen them"]![26]

In texts ranging from the Bible to Villehardouin, Robert de Clari, and Jan van Boendale, truth comes from the eyewitness. In fictitious narratives like Virgil's *Aeneid*, Chrétien's *Yvain*, the *Pseudo-Turpin* and its translations, the Prose *Merlin*, and the Prose *Lancelot*, the suggestion of veracity is created along the same lines: an alleged eyewitness narrator or a narrative construction featuring eyewitnesses is presented as the ultimate source of the romance. Thus fiction is masked as truth. That the disguise was successful is indicated by the authority of the *Pseudo-Turpin* throughout the Middle Ages and even by Jan van Boendale's firm belief in the truthfulness of Dares the Phrygian. With regard to the Prose *Lancelot*, however, I would like to believe that it may have been a challenge for a perspicacious medieval audience to see through—and enjoy—the hoax.

NOTES

*Bart Besamusca and Orlanda S.H. Lie read the first draft of this paper. I am grateful to them and to Erik Kooper, who allowed me to quote his translation (then unpublished) of Boendale's treatise. I also thank the participants in the discussion of the oral version of this article at the XVIIth International Congress of the Arthurian Society in Bonn for their comments and suggestions.

1. Jan van Boendale, *Der Leken Spiegel*, ed. M. de Vries, 3 vols. (Leiden: Du Mortier, 1844–48), Book III, chap. XV. For an English translation (by Erik Kooper) of the text, see W.P. Gerritsen, H. van Dijk, Orlanda S.H. Lie, and A.M.J. van Buuren, "A Fourteenth-Century Vernacular Poetics: Jan van Boendale's 'How Writers Should Write,'" in Erik Kooper, ed., *Medieval Dutch Literature in Its European Context* (Cambridge: Cambridge University Press, 1994), pp. 245–60. From this translation ll. 67–90 (p. 254) will be quoted here. See also W.P. Gerritsen, "The Benefits of *Clergie*: Laymen and Clerics as Participants in the Literary Culture of the Low countries around 1300," in Ann Rigney and Douwe Fokkema, eds., *Cultural Participation: Trends since the Middle Ages* (Amsterdam: Benjamins, 1993), pp. 13–19.

2. Jeanette M.A. Beer, *Narrative Conventions of Truth in the Middle Ages* (Geneva: Droz, 1981), p. 25. See also Alexandru Cizek, "L'Historia comme témoignage oculaire: Quelques implications et conséquences de la définition de l'historiographie chez Isidore de Séville" in Danielle Buschinger, ed., *Histoire et littérature au Moyen Age: Actes du Colloque du Centre d'Etudes Médiévales de l'Université de Picardie (Amiens 20–24 Mars 1985)* (Göppingen: Kümmerle, 1991), pp. 69–84. I owe the reference to this last article to Richard Trachsler.

3. The evangelist Luke describes himself and other narrators of the same events as trustworthy eyewitnesses; see Luke I: 1–4. See John XX: 24–29 for the disciple Thomas's "nisi videro, non credam" ("Unless I see [the scars of the nails in his hands and put my finger on those scars and my hand in his side], I will not believe," Good News Bible [n.p.: The Bible Societies/Collins/Fontana, 1976], New Testament, p. 146).

4. The quote is taken from the introduction of Virgil, *The Aeneid*, translated into English prose with an introduction by W.F. Jackson Knight (Harmondsworth: Penguin, 1981), p. 23.

5. The veracity of Aeneas's report, given as eyewitness-protagonist (cf. the next remark to be made in my text), may have been impaired by the fact that it contains an embedded report by a similar eyewitness-protagonist (Sino, cf. *Aeneid*, book II, ll. 76–198), which turned out to be untrue, his story being a hoax devised by Ulysses.

6. At the beginning of his narrative, Aeneas describes himself as eyewitness and protagonist (*Aeneid*, book II, ll. 5–6; cf. also ll. 500, 624). See also *Eneas: Roman du XIIe siècle*, ed. J.-J. Salverda de Grave (Paris: Champion, 1925), ll. 857–58, where Eneas states, "la verité vos an dirai, car jo i fui, sel vi et sai" ("I will tell you the truth, because I was there, and I saw it and know it").

7. See Chrétien de Troyes, *The Knight with the Lion, or Yvain (Le Chevalier au Lion)*, ed. William W. Kibler (New York: Garland, 1985), ll. 42–580; *Der Löwenritter (Yvain) von Christian von Troyes*, ed. W. Foerster (Halle: Niemeyer, 1887; rpt. Amsterdam: Rodopi, 1965), ll. 42–580, and *Les Romans de Chrétien de Troyes édités d'après la copie de Guiot (Bibl. nat, fr. 794). IV: Le Chevalier au lion (Yvain)*, ed. Mario Roques (Paris: Champion, 1982), ll. 42–580.

8. *Yvain*, ed. and trans. Kibler, ll. 169–74; cf. ed. Foerster, ll. 169–74 and ed. Roques, ll. 169–74. The reference to "fable and mançonge" and other intertextual references to Wace's *Roman de Brut* and *Roman de Rou* (esp. *Yvain*, ll. 577–78: "Ensi alai, ensi reving; au revenir por fol me ting" ["Thus I went, and thus I returned; upon returning I considered myself a fool"]) are discussed in Alois Wolf, "Fol i allai—fol m'en revinc! Der Roman vom Löwenritter zwischen mançonge und mære," in W. Fritsch-Rößler, ed., *Uf der mâze pfat*. Festschrift für Werner Hoffmann zum 60. Geburtstag (Göppingen: Kümmerle, 1991), pp. 205–25. Whereas Wolf stresses the fictional nature of the account of Calogrenant's adventure in Brocéliande, I would like to put forward its veracity within the confines of the *Yvain* narrative. See also Alexandre Leupin, *Le Graal et la littérature: Étude sur la vulgate arthurienne en prose* (Lausanne: l'Age d'Homme, 1982), pp. 18–19.

9. There is a strong emphasis on "seeing" ("veoir") in Calogrenant's report, cf. lines 195, 226, 228, 295, 315, 319, 331, 380, 390, 392, 397, 401, 412, 419, 432, 455, 460, 482, 537. See also Joan Tasker Grimbert, *Yvain dans le miroir: Une Poétique de la réflexion dans le Chevalier au lion de Chrétien de Troyes* (Amsterdam: Benjamins, 1988), p. 143 (and p. 208, n. 4) and Barbara Nelson Sargent-Baur, "'Avis li fu': Vision and Cognition in the *Conte du Graal*," in Norris J. Lacy and Gloria Torrini-Roblin, eds., *Continuations: Essays on Medieval Literature and Language in Honor of John L. Grigsby* (Birmingham, Alabama: Summa, 1989), pp. 133–44.

10. *Yvain*, ed. Kibler, ll. 526–27; cf. ed. Foerster, ll. 526–27 (and p. 283, n.) and ed. Roques, ll. 526–27.

11. *Yvain*, ed. Kibler, ll. 723–961; ed. Foerster, ll. 723–961; ed. Roques, ll. 723–961.

12. Cf. *Yvain*, ed. Kibler, ll. 800–901: "Puis erra jusqu'a la fontainne, si vit quanqu'il voloit veoir" ("Then he wandered until he came to the fountain, and he saw everything he wanted to see").

13. Robert de Boron, *Merlin: Roman du XIIIe siècle*, ed. Alexandre Micha (Geneva: Droz, 1979), par. 15, ll. 17–28 and par. 16, ll. 19–53.

14. *Merlin* (ed. Micha), par. 81, ll. 6–9. The word "nos" indicates the narrator and his audience, which means that there is an extra level in the narrative construction above those of Merlin and Blaise respectively, namely the level of the narrator. Cf. for the scriptor Blaise also par. 16, ll. 1–117; par. 23, ll. 1–71; par. 36, ll. 1–4; par. 44, ll. 1–22; par. 50, ll. 1–4; par. 69, ll. 2–4; par. 74, ll. 1–2.

15. *Merlin* (ed. Micha), par. 16, ll. 95–101.

16. Leupin, pp. 38–39; the quote discussed by Leupin was taken from the *Estoire de Merlin* (ed. Sommer), which does not differ in any significant way from the

Prose Merlin quote given above. For Merlin and Blaise, see also E. Jane Burns, *Arthurian Fictions: Rereading the Vulgate Cycle* (Columbus: Ohio State University Press, 1985), pp. 17–18.

17. See Erich Köhler, "Zur Entstehung des altfranzösischen Prosaromans," in his *Trobadorlyrik und höfischer Roman: Aufsätze zur französischen und provenzalischen Literatur des Mittelalters* (Berlin: Rütten and Loening, 1962), pp. 213–33, 294–96, and Walter Haug, *Literaturtheorie im deutschen Mittelalter: Von den Anfängen bis zum Ende des 13. Jahrhunderts, Eine Einführung* (Darmstadt: Wissenschaftliche Buchgesellschaft, 1985), pp. 235–49, esp. 242–47.

18. Ronald N. Walpole, ed., *The Old French Johannes Translation of the Pseudo-Turpin Chronicle: A Critical Edition* (Berkeley: University of California Press, 1976), p. 130, prologue, ll. 10–14. In ll. 2–6 a similar truth claim is expressed: "ci poez oïr la verité d'Espaigne selonc le latin de l'estoire que li cuens Renauz de Boloigne fist par grant estuide cerchier et querre es livres a monseignor Saint Denise" ("Here you may hear the truth about Spain according to the Latin version of the history for which count Renaut of Boloigne ordered a very industrious search in the books [of the monastery] of Monseigneur Saint Denis"). See par. LXII, LXVIII, and LXXVII for instances like "je, Torpins, arcevesques . . . " ("I, Turpin, the archbishop . . . "). The epilogue of the texts describes the death of Turpin "si con il fu tesmoigniez d'autre escripture et de plusors anciens clers qui certainemant le sorent, par cui il est mis en escrit et en memoire" ("as it is testified by other writings and by several ancient scholars who know it for certain, by whom it is written down and remembered," par. LXXVIII, ll. 19–21).

19. Walpole, xii. Cf. Gabriele Spiegel, "Pseudo-Turpin, the Crisis of the Aristocracy and the Beginnings of Vernacular Historiography in France," *Journal of Medieval History*, 12 (1986), 207–23. In fact, Einhard in his prologue presents himself as a trustworthy eyewitness: "quaeque praesens oculata"; see Einhard, *Vita Karoli Magni / The Life of Charlemagne*, ed. Evelyn Scherabon Firchow and Edwin H. Zeydel (Dudweiler: AQ-Verlag, 1985), p. 30, and Cizek, p. 80, n. 2.

20. Robert de Clari, *La Conquête de Constantinople*, ed. Philippe Lauer (Paris: Champion, 1956), par. CXX.

21. Cf. Jeanette Beer, "Author Formulae and the Differentation of Material in Villehardouin's *La Conquête de Constantinople*," *Romance Philology*, 32 (1979), 298–302, and her *Narrative Conventions of Truth*, pp. 35–46 (the chapter is entitled "Truth and Propaganda"). See also Villehardouin, *La Conquête de Constantinople*, ed. Edmond Faral (Paris: Les Belles Lettres, 1961), pp. xvi–xxxvii. The eyewitness narratives of the Crusades describe travels and strange new lands. It is interesting to note here that in travel stories (like those of Brendan and Marco Polo) the eyewitness narrator functions just as he does in historiography: he provides and guarantees a truthful account. See Dietmar Rieger, "Marco Polo und Rusticello da Pisa: Der Reisende und sein Erzähler," and Hannes Kästner, "Der zweifelnde Abt und die 'mirabilia descripta': Buchwissen, Erfahrung und Inspiration in den Reiseversionen der Brandan-Legende," both articles in Xenja von Ertzdorff and Dieter Neukirch, eds., *Reisen und Reiseliteratur im Mittelalter und in der Frühen Neuzeit* (Amsterdam: Rodopi, 1992), pp. 289–312, 389–416.

22. See *Lancelot: Roman en prose du XIIIe siècle*, ed. Alexandre Micha, 9 vols. (Geneva: Droz, 1978–83), IV, par. LXXX, 17 (hereafter, Micha's edition is abbreviated *M*) and *The Vulgate Version of the Arthurian Romances: Edited from Manuscripts in the British Museum*, ed. H.O. Sommer (Washington, D.C., 1908–16; rpt. New York: AMC, 1979), V, 130, l. 13–15 (hereafter *S*). In Chrétien's *Erec* (ed. Foerster, ll. 6474–510) and *Yvain* (ll. 2291–301), the protagonists describe their adventures to the king.

23. Edition: *M*, VIII, par. LXXIa, 48; translation by Carleton W. Carroll in Norris J. Lacy, ed., *Lancelot-Grail: The Old French Arthurian Vulgate and Post-Vulgate in Translation* (New York: Garland, 1993), II, 238.

24. In the "Préparation à la Queste" section of the *Lancelot*, King Arthur wishes to let his heirs hear of Lancelot's exploits, cf. *M*, VI, par. CI, 6 and *S*, V, 332, ll. 16–20.

25. *Lancelot do Lac: The Non-Cyclic Old French Prose Romance*, ed. Elspeth Kennedy (Oxford: Clarendon, 1980), p. 298, ll. 10–15, see also *M*, VII, par. LIa, 6 and *S*, III, 227, ll. 16–20. Translation: *Lancelot of the Lake*, trans. Corin Corley (Oxford: Oxford University Press, 1989), p. 257. Cf. Leupin, 43–46 (Leupin points out a number of inconsistencies in the narrative construction); Elspeth Kennedy, *Lancelot and the Grail: A Study of the Prose Lancelot* (Oxford: Clarendon, 1986), pp. 156–57; Emmanuèle Baumgartner, "Les Techniques narratives dans le roman en prose," in Norris J. Lacy, Douglas Kelly, Keith Busby, eds., *The Legacy of Chrétien de Troyes*, 2 vols. (Amsterdam: Rodopi, 1987–88), I, 172–77; E. Jane Burns, "La Voie de la Voix: The Aesthetics of Indirection in the Vulgate Cycle," in Lacy, Kelly, Busby, eds., *The Legacy of Chrétien de Troyes*, II, 151–58, and Katalin Halász, *Images d'auteur dans le roman médiéval (XIIe-XIIIe siècles)* (Debrecen: Kossuth Lajos Tudományegyetem, 1992), pp. 97–111.

26. The epilogue to the *Queste del saint Graal* states, "Quant il orent mengié, li rois fist avant venir le clers qui metoient en escrit les aventures aus chevaliers de laienz. Et quant Boorz ot contees les aventures telles come il les avoit *veues*, si furent mises en escrit et gardees en l'almiere de Salebieres, dont mestre Gautier Map les trest a fere son livre del Seint Graal por l'amor del roi Henri son seignor, qui fist l'estoire translater de latin en françois" ("When they had dined, King Arthur summoned his clerks who were keeping a record of all the adventures undergone by the knights of his household. When Bors had related to them the adventures of the Holy Grail as witnessed by himself, they were written down and the record kept in the library at Salisbury, whence Master Walter Map extracted them in order to make his book of the Holy Grail for love of his lord King Henry, who had the story translated from Latin into French," *La Queste del saint Graal*, ed. Albert Pauphilet [Paris: Champion, 1921], pp. 279–80; *The Quest of the Holy Grail*, trans. Pauline Matarasso [Harmondsworth: Penguin, 1969], p. 284).

Intertextuality Between Genres in the *Lancelot-Grail*

Elspeth Kennedy

In this chapter I propose to explore generic intertextuality in Arthurian romance and to compare our perceptions of it with those of the medieval public insofar as these can be determined. I shall focus this exploration on the *Lancelot-Grail* cycle not only because I have lived with this text for rather a long time but also because, like other complex literary works of the Middle Ages, it does not exist in splendid isolation, frozen in time and within a rigid concept of literary genre. I want to study it here as an example on a grand scale of intertextuality not only within that elusive genre of medieval romance, so resistant to firm definition, but also within a range of other types of literature; I shall be paying particular attention to interaction with the lyric, the chronicle, and the *chanson de geste* and to the way such interaction may also serve to bring out the differences between the handling of similar material that characterize the various genres. For an exploration of medieval perceptions of generic intertextuality, the following kinds of evidence might be of assistance. The first of these is the context in which a romance is placed within a manuscript volume. As we shall see, this can be suggestive in relation to Chrétien's romances but is not of much assistance in relation to a prose romance such as the *Lancelot-Grail* cycle, which is so vast that it leaves little room for other texts within one volume. Second, scribal interventions within the text itself can be illuminating. Third, readers' comments in the margin might be revealing. Fourth, comments in other near contemporary works might provide some clues. Fifth, the use made by later medieval writers of quotations from and allusions to the Arthurian romances could be of interest. Terms such as *estoire*, *roman*, *conte*, even *chanson* are not sufficiently clearly differentiated at this stage to be of much use in relation to genre.

I shall begin with the lyric. This might appear to be an unexpected choice, as at first sight there seems to be little connection between the lyric and the *Lancelot-Grail* cycle, which, unlike the Prose *Tristan* and the

Perceforest, contains no lyrics. It also lacks the love meditations, usually in the form of monologues, such as are to be found in the *Chevalier de la charrete*, and which so often echo the rhythms and the images of the lyric. Yet it is the interplay between the Lancelot romance in verse and that in prose that provides the main link, as it were at one remove, with the *chanson d'amor*.

Chrétien's work, as Sylvia Huot has pointed out, opens with an extended first-person statement of poetic service somewhat reminiscent of the trouvère lyric; in it the transition from prologue to narrative proper entails the transformation of this authorial persona into a third-person figure and suggests a conflation of the trouvère with the clerkly romance narrator.[1] The *Chevalier de la charrete* represents, from a certain point of view, a transposition into narrative terms of a situation typical of the *chanson d'amor*: the lover tries to convince his lady of the quality of his love, here not through song but through deeds of chivalry. Links with the lyric are, of course, also to be found in the exploration of the pain and joy of love in the monologues, which recall the vocabulary and images of the lyric. Reminiscent too of the lyric are the trances that exemplify the lover's total absorption in thoughts of his beloved and his lack of awareness of his surroundings and of the normal requirements of social conventions at that particular moment. The terms *pense* and *s'oblie* are used in relation to the lover's meditations in both the lyric and the verse romance.[2]

In the Prose *Lancelot*, in contrast, the hero as lover is usually singularly inarticulate; not only is he, as might be expected, struck dumb in the presence of his lady, but he does not even voice his feelings to himself in monologues. Yet the link with the lyric through allusion to Chrétien's romances is clearly made through the lover's trances to which are subject Lancelot and the other young lover, Hector.[3] A number of these—seven major trances and a number of briefer moments of abstraction—occur in the account of the events that ultimately lead up to Lancelot's installation as a knight of the Round Table.

Unlike the situation in Chrétien's romance, Lancelot's trances are not explicitly identified as those of a lover through reference to the thoughts that are passing through his mind or the physical sensations conventionally linked with love, but the terms *pense* and *s'oblie* are used, and the context and narrative framework given to the trance evoke specific episodes in the verse romances. For example, Lancelot twice falls into a trance by a river. The first of these trances is closely modeled on the *Charrete* episode of the meditation by the ford during which Lancelot fails to respond to a challenge and is rudely awakened from it by contact with water;[4] in the prose romance there is a second trance by water, brought on by a glimpse of the queen; this one leads Lancelot right into the river from which he is rescued by another of Chrétien's lovers, Yvain (*LK* 266–67).

There is also a more direct link made between one of Lancelot's achievements as a true lover and song in the episode of the *carole magique* into which those are drawn who love or have loved. Lancelot joins the *carole* and disports himself and sings, "s'anvoise et chante ausi com li autre font";[5] but, as the most loyal, the most handsome and best of all knights, he is destined to bring the *carole* to an end. Only on three occasions in the prose romance does Lancelot give eloquent expression to his feelings as a lover. When, after much tongue-tied hesitation, he finally declares his love for Guinevere, he does so in terms that echo the language and rhythms of the lyric, as he explains the effect that her words of farewell as he sets off on his first adventure ("A Deu, biaus douz amis") have had upon him:

> "Ne onques puis do cuer ne me pot issir. Ce fu li moz qui prodome me fera se gel suis. Ne onques puis ne vign an si grant meschief que de cest mot ne me manbrast. Cist moz m'a conforté an toz mes anuiz, cist moz m'a de toz mes maus garantiz et m'a gari de toz periz; cist moz m'a saolé an totes mes fains, cist moz m'a fait riche an totes mes granz povretez." (*LK*, 345–46)

> ["These words have been engraved on my heart ever since. These were the words that will make me a man of worth if I am to become one. Since then I have never been in such great straits that I did not remember these words. These words have comforted me in all my troubles, these words have preserved me from all ills and have saved me from all perils; these words have nourished me in my great hunger, these words have made me rich in my great poverty."]

He is goaded into a passionate verbal defense of his love when he rejects absolutely Guinevere's suggestion that his love for her has had a destructive effect upon him as a knight:

> "Dame, fait Lanceloz, vos dites mal. Sachiez que je ja ne fusse venuz a si grant hautesce com je sui, se vos ne fussiez, car je n'eusse mie cuer par moi au conmancement de ma chevalerie d'amprandre les choses que li autre laissoient par defaute de pooir. Mais ce que je baoie a vos et a vostre grant biauté mist mon cuer en l'orgueil ou j'estoie si que je ne poïsse trouver aventure que je ne menasse a chief: car je savoie bien, se je ne pooie les aventures passer par prouesce, que a vos ne vandroie

je ja, et il m'i couvenoit avenir ou morir. Dont je vos di vraiement que ce fu la chose qui plus acroissoit mes vertuz." (*LM*, LXXXV 3)

["Lady," said Lancelot, "what you say is not right. You should know that I would never have reached my present high status were it not for you, for at the beginning of my career as a knight I would never have had the heart to undertake the things that others did not attempt through lack of the power to succeed in them. But because I was aspiring toward you and your great beauty, this gave me the temerity to believe that I could not find an adventure that I would not achieve; for I knew that, if I could not complete the adventures through prowess, I would never reach you, and I had to reach you or die. This was in truth the source from which above all I drew increased strength."]

Finally, it is in his renunciation of this love in the *Queste* that he picks up and inverts the series of antitheses in his first avowal of love, a series that evoked those to be found in the lyric:

"Sire, fet Lancelot, il est einsi que je sui morz de pechié d'une moie dame que je ai amee toute ma vie, et ce est la reine Guenievre, la fame le roi Artus. Ce est cele qui a plenté m'a doné l'or et l'argent et les riches dons que je ai aucune foiz donez as povres chevaliers. Ce est cele qui m'a mis ou grant boban et en la grant hautece ou je sui. Ce est cele por qui amor j'ai faites les granz proeces dont toz li mondes parole. Ce est cele qui m'a fet venir de povreté en richece et de mesaise a toutes les terriannes beneurtez. Mes je sai bien que par cest pechié de li s'est Nostre Sires si durement corociez a moi qu'il le m'a bien mostré puis ersoir."[6]

["Sir," said Lancelot, "the position is that I am guilty of mortal sin with my lady whom I have loved all my life, that is Queen Guinevere, the wife of King Arthur. It is she who gave me in abundance the gold, silver, and rich gifts that I have on occasion given to poor knights. It is she who raised me up and gave me my present high status. It is for love of her that I have performed the deeds of prowess known throughout the world. It is she who brought me from poverty to riches and from hardship to great happiness on earth. But I know well that it is on account of this sin with her that I have incurred God's great wrath, as He showed me so clearly last night."]

This reluctant renunciation is linked to another echo of the lyric, for it is preceded by a spring opening similar to that found in secular lyrics, but here, according to Pauphilet,[7] recalling the different use made of the theme in religious texts, where the birds are the symbol of Christ:

> Et quant li jorz parut biaus et clers et li oiselet comencerent a chanter parmi le bois et li soleux comença a luire par mi les arbres, et il [Lancelot] voit le biau tens et il ot le chant des oisiaus dont il s'ert maintes foiz esjoiz, et lors se voit desgarni de toutes choses, et de ses armes et de son cheval, et bien set de voir que Nostre Sires s'est corrociez a lui; si ne cuide ja mes venir a cel point qu'il truist chose ou monde qui sa joie li poïst rendre. Car la ou il cuidoit joie trover et toutes honors terrianes a il failli, ce est as aventures dou Saint Graal; et ce est une chose qui mout le desconforte. (*Queste*, 62)

> [And when day broke, fine and clear, and the little birds started to sing in the woods and the sun began to shine through the trees and he [Lancelot] saw the fine weather and heard the song of the birds, which had in the past so often rejoiced his heart, and then he saw himself stripped of everything, of his arms and his horse, he knew well that God was angry with him. He thought that he would never reach a position where he might find anything in the world which could bring back his joy. For where he had thought he would find joy and all earthly honor, he had failed; that was in the adventures of the Holy Grail, and this was something which sorely grieved him.]

It is on that spring day that Lancelot comes to the hermitage where he is persuaded to confess to his love and to recognize in it the origin of his failure in relation to the Grail.

The Prose *Lancelot* therefore has, as it were, a coded system of allusions that refers reader or listener to the lovers of Chrétien's romances and back through them to the lyric. This is above all achieved by wordless pauses in the action, moments of silent withdrawal that, by implication, remind us that the inspiration of love lies behind Lancelot's every deed. In the Prose *Tristan*, which imitates and at the same time reacts against the Prose *Lancelot*, the lover no longer *s'oblie* silently, but the same effect of interruption in the narrative flow in order to dwell upon emotion is achieved when he *sings* of his love and lyrics are brought into the romance. Thus, suggestions implicit in the earlier romance are decoded and given full creative development by introducing lyrics as an integral part of the structure of the romance. Many of the lyrics are ascribed to Tristan himself and recall a specific event in the life of the lovers; a few have a direct effect on the progress of events. They are on occasion sung by him, but it is made clear that they have also become part of the general repertoire of love lyrics sung by damsels or minstrels, a repertoire of trouvère songs existing outside the romance itself, a supreme example of generic intertextuality.

The interplay between chronicle and Arthurian romance has often been discussed. The "historical" quality of Geoffrey of Monmouth's *Historia regum Britanniae* was doubted by some medieval chroniclers, such as William of Newburg, who writes in the *Prooemium* to his own history of England (ca. 1198) that Geoffrey "disguised under the honorable name of history, thanks to his Latinity, the fables about Arthur which he took from the ancient fictions of the Britons and increased out of his own head." However, other medieval chroniclers were not so critical and incorporated much of the *Historia* into their own works.[8] In the early seventeenth century, Speed includes in his *History of England* a drawing of the cross with the inscription referring to *rex Arturus* found above his alleged grave in Glastonbury. After criticizing some of the fictions that Geoffrey introduced into his account, he concludes: "Therefore of his person [that of Arthur] wee make no doubt, though his acts have been written with too lavish a pen."[9] For my purposes I propose to treat Geoffrey of Monmouth and the vernacular versions of his *Historia* as "historical" chronicles.

Chrétien's romances have often been treated as ahistorical, suspended in time and space, with the main emphasis being on the adventures of the individual hero and little direct link being made with the progress of events in Arthur's reign. Donald Maddox has recently explored the way in which Chrétien, while laying out the parameters of an "anterior" Arthurian order, "effected an ostentatious and emphatic turn away from the Arthurian world depicted by Geoffrey and Wace."[10] In *Cligés*, where the action is mainly centered on Byzantium rather than Britain, we catch a glimpse of the more active Arthur of the chronicles leading an expedition, more reminiscent in terms of geography, according to Rosemary Morris, of the activities of Henry II.[11] In the *Conte del Graal* a much more direct reference is made to historical events and to the passing of time, when Perceval's mother links his father's maiming and loss of land with the past, with the political and social unrest on the death of Uther, while the main adventures of the romance take place during Arthur's reign:

"Vostre peres, si nel savez,
Fu parmi la jambe navrez
Si que il mehaigna del cors.
Sa grant terre, ses grans tresors,
Que il avoit come preudom,
Ala tot a perdition.
Si chaï en grant povreté.
Apovri et deshireté
Et escillié furent a tort
Li gentil home aprés la mort
Uterpandragon qui rois fu
Et peres le bon roi Artu.
Les terres furent escillies
Et les povres gens avillies,
Si s'en fuï qui fuïr pot."[12]

["Your father, though you don't know this, was wounded in the thigh
and maimed, his great land, his great treasure, which he owned as a
man of worth, all lapsed into ruin, and he fell into great poverty. All
noble men were impoverished, disinherited, and wrongfully reduced
to penury after the death of Uther Pendragon, who was king and father of the good King Arthur. The lands were laid waste and the poor
people debased, and those who could fled."]

It should be noted that here the troubles of Perceval's father are associated
with his loss of physical strength through the wound, and the instability and
internal difficulties of the kingdom with the *death* of Uther rather than with
his illness. This is an interesting transposition of the chronicle tradition,
where the unwillingness of the British barons to fight against external enemies is associated with the illness of Uther and his subsequent delegation
of the task of repelling invaders to his nephew Loth. When Uther has himself carried into battle, his barons respond. Once Arthur is made king, which
happens immediately after the death of Uther, the need to repel external invaders is emphasized, but there is no mention of internal dissension or lack
of support from the barons. The theme of the suffering of the land through
the illness of its lord is in Chrétien's work focused on Perceval's family, first
his father and then his uncle, in a significant variation on the situation in
the chronicles. Later, a prose continuation of Chrétien's work, the *Roman
de Perlesvaus*, picks up again the theme of the land suffering through the
physical lethargy of its lord (here without the excuse of a wound) in rela-

tion to Arthur in the first branch of the work, while of course retaining the theme of the land of the Grail guardians suffering through the illness of the Fisher King.[13]

However, if, apart from the *Conte del Graal*, there are few internal historical references in Chrétien, it might well be considered that his work should be read with the *Brut* of Wace in mind even if in terms of contrast, for, to some degree at least, implicit within the romances is the idea of an Arthur who, in theory at least, is a great king, focus of chivalry, head of the Round Table. Such a view is confirmed by the passages in *Cligés* that in their praise of Arthur and his court recall similar passages in Wace.[14] Why else should anyone want to become a knight of the Round Table at Arthur's court? Indeed the fact that the Round Table itself is first to be found in Wace's *Brut* would seem to provide an important point of reference from Chrétien to that work, although there is as always an element of ambiguity in any interplay between Chrétien and Wace. Evidence that some medieval scribes or their patrons shared the view that Chrétien should not be read in isolation from the *Brut* is to be found in the contents and internal organization of some of the volumes including his works, where the romances are placed within a historical context, as if destined to be heard or read against a background of the *Roman de Brut* of Wace.

Lori Walters has studied in an important article the way that the copyist of MS. Paris, B.N. fr. 1450 presents Chrétien as a continuator of Wace.[15] He inserts Chrétien's romances into the narrative of the *Brut* at the moment when Arthur establishes peace within his kingdom,[16] introducing them in such a way that they appear as "témoignage véridique sur le règne d'Arthur." Walters points out that this is in contrast with Chrétien, who "ne privilégie plus la matière historique en tant que telle; c'est plutôt la *narratio* qu'il valorise." The scribe of 1450 returns to Wace after he has copied with certain interesting variants all five romances and the First Perceval Continuation. Two other manuscripts (that of Guiot, Paris, B.N. fr. 794, containing all five romances, and College of Arms, Arundell 14, including only the *Conte del Graal*) do not intercalate Chrétien's work within Wace, but nevertheless present it within a framework of other historical texts including Wace.

In Robert de Boron's work, which was to be of such great importance for the development of the prose romances, the Grail theme is set within the history of Britain. Robert may modify some important elements in the account given in Wace, including the reign in which the Round Table was founded (according to the *Merlin* of Robert,[17] that of Uther, not of Arthur), but the interaction with the chronicle tradition is clearly evident in this work, which was originally in verse, but seems soon to have been turned into prose.

The fact that prose versions of Robert's romances occur so early is also linked with the way that his work was perceived at the time. In the last years of the twelfth century and the early years of the thirteenth, a number of prose versions of "serious" texts such as *Les Vies des Pères* and the *Pseudo-Turpin* were commissioned because prose was said to be truer than verse and therefore suitable for historical texts, as the prologue to the second translation of the *Pseudo-Turpin* indicates:

> Et por ce que rime se feit afaitier de moz concueilliz hors de l'estoire, si voust li cuens [Renaud de Boulogne] que cist livres fust fait sans rime tot selonc le latin que Turpins l'arcevesques de Reims recita et ecrist.[18]

> [And because rhyme is made by plucking words from outside the subject matter, the Count (Renaud de Boulogne) wants this book to be composed without rhyme, keeping closely to the Latin text which Turpin the archbishop of Reims narrated and set down.]

Unlike Chrétien, the Prose *Lancelot* provides an abundance of allusions outward from the text, which link the tale of Lancelot with a wider historical tradition including the work of Robert de Boron as well as the Brut tradition. The story of Lancelot, which opens, "En la marche de Gaule et de la Petite Bretaigne," begins with an historical introduction in which the hero's loss of land and father and his upbringing in isolation from all contact with Arthur's court and with feudal society are explained in terms of the political instability after the death of Uther:

> Quant li rois Aramonz fu morz, et Uter Pandragons, et la terre de Logres fu an la main lo roi Artur, si sordirent guerres an Bretaigne la Grant en pluseurs leus et guerroierent lo roi Artu li plus des barons. (*LK*, 2)

> [When King Aramont and Uther Pendragon were dead and the land of Logres was in the hands of Arthur, wars broke out in Great Britain in many places, and most of the barons fought against King Arthur.]

Once again, as in Chrétien's Perceval romance, the internal troubles with the barons, here combined with attacks from invaders, are associated with the beginning of Arthur's reign rather than with the illness of Uther as in the chronicles. This is true not only in this historical introduction but in a whole series of allusions to Arthur's constant struggles against his enemies. For example, when Claudas comes to Britain, we are told that Arthur is at war with a number of his barons:

> En celui tans avoit li rois Artus guerre au roi Yon d'Irlande la Menor, et puis au roi Agu[is]çant d'Escoce, son coisin meesmes, et aprés au Roi d'Outre les Marches de Galone, et a mainz autres de ses barons. Et de toz vint au desus par l'aide Nostre Seignor qui en mainz leus li fu apareilliez, et par les preudomes qui de totes les terres de crestienté li venoient aidier por la grant vaillance de lui. (*LK,* 33)

> [At this time King Arthur was at war with King Yon of Irelande la Menor and with King Aguisçant of Scotland, his cousin, and with the Roi d'Outre les Marches de Galone, and with many others among his own barons. And he overcame them all with the help of Our Lord, which he received on many occasions, and with the assistance of all the men of worth who came to his aid from all over Christendom because of his merit and valor.]

Another example is to be found in the episode in which a *randu*, a former knight of King Uther, promises the two queens, the mother of Lancelot and the mother of Lyonel and Bohort, that he will go to Arthur's court to remind him of his duty to avenge the death of his vassals Ban and Bohort and the loss of their lands. Before he leaves, he explains to the two widows that Arthur has been under so much pressure from his enemies that he has been unable to fulfill his obligations. When the *randu* arrives at Arthur's court, the king has just come back from Scotland after having made peace with King Aguisçant at the end of his third war with him and having agreed to a short truce with another king. Arthur, when reproached for his failure either to help his vassals during their lifetime or avenge them after their death, also refers to the fact that he has been under constant attack and promises to make amends as soon as he has overcome his present troubles. This is a significant variation on the much more upbeat accounts of the early years of Arthur's reign in Geoffrey and Wace, with their emphasis on a succession of victories rather than on the obligations that cannot be fulfilled because of the constant wars, as is explained in the prose romance (*LK,* 52–56).

This modification of the chronicle tradition is linked with the particular role of Arthur within the work: the great king whose court attracts the best knights in all the world, but whose role is frequently restricted to a passive one as his knights set out to undertake adventures and to see that justice is done in his kingdom. It is also important in connection with this change that one of the central themes of the work is the love of Lancelot for Arthur's Queen Guinevere, a love that inspires him to great deeds; this means that the figure of Arthur has to be carefully handled if the love is to be given a positive role as it is in Lancelot's early adventures. Hence the emphasis on Arthur's failure to fulfill his obligations as lord both to Ban, who held his land from him and lost it through his loyalty to him, and to Ban's son, Lancelot; but this failure is explained by the pressures upon the king from external enemies and unruly barons and is to some extent counterbalanced by references outward to his activities, both those in the past in relation to the tale and those contemporary with the tale.

These references mention events not told in full within the romance, and they fit in in general terms with the wars against the Scots or Irish described in the chronicles. Within the Lancelot story itself, during the account of the hero's adventures as a young knight, Arthur is actively engaged in battles against the Saxons in a way that recalls Wace. However, in the romance, although he fights courageously, he needs the help of Lancelot to achieve victory. This interplay with the chronicle tradition, but with adaptations made to fit the particular demands of the Prose *Lancelot*'s themes and narrative structure, is characteristic of the relations between the romance and its intertext. In the last branch of the cycle, *La Mort Artu*, where interaction with the chronicle tradition is again very important, it is, as in the chronicles, Arthur who leads his army into battle and achieves victory against the Romans. It is again the king who plays the leading role in the final battle where, according to the romance, Lancelot's absence was one of the causes of the final tragedy. Here, as we shall see, these links with the historical tradition help to give an epic dimension to the romance.

The relationship between the historical tradition, as represented by Geoffrey and the vernacular *Brut*, and Chrétien and that between these chronicles and the *Lancelot-Grail* cycle are therefore very different, for in the prose work the Lancelot story becomes part of the history of Arthur's reign: Lancelot's loss of land and father and his childhood in the Lake are related to the beginning of Arthur's reign, his retirement from the world and final death to the end of Arthur's reign. The story of Lancelot is integrated into the more general history of an Arthurian feudal kingdom in two ways. First, there are a series of references to events lying outside the main narrative. Second, Lancelot's early adventures are directly involved with the fate of the Arthurian kingdom through the war with Galehot (not in the chronicles) and through the war with the Saxons in which Arthur performs the traditional role attributed to him in Geoffrey and Wace and still given him by Speed in the seventeenth century, that of defender of Britain against pagan Saxon invaders. Lancelot's last adventures too are linked closely to the pattern of events in the chronicles. The great romance cycle would have all the greater impact because of its relationship with the well-known and influential Brut tradition and with Robert de Boron.

In the *Lancelot-Grail*, the links with the chronicle are made explicitly within the romance, and these links are increased as the cycle evolves. The fully developed version begins with an early history of the Grail, written to prepare the way for the already existing *Queste del saint Graal*. Then follows the prose version of Robert de Boron's *Merlin*; this is linked to the beginning of Lancelot's story by a continuation that gives further information about Arthur's wars and his troubles with his barons, expanding on the brief allusions in the account of the childhood of Lancelot that I have already mentioned, although this additional material does not always correlate precisely with the chronology given there. Micha[19] suggests that some of the Arthurian "history" narrating the king's struggles with his barons may echo events in the reign of Philippe Auguste. They have no equivalent in the Brut tradition of Geoffrey and Wace with which the Vulgate *Merlin* continuation also interacts, adapting freely, when it inserts a war with the Romans at an early stage in Arthur's career.

Interplay with history is, therefore, further developed as the last branches are added to the cycle. There are other signs of a thirteenth-century recognition of this intertextuality between genres. For example, the existing historical links are picked up and further reinforced by the active scribe of MS. Paris, B.N. fr. 754, who copied the account of Lancelot's early adventures, breaking off after Lancelot's capture of the Dolereuse Garde and the second escape of its lord, Brandin des Isles. The links here are made with Robert de Boron rather than directly with the chronicles and also fit in with a special Vulgate *Merlin* continuation (similar to that in Paris, B.N. fr. 337). For example, the scribe adds a reference to the flight of the young Uther and his brother Aurelius Ambrosius Pandragon for fear of Vortigier, who had had their brother killed. Some light may also be shed on some early thirteenth-century perceptions of the Prose *Lancelot* by the fact that it is cited as an example of truth in the verse introduction to a prose chronicle of the reign of Philippe-Auguste, written about 1226:

> Issi vos an feré le conte
> Non pas rimé, qui an droit conte,
> Si con li livres Lancelot
> Ou il n'a de rime un seul mot,
> Por mielz dire la verité

Et por tretier sans fauseté;
 Quar anviz puet estre rimee
Estoire ou n'ait ajostee
Mançonge por fere la rime.[20]

[Thus I will relate this not in verse but in prose, which gives an accurate account, like the book of Lancelot where there is not a single rhyme. I shall do this the better to tell the truth and to treat the subject without deviation, for a history can scarcely be told in verse without lying additions, made to furnish the rhyme.]

If the tribute to the accuracy and truth of the *livre Lancelot* is confined to the verse prologue of this chronicle of the reign of Philippe-Auguste, material from the *Lancelot-Grail* cycle penetrates far more deeply into chronicles written in England. It is not perhaps surprising that historical works on Glastonbury should provide early examples of this, as James Carley has reminded us recently.[21] A marginal note of the mid- to late-thirteenth century in one of the manuscripts of William of Malmesbury's *De antiquitate Glastoniensis ecclesiae* adds an account of Joseph's journey to Britain and that of his son Josephés, as it was developed in the *Estoire del saint Graal* and other branches of the cycle. Joseph's journey to Britain was later incorporated in John of Glastonbury's Chronicle, with some of the romance elements eliminated, so that interplay between romance and chronicle continued.

Another example of this incorporation of material from romance into a "historical" work is to be found in the early fourteenth-century *Story of England* of Robert Mannyng of Brunne, which has been analyzed by Lesley Johnson[22] and explored further in a recent article by Ad Putter.[23] Putter examines "a strategy that medieval writers adopted to fit new Arthurian matter into the historical tradition, a strategy that depended on discovering or opening up in the chronicle periods of unused story-time." He points out that Mannyng incorporates allusions to the *verse* romances in the period of peace early in Arthur's reign that MS. Paris, B.N. fr. 1450 had used for the insertion of Chrétien's romances within the *Brut* of Wace, but places his material from the *prose* romances during the time Arthur spent in France.

Another example of romance material being brought into a history is the *Chronicle of John Hardyng*, which is mentioned by Putter and has been analyzed by Edward Kennedy[24] and more recently by Felicity Riddy.[25] As these examples suggest, there are two main categories of material introduced into or reintegrated into the historical texts: first, the elements of the Grail tradition that had been given a "historical" framework by Robert de Boron, then turned into prose and incorporated into the *Lancelot-Graal*; second, themes such as the death of Arthur that have their roots in the Brut tradition before being further developed in the *Lancelot-Grail*. This sheds an interesting light on medieval perceptions of distinctions between history and romance.

There is also interaction between the *chanson de geste* and the *Lancelot-Grail* cycle in that the romance sometimes explores similar themes. As we are all well aware, in the romances of Chrétien de Troyes, the traditional epic themes of the tension between the rugged individual's idea of his personal honor and the claims of society, the conflict between loyalty to the lord and the bonds of kinship, are not in the foreground, and the hero of romance tends to be engaged in a more solitary quest for self-discovery. On the other hand it would be a mistake to consider the Chrétien hero as totally isolated from problems of interest to contemporary society or to deny that there was interaction between *chanson de geste* and romance from the twelfth century onward.

On the stylistic level, a similar use of tenses linked with the present is to be found in the battle scenes of both Old French epic and romance. On the thematic level, common to both genres, as has often been pointed out, is a great interest in the law, in the means by which justice and order can be maintained. Conflict in loyalty is a theme central to Beroul's version of the Tristan story. Mark comes under pressure from some of his barons, who maintain that Tristan's adulterous relationship with Iseut constitutes a threat to the stability of the kingdom; Tristan himself is torn between his duty to his kinsman and king and his passion for Iseut. In the Tristan verse romances, the lovers are separated, and it is their deaths that constitute the final tragedy. In the *Mort Artu* the theme of adulterous love recalls that of Tristan and Iseut, as is made clear by a number of echoes of the Tristan story and by Bohort's direct reference to the fate of Tristan: "Et a nostre tens meïsmes, n'a pas encore cinc anz que Tristans en morut, li niés au roi Marc, qui si loiaument ama Yseut la blonde que onques en son vivant n'avoit mespris vers lui"[26] ("And in our own time, less than five years ago, Tristan died of it, the nephew of King Mark, who loved Yseut the fair so faithfully that never in his life was he false to her").

But in the prose romance this adulterous love between knight and queen is linked to the theme taken from the chronicles of the death of Arthur and the end of the Arthurian world. The epic quality thus given to the last branch of the Arthurian cycle has long been recognized, as can be seen in the work of Jean Frappier.[27] The traditional themes of conflict in loyalties, the struggle between the lineage of Ban and the lineage of Lot, Gauvain's unbridled grief and anger at Lancelot's accidental killing of his beloved brother, those passionate emotions that give rise to *desmesure*, the characteristic fault of a hero such as Roland or Raoul de Cambrai—all these elements remind one of the epic, as does Arthur's strong sense of his obligation as king and kinsman to support Gauvain in his efforts to avenge the death of his brother Gaheriet. So do the signs and portents that indicate the inevitability of the tragedy and its significance for the whole world: the dreams, visions, and prophecies. The signs from nature reinforce this and suggest that the final battle between Arthur and Mordred is one in which divine forces are involved. Thus when Arthur, having given Mordred his fatal blow, wrenches the lance out of the body of his son, a ray of sun passes through the wound and is identified as a sign of the wrath of God: "Et l'estoire dit que aprés l'estordre del glaive passa par mi la plaie uns rais de soleill si apertement que Girflet le vit, dont cil del païs distrent que ce avoit esté sygnes de corrouz de Nostre Seigneur" ("And the story says that after the lance was withdrawn, a ray of sunlight shone through the wound so clearly that Girflet saw it, wherefore those of that land said that it was a sign of the wrath of Our Lord," *Mort Artu*, §190, 56).

There is also the heavy rain, described as *moult merveilleuse,* which falls just before the boat arrives with Morgain and the other ladies to take Arthur away, but this does not have the same biblical resonances as does the darkness at noon that is linked to Roland's death.

Less attention had perhaps been paid to the interactions with the *chanson de geste* in that part of the cycle that begins, "En la marche de Gaule" and gives an account of the childhood of Lancelot and his early adventures, until I pointed out some forty years ago that in addition to a general emphasis on feudal relationships also characteristic of the *chanson de geste*, there were parallels between Pharien, vassal of Claudas and protector and *maître* of Lancelot's cousin Lyonel, and Guillaume d'Orange.[28] These parallels were re-explored more recently by Jean Dufournet.[29] The episodes dealing with Pharien link up not only with the *chanson de geste* but also with the lawbooks in the vernacular of the thirteenth century. Pharien, like Guillaume and Bernier, is a vassal whose lord's behavior leaves much to be desired, and it is through his words and actions that a theory of good vassalship is expounded. He has been placed in a peculiarly difficult situation. He was exiled for homicide by his old lord Bohort, a great maintainer of justice, father of Lyonel and uncle of Lancelot. Pharien has never formally renounced his homage to Bohort, who is now dead, leaving two young children, but he has a new lord, Claudas, who has given him land and appears to trust him. On the one hand, Pharien is greatly indebted to Claudas, but on the other, he has good reason to hate him, for not only has Claudas behaved treacherously toward the sons of Bohort, but he is also Pharien's wife's lover. The vassal is thus torn between his duty to Claudas and his duty to the children of Bohort:

> "Et cist est mes sires, comment que ge soie ses hom, si lo doi de mort et de honte garantir a mon pooir por la feauté garder et por l'omage que fait li ai; et les anfanz a mon seignor cui ge sui hom d'ancesserie doi ge garder en foi et por amor de norreture que j'ai en els et il en moi." (*LK*, 78)

> ["And this man is my lord, in whatever way I am his vassal, and it is my duty to save him from death and shame to the best of my ability in keeping with my oath of fealty and my act of homage; and the children of the lord whose vassal I was through my ancestors should be protected by me in loyalty to my oath and for the love I have for them through having brought them up."]

No matter what hostile feelings he may have toward Claudas, he cannot kill him without losing his honor, for in Pharien's eyes the greatest crime before God and man is for a vassal to kill his lord, as it is for Guillaume, who says in *Le Couronnement de Louis*: "Je ne vueil mie mon dreit seignor traïr. / Je nel fereie por les membres tolir" ("I will not betray my lord, not even were I to forfeit my limbs").[30] Bernier in *Raoul de Cambrai* says that his lord is "plus fel que Judas" ("more villainous than Judas"), but declares: "Ne li fauroie por l'onnor de Damas, / Tant qe tuit dient: Berniers, droit en as!" ("I wouldn't fail him, not even for the fief of Damascus, until such time as all can declare: 'Bernier, you are in the right!'").[31] However, if Pharien shares many of the same problems as a knight and vassal in a *chanson de geste*, he uses a very different style to talk of them, the written language of the law book rather than the oral style of the *chanson de geste*, as when in a speech to his fellow barons he gives a detailed exposition of the circumstances under which a vassal is justified in renouncing his allegiance and of the precise conditions that might justify him laying violent hands upon his lord:

> "Ne ge ne sai nule plus laide desleiauté que de son seignor ocirre. Mais se li sires mesprant vers son home o li mesfait, ses hom l'an doit a raison metre par ses parelz par lo terme d'une quarantainne, et se des lors nel puet rapeler a sa droiture, si li rande son homage devant ses pers, non pas en repost, car chose aperte porte tesmoign de leiauté et chose reposte senefie mauveitié et felenie." (*LK*, 86)

["And I know of no greater disloyalty than to kill one's lord. But if the lord wrongs his vassal and behaves badly toward him, the vassal should let his equals put his case for him, and if, when forty days have passed, the lord has not put things right, the vassal should renounce his homage in the presence of his peers, not secretly, for what is done openly bears witness to loyalty and what is done secretly signifies wickedness and treachery."]

This is to be compared with the passage in a later thirteenth-century lawbook of Beaumanoir,[32] where he discusses the procedure by which a wronged vassal may challenge his lord.

It is also perhaps of interest that Philippe de Novare, who served the Ybelins as a knight and also wrote a legal treatise, should have cited both Guillaume d'Orange and Pharien in his work. He refers to Guillaume in his *Mémoires*[33] in relation to Ybelin's appeal to his lord for help in return for his own faithful service. In *Les Quatre Ages de l'homme*[34] he uses a long paraphrase of a passage in the Prose *Lancelot* (*LK*, 85) to illustrate the need for the young *bachelier* to listen to the counsel of his elders; this is drawn from an episode in the romance in which Pharien has to restrain his young nephew Lambegues from raising his hand against his lord. Thus Philippe de Novare uses both a *chanson de geste* (*Foulke de Candie*) and the Prose *Lancelot* within a context of feudal relations. Beaumanoir too follows closely a passage from the Lady of the Lake's explanation of the origins of chivalry (*LK*, 142–45) in his account of the origin of kings and the role of the *gentilhommes* in relation to the governing of a kingdom in *Coutumes de Beauvaisis* (II, xlv, 1453). Thus the allusions made to the Prose *Lancelot* by two thirteenth-century writers serve to illustrate the continuing interplay between *chanson de geste*, romance, and lawbook.

There are also links with another well-known type of book, the *Miroir des princes*. The prose romance draws on this tradition in an episode in which a *preudomme* interprets three dreams of Arthur. The *preudomme* gives Arthur advice on how he should govern his kingdom and win back the hearts of his vassals from the highest to the lowest. The Scottish *Lancelot of the Laik* picks up this theme and explores it further with reference to contemporary political circumstances, as Sally Mapstone has shown in her doctoral thesis, soon to be published. In a similar way the Prose *Lancelot* links up with an existing tradition of works on the order of chivalry in the Lady of the Lake's discourse on chivalry and is itself drawn upon by Ramon Lull in his book on chivalry, later translated by Caxton.[35] Other passages in the Prose *Lancelot* are echoed in the statutes of the Compaignie de l'Etoile as these are recorded by Jean le Bel; that is, those passages that describe the custom that before Arthur's knights leave court on adventure, they must all swear that on their return they will give a truthful account of their adventures whether to their honor or their shame (*LK*, 298, 406); also those passages that explain that these reports are recorded in writing in a great book (*LK*, 571).[36]

Finally a brief mention of an important aspect of the *Lancelot-Grail* that has been explored by a number of scholars; as Jane Burns has pointed out: "Several branches of the cycle reproduce select elements of the medieval Scriptural tradition only to undermine their significance."[37] It should also not be forgotten that Adam de la Halle brings Morgain la Fée and the Wheel of Fortune onto the stage and mocks the way that the *haute bourgeoisie* imitates the heroes of Arthurian romance in that play that is a splendid example of interplay between genres, *Le Jeu de la Feuillee*.

Michelle Szkilnik in her book on the *Estoire del saint Graal* has described this first branch of the complete cycle in the following terms: "Elle semble surtout se situer au carrefour de bien des genres littéraires, qu'elle juxtapose ou combine, parfois de manière surprenante, ce qui lui a valu sa réputation d'œuvre mal construite."[38] Interchange between genres, as has been seen, is not confined to this branch, according to the perceptions of both medieval and modern readers. However, in the cycle as a whole it is not so much a case of startling juxtapositions, but rather of more subtle variations on themes or forms characteristic of other genres, or of allusions outward that set the prose romance within a wider literary or historical context.

The romance itself is not just a kind of tutti frutti, full of conflicting flavors; it functions as a literary structure in relation to a set of conventions and a particular range of linguistic and stylistic registers. As a result it can achieve certain effects by the deliberate and occasional failure to fulfill the expectations of a medieval reader of romance. The interplay with other genres to be found in the *Lancelot-Grail* cycle does not usually operate in terms of introducing elements of surprising contrast; rather, it helps to enrich the texture of the romance, sometimes giving it a depth in time or a wider setting, as with some of the historical references, sometimes underlining key themes such as that of love through echoes of the lyric. These intertextual allusions are not therefore straight borrowings, but always transform and adapt in a way that characterizes the particular literary structure of the romance and sets it in parallel and contrast within the context of other familiar literary structures. The kingdom of Arthur as it is to be found in prose romance is not presented as an isolated world but as one at the center of a whole network of traditions, literary and historical, political and legal, even, on occasion, religious. It is not surprising, therefore, that Arthurian prose romance was itself drawn on for a whole range of different purposes and in relation to different genres by medieval kings, knights, legists, and moralists.

NOTES

1. Sylvia Huot, *From Song to Book: The Poetics of Writing in Old French Lyric and Lyrical Narrative Poetry* (Ithaca: Cornell University Press, 1987), pp. 42, 192.

2. For a study of the vocabulary of love meditations, see D.R. Sutherland, "The Love Meditation in Courtly Literature," in *Studies in Medieval French Presented to Alfred Ewert* (Oxford: Oxford University Press, 1961), pp. 165–93.

3. For a list of these trances and an analysis of their function in the romance, see Elspeth Kennedy, "Royal Broodings and Lovers' Trances in the First Part of the Prose *Lancelot*," in *Mélanges de philologie et de littérature romanes offerts à Jeanne Wathelet-Willem, Marche Romane*, 1978, pp. 301–14.

4. *Lancelot do Lac: The Non-Cyclic Old French Prose Romance* [hereafter *LK*], 2 vols. (Oxford: Oxford University Press, 1980), p. 179.

5. *Lancelot: roman en prose du xiiie siècle* [hereafter *LM*], ed, Alexandre Micha, 9 vols. (Geneva: Droz, 1978–83), Chap. LXXXIII, par. 1.

6. *La Queste del Saint Graal*, ed. Albert Pauphilet (Paris: Champion, 1923), p. 66.

7. Albert Pauphilet, *Études sur la Queste del Saint Graal attribuée à Gautier Map* (Paris: Champion, 1921), p. 109.

8. See Robert Huntington Fletcher, *The Arthurian Material in the Chronicles, Especially Those of Great Britain and France* (Boston: Ginn, 1910), chap. IV, VI and VII.

9. John Speed, *History of England*, 3rd ed. (London: George Humble, 1632), p. 271.

10. Donald Maddox, *The Arthurian Romances of Chrétien de Troyes: Once and Future Fictions* (Cambridge: Cambridge University Press, 1991), p. 5.

11. Rosemary Morris, "Aspects of Time and Place in the French Arthurian Verse Romances," *French Studies*, 42 (1988), 257–77.

12. Chrétien de Troyes, *Le Roman de Perceval ou le Conte du Graal*, ed. William Roach (Geneva: Droz, 1956), ll. 435–49.

13. *Le Haut Livre du Graal: Perlesvaus*, ed. William A. Nitze and T. Atkinson Jenkins, 2 vols. (Chicago: University of Chicago Press, 1932–37), pp. 26, 117.

14. See Elspeth M. Kennedy, "King Arthur in the First Part of the Prose *Lancelot*," in *Medieval Miscellany Presented to Eugène Vinaver by Pupils, Colleagues and Friends* (Manchester: Manchester University Press, 1965), p. 188.

15. Lori Walters, "Le Rôle du scribe dans l'organisation des manuscrits des romans de Chrétien de Troyes," *Romania*, 106 (1985), 303–25.

16. Wace, *Le Roman de Brut*, ed. Ivor D.O. Arnold, 2 vols. (Paris: Droz, 1938–40), l. 9798.

17. Robert de Boron, *Merlin: roman du xiii siècle*, ed. Alexandre Micha (Paris: Droz, 1980), pp. 185–90.

18. Quoted by Brian Woledge and H.P. Clive, *Répertoire des plus anciens textes en prose française depuis 842 jusqu'aux premières années du xiiie siècle* (Geneva: Droz, 1964), p. 29.

19. Alexandre Micha, "Les Sources de la Vulgate du *Merlin*," in his *De la chanson de geste au roman* (Geneva: Droz, 1976), pp. 299–387.

20. Quoted by Woledge and Clive, p. 30, from an article by Paul Meyer in *Romania*, 6 (1877), 498.

21. James P. Carley, *Glastonbury Abbey: The Holy House at the Head of the Moors Adventurous* (Woodbridge: Boydell, 1988), pp. 92–93.

22. Lesley Johnson, "Robert Mannyng's History of Arthurian Literature," in *Church and Chronicle: The Middle Ages*, ed. I. Wood and G. Loud (London: Hambledon, 1991), pp. 129–47.

23. Ad Putter, "Finding Time for Romance: Mediaeval Arthurian Literary History," *Medium Ævum*, 63, No. 1 (1994), 1–16.

24. Edward Kennedy, "Malory and his English Sources," in *Aspects of Malory*, ed. Toshiyuki Takamiya and Derek Brewer (Woodbridge: Boydell and Brewer, 1981), pp. 27–55.

25. Felicity Riddy, "Glastonbury, Joseph of Arimathea and the Grail," in *The Archaeology and History of Glastonbury Abbey: Essays in Honour of the Ninetieth Birthday of C.A. Ralegh Radford* (Woodbridge: Boydell and Brewer, 1991), pp. 317–31.

26. *La Mort le roi Artu*, ed. Jean Frappier, 3rd ed. (Geneva: Droz, 1964), §59.

27. See, for example, Jean Frappier, *Étude sur la Mort le roi Artu*, 3rd ed. (Geneva: Droz, 1972), pp. 200–202.

28. Elspeth Kennedy, "Social and Political Ideas in the French Prose *Lancelot*," *Medium Ævum*, 26 (1957), 90–106.

29. Jean Dufournet, "Un Personnage exemplaire et complexe du *Lancelot* en prose," in *Approches du Lancelot en prose*, ed. Jean Dufournet (Paris: Champion, 1984), pp. 137–56.

30. *Le Couronnement de Louis*, ed. Ernest Langlois (Paris: Champion, 1920), ll. 2535–36.

31. *Raoul de Cambrai*, ed. Sarah Kay (Oxford: Oxford University Press, 1992), ll. 1207–08.

32. Philippe de Beaumanoir, *Coutumes de Beauvaisis*, ed. Am. Salmon, 2 vols. (Paris: Picard, 1899–1900), II, lxi, 1734.

33. Philippe de Novare, *Memoires (1218–1243)*, ed. C. Kohler (Paris: Champion, 1970, rpt. with corrections), p. 54.

34. Philippe de Novare, *Les Quatre Ages de l'homme: Traité moral de Philippe de Navarre, publié pour la première fois d'après les manuscrits de Paris, de Londres et de Metz*, ed. Marcel de Fréville (Paris: Didot, 1888), §37–38.

35. *Le Libre del orde de cavalleria*, in *Obres de Ramon Lull*, ed. Antoni M. Alcover, Mateu Obrador, and Bennassar (Palma de Mallorca: Comissio Editora Lulliana, 1906), I, 208.

36. *Chronique de Jean le Bel*, ed. J. Viard and E. Deprez, 2 vols. (Paris: Renouard, 1904), II, 204–06.

37. E. Jane Burns, *Arthurian Fictions: Rereading the Vulgate Cycle* (Columbus, Ohio: Ohio State University Press, 1985), p. 79.

38. "It seems, in particular, to situate itself at the intersection of a good many literary genres, which it juxtaposes or combines, sometimes in a surprising manner, and that is what has earned for it its reputation as a poorly constructed work." In *L'Archipel du Graal: Étude de l'Estoire del saint Graal* (Geneva: Droz, 1991), p. 111.

MORGAIN LA FÉE IN *SIR GAWAIN AND THE GREEN KNIGHT*

FROM TROY TO CAMELOT

Michael W. Twomey

Like so much of the Arthurian corpus, *Sir Gawain and the Green Knight* (hereafter *SGGK*) is richly intertextual. *SGGK*'s intertextual relations with the other three poems of the manuscript, London, B.L. Cotton Nero A.x., are one reason why the four poems are generally presumed to be by one author.[1] There are also links with other Middle English alliterative verse. For instance the Trojan history that encloses *SGGK* is found also in the closing lines of the *Alliterative Morte Arthure* and in the opening lines of *Winner and Waster*. If William Cook is correct in placing *SGGK* in the middle of the fourteenth century rather than at the end, then *Winner and Waster*'s Trojan prologue would seem perhaps to parody the one in *SGGK*.[2] Like *The Parlement of the Thre Ages*, as well as like *Pearl* and *Patience*, *SGGK* echoes its opening line in its conclusion. Like *Somer Soneday* and other poems, it uses long alliterative lines together with a "bob" and a "wheel."[3]

Intertextuality is a feature of any literature; but it is particularly pronounced in a literary culture in which originality means reworking older texts, retelling tales that have always already been told. Peter Haidu has observed, "It is the very nature of a conventional aesthetic to be intertextual, and only the beginnings of the study of medieval intertextuality have been accomplished; further studies of the multiple codes, their concrete embodiments, and their multiple intersections are needed."[4] Intertextuality is not source study.[5] Intertextuality considers the writer as reader—as the shaping mind negotiating between the present text (or "intertext") and the texts that surround it in its literary culture. Source study sees the writer as an object of influence. Useful as source study is, it diminishes the role of the author and tends to view the text as a record of its predecessors, thus removing the text from its contemporary literary context. Furthermore, it tends to dismember the text into a collection of motifs removed from their narrative context. Carried to an extreme, source study assumes that the text is an etiolated version of its original. In scholarship on *SGGK*, source study has focused chiefly on Celtic antecedents of the narrative and of the figures of Gawain and the Green Knight, with terms such as "beheading game," "temptation scenes," and "exchange of winnings" still current and influential in our discourse about the poem.[6] Elisabeth Brewer's *Sir Gawain and the Green Knight: Sources and Analogues*, recently reissued, is the latest entrant to this crowded field.[7]

The case of Morgain la Fée is an excellent demonstration of intertextuality in *SGGK* that has been overlooked on account of the emphasis that source study has put on Gawain and the Green Knight. Because I will be returning frequently to this passage in this essay, I quote it here in full:

> "Syn ȝe be lorde of þe ȝonder londe þer I haf lent inne
> Wyth yow wyth worschyp—þe wyȝe hit yow ȝelde
> Þat vphaldez þe heuen and on hyȝ sittez—
> How norne ȝe yowre ryȝt nome, and þenne no more?"
> "Þat schal I telle þe trwly," quoþ þat oþer þenne,
> "Bertilak de Hautdesert I hat in þis londe,
> Þurȝ myȝt of Morgne la Faye, þat in my hous lenges,
> And koyntyse of clergye, bi craftes wel lerned,
> Þe maystrés of Merlyn mony hatz taken—
> For ho hatz dalt drwry ful dere sumtyme
> With þat conable klerk, þat knowes alle your knyȝtez
>   at hame;
>   Morgne þe goddes
>   Þerfore hit is hir name:
>   Weldez non so hyȝe hawtesse
>   Þat ho ne con make ful tame—
>
> Ho wayned me vpon þis wyse to your wynne halle
> For to assay þe surquidré, ȝif hit soth were
> Þat rennes of þe grete renoun of þe Rounde Table;
> Ho wayned me þis wonder your wyttez to reue,
> For to haf greued Gaynour and gart hir to dyȝe
> With glopnyng of þat ilke gome þat gostlych speked
> With his hede in his honde bifore þe hyȝe table.
> Þat is ho þat is at home, þe auncian lady;
> Ho is euen þyn aunt, Arþurez half-suster,
> Þe duches doȝter of Tyntagelle, þat dere Vter after
> Hade Arþur vpon, þat aþel is nowþe." (2440–66)[8]

["Since you are lord of the yonder land where I have stayed
With you honorably—may the man
Who holds up the heaven and on high sits repay it to you—
How do you call yourself rightly, and then no more?"
"That shall I tell you truly," said that other one then,
"Bertilak de Hautdesert I am called in this land,
Through the might of Morgain la Fée who dwells in my house,
And [who] has taken the skill of learning, by crafts well learned,
The many arts of Merlin.
For she once had most a pleasant love affair
With that excellent sage, who knows all your knights
     at home;
   Morgain the goddess
   Therefore is her name:
   No one has such high pride
   That she cannot completely tame him.

"She sent me in this fashion to your beautiful hall
In order to make trial of the pride, [to see] if it were true
What circulates about the great renown of the Round Table;
She sent this marvel to take away your wits,
In order to afflict Guinevere and cause her to die
With dismay at that same man who spoke like a phantom
With his head in his hand before the high table.
That is she who is at home, the aged lady;
She is indeed your aunt, Arthur's half-sister,
The daughter of the duchess of Tintagel on whom noble Uther later
Begot Arthur, who is now noble."]

Allegiance to the view of *SGGK* prompted by source study has encouraged scholars to disparage Morgain's deployment at the conclusion of
the poem as an aesthetic flaw. Bertilak's revelation that Morgain is the only
begetter of Gawain's adventure, which comes three stanzas before the end
of the poem, is for many readers a *dea ex machina*—unmotivated in the plot,
unforeshadowed, and insufficient to explain the action of the story. For these
readers of the poem, the narrative concerns nothing but Sir Gawain and the
Green Knight, as if the editorial title were an authorial title, and Bertilak's
revelation about Morgain is simply an adjunct to the authentic tale of the
two male figures. George Lyman Kittredge speaks for this entire group of
readers, saying in 1916 that Bertilak's revelation about Morgain's role is "the

one weak spot of the superb English romance."[9] Kittredge's book was reprinted in 1960. The Morgain question was virtually ignored in the surveys of scholarship by Morton Bloomfield in 1961, Robert Ackerman in 1968, and Donald Howard in 1971.[10] In 1976 Derek Brewer proclaimed that *SGGK* is "self-evidently the story of Gawain: Morgan and Guinevere are marginal, whatever their significance to Gawain" (Brewer, 570).[11] In 1991, arguing for a ring structure in *SGGK*, Stephanie Trigg dismissed Morgain, saying, "this motivation seems to receive very little narratorial support and does not provide unambiguous answers to many of the poem's concerns."[12]

Kittredge and company held *SGGK* accountable to an alleged source. Albert Friedman and Larry Benson, for example, considered *SGGK* a disenchantment tale from which the poet at the last minute dropped the required unspelling of the ogre by decapitation. In the hypothetical model to which Friedman compared *SGGK*, "the hero, after surviving the token return blow and thus proving his courage and fidelity, is asked by the giant challenger to strike off his head for the second time. The hero complies, and the giant by this act is unspelled, resuming his normal human size, appearance, and disposition" (Friedman, 269). Benson compared *SGGK* specifically to *Le Livre de Caradoc*, part of the First Continuation of Chrétien's *Perceval*, citing details shared by *Caradoc* and *SGGK* that suggested to him that the French poem inspired the so-called beheading game of the English poem. Benson considered Morgain a necessity only because the poet had replaced Caradoc with Gawain in *SGGK*, but he dismissed her on the grounds that she appears too late in the narrative (Benson, 16–37).

Yet, from the beginning, Morgain and her magic are anticipated in the narrative. In line 30 the poet calls his tale a *laye*, which indicates that the plot will involve magic and love, and quite likely a fay as well. Calling it an adventure in lines 27, 29, and 2522 reinforces the audience's expectation of fairy magic when one considers the notion in the prose romances that the time of Arthur was especially marked by enchantments known as "the adventures (of Britain / Logres)."[13] The Green Knight's color is perhaps a "fairy color."[14] Arthur's courtiers take the Green Knight to be "fantoum and fayryȝe" (240), in which *fayryȝe* can mean generally "magic" or specifically "something from the fairy-realm," the latter being more likely in view of the court's fear of what the "aluisch mon" (681) will do to Gawain.[15] The Green Knight's disappearances in ll. 460–61 and 2477–78—"To quat kyth he becom knwe non þere, / Neuer more þen þey wyste queþen he watz wonnen" ("No one there knew to what place he went / Any more than they knew whence he had come"); "And þe knyȝt in þe enker grene / Whiderwarde-soeuer he wolde" ("And the knight in the bright green / [Went] whichever way he wished")—may be another indication of an enchantment.[16] When Morgain herself is introduced along with the Lady, the ugly old woman is singled out by her special relationship with the Lady and with Bertilak. In line 2463, Bertilak refers to her honorifically as the "þe auncian lady," which recalls that *auncian* is also the narrator's word for Morgain in her earlier appearance, when Gawain first sees her. Here she leads Bertilak's wife by the left hand, and the poet observes that Morgain "watz alder þen ho, an auncian hit semed, / And heȝly honowred with haþelez aboute" ("was older than she, an aged one she seemed, / And highly honored by the men about her," 948–49). Moreover Morgain is seated at the highest place at table, where Bertilak accompanies her: "Þe olde auncian wyf heȝest ho syttez, / Þe lorde lufly her by lent, as I trowe" ("The old, aged woman sat at the highest place, / The lord courteously took his place by her, as I believe," 1001–2). Bertilak's claim that Morgain enchanted him and sent him to Arthur's court to test the Round Table should perhaps be taken seriously.

Morgain la Fée has had her share of defenders over the years, but their impact has been as marginal as the fay herself. The essays of Denver Ewing Baughan, Mother Angela Carson, Douglas M. Moon, and Ivo Kamps unfortunately misconstrue literary facts.[17] The essays of T.P. McAlindon and Dennis Moore make more viable claims for attention. McAlindon reads *SGGK* as a romance version of a saint's life, in which Gawain takes the part of the saint and Morgain and Bertilak share the role of the devil. Following the narrative theories of Roman Ingarden, Moore argues that reading *SGGK* is a process of constant reevaluation, and that the reader must resist the urge to draw premature conclusions.[18]

The most recent essays on Morgain's role come from Sheila Fisher and Geraldine Heng, both of whom read *SGGK* through feminist theory.[19] Fisher and Heng remove Morgain from the margins of the story, arguing that she and the Lady set the plot in motion by creating what Fisher calls "systems of exchange" between women and men (Fisher, "Taken Men," 72). Both essays also consider all the women in the poem as aspects of a universal feminine principle. Fisher regards the women in *SGGK* as token figures with limited power. Since Morgain and the Lady threaten "to subvert the [political and economic] exchange systems of Christian feudalism" (Fisher, "Taken Men," 80), Bertilak displaces them at the end of the narrative, claiming that the girdle, the Lady, and the testing were all his. In contrast, Heng considers the action of *SGGK* to be a plan initiated by Morgain, directed at Guinevere, performed by the Lady, and modulated by the Virgin Mary, with Gawain as "a player drawn into Morgain's game" (Heng, 501). Whereas Fisher argues that Gawain extricates himself from the lady's power by making the girdle into his personal symbol, Heng emphasizes that, by calling the girdle a "love-lace" in line 2438, Gawain accepts the erotic significance assigned to it by the Lady in their last encounter in his bedroom.

The essays of Fisher and Heng demonstrate significant narrative patterns that have been overlooked by readers who think of *SGGK* strictly as a confrontation between Gawain and a Green Knight. As such, they provide a valuable corrective to the view of Morgain encouraged by source study, and they point up the fallacies of the belletristic and New Critical assumptions about narrative unity that have guided many readers of the poem. On the other hand, an intertextual reading of Morgain enables an historical reading of her agency in the poem. If we are to explain Morgain's presence in the poem, we should consider Morgain's script in *SGGK* in the light of the narrative practice of medieval writers for whom she was an available literary property.

Bertilak's speech in *SGGK* 2440–66 identifies Morgain genealogically and biographically via her involvement in a larger narrative. Genealogically Morgain is identified three ways: as Gawain's aunt, as Arthur's half-sister, and as the daughter of the duchess of Tintagel (2463–66). This duchess is of course Igern, the story of whose seduction by Uther Pendragon was first told in Geoffrey of Monmouth's *Historia regum Britanniae* 8.19. Biographically Morgain is identified by her relationship with Merlin (2447–51) and by her age ("þe auncian lady," 2463), which puts that relationship somewhat in the past. When Bertilak says that Morgain had learned the "arts of Merlin" and had had a love affair with him, his statement refers to an episode in the Prose *Lancelot* of the *Lancelot-Grail* (or Vulgate) Cycle, where Morgain learns Merlin's magic after she has been driven from Arthur's court by Guinevere on account of a love-affair with a young courtier named Guiomar, Guinevere's cousin.[20] Exiled from court and set on revenge against Guinevere, Morgain takes up residence in the Val sans Retour—the "valley of no return"—where she builds a chapel that traps all knights who have been faithless in love. The wilderness setting and the chapel anticipate the wilderness setting and the Green Chapel of *SGGK*, whereas Morgain's test of faithfulness in the *Lancelot* anticipates the test of Gawain's *trawþe* in *SGGK*. This section of the *Lancelot* also provides a parallel for the three temptation scenes in *SGGK*, since in it Morgain sends a seductress to Lancelot three times without success. Both in the *Lancelot* and in *SGGK*, Morgain operates through intermediaries, and the seductress serves as Morgain's accomplice. It is during this section of the *Lancelot* that Morgain learns her magic from Merlin. The Prose *Lancelot* accounts for these details in Morgain's genealogy and biography in two rather close passages. In de-

scribing the Val sans Retour it identifies Morgain as "Morgain la déesse"—
"Morgain the goddess," as in *SGGK* 2452. This much is found in Paton
(*Fairy Mythology*, 165, n. 1) and in the notes to the edition of Tolkien-Gordon-Davis.[21] However, only a few manuscript folios later the *Lancelot* also
gives the rest of Morgain's history found in *SGGK* 2465–66:

> Il fu voirs que Morgue le suer al roi Artu sot d'enchantement. . . . par
> tot le païs ne disoient mie qu'ele fu feme, ançois l'apeloient Morgue
> la dieuesse. . . . Morgue fu fille al duc de Tintajuel et a Egerne sa feme,
> qui puis fu roine de Bretaigne et feme Uterpandragon, et de li fu nes
> li rois Artus qui en li fu engendrés al vivant le duc par la traïson que
> Merlins fist. . . . Li dux estoit molt lais chevaliers et Morgue retraioit
> a lui, kar molt estoit laide. . . . [After leaving court she sought Mer-
> lin] et ele en avoit mené molt grant avoir et molt grant chevalcheure;
> si s'acointa de Merlin qui l'ama plus que nule rien, si li aprist tant de
> caraies et d'enchantemens com ele sot puis et demora avec lui grant
> piece. Et li enfés qu'ele ot de Guiamor fu puis chevaliers de grant
> proesce. Por ce fu la haine qu'ele ot envers la roine Genievre tos les
> jors de sa vie. (ed. Micha, I, sections XXII.1 and XXIV.39, 42)

[It was true that Morgan the sister of Arthur knew enchantment. . . .
throughout the country, no one said that she was a woman, rather
they called her Morgain the goddess. . . . Morgain was the daughter
of the duke of Tintagel and of Igern, his wife who afterwards was the
queen of Britain and the wife of Uther Pendragon; and from her was
born King Arthur, who was engendered in her while the duke still
lived through the treachery that Merlin devised. . . . The duke was a
very ugly knight and Morgain took after him, for she was very
ugly. . . . (After leaving court she sought Merlin) and she had brought
with her a very great fortune and a very great mounted troop; she
had a liaison with Merlin, who loved her more than anything and
taught her all the magic and enchantments that she knew afterwards,
and she stayed with him a long while. And the infant that she had of
Guiomar was later a knight of great prowess. This was the reason
for the hatred that she bore against Guinevere all the days of her life.]

The *Lancelot-Grail* cycle thus also suggests a solution to the problem of Morgain's motives as they are explained by Bertilak in *SGGK* 2459–
62. Guinevere did *not* die, as Morgain had hoped, but Morgain's motive is
credible when it is considered in connection with the *Lancelot-Grail* cycle.

Earlier scholars expected Morgain and her motives to come from within the plot of *SGGK*, even though they recognized a correlative in the Prose *Lancelot*'s story of Morgain and Guiomar. Kittredge and Hulbert believed that Bertilak's revelation about Morgain was due to a clumsy interpolation in the (supposed) lost Anglo-Norman original by the English poet (Kittredge, 132, 136; Hulbert, "*Syr Gawayne*," 454, "Name," 16).

In effect, an explanation for Morgain la Fée's appearance in *SGGK* has been available for most of this century, but scholars looking for a direct lineal antecedent to *SGGK* would not consider the significance of the parallels they had uncovered between the Prose *Lancelot* and *SGGK*. However, having located Morgain's biography and genealogy in a passage from the Prose *Lancelot*, I must hasten to add that I am not suggesting that we fit *SGGK* into any one section of the *Lancelot-Grail* cycle, nor do I consider it necessary to do so.[22] Although *SGGK* could very well have been conceived as an episode from the Prose *Lancelot*, as soon as we begin thinking of the *Lancelot* as the source for *SGGK*, we must certainly be frustrated because, as an earlier generation of scholars found, the fit is far from neat. For this reason *SGGK* scholarship is littered with lost sources and missing links.

Intertextuality differs from source study in that it can also consider the adaptation of patterns or structures from one text or group of texts to another without having to lay claim to a specific text as a source. This is a way of describing what kind of narrative we are dealing with and of delimiting our expectations for it. The intertextuality of Morgain la Fée in *SGGK* may extend beyond the main narrative to its Trojan historical frame. This frame provides another context for Morgain's role in *SGGK* and links the Matter of Britain with the Matter of Antiquity. The proem moves from the Trojan war, through the founding of Britain by Aeneas's descendant Brutus, and on to Arthur. The conclusion reverses that historical sequence, as if to return the tale to its Trojan roots:

> Siþen þe sege and þe assaut watz sesed at Troye,
> Þe borȝ brittened and brent to brondez and askez,
> Þe tulk þat þe trammes of tresoun þer wroȝt
> Watz tried for his tricherie, þe trewest on erthe:
> Hit watz Ennias þe athel, and his highe kynde,
> Þat siþen depreced prouinces, and patrounes bicome
> Welneȝe of al þe wele in þe west iles.
> Fro riche Romulus to Rome ricchis hym swyþe,
> With gret bobbaunce þat burȝe he biges vpon first,
> And neuenes hit his aune nome, as hit now hat;
> Tirius to Tuskan and teldes bigynnes,

Langaberde in Lumbardie lyftes vp homes,
And fer ouer þe French flod Felix Brutus
On mony bonkkes ful brode Bretayn he settez
  wyth wynne.
    Where werre and wrake and wonder
    Bi syþez hatz wont þerinne,
    And oft boþe blysse and blunder
    Ful skete hatz skyfted synne.

Ande quen þis Bretayn watz bigged bi þis burn rych,
Bolde bredden þerinne, baret þat lofden,
In mony turned tyme tene þat wroȝten.
Mo ferlyes on þis folde han fallen here oft
Þen in any oþer þat I wot, syn þat ilk tyme.
Bot of alle þat here bult, of Bretaygne kynges,
Ay watz Arthur þe hendest, as I haf herde telle. (1–26)

[After the siege and the assault had ceased at Troy,
The city broken up and burned to brands and ashes,
The man who contrived the devices of treason
Was tried for his treachery, the truest on earth.
It was Aeneas the noble and his illustrious offspring
Who later conquered provinces and acquired patrimonies
Of well-nigh all the wealth in the western isles.
Then rich Romulus hastens himself to Rome,
With great splendor he founds that city at once,
And names it with his own name, as it is now called;
Tirius goes to Tuscany and establishes dwellings,
Longobardus in Lombardy lifts up homes,
And far over the French Flood, Felix Brutus,
On many banks full broad, Britain he sets
  with joy;
    Where war and wrack and wonder
    At times have happened therein,
    And oft both good and bad fortune
    Full swiftly have changed places since.

And when this Britain was built by this noble man,
Bold men who loved combat were bred therein,
And [they were men] who wrought misery in many a time past.

More marvels in this earth have fallen here often
Than in any other that I know, since that very time.
But of all that here built, of Britain's kings,
Ever was Arthur the most courteous, as I have heard tell.]

Þus in Arthurus day þis aunter bitidde,
Þe Brutus bokez þerof beres wyttenesse;
Syþen Brutus, þe bolde burne, boȝed hider first,
After þe segge and þe asaute watz sesed at Troye,
      iwysse,
    Mony aunterez here-biforne
    Haf fallen suche er þis.
    Now þat bere þe croun of þorne,
    He bryng vus to his blysse! Amen. (2522–30)

[Thus in Arthur's day this adventure occurred,
The Brut books bear witness to it;
Since Brutus, the bold warrior, first came hither
After the siege and assault had ceased at Troy
      indeed.
    Many adventures here before
    Have befallen such men before this—
    Now that one that bore the crown of thorns,
    May he bring us to his bliss! Amen.]

The story of Troy's betrayal alluded to in the opening lines of *SGGK*
most likely comes from the Old French *Roman de Troie* (henceforth *RT*) by
Benoît de Sainte-Maure, written about 1160, or from Guido delle Colonne's
Historia Destructionis Troiae, dated 1287. Scholarly consensus now seems
to be that the "man who contrived the devices of treason," who was "tried
for his treachery" and yet remained the "truest on earth" in *SGGK* 3–4 is
Aeneas as he is portrayed by Benoît and by Guido.[23] On the other hand, the
reference to the Brut books in 2523 seems to be a red herring because neither Geoffrey of Monmouth nor the many so-called Brut chronicles that
succeeded him contain a story like *SGGK*, and the poet here contradicts his
own earlier statement in line 31 that he heard his story told "in town"—
although that, too, may be a pose.
    Earlier I argued that when Morgain la Fée is formally introduced
in *SGGK* 2440–66, she is identified via her genealogy and her fictional biography from the *Lancelot-Grail* cycle. By observing the same genealogies

and biographies from text to text over a period of years, as has largely been the case since the *Lancelot-Grail* cycle, Arthurian romances created a consistent fictional history for themselves. Another historicizing strategy is to anchor the fiction within a secure historical context, as Geoffrey of Monmouth did in the *Historia regum Britanniae* by setting his Arthurian material in among the narratives of the Roman withdrawal from Britain and the subsequent Saxon invasions. The Trojan ancestral epitome that frames *SGGK* in this way historicizes the Arthurian narrative. Enfolded within this context the Arthurian matter of Britain becomes "an aspect of the larger matter of Troy" as Theodore Silverstein once observed (191), inviting us to read the main narrative and the frame through each other. The Troy frame may have typological significance, foreshadowing Gawain's threatened fate, in that the verb *britten*, which happens to pun nicely on the name of the island "Britain," is applied to Troy in line 2, to Gawain in line 680, and to the deer and the boar that Bertilak hunts in lines 1339 and 1611. In the allegorical tradition, the burning of Troy was often regarded as an exemplum of the humbling of pride—for example, in Dante's *Inferno*, I, 75, where Virgil identifies himself as the poet who "'cantai di quel giusto / figliuol d'Anchise che venne di Troia, / poi che 'l superbo Ilïón fu combusto'" ("sang of that just son of Anchises who came from Troy after proud Ilium was burned,") and *Purgatorio*, XII, 61–63, where Dante sees Troy in ashes sculpted in the pavement of the terrace of the proud.[24] In *SGGK* Bertilak says that Morgain's purpose is to "'assay þe surquidré'" ("make trial of the pride," 2457; cp. 311) of the Round Table, and that "'Weldez non so hyȝe hawtesse / Þat ho ne con make ful tame'" ("no one possesses such high pride that she cannot completely tame him," 2454–55).

The story of Troy in its medieval form surprisingly contains an Arthurian subtext in some manuscripts of Benoît's *RT* and in some manuscripts of a fourteenth-century prose translation called the *Histoire de Troie* that is found interpolated in the early thirteenth-century *Histoire ancienne jusqu'à César*. Before the Trojans go out for the second battle, Benoît describes Hector and his brothers. As Hector mounts his horse, Galatée, Benoît mentions that the horse was a gift of Morgain la Fée, who loved him in vain. Her love turned to hatred when he spurned her:

> Hector monta sor Galatee,
> Que li tramist Orva [6 MSS.: Morgain] la fee,
> Que mout l'ama e mout l'ot chier
> Mais ne la voust o sei couchier:

Empor la honte qu'ele en ot,
L'en haï tant come el plus pot.
Ço fu li tres plus beaus chevaus
Sor que montast nus hom charnaus,
E li mieudre e li plus coranz,
Li plus hardiz e li plus granz:
Si bele rien onc ne fu nee. (8023–33)[25]

[Hector mounted on Galatée,
Which Morgain la Fée had given him,
For she loved him greatly and held him dear,
But he would not sleep with her;
Because of the shame she felt on account of it,
She hated him as much as she could.
That was the most beautiful horse
That any mortal man ever mounted,
And the best and the fastest,
The hardiest and the biggest:
So beautiful a thing was never born.]

Lucy Allen Paton first called attention to Morgain in this passage (*Fairy Mythology*, 6, 21). In 1911 J.D. Bruce suggested that although the name "Morgain" appears in only six of eighteen manuscripts at this point, "Morgain" was nevertheless authorial.[26] In 1945 Roger Sherman Loomis confirmed this opinion (Loomis, "Celtic Goddesses," 185). One argument is that the name "Morgain" or a variant of it appears in all of the manuscript families of the *RT*. The appearance of Morgain in three manuscripts of the *Histoire de Troie* in the second redaction of *Histoire ancienne jusqu'à César,* which Paton, Bruce, and Loomis did not know, to some extent corroborates this hypothesis.[27] The fay's other name, Orva, occurs in so many variations in the manuscripts as to suggest that the name meant little or nothing to scribes. On the other hand, the name "Morgain" is not significantly varied, suggesting that to scribes it was a meaningful name. Finally, Benoît was well acquainted with the Matter of Britain. He refers to Breton *lais* in line 23,599. In the same section in which Morgain appears, Benoît names Hector's illegitimate brothers, four of whom have names from Wace's *Brut* (Loomis, "Celtic Goddesses," 184–85): Cadorz de Liz (8125), Cassibilant (8007), Gilor d'Agluz (8121), and Duglas (8123). It is thus quite possible that Benoît wrote "Morgain" in line 8024. We can certainly say that to the scribes and readers of six manuscripts of the *RT* and three manuscripts of the *Histoire de Troie*, the fay who loved Hector was Morgain.

The manner in which Morgain occurs in the *RT*, as part of a gloss on a narrative element associated with the hero, is consistent with her employment in other texts outside the *Lancelot-Grail* cycle. In her first appearance, Geoffrey of Monmouth's *Vita Merlini* (ca. 1150, ll. 908–40), she conducts Arthur to the Isle of Apples. This is repeated by Laȝamon, Gervaise of Tilbury, and Giraldus Cambrensis.[28] In Chrétien's *Erec et Enide*, 1904–8, she is said to be the mistress of Guigomar, lord of Avalon, in the list of wedding guests; in 2353–66 she is said to have embroidered the gown that Guinevere gave to Enide as a wedding gift; in 4193–204 she is said to be Arthur's sister and a skilled healer—as in *Yvain* 2947–51.[29]

Although Geoffrey of Monmouth's *Vita Merlini* is the only earlier written attestation of Morgain la Fée, already in the *RT* Morgain is a type of character that Theodore Ziolkowski dubbed a "figure on loan"—a figure transferred from one text to another in a process that Wolfgang Müller has called "interfigurality."[30] Interfigurality is a kind of intertextuality that specifically involves characters or figures. Once borrowed, a figure both is and is not the same as before, for as Müller says, "If an author takes over a figure from a work by another author into his own work, he absorbs it into the formal and ideological structure of his own product, putting it to his own uses" (Müller, 107). To apply this to Morgain, once she is Trojanized, she remains recognizable as Morgain la Fée but is also an adapted figure—an allomorph of her Arthurian forms.

The implied story of Hector and Morgain la Fée abstracts a plot that Paton and Loomis each in turn derived from the Irish legend of Cuchulainn and the fay Macha (Paton, 161; Loomis, "Survey," 283–84), but which could have been known to the poet of *SGGK* through a number of vehicles. In *Les fées au moyen âge*, Laurence Harf-Lancner proposes two narrative types that she labels the *conte melusinien* and the *conte morganien,* named respectively for Melusine and Morgain.[31] The *conte morganien* is in effect a *conte melusinien* in a derogated form. Both types involve a fay and her human lover. What distinguishes "Melusinian" from "Morgainian" narratives is simply that in "Melusinian" narratives the fay's desire for a human male is beneficent, whereas in the "Morgainien" narratives the fay's desire is dangerous and destructive: "En Morgue, la 'femme fatale,' s'incarne la féminité maléfique: ravisseuse inexorable, qu'elle prenne le doux visage de l'amante de Lanval ou les traits repoussants de la fée luxurieuse des romans en prose, Lorelei ou sirène, elle s'identifie toujours à la Mort" ("In Morgue, the 'femme fatale,' malevolent feminity is incarnated: an unrelenting abductress, whether she adopts the sweet visage of Lanval's lover or the repulsive traits of the lecherous fay of the prose romances—Lorelei or Siren—she is always identified with death," Harf-Lancner, 434).

Harf-Lancner (203–375) and Roger Sherman Loomis ("Celtic Goddesses," passim) cite numerous examples of stories involving fays and mortal men. The "lais féeriques" such as *Lanval* (and its Middle English versions), *Graelent, Désiré, Guingamor, Tyolet,* and the Middle English *Sir Orfeo* examine the relationship between a knight and a fay who seeks to remove the knight from the court and take him with her forever into the Other World (203–14). The story of Morgain taking the mortally wounded Arthur to Avalon would seem to be an implicit version of this narrative, as would be the allusion to Morgain in the *RT*.[32] Focusing only on stories in which Morgain is named as the fay, the *contes morganiens* provide certain general features that also occur in *SGGK*: the revenge motive, the wilderness castle, and the detainment of the knight by the fay or her accomplice.[33] In the Prose *Lancelot* the abduction theme of the *lais* has been preserved *in malo*, and the Other World has been rationalized into Morgain's wilderness castle, where four times altogether Morgain imprisons Lancelot—twice out of revenge against Guinevere, twice out of desire for Lancelot—and each time Lancelot escapes.[34] The Val sans Retour appears also in the *Livre d'Artus*, where it is Gawain's discovery of Morgain and Guiomar *in flagrante delicto* that brings about Morgain's flight to the wilderness.[35] Another narrative embodying the *conte morganien* is the story of Morgain and Alixandre l'Orphelin in the *Prophécies de Merlin* (ca. 1275).[36] In the *Suite du Merlin*, a source for Malory, Morgain's plots focus on Arthur in the tale of Accolon and the tale of the poisoned cloak.[37] In the Prose *Tristan*, Morgain is said to have loved Lancelot, but he, like Alixandre and like Hector in the *RT*, has spurned her, and her love has turned to hate; she seeks her revenge both against Lancelot and against Tristan.[38] Like the Prose *Lancelot* and *SGGK*, the Prose *Tristan* prominently features Morgain's castle and her use of imprisonment in her revenge plots against the court. The fourteenth-century Italian *cantari* provide an apposite example in the *Ponzela Gaia*, in which Gawain's affair with Morgain la Fée's daughter Ponzela Gaia is thwarted by Morgain. When she discovers the affair, Morgain puts her daughter in prison, and it takes Gawain six months to find Ponzela Gaia and release her. As Marie-José Heijkant has observed, "Depuis le *Lancelot*, Morgane a la réputation d'être une méchante fée. Indissociablement liée à sa personne est la notion d'emprisonnement, moyen habituel pour elle de soustraire le héros au monde des femmes" ("After the *Lancelot*, Morgain has the reputation of being a wicked fay. Inextricably tied to her character is the notion of imprisonment, her usual way of removing the hero to the world of women").[39]

In 1399 or 1400 Christine de Pisan adapted the story of Hector, Morgain, and the horse Galatée as part of the gloss to her *Epistle of Othea to Hector*. Like Benoît de Sainte-Maure, Christine only cited the story and did not narrate it. Allegorizing the story of Hector into a paradigm for human life, Christine changed Morgain into Othea, the goddess of prudence. Othea comes to the young Hector with a letter that, by retelling various Ovidian myths and looking ahead to the fall of Troy, counsels Hector on the importance of prudence.[40] As P.G.C. Campbell showed many years ago, Christine's source for the legend of Troy is the prose translation of the *RT* found in the *Histoire de Troie* section of the *Histoire ancienne jusqu'à César*.[41] The untold story of Trojan Hector and Morgain la Fée may have been transferred to the Arthurian Hector as well. In the version of the thirteenth-century romance *Palamedes* by Rusticiano da Pisa, which is an expansion of the Prose *Tristan*, there is oblique reference to Morgain's wish to avenge the shame that Hector "spoke to her long ago." She enacts her revenge by imprisoning Lionel in her castle.[42]

The *RT*'s allusion to Morgain refers not to an isolated, anomalous episode but to a well-known and productive plot whose occurrence in the *RT* stands at the beginning of a French romance tradition, as well as at the end of a Celtic mythic one—the *conte morganien* of the fairy mistress seeking to sever the knight from his male cohort. But nowhere do we find the story of Hector and Morgain told: it exists only in the form of a citation whose purpose is to gloss or explain something in the narrative. Since Morgain's appearance in the *RT* is only her second appearance in literature after Geoffrey of Monmouth's *Vita Merlini*, Roger Sherman Loomis quite reasonably argued that here was a "stock motif, employed very early by the Arthurian *conteurs* and the composers of Breton lais," from whom Benoît must have learned it (Loomis, "Celtic Goddesses," 189). Thus, if Morgain is a "figure on loan" in the *RT*, we do not have a written text from which she might have been borrowed.

Yet, in order for Morgain's love affair with Hector to be meaningful, it must refer to something intelligible to the reader. Supposed oral sources notwithstanding, Morgain's function in the *RT* is as a gloss on Hector. She is a figure haunting the margins whose personal history in relation to Hector defines Hector in his heroic role. An intertextual reading of Bertilak's speech about Morgain in *SGGK* together with the Morgain citation of the *RT* would thus consider both as narrative glosses based on the *conte morganien* of the fay and the knight.

Gawain and Hector, both propelled to their destinies by Morgain la Fée, embody the constitutive values of their chivalric worlds. Both are bribed with gifts from the fay. Hector is bribed directly, when Morgain gives him the horse so that he will sleep with her, which he does not do. Gawain is bribed by an intermediary when Morgain's agent, the Lady, offers him kisses, a ring, and finally a magic girdle, also expressing her desire to sleep with Gawain. In the *RT* Hector keeps the horse Galatée, but breaks faith with Morgain; in *SGGK* Gawain keeps the green girdle and holds himself guilty of *vntrawþe* for his double breach of promises to the Green Knight, Morgain's other agent (2383, 2509). Gawain's response is psychologically richer than Hector's, of course, because the encounter with Morgain is much closer to the bone for him—Morgain is, after all, Gawain's aunt and Arthur's half-sister. But also Morgain is ultimately the engenderer of the plot in *SGGK*, whereas in the *RT* Morgain is part of an aside whose purpose is also to get Hector on his horse.

In this essay I have been suggesting that scholars have neglected or dismissed the intertextual relations implied in Bertilak's speech about Morgain la Fée. The intertextuality of Morgain imbeds her and *SGGK* in the larger narrative of the *Lancelot-Grail* cycle. I have also suggested that the plot of *SGGK* is an example of a *conte morganien*, in which the fay seeks to lure a knight away from his male cohort, and that this is also the case with Lancelot in the Val sans Retour episode of the *Lancelot* and with Hector in the *RT*. I am thus calling for a reorientation of critical perspective on *SGGK*, such that we begin to see it not simply as an exchange between Gawain and a Green Knight, but also—perhaps primarily—as a *conte morganien* involving Gawain and Morgain.

Certainly this is how Gawain himself sees his adventure, even before he learns of Morgain. In lines 2400–2407, Bertilak invites Gawain to return to his castle for the rest of the New Year's feast, offering to reconcile Gawain and the lady of the castle:

> "And 3e schal in þis Nwe 3er a3ayn to my wonez,
> And we schyn reuel þe remnaunt of þis ryche fest
> ful bene."
> Þer laþed hym fast þe lorde
> And sayde: "With my wyf, I wene,
> We schal yow wel acorde,
> Þat watz your enmy kene."

["And you shall in this New Year again go to my lodgings,

And we shall revel the remnant of this rich feast
very pleasantly."
The lord invited him insistently
And said, "With my wife, I expect,
We shall accord you well,
Who was your enemy keen."]

Here Gawain is invited to stay, but he declines, and he begins to take his leave, commending himself to "'Boþe þat on and þat oþer, myn honoured ladyez, / Þat þus hor kny3t wyth hor kest han koyntly bigyled'" ("Both the one and the other, my honored ladies, / Who thus with their trick have neatly beguiled their knight," 2411–13). Gawain concludes that he has been beguiled by both the young lady and old lady. Line 2413 recognizes the two women's power over him via the balanced phrases "hor kny3t" and "hor kest," the possessive pronoun *hor* "their" linking "their knight" to "their trick." Has he realized that the *auncian* lady is Morgain la Fée? Then Gawain compares himself to other "deluded" men, setting himself in an historical pattern that begins chronologically with Adam and ends with himself:

"Bot hit is no ferly þa3 a fole madde,
And þur3 wyles of wymmen be wonen to sor3e,
For so watz Adam in erde with one bigyled,
And Salamon with fele sere, and Samson eftsonez—
Dalyda hym dalt hys wyrde—and Dauyth þerafter
Watz blended with Barsabe, þat much bale þoled." (2414–19)

["But it is no marvel if a fool go mad,
And be brought to misery by the wiles of women.
For so was Adam beguiled by one on earth,
And Solomon with many various ones, and Samson as a second
instance—
Delila dealt him his fate—and David thereafter,
Who suffered much misery, was blinded by Bathsheba."]

The histories of Morgain, Arthur, and Gawain converge with Trojan and biblical history in this moment when Gawain recognizes the power of his aunt and the Lady. The genealogy of Morgain connects Morgain and Gawain to the pre-Arthurian generation in history; the story of Troy that begins and ends *SGGK* in turn links the Arthurian lineage to Troy; and finally, the Biblical scheme in Gawain's antifeminist outburst in the lines above links Gawain to Adam. These three schemes in effect join the action of the poem to all of history, from the Arthurian present backward to the Fall of mankind, and all three have Gawain in the "modern" or "contemporary" position. The family history of Igern leads through Morgain to her nephew, Gawain. Trojan history leads to Arthur, whose nephew Gawain also is. The pentangle on Gawain's shield was established by Solomon (625), and Gawain now sees himself at the end of a biblical line of men, including Solomon, who were beguiled by women. All history, in a sense, leads to Gawain.

The various historical schemes of *SGGK* are "about" deception: Troy was brought down by the treachery of Aeneas; Adam and his successors are said to be deceived by women; Arthur's court and Gawain have been deceived by Morgain la Fée. Focusing more specifically on the sexual desire by which Gawain was tried in the bedroom scenes and which implicated him in the deception of the green girdle, adultery is concealed in all three histories. The Trojan war begins with Paris's abduction of Helen. The Arthurian world begins when Merlin's enchantment enables Uther to beget Arthur on Igern, a fact to which Bertilak alludes in lines 2465–66. In the *Lancelot-Grail* cycle, the Arthurian world ends because of the adultery of Lancelot and Guinevere. The biblical line of men in 2414–19 includes the adultery of David and Bathsheba. Again, what happens to Gawain in *SGGK* is part of a larger historical pattern that stretches back to the earliest time.

What launches Gawain's antifeminist speech is the Green Knight's invitation to return to his castle for the rest of the New Year with his wife, whom he calls Gawain's "enmy kene" in line 2406. At those words Gawain responds courteously and amicably to his host, while speaking nothing but ill of women. Gawain's anger is directed at Morgain and the Lady, not at the Green Knight, even though the Green Knight tells him in lines 2361–62 that he set his wife on Gawain: "'I wroȝt hit myseluen. / I sende hir to asay þe . . . '" ("I did it myself. / I sent her to test you . . . "). He turns down the Green Knight's invitation by politely doffing his helmet and commending himself to the ladies in the castle. But when he thinks of those ladies, he jumps to the conclusion that both of *them*—not the Green Knight—were his deceivers: "'And comaundez me to þat cortays, your comlych fere, / Boþe þat on and þat oþer, myn honoured ladyez, / Þat þus hor knyȝt wyth hor kest han koyntly bigyled'" ("And commend me to that courteous one, your comely companion, / Both the one and the other, my honored ladies, / Who thus with their trick have neatly beguiled their knight," 2411–13).

Gawain implicitly recognizes the erotic undercurrent of his ensnarement by Morgain and the Lady when he likens himself to the biblical lovers. Even as he attempts to define the girdle as the token of his guilt, his language cannot escape this insinuation: "'And þus, quen pryde schal me pryk for prowes of armes, / Þe loke to þis luf-lace schal leþe my hert'" ("And thus when pride shall spur me on account of prowess of arms, / Looking at this love-lace shall humble my heart," 2437–38). In calling the girdle a "love-lace," he accepts not its magical significance but its erotic significance as a love token given to him by the lady in his bedroom the previous day, and he allows that relationship to define his adventure with her husband as a *conte morganien*. Bertilak's subsequent revelation about Morgain's role in the adventure in lines 2440–66 only confirms what Gawain has already suspected.

It is Gawain's request to know Bertilak's name that prompts Bertilak to speak of Morgain. Naming himself forces Bertilak to identify his role as Morgain's minister—because a full disclosure of his identity necessitates the admission that he is in a sense not the lord of his domain, as Gawain thinks he is, but the vassal of a higher power, Morgain la Fée. Thus Gawain's assumption in line 2440 that Bertilak is "lorde of þe ȝonder londe" at the castle induces Bertilak in line 2445 to tell him his proper identity "in þis londe." This admission is necessary because Morgain's particular power, as Bertilak explains in lines 2454–55, is humbling the proud and that one of the purposes of his mission as the Green Knight sent by Morgain was to "'assay þe surquidré, ȝif hit soth were / Þat rennes of þe grete renoun of þe Rounde Table'" ("make trial of the pride, [to see] if it were true / What circulates about the great renown of the Round Table," 2457–58). For Bertilak to identify himself without explaining his relationship to Morgain would be surquidry—like Gawain taking the axe from the Green Knight without acknowledging that he was doing it on behalf of his uncle Arthur (see 339–65).

The reading of *SGGK* set forth in the present essay puts Morgain la Fée and her nephew Gawain at the very center of the poem. Though she is absent, her presence has been felt in the narrative, and, through her genealogical connection to Gawain, in Gawain as well. If Morgain's plot fails to scare Guinevere to death, then this is in accordance with the fictional history of Guinevere's death presented in the *Lancelot-Grail* cycle, where, in the *Mort Artu*, Guinevere, who has been a virtual prisoner of Mordred in the Tower of London, flees to the forest, finds refuge in a nunnery, and dies in the nunnery three days before Lancelot's battle with the two sons of Mordred, which takes place after Arthur's death on Salisbury Plain. Because *this* is the canonical version of Guinevere's death, in *SGGK* Morgain could no more kill Guinevere than the Green Knight could kill Gawain. Thus I would suggest that Morgain's role in *SGGK* makes sense if we think of it as a poem deeply invested in the fictional truths of Arthurian history, a history that is embodied in the relationship of Morgain la Fée and Gawain.[43]

1. The single-author hypothesis is based on formal, thematic, and lexical similarities. The best introduction to the question is now in R.A. Cooper and Derek Pearsall, "The *Gawain* Poems: A Statistical Approach to the Question of Common Authorship," *Review of English Studies*, NS 39 (1988), 365–85.

2. See W.G. Cooke, "*Sir Gawain and the Green Knight*: A Restored Dating," *Medium Ævum*, 53 (1989), 34–48; here citing 37.

3. "Somer Soneday," ed. Rossell Hope Robbins in *Historical Poems of the XIVth and XVth Centuries* (New York: Columbia University Press, 1959), pp. 98–102. See further J.P. Oakden, *Alliterative Poetry in Middle English*, 2 vols. (Manchester: Manchester University Press, 1930), I, 217–32.

4. "Romance: Idealistic Genre or Historical Text?" in *The Craft of Fiction: Essays on Medieval Poetics*, ed. Leigh A. Arrathoon (Rochester, Michigan: Solaris, 1984), pp. 37–38.

5. Julia Kristeva, who coined the term, came to prefer "transposition" when "intertextuality" was corrupted into a synonym for source study: *Revolution in Poetic Language*, trans. Margaret Walker (New York: Columbia University Press, 1984), pp. 59–60.

6. For example, see the entry on *SGGK* in *The New Arthurian Encyclopedia*, ed. Norris J. Lacy et al. (New York: Garland, 1991), pp. 419–21. The incorporation of the conclusions of early source studies into the entry on *SGGK* in the Severs *Manual* ensured the preservation of this approach and its terms for the forseeable future: see *A Manual of the Writings in Middle English 1050–1500*, ed. J. Burke Severs et al. (New Haven: Connecticut Academy of Sciences, 1967–), I, 54–57. Fanni Bogdanow's assessment of Morgain scholarship up to 1969 applies equally to *SGGK* scholarship: "For a long time scholars tended to treat the Arthurian romances not as works of imagination produced by successive writers, but as a 'treasure house of fairy lore,' 'a source of information in regard to the otherworld and its inhabitants'": "Morgain's Role in the Thirteenth-Century Prose Romances of the Arthurian Cycle," *Medium Ævum*, 38 (1969), 123–33; here quoting 123, which in turn quotes from Lucy Allen Paton, *Studies in the Fairy Mythology of Arthurian Romance*, Radcliffe College Monographs, No. 13 (1903), 2nd ed. enlarged by a "Survey of Scholarship on the Fairy Mythology Since 1903" and a bibliography by Roger Sherman Loomis (New York: Burt Franklin, 1960), p. 1.

7. Brewer, *Sir Gawain and the Green Knight: Sources and Analogues* (Cambridge: Brewer, 1992), reprints her earlier *From Cuchulainn to Gawain* (Cambridge: Brewer, 1973), which follows traditional motif analysis by providing parallels to the feast, the beheading game, the passing of the year, etc. The most complete summary of source study of *SGGK* is in Larry D. Benson, *Art and Tradition in Sir Gawain and the Green Knight* (New Brunswick, New Jersey: Rutgers University Press, 1965). See also Laura Hibbard Loomis, "*Gawain and the Green Knight*," in Roger Sherman Loomis, ed., *Arthurian Literature in the Middle Ages: A Collaborative History* (Oxford: Clarendon, 1959), pp. 528–40, here citing 530–37, reprinted in Donald R. Howard and Christian Zacher, eds., *Critical Studies of Sir Gawain and the Green Knight* (Notre Dame: University of Notre Dame Press, 1968), pp. 3–23, here citing pp. 7–18. Sources and analogues are also discussed passim in J.A. Burrow's excellent book, *A Reading of Sir Gawain and the Green Knight* (London: Routledge and Kegan Paul, 1965).

8. All citation to *SGGK* is to the edition of J.R.R. Tolkien and E.V. Gordon, 2nd ed., rev. Norman Davis (Oxford: Clarendon, 1967); translations are my own, and occasionally, as in line 2445, I have repunctuated for greater grammatical clarity.

9. George Lyman Kittredge, *A Study of* Sir Gawain and the Green Knight (1916; rpt. Gloucester, Massachusetts: Peter Smith, 1960), p. 136. See also J. R. Hulbert, "*Syr Gawayn and the Grene Knyȝt*," MP, 13 (1915), 433–62, here citing 454;

Albert B. Friedman, "Morgan le Fay in *Sir Gawain and the Green Knight,*" *Speculum,* 35 (1960), 260–74; Benson, pp. 18–37. One exception to this trend is J.A. Burrow, whose more benign view was that Morgain had "the older, less interesting, and in part untransposable aspects of the tester's role" (168).

10. Morton W. Bloomfield, "*Sir Gawain and the Green Knight*: An Appraisal," *PMLA,* 76 (1961), 7–19; Robert W. Ackerman, "*Sir Gawain and the Green Knight* and Its Interpreters," in John W. Ehrstine, John R. Elwood, and Robert C. McLean, eds., *On Stage and Off: Eight Essays in English Literature* (Seattle: Washington State University Press, 1968), pp. 66–73; Donald R. Howard, "*Sir Gawain and the Green Knight,*" in J. Burke Severs, ed., *Recent Middle English Scholarship and Criticism: Survey and Desiderata* (Pittsburgh: Duquesne University Press, 1971), pp. 29–54.

11. Derek Brewer, "The Interpretation of Dream, Folktale, and Romance, With Special Reference to *Sir Gawain and the Green Knight,*" *Neuphilologische Mitteilungen,* 77 (1976), 569–81, here quoting 570.

12. Stephanie Trigg, "The Romance of Exchange: *Sir Gawain and the Green Knight,*" *Viator,* 22 (1991), 251–66, here quoting 259. Trigg supports her point by reference to Friedman 260 and 274, and later she reaffirms Morgain's dismissal, saying that the poem's female figures are "at once powerful yet contained within the dominant patriarchal ideology" (263). Further on this notion see the articles by Fisher cited below.

13. On Middle English genre terms, see Paul Strohm, "*Storie, spelle, geste, romaunce, tragedie*: Generic Distinctions in the Middle English Troy Narrative," *Speculum,* 46 (1971), 348–59, who observes (348) that Middle English writers would apply more than one designation to their works. On "the adventures (of Britain / Logres)" see Christine Archer-Ferlampin, "Magie et surnaturel dans les romans de chevalerie français en prose aux XIIIe et XIVe siècles" [summary of dissertation], *Perspectives Médiévales,* 18 (1992), 104–08; Charles Méla, "Life in *La Mort le roi Artu,*" in Christopher Baswell and William Sharpe, eds., *The Passing of Arthur: New Essays in Arthurian Tradition* (New York: Garland, 1988), pp. 5–14; Jacques Ribard, "*L'aventure* dans la *Queste del Saint Graal,*" in *Mélanges de langue et de littérature médiévales offerts à Alice Planche* (Nice: Les Belles Lettres, 1984), pp. 415–23; Eugène Vinaver, "La Fée Morgain et les aventures de Bretagne," in *Mélanges de langue et de littérature du moyen âge et de la renaissance offerts à Jean Frappier,* 2 vols. (Geneva: Droz, 1970), II, 1077–83.

14. Pointed out by, e.g., Hulbert, "*Syr Gawayne,*" 440, 455–57.

15. Pointed out by Martin Puhvel, "Art and the Supernatural in *Sir Gawain and the Green Knight,*" *Arthurian Literature V* (1985), 12.

16. Malcolm Andrew and Ronald Waldron compare these lines to *Sir Orfeo* 288 and 296 ("No never he nist whider thai bicome" and "Ac never he nist whider thai wold"); *The Poems of the Pearl Manuscript* (Berkeley: University of California Press, 1978), n. to 460f.

17. See Denver Ewing Baughan, "The Role of Morgan la Fay in *Sir Gawain and the Green Knight,*" *English Literary History,* 17 (1950), 241–51; Mother Angela Carson, "Morgan la Fée as the Principle of Unity in 'Gawain and the Green Knight,'" *Modern Language Quarterly,* 23 (1962), 3–16; Douglas M. Moon, "The Role of Morgan la Fée in *Sir Gawain and the Green Knight,*" *Neuphilologische Mitteilungen,* 67 (1966), 31–57; Ivo Kamps, "Magic, Women, and Incest: The Real Challenges of *Sir Gawain and the Green Knight,*" *Exemplaria,* 1 (1989), 313–36. Baughan believed that Arthur took a few swings at the Green Knight before giving the axe to Gawain. Carson believed that Bertilak was Urien—the father of Yvain. Moon believed that Gawain was having an affair with Guinevere. Kamps regarded Morgain as a scapegoat figure onto whom the Arthurian world in *SGGK* "displaces its own antisocial impulses" (314), a thesis whose demonstration led Kamps to argue rather fancifully that Arthur's incest with Morgawse and the coming treachery of Mordred both somehow are implicated in the narrative of *SGGK.* See also Charles Moorman, *The Pearl Poet* (New York: Twayne, 1968), pp. 106–07.

18. T.P. McAlindon, "Magic, Fate, and Providence in Medieval Narrative and *Sir Gawain and the Green Knight,*" *Review of English Studies,* NS 16 (1965), 121–39; Dennis Moore, "Making Sense of an Ending: Morgan le Fay in *Sir Gawain and the Green Knight,*" *Mediaevalia,* 10 (1988 for 1984), 213–33.

19. Sheila Fisher, "Leaving Morgan Aside: Women, History, and Revisionism in *Sir Gawain and the Green Knight,*" in *The Passing of Arthur,* pp. 129–51; rpt. in Stephanie Trigg, ed., *Medieval English Poetry* (London: Longman, 1993), pp. 138–55; Sheila Fisher, "Taken Men and Token Women in *Sir Gawain and the Green Knight,*" in Sheila Fisher and Janet E. Halley, eds., *Seeking the Woman in Late Medieval and Renaissance Writings: Essays in Feminist Contextual Criticism* (Knoxville: University of Tennessee Press, 1989), pp. 71–105; Geraldine Heng, "Feminine Knots and the Other *Sir Gawain and the Green Knight,*" *PMLA,* 106 (1991), 500–14.

20. *Lancelot: Roman en prose du XIIIe siècle,* ed. Alexandre Micha, Textes Littéraires Français, 9 vols. (Geneva: Droz, 1978–83), I, section XXIV.

21. On Morgain as goddess, see Paul Mertens-Fonck, "Morgan, fée et déesse," in *Mélanges offerts à Rita Lejeune, professeur à l'Université de Liège,* 2 vols. (Gembloux: Duculot, 1969), II, 1067–76; and Paton, *Fairy Mythology,* p. 165, n. 1.

22. Since the nineteenth century, scholars now and again have argued that the *Lancelot-Grail* cycle is in some way a source for *SGGK.* Although there is little agreement (and much repetition) among these scattered attempts, this body of work does point the way to potentially rich further study. The most important for the present discussion are the suggestions of Smithers, who derived the scene at the Green Chapel from the *Queste del Saint Graal,* and of Laura Hibbard Loomis and Marjory Rigby, who individually derived the "temptation scenes" from the Val sanz Retour episode of the Prose *Lancelot.* Rigby further drew a connection between Morgain's affair with Merlin and her hatred of Guinevere in the Prose *Lancelot* and *SGGK*'s information about Morgain in 2447–49 and 2460. See Kittredge, pp. 131–35; J.R. Hulbert, "The Name of the Green Knight: Bercilak or Bertilak," in *The Manly Anniversary Studies in Language and Literature* (1923; rpt. Freeport, New York: Books for Libraries, 1968), pp. 12–19; Laura Hibbard Loomis, "*Gawain and the Green Knight,*" pp. 534–35; G.V. Smithers, "What *Sir Gawain and the Green Knight* Is About," *Medium Ævum,* 31 (1963), 171–89; Tolkien-Gordon-Davis, ed. cit., notes to 39, 44, 552, 2445, 2452, 2460, 2494 ff.; Richard R. Griffith, "Bertilak's Lady: The French Background of *Sir Gawain and the Green Knight,*" in Madeleine Pelner Cosman and Bruce Chandler, eds., *Machaut's World: Science and Art in the Fourteenth Century* (New York: New York Academy of Sciences, 1978), pp. 249–66; Robert L. Kelly, "Allusions to the Vulgate Cycle in *Sir Gawain and the Green Knight,*" in Patricia W. Cummins, Patrick W. Conner, and Charles W. Connell, eds., *Literary and Historical Perspectives of the Middle Ages: Proceedings of the 1981 SEMA Meeting* (Morgantown: West Virginia University Press, 1982), pp. 183–99; Marjory Rigby, "*Sir Gawain and the Green Knight* and the Vulgate *Lancelot,*" *Modern Language Review,* 78 (1983), 257–66; Elizabeth Gee, "The Lists of Knights in *Sir Gawain and the Green Knight,*" *AUMLA: Journal of the Australasian Universities Language and Literature Association,* 62 (1984), 171–78.

23. In addition to Tolkien-Gordon-Davis, notes to 3–5, 6, and 11, see Alfred David, "Gawain and Aeneas," *English Studies,* 49 (1968), 402–09, and Theodore Silverstein, "*Sir Gawain,* Dear Brutus, and Britain's Fortunate Founding: A Study in Comedy and Convention," *Modern Philology,* 62 (1965), 189–206.

24. Text and translation from *The Divine Comedy,* ed. Charles S. Singleton, 3 vols. (Princeton: Princeton University Press, 1970–75). This tradition ultimately stems from the *Aeneid* itself: "ceciditque superbum / Ilium et omnis humo fumat Neptunia Troia" ("proud Ilium fell, and all Neptune's Troy smokes from the ground," 3.2–3).

25. *Le Roman de Troie,* ed. Leopold Constans, Société des Anciens Textes Français, 6 vols. (Paris: Didot, 1904–12), I, 434. Constans's text reads "Orva" for "Morgain" at this point, but six of the twelve manuscripts of the *RT* give the name

Morgain or a variant: Morgain: Paris, B.N. fr. 783; Montpellier, Bibl. de la Faculté de Médecine 251. Morguein: Paris, B.N. nouv. acq. 6534. Morgan: Paris, B.N. fr. 2181; Rome, Vatican Regina 1505. Morganz: Paris, B.N. fr. 794. Roger S. Loomis, "Morgain la Fee and the Celtic Goddesses," *Speculum*, 20 (1945), 183–203, here citing 184–85 (rpt. in *Wales and the Arthurian Legend* [Cardiff: University of Wales Press, 1956]), considers the name "Orva" and its variants to be a corruption of the name "Morgain."

26. Bruce, "Some Proper Names in Laʒamon's *Brut* Not Represented in Wace or Geoffrey of Monmouth," *Modern Language Notes*, 26 (1911), 65–69, here citing 66–67.

27. These manuscripts are described in Clem C. Williams, "A Case of Mistaken Identity: Still Another Trojan Narrative in Old French Prose," *Medium Ævum*, 53 (1984) 59–72, here citing 62. The three manuscripts are Paris, B.N. fr. 301 (ca. 1400); London, B.L. Royal 20.D.I (ca. 1340, from Naples); Oxford, Bodley Douce 353 (fifteenth century).

28. *Vita Merlini*, ed. John Jay Parry (Urbana: University of Illinois Press, 1925); Laʒamon, *Brut*, ll. 14,277–82 in the edition of G.L. Brook and R.F. Leslie (London: Oxford University Press, 1963, 1978); Gervaise of Tilbury, *Otia imperialia*, in *Radulphi de Coggeshall Chronicon Anglicanum*, etc., ed. Joseph Stevenson, Rolls Series, 66 (London: Trübner, 1875), p. 438; Giraldus Cambrensis, *Speculum ecclesiae*, dist. 2, chap. 9 in *Giraldus Cambrensis Opera*, ed. Joseph S. Brewer, 8 vols. (London: Longman, 1861–91), 4.49–49 and *De principis instructione*, dist. 1 in the edition of Brewer, VIII, 128.

29. *Les Romans de Chrétien de Troyes, I: Erec et Enide*, ed. Mario Roques (Paris: Champion, 1970); *IV: Le Chevalier au Lion (Yvain)*, ed. Mario Roques (Paris: Champion, 1971).

30. Ziolkowski, "Figures on Loan," in *Varieties of Literary Thematics* (Princeton: Princeton University Press, 1983), pp. 123–51. Müller, "Interfigurality: A Study on the Interdependence of Literary Figures," in Heinrich F. Plett, ed., *Intertextuality* (Berlin: de Gruyter, 1991), pp. 101–21.

31. Laurence Harf-Lancner, *Les Fées au moyen âge: Morgane et Mélusine, La Naissance des fées* (Paris: Champion, 1984). On pp. 267–68, n. 15, are listed the chief studies on Morgain since Paton's *Fairy Mythology*. On the basis of comparisons with *La Mule sans frein* and *Diu Krône*, Hulbert ("*Syr Gawayne*," 433–62) considered *SGGK* a beheading narrative joined to a fairy-mistress narrative. However, for Hulbert the significance of this was that it enabled him to reconstruct what he believed to be the lost archetype, in which a fay who loved Gawain sent her thrall to lure Gawain to the Other World, where he underwent the beheading game successfully and stayed with the fay. She then gave him the green girdle and allowed him to return to his world.

32. Only in the *Gesta regum Britanniae* (ca. 1235) is Arthur said to be Morgain's lover (Harf-Lancner, pp. 267, citing Paton, *Fairy Mythology*, p. 28). In view of the lingering notion that Morgain derives from the Celtic Morrigan or Modron, Harf-Lancner prudently suggests: "Au lieu de voir dans le séjour d'Arthur blessé à Avalon le vestige d'une légende qui ferait du roi l'amant d'une femme surnaturelle et de reconstituer cette conjecturale légende à partir de textes postérieurs, il est plus sage de voir dans les textes du XIIe siècle les premiers témoignages d'une légende en train de se former. Il est vain de chercher l'origine de chacun des traits de Morgane dans les traditions antérieures: la fée Morgue, telle qu'elle apparaît dans les romans français, est une création du XIIe et du XIIIe siècles" ("Instead of seeing, in the wounded Arthur's sojourn at Avalon, the vestige of a legend that makes the king the lover of a supernatural woman, and instead of reconstructing this conjectural legend on the basis of later texts, it is more sensible to see in the twelfth-century texts the first evidence of a legend in the process of being formed. It is useless to search for the origin of each of Morgain's traits in the earlier traditions: the fay Morgue, such as she appears in the French romances, is a creation of the twelfth and thirteenth centuries," 265).

33. These have been summarized for the most part by Bogdanow, "Morgain's Role."

34. See the edition of Micha: vol. 1, section XXIV.47–XXVI.9 and XXVIII.22–XXXI.10; vol. 4, section LXXVIII.1–14; and vol. 5, section LXXXVI.14–LXXXVIII.5. For a summary see Harf-Lancner, pp. 270–72 or Bogdanow, 124–26. See further Laurence Harf-Lancner, "Le Val sans retour, ou la prise du pouvoir par les femmes" in Danielle Buschinger and André Crépin, eds. *Amour, mariage, et transgressions au Moyen Age: Université de Picardie Centre d'Études Médiévales, Actes du Colloque des 24, 25, 26, et 27 mars 1983* (Göppingen: Kümmerle, 1984), pp. 185–93.

35. *The Vulgate Version of the Arthurian Romances*, ed. H. Oskar Sommer, 8 vols. (Washington, D.C.: Carnegie Institution, 1909–16), VII, 135–36.

36. *Les Prophesies de Merlin (Cod. Bodmer 116)*, ed. Anne Berthelot (Cologny: Fondation Martin Bodmer, 1992), pp. 325–77. See also Cedric E. Pickford, "Miscellaneous French Prose Romances," in *Arthurian Literature in the Middle Ages*, pp. 353–54; *Alixandre l'Orphelin: A Prose Tale of the XVth Century*, ed. Cedric E. Pickford (Manchester: Manchester University Press, 1951), pp. 10, 26–27; Jeanne Wathelet-Willem, "La Fée Morgain dans la chanson de geste," *Cahiers de Civilisation Médiévale*, 13 (1970), 209–19, here citing 218.

37. *Les Enchantemenz de Bretaigne: An Abstract from a Thirteenth Century Prose Romance—"La Suite du Merlin,"* ed. Patrick Coogan Smith (Chapel Hill: University of North Carolina Department of Romance Languages, 1977), pp. 9–31 (Accolon) and 47–50 (poisoned cloak).

38. At one point Morgain has imprisoned Tristan in the room whose walls Lancelot had once decorated with the story of his affair with Guinevere (also referred to in the *Mort Artu*, ed. Jean Frappier [Geneva: Droz, 1964], sections 48–53). When Tristan tells her that Lancelot plans to appear at an upcoming tournament, "ele souspire de cuer parfont, com chele ki tant haoit Lanselot qu'ele nel pooit oublier. . . . Ele le haoit de grant haïne et si l'avoit amé jadis et encore l'amoit, mais che estoit encontre sa volenté meïsmes, pour ce qu'ele l'avoit veü si bel, et si le haoit mortelment pour ce k'il l'avoit refusee. Ensi amoit ele et haoit tout ensamble Lanselot" ("she sighed from deep in her heart, like one who hated Lancelot so much that she could not forget him. . . . she hated him with a great hate, and on the one hand she loved him once and still she loved him, though this was against her own will, because she had seen him to be so beautiful, and on the other hand she hated him mortally because he had refused her. Thus she hated and loved Lancelot all at once"; *Le Roman de Tristan en prose*, ed. Philippe Ménard et al., 7 vols. to date (Geneva: Droz, 1987–1993), vol. 2, section 174.15–24. For Morgain's wish for revenge against Lancelot and Tristan, see vol. 2, sections 23–35 and 72–77 respectively. For the imprisonment of Tristan, see vol. 3, sections 167–82. Morgain also has Lancelot imprisoned in vol. 6, sections 35 and 67–68. For a summary, see Bogdanow, 126–27.

39. *Ponzela Gaia: Cantare dialettale inedito del sec. XV*, ed. Giorgio Varanini (Bologna: Commissione per i Testi di Lingua, 1957; corr. publ. in 1958). For a summary see Edmund G. Gardner, *The Arthurian Legend in Italian Literature* (London: Dent; New York: Dutton, 1930), pp. 241–47. On resemblances between the *cantari* and the "lais féeriques," see Maria Bendinelli Predelli, "Fonti e struttura: il caso del 'cantare fiabesco' italiano," in *I Cantari: struttura e tradizione, Atti del Convegno Internazionale di Montreal, 19–20 marzo 1981* (Florence: Olschki, 1984), pp. 127–41, here citing 130–37. Other *cantari* of this narrative type are *Liombruno* and *Bel Gherardino*; see Gardner, p. 247. The story of Ponzela Gaia is alluded to in the fourteenth-century *Tavola Ritonda, o l'istoria di Tristano*, ed. Filippo-Luigi Polidori, 2 vols. (Bologna: Romagnoli, 1864–66), I, 487. I am indebted to Dr. Heijkant for a copy of her paper, "La transformation du personnage du Gauvain en Italie," read at the XVIIIth International Congress of the Arthurian Society, Bonn, 1993, from which I drew this information and from which I quote (p. 7).

40. There is no modern edition of the *Epistle of Othea*; sixteenth-century editions bear the title *Cent histoires de Troie*. The forty-three manuscripts were described by Gianni Mombello, "Per un'edizione critica dell' 'Epistre Othea' di Christine di

Pizan," *Studi Francesi*, 24 (1964), 401–17 and 25 (1965), 1–12, but the promised edition did not appear. I refer here to *Christine de Pizan's Letter of Othea to Hector*, trans. Jane Chance (Newburyport, Massachusetts: Focus Information Group, 1990), p. 37.

41. P.G.C. Campbell, *L'Épitre d'Othea: Étude sur les sources de Christine de Pisan* (Paris: Champion, 1924), pp. 80–109.

42. See the summary in Eilert Löseth, *Le Roman en prose de Tristan* (Paris, 1891), pp. 423–75, 487–91, here citing p. 430; see further Cedric E. Pickford, "Miscellaneous French Prose Romances," in *Arthurian Literature in the Middle Ages*, pp. 350–52. Although Rusticiano was an Italian, he claims in his prologue and epilogue that he translated from a book in an unnamed language that was given to him by King Edward I of England while Edward was on Crusade, which was between 1270 and 1274. This book has not been found. On Edward's Arthurian interests, see Loomis, "Edward I, Arthurian Enthusiast," *Speculum*, 28 (1953), 114–27, and Loomis, "Arthurian Influence in Sport and Spectacle," in *Arthurian Literature in the Middle Ages*, pp. 554, 558–59.

43. I gratefully acknowledge the suggestions of Professors Alice Colby-Hall and Nicole Clifton and of my former student Stephanie Overcash on several points.

FOOD FOR HEROES

THE INTERTEXTUAL LEGACY OF THE *CONTE DEL GRAAL*

Sara Sturm-Maddox

The Arthurian court as represented in medieval romance is, as we all know, much given to feasting and little to fasting. Chrétien's romances establish the pattern: Arthur's celebrations of the great feast days punctuate the adventures of the chivalric heroes, or their adventures punctuate his celebration, as accounts of their deeds are related by subjugated enemies or adventures erupt unannounced upon a court at table. Far-flung reaches of the realm and beyond are seldom different: knights who depart *en aventure* find hospitality characterized by the rituals of wining and dining in even the most unlikely of places.[1] None of this is suggested as problematic in these early courtly texts. On the contrary: where abundance is the rule, departures from it—by siege, by famine, by the evil practices of a *coutume*—are to be abolished, their victims rescued; one recalls at once the deprivation occasioned by the siege of Blancheflor's castle in the *Conte del Graal* and the feasting that follows its ending.[2] It is noteworthy, then, that when in Chrétien's final romance we are offered a glimpse of a world truly "other" that stands in contradistinction to the Arthurian world, that otherness is doubly marked in terms of sustenance: the Grail procession in the *Conte del Graal*, affording its unique nourishment to the aged Grail King, occurs while the unwitting hero is seated with his host at a lavish banquet.

Readers will recall Perceval's first "adventure" in that text, the visit of the destined but as yet unwitting hero to a maiden whom he finds sleeping in a luxurious tent. Having forcibly kissed the maiden and taken possession of her ring, according, as he thinks, to the instructions of his mother, he ignores both her protests and her warnings and looks about for food: "Li vallés a son cuer ne met / Rien nule de che que il ot, / Mais de che que jeüné ot / Moroit de fain a male fin" ("The youth took to heart nothing he heard. Since he had not eaten in a long time, he was dying of hunger," ll. 734–37). When he finds it, the account of his partaking of the wine and the "bons pastez de chievrol fres" is colored by the comic of his unself-conscious appetite:

> Et dist: "Pucele, cist pasté
> N'estroient hui par moi gasté.
> Venez mengier, qu'il sont molt buen,
> Assez avra chascuns del suen,
> S'en i remandra uns entiers." (ll. 751–55)

["Maiden, I shall not let these pies be wasted today. Come and eat. They are very good. Each of us will have a share, and a whole one will still be left."]

Here the emphasis on food is doubled by an emphasis on appetite, one that reemerges as a prominent feature of the characterization of the hero in this text; "amazingly," Madeleine Pelner Cosman remarks, "Perceval's every major adventure but one is inextricably bound with food."[3]

This association of Perceval with appetite is to remain constant in his reappearances in later texts. Noting that in Manessier's sequel to Chrétien's unfinished romance the very first words of the Fisher King as he welcomes Perceval back at last to the Grail Castle are "'Mangiez, biau sire'" ("Eat, good sir"), John L. Grigsby calls attention to the recurrent motif of "Perceval, the avid eater."[4] Heroic appetite is of course an attribute of other Arthurian heroes and a trait of classical heroes as well. Of particular interest here, however, is that the trait is not univocally invested in the texts in which Perceval will reappear, and the fact is not without significance. Chrétien's tent-maiden episode no doubt renders, with an authorial wink to the reader, a cultural clash of sorts, between the satisfaction of a heroic appetite and the "effort de discipline courtoise" necessary for proper chivalric conduct.[5] In the diverging reinvestments of this motif, however, in the works known as the *Perceval Continuations* on the one hand and the *Queste del saint Graal* on the other, we find evidence of a broader cultural conflict, if not of its resolution.

In the scene in the *Conte del Graal* that makes food and its consumption central to the romance as a whole, that in which Perceval is offered the hospitality of his uncle the Fisher King, the rhythm of the lavish banquet is one with that of the mysterious Grail procession, which passes and repasses as the courses are served:[6]

> Qu'a chascun mes que l'on servoit,
> Par devant lui trespasser voit

Le graal trestot descovert,
Ne ne set pas cui l'en en sert
Et si le volroit il savoir. (ll. 3299–303)

[As each course was served, he saw the bowl pass before them completely uncovered, but did not know who was served from it, and he
would have liked to know.]

Despite his desire to know for whom the service of the mysterious vessel
is destined, Perceval does not ask, intent on the food and drink set before
him: "S'enten[t] al boire et al mengier" ("He set about eating and drinking," l. 3311). His failure to put the question is not attributed by the narrator to this concentration on the satisfaction of his appetite; other causes—
his chivalric mentor's admonition against asking too many questions, the
"pechié sa mere"—impede his natural impulse to satisfy his curiosity. The
feast upon which he is intent, however, is a particularly lavish one, in sharp
contrast with that other, contemporaneous scene about which the youth
wonders but does not inquire, a scene in which, as he later learns, the figure of an aged king is served by the Grail with "une sole oiste," his unique
sustenance:

Mais ne quidiez pas que il ait
Lus ne lamproie ne salmon;
D'une sole oiste le sert on,
Que l'en en cel graal li porte;
Sa vie sostient et conforte,
Tant sainte chose est li graals. (ll. 6420–25)

[Do not imagine that it holds pike, lamprey, or salmon. With a
single host carried to him in the bowl, we know, he sustains and
nourishes his life. Such a holy object is the bowl.]

If the alimentary contrast in this scene is suggestive of a dichotomy between
carnality and spirituality, that suggestion will receive prominence only at that
much later date when Perceval's hermit uncle elucidates it:

Et il, qui est esperitax
Qu'a sa vie plus ne covient
Fors l'oiste qui el graal vient,
Douze ans i a esté issi . . . (ll. 6426–29)

[. . . so pure in spirit is he himself that his life requires no further nourishment than the host that comes in the bowl. For fifteen years now he has been served in this manner.]

A precise liturgical significance of the event is not advanced here, as it is in other texts, in particular in the *Joseph* of Robert de Boron and the *Didot Perceval*. While Perceval's visit to his hermit uncle in Chrétien's romance culminates in the Easter ritual of communion, the significance of the act is not disclosed in the unfinished text, in which it marks his final appearance. Yet it is apparent here too that because of the connection of food with the sacred ritual in the medieval centuries, the act of eating in itself "focused the Christian paradox of carnality in an acute way."[7]

That paradox is fundamental to the *Queste del saint Graal*. In the *Queste*, moreover, as William Boletta points out, food is among the motifs that convey the transformation of Perceval from earthly to celestial knight.[8] Perceval's singular lack of hunger or thirst during his encounter with a holy man reinforces this emphasis, which he himself explores. More dramatically, food and drink are leitmotifs in the temptation to which he is subjected in his island retreat: the devil who appears to him as a beautiful lady attempts to shake him from his professed indifference to food, and his eventual eating and drinking lead to an intoxication that almost results in his acquiescence in the seduction intended. The episode, which illustrates the appropriateness of Augustine's warnings in the *Confessions* that oppose the spiritual to the carnal appetite (Nichols, 847–51), concludes in a reference to spiritual nourishment. When the holy man returns, Perceval declares to him: "Se sai de voir, se vos demoriez toz dis o moi, je n'avroie ja ne fain ne soif . . . je diroie que vos estes li Pains vis qui descent des ciex, dont nus ne menjue dignement qui pardurablement ne vive" ("I know beyond question that if you stayed with me for ever I should know neither hunger nor thirst . . . I would say that you are the Living Bread that comes down from heaven, which is a pledge of everlasting life to all who partake worthily thereof").[9]

We recall that in the *Queste* the departure of the questing knights from Camelot had itself been associated with alimentary images. Their exodus followed the marvelous appearance of a cornucopian Grail that passed before the tables to feed the companions: ". . . et tout einsi come il trespassoit par devant les tables, estoient eles maintenant raemplies endroit chascun siege de tel viande come chascuns desirroit" ("It circled the hall along the great tables and each place was furnished in its wake with the food its occupants desired," *Queste*, 15). This scene of feasting, like analogues in the Continuations, may have distant origins in Celtic tales of superabundance afforded by magical vessels of plenty.[10] In this text, however, it yields to the metaphors of appetite familiar from a devotional literature in which the faithful are enjoined to "hunger and thirst after righteousness," which both afford a measure for the qualification of the more worthy knights and, more generally, mark the passage from carnal to spiritual understanding. When the knights vow that they will never abandon their quest until they are seated at the high table where "si douce viande" as that they have just enjoyed is presented every day, already Gauvain has voiced a caution: they have not seen clearly, not seen "la vraie semblance" (16). And for most of them it will remain hidden: at the conclusion of the quest, when the host itself is described as "la haute viande" (270), the elect communicants who are the beneficiaries of the vessel's munificence are few indeed.

The motif as introduced in the First Continuation of Chrétien's *Perceval* at first appears very similar: Gauvain on his visit to the Grail Castle marvels at the lavish service provided to the entire company by the vessel (II, 518–19).[11] He then learns, in a retelling of the story told also by Robert de Boron and others, of the miraculous nurture long ago afforded Joseph of Arimathea and his companions. Finding themselves besieged and in need of food, they prayed that God accord them the Grail and prepared themselves to dine:

> Et li Graaux par tot aloit
> Et pain et vin par tot portoit,
> Et autres mes a grant planté,
> Ce que chascun venoit a gre. (II, 528)

> [The Grail went about everywhere and everywhere it bore bread and wine and great plenty of other dishes, that which was to the liking of each.]

A similar story is recounted in Gerbert's Continuation, where the captors of these guardians of the Grail thought to destroy them by depriving them of food. For forty days the Grail afforded them not only sustenance but abundance, "de toz biens si grant planté / Qu'il estoient tout raempli, / Et tout lor voloir acompli" ("such plenty of all good things that they were well filled, and all their desire fulfilled," ll. 10,444–46).[12]

In the Continuations, in contrast, the progressive passage from a literal (carnal) to a metaphorical (spiritual) reading of the sustenance afforded by the Grail is absent. Highly suggestive is a near analogy between the island temptation scene in the *Queste* cited above and that in Manessier's Continuation.[13] Again Perceval is said to eat heartily on this occasion, but that detail is not now attributed to the lady's seductive urging or to diabolic temptation. It results rather from his natural appetite, and that appetite is evoked without reprobation. On the contrary: the text tells us "Et il an avoit grant mestier, / Car de trestout le jor antier / N'avoit ne mangié ne beü / Et avoit maint corroz eü" ("He had great need of it, for throughout the whole day he had had no food or drink, and he had suffered many hardships," V, 195).

Or consider the scene of Perceval's final visit to the Grail Castle, the scene that sutures together two Continuations, bringing the Second Continuation to a close and opening that of Manessier. The former rewrites Chrétien's scene, but with differences. No longer is Perceval "entent al boire et al mengier" ("intent upon eating and drinking"); on the contrary he is so rapt in his attention to the Grail procession that he finds himself without appetite. But the Fisher King urges him to eat, an urging continued with Manessier's opening "Mangiez, biau sire." While these words indeed call attention to the motif of Perceval the avid eater, they also valorize both his appetite and the feasting that follows, for its bounty is attributed, as in the First Continuation, to the presence of the Grail itself: "Lors furent de mes deletables / Repleni tuit conmune[me]nt" ("Then they were all filled with delectable dishes," V, 321). Now the lavish progression of courses is not only coordinated with the passage of the Grail procession, as in Chrétien's scene, but results from it. Manessier will heighten the emphasis in his rendering of the subsequent return of Perceval to Arthur's court, where *all* the knights are served during an entire month by the Grail (V, 338–39).[14]

It is evident that the *Queste* and the Continuations, while maintaining their intertextual resonance with Chrétien's romance, reflect the influence of different cultural matrices, adapting the same elements of the *Conte del Graal* as effective vehicles of divergent ideological objectives.[15] Perceval's characterization in the Continuations with regard to food and its consumption is of particular interest because it is here, and not in the prose tradition, that it is he who is destined to accomplish the quest. As Grigsby noted, all of Chrétien's continuators who focus on the adventures of Perceval retain the trait of voracious appetite attributed to the healthy if ill-mannered youth of Chrétien's Tent Maiden episode. Lavish meals are repeatedly set forth for Perceval, some described in considerable detail.[16] The contrast of this regimen with simpler fare is not lacking: hermits and other religious figures, often reminiscent of the hermit uncle in Chrétien's romance, partake of humble meals, and these are sometimes shared by the hero; the association of such fare with purity is such a commonplace that in the Second Continuation, when Perceval and his sister dine with a saintly hermit on bread and water, these are said without further comment to be brought each day by an angel and to constitute their host's only nourishment (IV, 191). Following this rigorously ascetic meal, however, the siblings proceed to another lodging where they gratefully enjoy a bountiful repast, one indication among many that these texts do not valorize ascetic fare for the chivalric hero:

> Bars et saumons, perches et lus
> Ont eü a molt grant planté,
> Car la nuit n'ont de char gouté.
> Quant ont mangié par grant d[el]it . . . (IV, 195)

[They had great plenty of bar and salmon, perch and pike, for that night they had had no meat; they ate with great pleasure.]

The motif of Perceval's appetite achieves its greatest prominence in the Continuation interpolated in two manuscripts between the Second Continuation and that by Manessier, a text whose author identifies himself only as Gerbert. Here Perceval is constantly hungry. Indeed he is preoccupied with food, and the text shares that preoccupation, supports it, we might say nourishes it: entire episodes have no apparent function other than to afford food to the hero. His own concern with food is repeatedly underlined: where is his next meal coming from? His need or desire for food and the satisfaction of his appetite are constants in the long series of adventures that separate his second from his third visit to the Grail Castle, adventures ranging from the banal brutality of chivalric contest to the theological subtlety of clerical exegesis, as conventional scenes of hospitality are supplemented by others less conventional.[17] The emphasis is particularly striking in its contrast to other elements of Gerbert's characterization of Perceval—his unconsummated marriage to Blancheflor, for example—that accentuate his capacity for sacrifice and the renunciation of worldly pleasures.[18] The interest of these scenes lies not in their depiction of the food afforded the hero, which, while sometimes extensively described, is also often passed over in silence.[19] The particular interest of Gerbert's poem in this regard lies rather in its reflection and commentary on the nurturing of the hero, and these bring cultural presuppositions that remain implicit in the other Continuations into unusual focus.

Let us compare a central scene in Gerbert with its model in the *Conte del Graal*. When Chrétien's Perceval, repentant for his forgetfulness of God, begs counsel of his hermit uncle in the final episode in which he figures in that text, the holy man not only advises him in the practices that will enable him to "monter en pris" and move toward his salvation, but prescribes that Perceval remain with him for two days "Et que en penitance praignes / Tel vïande com est la moie" ("and in penance eat such food as is mine," ll. 6478–79). This diet is described in some detail:

> Icele nuit a mengier ot
> Ice qu'al saint hermite plot;
> Mais il n'i ot se betes non,
> Cerfueil, laitues et cresson
> Et mill, et pain d'orge et d'avaine,
> Et iaue de clere fontaine. (ll. 6499–504)

[For food that night he had what pleased the hermit, nothing but beets and chervil, lettuce, cress and millet, bread made from barley and oats, and clear spring water.]

Certainly acceptable vegetarian nourishment, and Charles Foulon, suggesting that Perceval's progress is discernible in what he eats and drinks as well as in his deeds, finds in his acceptance of this ascetic fare a signal of his encounter with an ideal of purity and renunciation (173). In Gerbert's Continuation, however, when Perceval again dines with a hermit on similar, yet even simpler fare, he eats it with difficulty: "Fontaine, cresson et pain d'orge / Qui Percheval colpast la gorge, / N'en peüst une mie user. . . . " ("Spring water, cress and barley bread that cut his throat, he could not swallow a bit of it," ll. 7119–21).

Chrétien's Yvain, even in his "savage" state, had found a hermit's coarse bread "fort" and "aspre" (ll. 2845–49).[20] It is not uncommon, nor is it particularly surprising, for the refined appetite of romance heroes and heroines to revolt when confronted with the coarse food to which the poor are accustomed;[21] such an experience helps to convince the wayward youth in *Courtois d'Arras* to return to the paternal fold.[22] In very similar terms Perceval's fair companion rescued from a brutal suitor in Gerbert's Continuation complains openly of the rough bread again offered: "Hé! las! or me riffle la gorge, / Ainc mais ne mengai de son per . . . " ("Oh! Alas! it hurts my throat, I have never eaten anything like it!" ll. 7406–7). Soon thereafter Perceval again takes shelter with hermits, now with a group of thirteen whom he finds in the act of cutting their single loaf of hard bread into thirteen pieces. The scene has suggested to some readers an image of the Last Supper shared by Christ with his disciples,[23] but its emphasis remains gustatory:

Perceval is duly offered a share, but he eats little, the narrator tells us, because he finds nothing to his liking: "Menga petit, car il n'avoit / rien nule dont eüst covoit, / car del pain ne pooit gouster" ("He ate little, for there was nothing that he wanted, as he could not appreciate the bread," ll. 8463–65). This pattern of aversion emphasizes for the reader that Perceval's habitual nourishment is markedly different from that of priests, hermits, or members of religious communities.[24] If the progress of the elect knights in the *Queste* ultimately blurs the distinction, the Continuations confidently reaffirm its appropriateness.

What are the consequences for Chrétien's hungry young Perceval as transtextual hero? The pervasive medieval connection between food and spirituality, Cosman comments, was such that "eating habits determined a human being's association with a pantheon of virtues and vices" (see 116–23). Is Perceval's disdain of frugal nourishment then one sign among others, not only of his worldliness, but of a sense of superiority, of pride, of vainglory—of the sin that must be expiated and overcome before he can return successfully to the Grail Castle? Such a reading would be inevitable for the Perceval of the *Queste*, and it has been suggested with regard to Gerbert's text as well (Larmat, 551–57). Subsequent events, however, cast doubt on its pertinence here. As Perceval is in the company of a group of hermits, enter a *pucele* bearing a white shield with a red cross and an inscription indicating that the Grail quest will be accomplished only by the knight who can take possession of the shield. Perceval readily appropriates the shield, and the spiritual significance of his act is spelled out at his request by the leader of the colony of hermits. But not before we learn that the maiden has brought provisions as well: "Si fait destorser son cheval / De deus bareus toz plains de vin / Et de deus pastez de conin / Qu'ele ot torsez en une nape" ("She had taken down from her horse two casks brimful of wine, and two rabbit pies that she had wrapped up in a cloth," ll. 8520–23). When this welcome fare is placed before Perceval, he politely proposes to share it with his hermit hosts, only to be told that while they eat no meat and drink no wine, he should nonetheless enjoy his meal and satisfy his appetite: "'Or mengiez a liie chiere'" ("Now eat in good spirits," l. 8541).

Following closely upon this episode, Perceval and yet another maiden pass the night in the refuge of a group of nuns who are reduced by the malice of a cruel knight to eating "rachines et pomes salvages" ("roots and wild apples," l. 9084), and few of those. The nuns are saddened by their inability to produce "un bel souper" for their guests, but once again the hero is fortunate: when he departs the next day to challenge the nuns' oppressor, a great storm obliges a halt for a convoy laden with food, whose drivers are in a rebellious mood against that same tyrant-master. Enter Perceval, who arranges for a generous meal of "pain et vin et poisson et char" ("bread and wine and fish and meat," l. 9266).

These episodes in Gerbert's text are particularly suggestive for two reasons. First, in each of them the food afforded Perceval is explicitly contrasted with another sort of fare, that of a religious individual or community, and second, no negative value is attached, through this contrast, to the hero's gastronomic preference. This thematic configuration stands in sharp contrast to the lesson learned by Perceval in the dramatic island encounter in the *Queste*, a lesson that recurs in that text in more carnally explicit terms in the exegesis offered to another of the elect knights by a venerable *prestres*. Sin, he explains to Boors, is receiving and eating of the devil, confession is vomiting out that food, to receive that of Christ. God, he explains, had long provided "la chevalerie terriane" ("earthly chivalry") with "la viande del cors" ("the food of the body"); now he has afforded them "la viande del Saint Graal, qui est repessement a l'ame et sostenement dou cors." And now just as "la viande terriane s'est changiee a la celestiel, tout ausi covient il que cil qui jusqu'a cest terme ont esté terrien, ce est a dire que cil qui jusqu'a cel terme ont esté pecheor, soient changié de terrien en celestiel, et lessent lor pechié et lor ordure et viegnent a confession et a repentance . . ." ("the earthly food has been changed for that of heaven, even so must those whose affections have been earthbound until now [meaning that they were sinners], transmute them to the heavenly plane, and must leave their sins and wickedness and come to confession and repentence," *Queste*, 163). As Boors gladly receives the bread and water, the holy man admonishes him: "Sire, de tel viande doivent li chevalier celestiel pestre lor cors, non pas de grosses viandes qui l'ome meinent a luxure et a pechié mortel" ("Sir, it is with such food as this that the knights of heaven should sustain their bodies, not with strong meats that rouse a man to lust and mortal sin"). Such a regimen, he assures the knight, will be sufficient to sustain not only his soul but his body as well, and Boors accordingly vows that he will consume nothing but bread and water until the much-desired appearance of the Holy Grail (165–66).

Not so in the Continuations generally, where the chivalric and the ascetic spheres are related by reciprocity and engaged in covalorization. And not so, explicitly, in Gerbert's Continuation. On the contrary: while the prominence of *nourriture* figures here as in the *Queste* among the indices that distinguish the secular from the religious domain, here the contrast between the food suitable for knights and ladies and that of those engaged in the religious life is explained in practical rather than spiritual terms. Perceval offers this response to his complaining companion:

Dist Perchevaus: "Ma dolce dame,
Cist hermites doit meillor ame
Rendre a Dieu que nous ne devons,
Car par aventure vivons:
Vïandes volons a sozhait,
Car le cors ne chaut fors qu'il ait
Assez por sostenir sa vie . . ." (ll. 7411–17)

[Perceval said: "My sweet lady, this hermit must render to God a soul better than ours, for we live through adventure: we require meat to satisfy our needs, for the body is not warmed unless it has enough to sustain its life."]

It is clear that the alimentary code does not function here, as in the *Queste*, to subordinate the chivalric sphere to the ascetic.[25] While Perceval piously observes that their hermit host has greater merit than those who seek only to "aesier lor cors" ("content their bodies"), the practice of gastronomic asceticism is not appropriate for those who live "par aventure," a fact emphasized by the description of the thirteen hermits soon encountered as "molt enpalis" ("very pale," 8430). This acceptance of the appropriateness of the two contrastive regimens finds an interesting epic parallel in the *Moniage Guillaume II*, where, as Jean Larmat notes, "à chaque fonction sociale convient sa nourriture:" the chivalric hero-become-hermit, obliged to take up his arms again to come to the king's defense, temporarily renounces the eremitic regimen.[26] The diet suitable for knights such as Perceval is in fact prescribed in Gerbert's Continuation. In anticipation of a chivalric combat, he dines with prudent moderation:

Petit a mengié et beü
Perchevaus, car de trop mengier
Ne se doit nus preudom cargier
Por tant que se doie combatre,
Car trop en puet son pris abatre. (ll. 9274–78)

[Perceval ate and drank little, for no valiant man should load himself down when he is to fight, for he might greatly diminish his worth.]

"Don't fight on a full stomach"—but on the other hand, fighting on an empty stomach is not to be recommended either. When Perceval spends a night with a hospitable vavasor, the evening meal is only summarily noted, but as he is arming himself for departure the following morning his host insists that he once again accept an appropriate repast:

> "Biax sire, or ne vous soit anois,
> ainz que metés le hiaume el chief,
> que un petit ne vous soit grief,
> mengerez ainchois une soupe
> et un pasté, et plaine colpe
> d'un vin sain, fort, novel et cler;
> s'arez le cuer plus sain et cler
> et mix tenrez vostre jornee." (ll. 16,526–33)

[Good sir, may it not displease you, before you put on your helmet, for a little will not harm you, first eat some soup and a pie, and a full ration of a wine that is hearty, strong, new and clear; your heart will be the more hearty and sure for it, and you will fare better during your day.]

Sound and practical advice, no doubt, but unambiguously worldly: it is quite evident here, as elsewhere in the Continuations, that "terrestrial" chivalry will not be transformed into "celestial" chivalry through symbolic renunciation of earthly sustenance.

What, to put the question once again, are the consequences for Perceval as transtextual hero? Paradoxically it is not in the *Queste* but in the Continuations, where his healthy appetite is not disciplined and subdued through the awakening of an enlightened spiritual hunger, that it is he who accomplishes the Grail quest; it is here, moreover, that he fulfills what many readers have assumed to be the intended destiny of Chrétien's Perceval in the unfinished *Conte del Graal*, in assuming the rule of the lands of the Fisher King. But there is more. One hermit with whom he shares a simple meal in Gerbert's Continuation exclaims that "C'est damages que tiex vassax / est atornez a tel mestier; / mix devez amer le mostier" ("It is a pity for such a fine young man to be engaged in such an occupation; you should prefer the monastery," ll. 15,832–34), and these words, while they have no sequel in Gerbert's text, anticipate the end of Manessier's Continuation, where Perceval himself becomes a hermit: "de cest siecle se demist" ("He abandoned this secular world"). Not merely does he renounce a hearty chivalric diet in favor of meager monastic fare. Thereafter, as if to close the circle suggested by the alimentary allusions of the *Conte del Graal*, the paragon of chivalric appetite will enjoy a privileged state in which the alimentary code is once again accessory to a transcendant spirituality: for the subsequent ten years until his death, like Chrétien's old Grail King, he will be sustained exclusively by the Grail.

NOTES

1. For the succession of conventional elements that frequently combine in what Matilda Tomaryn Bruckner identifies as "Suppertime," a subunit of a narrative sequence defined as "Hospitality," see *Narrative Invention in Twelfth-Century French Romance: The Convention of Hospitality (1160–1200)* (Lexington, Kentucky: French Forum, 1980), pp. 60–94.

2. All references are to *Le Roman de Perceval ou le Conte du Graal*, ed. William Roach (Geneva: Droz, 1959); see ll. 1921–22, 2574–77. Translations are from David Staines, trans., *The Complete Romances of Chrétien de Troyes* (Bloomington: Indiana University Press, 1990).

3. See *Fabulous Feasts: Medieval Cookery and Ceremony* (New York: Braziller, 1976), pp. 35–37; here p. 35.

4. See "Heroes and Their Destinies in the Continuations of Chrétien's *Perceval*," in Norris J. Lacy, Douglas Kelly, and Keith Busby, eds., *The Legacy of Chrétien de Troyes*, 2 vols. (Amsterdam: Rodopi, 1987–88), II, 49.

5. Marie-Luce Chênerie, *Le Chevalier errant dans les romans en vers des XIIe et XIIIe siècles* (Geneva: Droz, 1986), pp. 533–34.

6. For the emphasis on this feast, which falls not only on rich food and drink but also on spices and other aids to their digestion, see Charles Foulon, "Les quatre repas de Perceval," *Mélanges de philologie et de littératures romanes offerts à Jeanne Wathelet-Willem* (Liège, *Marche Romane*, 1978), 169–73. Chênerie proposes instead that the latter function "en rapport avec l'impossible guérison du Roi Méhaigné" (p. 545).

7. Stephen G. Nichols, "Seeing Food: An Anthropology of Ekphrasis, and Still Life in Classical and Medieval Examples," *Modern Language Notes*, 106 (1991), 847.

8. William L. Boletta, "Earthly and Spiritual Sustenance in *La Queste del saint Graal*," *Romance Notes*, 10 (1968–69), 384: "its importance in the ubiquitous banquets of Arthurian literature labels food as one of the terrestrial attributes of life in terms of the *Queste*."

9. *La Queste del saint Graal*, ed. Albert Pauphilet (Paris: Champion, 1965), p. 115; all citations refer to this edition; translations are from *The Quest of the Holy Grail*, trans. P.M. Matarasso (London: Penguin, 1969). See Boletta, 388.

10. See Roger Sherman Loomis, "The Origin of the Grail Legends," in Roger Sherman Loomis, ed., *Arthurian Literature in the Middle Ages: A Collaborative History* (Oxford: Clarendon, 1959), pp. 274–94.

11. The Continuations, with the exception of Gerbert, are cited from *Continuations of the Old French Perceval* (Philadelphia: American Philosophical Society): The First Continuation: vol. I, ed. William Roach (1949, rpt. 1965), vol. II, ed. Roach and Robert H. Ivy, Jr. (1950, rpt. 1965), vol. III, Part I, ed. Roach (1952, rpt. 1970), Part II, ed. Roach and Lucien Foulet (1955, rpt. 1970); The Second Continuation, vol. IV, ed. Roach (1971); The Third Continuation, vol. V, ed. Roach (1983). Citations are by volume and page number; translations mine.

12. Gerbert de Montreuil, *La Continuation de Perceval* (Paris: Champion): vol. I, ll. 1–7020, ed. Mary Williams, 1922; vol. II, ll. 7021–14,078, ed. Mary Williams, 1925; vol. III, ll. 14,079–end, ed. Marguerite Oswald, 1975; all citations are from this CFMA edition; translations mine.

13. On the parallels and speculation concerning the relation between Manessier's text and the *Queste* see Jean Marx, "Étude sur les rapports de la troisième continuation du *Conte du Graal* de Chrétien de Troyes avec le cycle du *Lancelot en prose* en général et la *Queste del saint Graal* en particulier," *Romania*, 84 (1963), 451–77; Corin Corley, "Manessier's Continuation of *Perceval* and the Prose *Lancelot* Cycle," *Modern Language Review*, 81 (1986), 574–91. Gerbert's abridged version of this temptation scene (ll. 2516–89) omits the mention of food.

14. For this opposition between the exclusive nature of the Grail's service in the prose tradition and the "ouverture du Graal vers la communauté" in the Second Continuation-Manessier see Colette-Anne Van Coolput, "La Réaction de quelques romanciers postérieurs," in Lacy, Kelly, and Busby, eds., *The Legacy of Chrétien de Troyes*, II, 111–12.

15. Anita Guerreau-Jalabert suggests that the earthly abundance afforded by an earthly vessel associated with the Eucharist in the Continuations discloses as ideological objective "une affirmation vigoureuse et réfléchie de la légitimité des valeurs chevaleresques et des prétensions de l'aristocratie à occuper le premier rang dans une société où prédominent les modèles chrétiens et ecclésiastiques'"; see "Aliments symboliques et symbolique de la table dans les romans arthuriens (XIIe–XIIIe siècles)," *Annales* (Ec.- Soc - Civ.), 47 (1992), 584–87. She suggests that Robert de Boron may have had a similar project in attributing "la création de la principe même de la messe . . . à un chevalier laïc" ("the creation of the very principle of the mass . . . to a lay knight," p. 585).

16. See the Second Continuation (IV, 211–12, 239–40); in Manessier, Perceval's companions in the Quest are similarly entertained.

17. These proliferate in particular near the end of the text; see in vol. III his encounter with a pilgrim, ll. 15,269–95; his brief sojourn at "une forтереche," ll. 15,617–736; and at "un chastelet," ll. 16,050–124.

18. Luciana Cocito's study of Gerbert's poem insists on these "saintly" qualities attributed to Perceval, his chastity and austerity; see *Gerbert de Montreuil e il poema del Graal* (Genoa: Bozzi, 1964), esp. pp. 59–71.

19. For this "scrupule" of the poet who refrains from elaborating on details of menus and the coexisting tendency to elaborate at length see Grégoire Lozinski's introduction to *La Bataille de Caresme et de Charnage* (Paris: Champion, 1933), pp. 62–84.

20. On this episode see Jacques Le Goff and P. Vidal-Naquet, "Lévi-Strauss en Brocéliande: Esquisse pour une analyse d'un roman courtois," in Jacques Le Goff, *L'Imaginaire médiéval* (Paris: Gallimard, 1985), pp. 151–87.

21. See for example the lament of the famished fugitive countess in Jehan Maillart, *Le Roman du Comte d'Anjou*, ed. Mario Roques (Paris: Champion, 1974), ll. 1102–62.

22. "Ha! Dieus, com cis pains me dehaite! / Je cuic k'i soit d'avaine u d'orge: / ja m'aront trenchie la gorge / les pailles et li festu lonc. / Je morroie de fain selonc, / je ne m'i porroie assentir." *Courtois d'Arras*, ed. Edmond Faral (Paris: Champion, 1980), ll. 508–11.

23. See Jean Larmat, "Le Péché de Perceval dans la *Continuation* de Gerbert," *Mélanges d'histoire littéraire, de linguistique et de philologie romanes offerts à Charles Rostaing* (Liège: Association Intercommunale de Mécanographie, 1974), I, 547.

24. Guerreau-Jalabert notes the regular distribution of the elements of these meals in an oppositional organization of the alimentary field in terms of two symbolic triangles: the chivalric (bread, wine, meat) and the eremitic (bread, water, vegetables) (pp. 562, 566).

25. For the overall contrast between the verse and prose traditions deriving from Chrétien, see Chênerie. While the latter reveal the failures of earthly chivalry,

she observes, the former retain the worldly features of the model; in them even the Grail heroes "trouvent ici-bas un sens à leur chevalerie" ("here in this world find meaning in their chivalry," pp. 683–84).

26. See "Manger et boire dans le *Moniage Guillaume* et dans le *Moniage Rainouart*," in *Manger et boire au Moyen Age* (Actes du Colloque de Nice, 1982), I (Nice: Les Belles Lettres, 1983), p. 400.

DANTE AND THE ROMAN DE LANCELOT

Daniela Delcorno Branca

At the outset of his journey recounted in the *Commedia*, Dante encounters two lovers, Francesca da Rimini and her brother-in-law, Paolo Malatesta, in the circle of the lustful. The woman introduces herself to Dante, and when he asks her how she and her lover first became aware of their feelings for each other, "a che e come concedette Amore / che conosceste i dubbiosi disiri?" ("With what and in what way did Love allow you / to recognize your still uncertain longings?" *Inf.* V, 119–20),[1] she recalls that it was while they were reading *Roman de Lancelot*, in particular the scene in which the protagonist and Queen Guinevere first kiss.

> " . . . Noi leggiavamo un giorno per diletto
> di Lancialotto come amor lo strinse;
> soli eravamo e sanza alcun sospetto.
> Per più fiate li occhi ci sospinse
> quella lettura, e scolorocci il viso;
> ma solo un punto fu quel che ci vinse.
> Quando leggemmo il disiato riso
> esser basciato da cotanto amante,
> questi, che mai da me non fia diviso,
> la bocca mi basciò tutto tremante.
> Galeotto fu 'l libro e chi lo scrisse:
> quel giorno più non vi leggemmo avante."
> Mentre che l'uno spirto questo disse,
> l'altro piangea; sì che di pietade
> io venni men così com'io morisse.
> E caddi come corpo morto cade. (*Inf.* V, 127–38)

["... One day, to pass the time away, we read
of Lancelot—how love had overcome him.
We were alone, and we suspected nothing.
And time and time again that reading led
our eyes to meet, and made our faces pale,
and yet one point alone defeated us.
When we had read how the desired smile
was kissed by one who was so true a lover,
this one, who never shall be parted from me,
while all his body trembled, kissed my mouth.
A Gallehault indeed, that book and he
who wrote it, too; that day we read no more."
And while one spirit said these words to me,
the other wept, so that—because of pity—
I fainted, as if I had met my death.
And then I fell as a dead body falls.]

This episode from Dante is very famous and has justifiably been singled out as a harsh moral and literary condemnation of the ideology of courtly love underlying Dante's previous work as well: as a prominent scholar, Gianfranco Contini, puts it, it is "una tappa simpatetica e respinta," a stop that moves and repels the character-poet Dante at the beginning of his journey of purification through the kingdoms of the otherworld.[2] It is not surprising that in the dialogue with Francesca the pilgrim's agitation mounts and culminates in his fainting (*Inf.* V, 142).

Despite numerous critical studies on this episode, several problems remain open to debate.[3] For instance, why was this particular Arthurian romance chosen by Dante? Which version of *Lancelot* had Dante read and how was it used in the economy of his poem?

The two greatest Arthurian romances in French prose, *Lancelot* and *Tristan*, met with immediate and enduring success in Italy, as abundant literary, iconographic, and paleographic materials attest. Between the thirteenth and fourteenth centuries these texts were generally read in French, and the placing of them in the hands of two members of the Court of Malatesta of Rimini confirms that they enjoyed wide circulation at the time.[4] Of the two texts, however, *Tristan* was particularly popular among the educated classes, as is evidenced by the numerous translations into Italian (mainly Tuscan and Venetian) from the end of the thirteenth century and throughout the following one: *Tristano Riccardiano*, *Tristano Panciatichiano*, *Tavola Ritonda*, *Tristano Corsiniano*, *Tristano Veneto*, and cantari, to name only the most important ones.[5] On the contrary if we consider the *Lancelot-Graal* cycle (that impressive, composite system of five romances that trace the development of the Arthurian legend from beginning to end: *Estoire del saint Graal, Merlin, Lancelot, Queste, Mort Artu*), there exist only single and fragmentary translations of some sections, whereas at the moment we know of no Italian translation of *Lancelot*, the oldest and most important nucleus of this cycle.

At a time when the success of *Tristan* was firmly established among the bourgeoisie of the "comune" of Tuscany, Dante does not exploit this romance, despite a series of notable analogies of the Tristan story with the story of Paolo and Francesca, such as the unlawful love between kin and the violent death brought about by a betrayed husband. Boccaccio, in commenting on the Dantesque episode in his *Esposizioni* on Dante, does not fail to point out these analogies:[6] Dante, however, had presented the two lovers engrossed in reading another romance, *Lancelot*, on which they model their conduct. In Dante's work, Tristan's name is mentioned only once, though emblematically, at the end of the list of those who died for love, which precedes his encounter with Paolo and Francesca (*Inf.* V, 67). On the contrary, there are in Dante's work several precise references to the *Lancelot-Graal*, twice to *Lancelot* and twice to *Mort Artu*, the closing romance of the whole cycle. It may be useful to recall these passages, starting with the ones referring to *Mort Artu*. In the *Convivio* (IV, 28, 7–8)[7] Lancelot's retreat to a hermitage after King Arthur's death is presented as a positive example of a man in his prime who abandons mundane life to devote himself completely to God; in the *Commedia* (*Inf.* XXXII, 61–62) in the circle of the betrayers, the detail of the sunray piercing the slashed chest of the betrayer, Mordret, becomes a poignant periphrasis of him.[8] As for *Lancelot*, besides the episode of Paolo and Francesca in the fifth canto of the *Inferno* mentioned above, we have to recall an episode from *Paradiso* (XVI, 14–15): "Onde Beatrice ch'era un poco scevra, / ridendo, parve quella che tossio / al primo fallo scritto di Ginevra" ("At this word, Beatrice, somewhat apart / smiling, seemed like the woman who had coughed— / so goes the tale—at Guinevere's first fault"). Beatrice, who regards the vainglorious "you" used by the protagonist with disdain, is compared to the Lady of Malehaut, who discreetly signals her presence to the two lovers, Lancelot and Guinevere, by coughing. In actual fact, the two passages from Dante refer to the same episode in the romance of *Lancelot*, that is, the meeting between Lancelot and Guinevere. This encounter is arranged by Prince Galehaut, who meanwhile stands by and entertains the Lady of Malehaut and two other ladies. Only when the queen's close interrogation of Lancelot becomes too insistent and distressing does he come to his friend's aid, convincing Guinevere to seal their bond with a kiss now that Lancelot has at last revealed his love for her (PL 339–49; LM chap. LIIa, 99–117).[9] The Lady of Malehaut's cough is a detail that, after the first and more relevant quoting of *Lancelot* in the *Inferno*, cannot but confirm the extent to which this episode gripped Dante's imagination. It may be interesting to note, however, that the two quotations are placed in opposition to each other, where the same episode is recalled along the axis of the male characters first (Lancelot who kisses the queen, Galehaut who acts as an intermediary) and then along the axis of the female characters (the meeting is defined "il primo fallo scritto di Ginevra," the Lady of Malehaut is remembered for her cough).

Since the beginning of the twentieth century, eminent scholars and philologists (Torraca, Novati, Toynbee, Rajna, Crescini, Zingarelli, and Bertoni, to name but a few)[10] have repeatedly debated which version of *Lancelot* Dante had read and, above all, the discrepancy between what Francesca claims to have read "quando leggemmo il disiato riso esser basciato da cotanto amante" (*Inf.* V, 133–34) and what the romance says: "Et la reine voit que li chevaliers n'an ose plus faire, si lo prant ele par lo menton, si lo baise devant Galehot assez longuement, si que la dame de Malohaut sot que ele lo baisoit" ("And the queen sees that the knight does not dare to do more, and she takes him by the chin and kisses him in the presence of Galehot until the lady of Malohaut knew that she was kissing him," PL 348, 28–30).

Some scholars claim that Dante's recollection of the text was imperfect—this convenient hypothesis however is contradicted by the accuracy of detail in the passage referring to the Lady of Malahaut's cough, *Par.* XVI, 14–15—while others argue that Dante deliberately manipulated the text. The latter solution is simplistic, though possible; however, it too is impossible to demonstrate. In this connection the most constructive and insightful contribution was made by Rajna who pointed out in a manuscript of the Biblioteca Laurenziana in Florence (Pl. 89 inf., 61) the variant "si que la dame de Malahaut sot quil la besoit" ("she realized he was kissing her," Rajna, 231–32). This element seems even more important now that we know that the manuscript is probably Italian and that in ancient times it belonged to the Tuscans.[11] Of course it would be naive of us to believe that this was the text Dante actually read: however, the variant can be found in a number of manuscripts (e.g., PL, variants 348, 29–30; II, 236–37), several of which were written by Italian scribes (besides the Laurenziano, Paris, Bibliothèque Nationale fr. 773 and Modena, Archivio di Stato, Biblioteca, framm. b. 11, 5, p. 20).[12] Dante's recollection of the fictional episode is not vague; rather, his utilization of *Lancelot* was based on the text circulating in Italy at the time. As some scholars have already pointed out (e.g., Toynbee and Morf),[13] line 137 "Galeotto fu il libro e chi lo scrisse" also contains an allusion to another textual particularity in the identification between the character who promotes the encounter/revelation between Lancelot and the queen, and the book that carries out the same function between Paolo and Francesca: the title *Galehaut* is assigned in the manuscripts to one of the initial sections of the romance, in different ways but rather frequently.

Having established that Dante was a careful or even scrupulous reader of *Lancelot*, it may be useful to reexamine the relationship between the Arthurian episode from Dante beyond the context of the moral and literary criticism of courtly ideology and of the romance tradition of "fole amor," which has already been trenchantly analyzed by Contini and Avalle. The dialogue between Lancelot and Guinevere takes place when the protagonist, having been raised by the Lady of the Lake and having been knighted by King Arthur, has already accomplished marvelous deeds incognito (such as the liberation of the Dolorous Guard, victories in tournaments, reconciliation between Galehaut and Arthur), thus arousing such curiosity as to induce Arthur's knights to set out in search of him. Once the secret of his identity has been disclosed, Guinevere decides to speak to the "newly dubbed knight" and Galehaut, who knows of his friend's love for the queen, arranges for them to meet. While Galehaut discreetly stands aside in the company of the Lady of Malahaut, Guinevere begins to question Lancelot so as to make him reveal his identity, his deeds, and in whose service these deeds were carried out. The dialogue is pressing on the one hand and reticent on the other, consisting mainly of short sentences, as the following examples show (PL, 341, 14–30 and 342, 28–37: cf. LM, chap. LIIa 102 and 104):

> Et la reine met an paroles lo chevalier et si li dit:
> "Biaus dolz sire, por quoi vos celez vos vers moi? Certes il n'i
> a mies por quoi. Et neporqant, tant me poez vos bien dire se vos
> iestes li chevaliers qui l'asenblee vainquie avant ier."
> ["Dame, fait il, naie."]
> "Coment? fait ele; n'aviez vos mies unes armes noires?"
> ["Dame, fait il, oïl."]
> "Donc n'estiez vos ce qui porta les armes Galehot au darien jor?"
> "Dame, fait il, c'est veritez, oie."
> "Donc n'iestes vos cil qui [l'asenblee] vainqui lo secont jor?"
> "Dame, fait il, no suis, voir."
> Lors s'apercut la reine que il ne voloit mies conoistre que il [l']aüst

vaincue, si l'an prise mout. "Or me dites, fait ele, qui vos fist chevalier."

"Dame, fait il, vos."

[And the queen said to the knight, "Good sir, why do you conceal
yourself from me? Truly there is no reason; you can at least tell me
whether it was you who carried the day in the recent battle."

"My lady," he said, "it was not."

"What?" she exclaimed. "Were you not wearing black armor?"

"My lady," he said, "yes."

"Are you not he who wore Galehaut's armor, on the last day?"

"Yes, my lady," he said, "that is true. I am."

"And are you not he who was the victor of the second day?"

"My lady," he said, "indeed I'm not."

Then the queen saw that he did not wish to acknowledge that he
had carried the day, and she esteemed him highly for that. "Now
tell me," she asked, "who made you a knight?"

"You, my lady."][14]

[Guinevere] "Mais or me dites ou alastes vos d'iluec."

"A la Dolereuse Garde."

"Et qui la conquist?"

"Dame, g'i antrai."

"Et vos i vi ge onques?"

"Dame, oïl, plus d'une foiz."

"An quel leu?" fait ele.

"Dame, un jor que ge vos demandai se vos voudriez antrer, et vos
deïstes que oïl, si estoiez mout esbahie par sanblant. Et ce vos dis ge
par deus foiz."

["But tell me now, where did you go from there?"

"To Dolorous Guard," he said.

"And who conquered it?"

"My lady, I entered there."

"And did I ever see you there?"

"Yes, my lady, more than once."

"In what place?"

"My lady, one day I asked you whether you wished to enter there;
you said you did, but you seemed very frightened, and I asked you
this twice."]

All of the events of the first part of the romance (the dubbing, the conquest of the Dolorous Guard, the war between Arthur and Galehaut) are retraced in slow motion, as it were, until Guinevere asks the question, "d'ou vint cele amors que vos avez en moi mise?" ("What is the source of this love that you have given to me?"). (It is at this point that the Lady of Malahaut signals her presence by coughing.) This question forces the reluctant Lancelot to remember when it was that he began to love her: it was at the moment of the queen's farewell after he had been knighted.

> [Lancelot] "Et ge dis: 'A Deu, dame.' Et vos deistes: 'A Deu, biaus douz amis.' Ne onques puis do cuer ne me pot issir. Ce fu li moz qui prodome me fera se gel suis. Ne onques puis ne vign an si grant meschief que de cest mot ne me manbrast. Cist moz m'a conforté an toz mes anuiz cist moz m'a de toz mes maus garantiz et m'a gari de toz periz; cist moz m'a saolé an totes mes fains, cist moz m'a fait riche an totes mes granz povretez." (PL, 345, 36–346, 3; LM, LIIa, 109)

> ["Then I said, 'Farewell, my lady,' and you said, 'Farewell, dear friend.' Since then those words could never leave my heart; those were the words that made me a worthy knight, if I am one; never have I been so badly off that I did not remember those words. They comfort me in all my troubles; they have kept me from all evil and saved me from all dangers; those words satisfied me in all my hunger, and made me rich in my great poverty."]

The monosyllabic and trembling replies of the preceding dialogue give way to this open and rhetorically sustained praise of Guinevere's "farewell." (How can one avoid recalling the importance of Beatrice's "dolcissimo salutare" in Dante's *Vita Nuova*?) The queen persists in her skirmishing until Lancelot is on the verge of fainting; and it is then that Galehaut decides to intervene on his friend's behalf, urging the queen to grant him a kiss.

What Dante has Paolo and Francesca read is not merely a love story considered unlawful according to the Christian code of ethics: it is the episode in which the "dubbiosi disiri" are revealed, everything that had happened before appears in a new light. The page of *Lancelot* is a page of high tension and of remarkable narrative effectiveness, functional to the romance as a whole. The mimesis of the two brothers-in-law toward Lancelot and Guinevere is contained in that reading made of pauses, pallor, and the unspoken: "per più fiate gli occhi ci sospinse / quella lettura, e scolorocci il viso" ("And time and time again that reading led / our eyes to meet, and made our faces pale," *Inf.* V, 130–31). The episode from *Lancelot* is evoked here in its stylistic cipher as a tormented and reticent dialogue made of silence and truths painfully surfacing. Thus, the traditional physical effects of love found in the fifth canto of the *Inferno* appear less discounted. In the romance, trembling, bewilderment, pale faces, bowed heads, tears, silence, and faintness obsessively punctuate Lancelot's behavior before the queen:

Atant vienent devant la reine. Et li chevaliers *tranble si durement que a poines puet la reine saluer, et a tote la color perdue*, si que la reine s'an mervoille. Lors s'agenoillent anbedui. Et li seneschauz la salue, et li autres, mais c'est mout povrement, et *fiche ses iauz an terre comme hontous*. [Then they came before the queen. The knight was trembling so violently that he could scarcely greet her; his face had lost all color, which astonished the queen. Then both knelt down; the seneschal greeted her, as did the other, but this was very poorly done, and he kept his eyes cast down, like a man ashamed; PL, 340.]

Et cil respont qu'il ne set, *qui onques une foiz ne la regarda anmi lo vis*. Et la reine se mervoille mout que il puet avoir, et tant que ele sopece une partie de ce que il a. Et Galehoz, qui *hontos* lo voit et *esbahi*. . . . [He replied that he did not know, and not once did he look at her face. The queen was most curious to know what might be wrong with him, but at length she began to suspect part of what it was. Galehaut, seeing that the knight was embarrassed and ill at ease . . . ; PL, 341].

Et il l'esgarde, si la conut, si an ot *tel paor et tel angoise* an son cuer que il ne pot respondre a ce que la reine disoit; *si commance a sospirer mout durement, et les lermes li corrent tot contraval les joes* si espessement que li samiz dont il estoit vestuz an fu moilliez jusque sor les genoz. [He looked at her and recognized her, and was so overcome with fear and anguish in his heart that he could not respond to what the queen had said. He began to sigh deeply, and the tears flowed from his eyes so abundantly that the samite he was wearing was wet down to the knees; PL, 345].

Et cil *an fu si angoissos que par un po ne se pasma*, mais la paors des dames qu'il regardoit lo retint. Et la reine meïsmes lo dota, qui lo vit muer et changier; si lou prist par la chevecaille que il ne chaïst, si apelle Galehot. [He was so full of anguish at this that he was near to fainting. But his fear concerning the ladies held him back. And the queen herself feared for him, seeing him change so; she grasped him by the shoulder, to keep him from falling, and called to Galehaut; PL, 346].

Conversely in the fifth canto of the *Inferno*, the reaction of Dante the pilgrim to the listing of famous figures who died for love (ending with the names of Paris and Tristan) is described as follows: "pietà mi giunse e fui quasi smarrito" ("pity seized me, and I was like a man astray," l. 72); after Francesca has introduced herself and introduced the tragic story of her love for Paolo, Dante becomes pensive: "Quand'io intesi quell'anime offense / china 'l viso, e tanto il tenni basso / fin che 'l poeta mi disse 'che pense?'" ("When I had listened to those injured souls / I bent my head and held it low until / the poet [Virgil] asked of me: 'What are you thinking?'" ll. 109–11). "Dirò come colui che *piange e dice*" ("I shall tell my tale to you as one who weeps and speaks"), Francesca says, introducing her recollections of the reading of *Lancelot* (l. 126). She describes its effects as follows: "Per più fiate *gli occhi ci sospinse* quella lettura e *scolorocci il viso*," (ll. 130–31); "questi [Paolo] la bocca mi basciò *tutto tremante*" (l. 136). The woman's story is accompanied by the silent weeping of Paolo, her companion in sin and damnation, and on hearing her story, Dante faints: "Mentre che l'uno spirto questo disse / l'altro *piangea*; sì che *di pietade / io venni men così com'io morisse / e caddi come corpo morto cade*" (ll. 139–42). In the episode from Dante, the paleness, trembling, silence, bowed heads, tears, and faintness, redistributed among the protagonists and the pilgrim who is their double, sound like a further allusion to the Arthurian romance, transferring the reticent and bewildered rhythm of it to Dante's page, well beyond Francesca's words. In his reading of *Lancelot* Dante was undoubtedly attentive not only to the details of the story but also to the unique narrative and stylistic texture of the romance, to the ambages justifiably defined in his *De vulgari Eloquentia* as "pulcherrime." (I, X, 2).[15]

Within the framework of the Italian tradition, Dante's use of the figure of Prince Galehaut, the courteous friend who does his utmost to have Lancelot and Guinevere meet, is similarly unique. When speaking of Galehaut, Italian texts prior to the *Commedia* highlight the episode of the reconciliation, thanks to Lancelot, between the prince and Arthur. And so Rustichello da Pisa (1275) includes it among the exemplary Arthurian tales in his *Compilazione* placing it last, as a climax, because—he says—it is the "greignor aventure."[16] The versifier Lapuccio Belfradelli cites it as an example of unconditioned loyalty: Galehaut keeps his promise to Lancelot to submit to King Arthur despite having defeated him (Gardner, 33). In the

Conti di antichi cavalieri (*Conto di Brunoro e di Galeotto suo figlio*), a similar reading is found where Galehaut is presented as a just, wise, and valiant prince, a positive model for the rulers of the "comune" to follow.[17] None of these texts recalls Galehaut's role as intermediary between Lancelot and Guinevere; nor is it mentioned in the most important Arthurian text in Italian, the *Tavola Ritonda*.[18] Dante decidedly dismissed this exemplary reading of the character, endowed with political and civil implications, to identify Galehaut with courtly literature itself, the ambiguous intermediary of romantic encounters and of fictional projections onto life. Such a daring and original use could not escape Boccaccio, who promptly proposed this identification anew, without any moral undertones however, in the subtitle of his *Decameron*: "Comincia il libro chiamato Decameron cognominato Prencipe Galeotto" ("Here begins the book called Decameron also known as Prince Galeotto").[19]

Further evidence of Dante's apparent preference for the *Roman de Lancelot* over *Roman de Tristan*, may come, paradoxically enough, from an author who was as wary of Dante as he was of Breton romances. Petrarch's explicit stand against Arthurian romances is perhaps too exaggerated to be considered definitive and complete: "Ecco quei che le carte empion di sogni / Lancilotto, Tristano e gli altri erranti / ove convien che'l vulgo errante agogni. / Vedi Ginevra, Isolda e l'altre amanti / e la coppia d'Arimino che 'nseme / vanno facendo dolorosi pianti" (*Triumphus Cupidinis*, III, 79–84).[20] For Petrarch the limit of this love and of this kind of literature essentially lies in its being a "fabula vulgi" (a tale for the common people), but it is symptomatic that the two classic Arthurian couples are juxtaposed to the couple "d'Arimino" (Paolo and Francesca). In the Italian tradition the Dantesque episode is an inevitable filter for those who prefer to consider Breton romances more than mere evasion.

One of the few Arthurian elements clearly identified in Petrarch's work refers to *Roman de Lancelot*: it is the ecstasy of love, so great that the lover is estranged from the surrounding world to fall into a waterway then to be brusquely brought back to reality. In sonnet 67 of the *Canzoniere*, the poet, having landed in Italy, sees a laurel on the shore; engrossed in the thoughts of his beloved (the laurel is the symbol of Laura), he runs toward the plant but "in un rio che l'erba asconde / caddi non già come persona viva" ("I fell like a dead person into water hidden by the grass," 7–8); the symbolic vision of the "doe of purest white" (sonnet 190) is abruptly interrupted by something similar ("Et era il sol già volto al mezzo giorno; / gli occhi miei stanchi di mirar non sazi / quand'io caddi ne l'acqua et ella sparve"; "The sun by now had climbed the sky midway; / my eyes were tired but not full from looking / when I fell into water, and she vanished," ll. 12–14). Since the sixteenth century these verses have puzzled and amazed scholars of Petrarch, torn between realistic and daring interpretations and unlikely transpositions of meaning.[21] Once the connection with Lancelot's "ensongements" has been made, however, their symbolic meaning becomes transparent (Caldarini). In the romance by Chrétien de Troyes, *Le Chevalier de la charrete* (ll. 767–71), Lancelot appears completely absorbed by the thoughts of the queen and is thrown into a ford by a knight; in the prose romance, the water Alybon throws in his face distracts him from his thoughts of love (PL, 179); in another example from the same text, he is dragged into the river by his horse and risks drowning while he gazes upon Guinevere, who is at her window (PL, 265–67).

Therefore, even a declared nonreader of Arthurian literature like Petrarch draws from *Lancelot*, the most refinedly constructed of the Arthurian romances, as Dante had done before him, grasping one of the characteristic themes, the ecstasies of love, which are—as Elspeth Kennedy has shown[22]—deeply functional to the very structure of the story and perhaps more congruent to the *Canzoniere* language. *Lancelot* seems to act on Dante and Petrarch principally because of its stylistic quality. In *Tristan*, the original myth was somehow subdued to constitute a socially integrated exemplary ethics within the grasp of a bourgeoisie, like the Italian one, nostalgic for chivalry. This accounts for its growing success between the thirteenth and fifteenth centuries and for the numerous translations into Italian mentioned before. The tragic fate of Tristan and Isolde, united in death and in the grave, was read as yet another triumph of love over death, the love potion constituting an excellent excuse for absolving them from adultery. On the other hand *Lancelot* (and even more so *Lancelot-Graal*) in its design of vast scope and in its refined structural pattern, presented a tension between sacred love and profane love, between sin and conversion in some way similar to the secret mainspring of works like the *Commedia* or the *Canzoniere*. Of course, chivalric adventures, the dynamics between court and knight, the ritual of courtly love, may have seemed dated to Dante and Petrarch, but the character of Lancelot could nonetheless still be an example of those who live love to the fullest, but who also experience its limits and vanity.

The Lancelot of the *Convivio*, repentant and solitary, is the end point of the trembling and ecstatic Lancelot in the *Inferno*. According to Gardner (pp. 150–51), the harsh phrase with which Beatrice addresses Dante when she meets him at the top of the mountain in the *Purgatorio*, "Come degnasti di accedere al monte?" ("How hast thou deigned to climb the hill?" *Purg.* XXX, 74), might be a parallel to the stern reproach of the hermit in the

Queste del saint Graal, who demonstrates to Lancelot how his love for Guinevere is preventing him from gaining access to the Grail: "Lancelot plus durs que pierre, plus amer que fuz plus nus et plus despris que figuiers, coment fus tu si hardiz que tu ou leu ou li sainz Graalx reperast osas entrer?" ("Lancelot, harder than stone, more bitter than wood, more naked and exposed than a fig tree, how dare you enter a place where the Holy Grail has been?")[23] This sermon-like speech and the confession of the confused Lancelot, who is forced to reconsider his life in the light of the parameters of the Christian ethical code and to acknowledge the vanity of everything he had considered precious until then (*Queste*, 65–69), present a series of analogies with several passages of the third book of Petrarch's *Secretum*.[24] For example in one of these passages, St. Augustine forces Francesco to consider the splendid abyss into which Laura has plunged him (Petrarch, *Prose*, 144–47). Is it the suggestiveness of Petrarch's youthful readings? one could ask. For Petrarch, as for Dante, Lancelot may have represented above all the human paradigm of the journey from sin to conversion.

NOTES

1. Dante Alighieri, *La Commedià secondo l'antica vulgata*, ed. Giorgio Petrocchi (Milan: Mondadori, 1966). All quotations are from this edition. All translations of the *Commedia* are taken from Allen Mandelbaum, *The Divine Comedy* (Toronto: Bantam, 1986). Abbreviations are *Inf.*: Inferno; *Purg.*: Purgatorio; *Par.*: Paradiso.

2. Gianfranco Contini, "Dante come personaggio-poeta della *Commedia*," ID. *Varianti e altra linguistica* (Turin: Einaudi, 1970), pp. 335–61.

3. Daniela Delcorno Branca, "Romanzi arturiani," *Enciclopedia Dantesca* (Rome: Istituto dell'Enciclopedia Italiana, 1973), IV, 1028–30; D'Arco Silvio Avalle, *Modelli semiologici della Commedia di Dante* (Milan: Bompiani, 1975), pp. 97–121.

4. Edmund G. Gardner, *The Arthurian Legend in Italian Literature* (London: Dent/Dutton, 1930); Daniela Delcorno Branca, "Tavola Rotonda," *Dizionario critico della Letteratura Italiana*, ed. Vittore Branca (Turin: Utet, 1986), IV, 270–76 (see bibliography).

5. The best work about *Tristan* in Italy is now Marie-José Heijkant, *La tradizione del Tristan in prosa in Italia e proposte di studio sul Tristano Riccardiano* (Nijmegen: Sneldruk Enschede, 1989); see also her edition of the *Tristano Riccardiano* (Parma: Pratiche, 1991), with an important preface.

6. Giovanni Boccaccio, *Esposizioni sopra la Commedia*, ed. Giorgio Padoan, in Boccaccio, *Tutte le Opere*, ed. Vittore Branca (Milan: Mondadori, 1965), VI, 313–25.

7. See Dante Alighieri, *Opere minori*, vol. I, ed. Cesare Vasoli and Domenico De Robertis (Milan: Ricciardi, 1988).

8. "non quelli a cui fu rotto il petto e l'ombra / con esso un colpo per la man d'Artù" ("not him who, at one blow, had chest and shadow / shattered by Arthur's hand").

9. PL refers henceforth to *Lancelot do Lac*, ed. Elspeth Kennedy (Oxford: Clarendon, 1980); LM identifies *Lancelot: Roman en prose du XIII siècle*, ed. Alexandre Micha (Paris: Droz, 1978–83). References to the first are by pages and, where necessary, lines; to the latter by chapter and paragraphs.

10. Francesco Novati, "Vita e poesia di corte nel Dugento" in *Arte, Scienza e Fede ai tempi di Dante* (Milan, 1901), pp. 251–84; Francesco Torraca, *Studi Danteschi* (Naples: Perrella, 1912), pp. 399–442; Paget Toynbee, *Ricerche e Note Dantesche*

(Bologna: Zanichelli, 1904), pp. 1–23; Pio Rajna, "Dante e i romanzi della Tavola Rotonda," *Nuova Antologia*, 55 (1920), Vol. 290, pp. 223–47; Vincenzo Crescini, "Il bacio di Ginevra e il bacio di Paolo," *Studi Danteschi*, 1 (1920), 65–90; Nicola Zingarelli, "Le reminiscenze del Lancelot," *Studi Danteschi*, 3 (1921), 5–57; Giulio Bertoni, *Studi su vecchie e nuove poesie e prose d'amore e di romanzi* (Modena: Orlandini, 1921), pp. 175–81. A survey of these different hypotheses is in Anna Hatcher and Mark Musa, "The Kiss: *Inferno V* and the Old French Prose *Lancelot*," *Comparative Literature*, 20 (1968), 97–109, which provides a too subtle and scarcely convincing interpretation.

11. *Mostra dei codici romanzi delle Biblioteche fiorentine* (Florence: Sansoni, 1957), pp. 59–61.

12. Daniela Delcorno Branca, "Tradizione italiana dei testi arturiani: Note sul *Lancelot*," *Medioevo Romanzo*, 17 (1992), 215–50, esp. 220–23.

13. Heinrich Morf, "Galeotto fu il libro e chi lo scrisse," *Sitzungberichte der K. preussische Akademie der Wissenschaften*, 43 (1916).

14. All translations of *Lancelot-Grail* material, except from the *Queste*, are by Carleton W. Carroll; they are taken (with adaptation as necessary) from Norris J. Lacy, ed., *Lancelot-Grail: The Old French Arthurian Vulgate and Post-Vulgate Cycles in English*, 5 vols. (New York: Garland, 1993–96), Vol. II (1993).

15. Dante Alighieri, *De vulgari eloquentia*, ed. Pier Vincenzo Mengaldo, in *Opere Minori* (Milan: Ricciardi, 1979), II, 82–84.

16. *Il romanzo arturiano di Rustichello da Pisa*, ed. Fabrizio Cigni (Pisa: Pacini, 1994), p. 277 (chapter 162, 13).

17. *Conti di antichi cavalieri*, ed. Alberto Del Monte (Milan: Cisalpino-Goliardica, 1972), pp. 149–54; Gardner, 85–87.

18. *La Tavola Ritonda o l'Istoria di Tristano*, ed. Filippo Luigi Polidori (Bologna: Romagnoli, 1864–66), I, 13–31.

19. Daniela Delcorno Branca, *Boccaccio e le storie di re Artù* (Bologna: il Mulino, 1991), pp. 15–19.

20. "Here are those who fill the pages with dreams: Lancelot, Tristan, and the other knights-errant for which it is meet that the erring vulgar herd yearn. See Guinevere, Iseult, and the other lovers and the couple of Rimini, who go together uttering mournful laments." For the original see Francesco Petrarca, *Triumphi*, ed. Marco Ariani (Milan: Mursia, 1988), pp. 146–47 (with a good commentary).

21. Francesco Petrarca, *Le Rime*, ed. Giosue Carducci and Severino Ferrari, presentazione di Gianfranco Contini (Florence: Sansoni, 1984), pp. 97, 274–75; Ernesta Caldarini, "Da Lancillotto a Petrarca," *Lettere Italiane*, 27 (1975), 373–80. The English translation is taken from Petrarch, *Selections from the Canzoniere*, trans. Mark Musa (Oxford: Oxford University Press, 1985), p. 57.

22. Elspeth Kennedy, "Royal Broodings and Lovers' Trances in the First Part of the *Prose Lancelot*," *Mélanges Jeanne Wathelet-Willem*, *Marche Romane* (1978), pp. 301–14.

23. *La Queste del saint Graal*, ed. Albert Pauphilet (Paris: Champion, 1949), p. 61. Translation by E. Jane Burns in Lacy, ed., *Lancelot-Grail*, IV (1995), 21 [see above, n. 14].

24. Francesco Petrarca, *Prose*, ed. Guido Martellotti, Pier Giorgio Ricci, Enrico Carrara, and Enrico Bianchi (Milan: Ricciardi, 1965), pp. 130–215.

IRONIC JUXTAPOSITION AS INTERTEXTUALITY IN THE PROSE *TRISTAN*[1]

Janina P. Traxler

Intertextuality in Arthurian literature is especially evident in the Prose *Tristan*, which mixes well-known twelfth-century verse material and thirteenth-century prose material with content *created* for the Prose *Tristan*. Moreover, the Tristan story illustrates multigenerational or reciprocal intertextuality: the original Tristan story probably influenced the Lancelot story of the late twelfth century; then the Arthurian Vulgate heavily inspired the Prose *Tristan*; and finally, by retelling the Grail quest, the *Tristan* author[2] changed that Vulgate story, especially Galaad's character. Intertextuality thus constitutes a complex, fascinating aspect of the Prose *Tristan*'s construction. By calling our attention to the treatment of the Grail quest in the *Tristan*, Colette-Anne Van Coolput has signaled an especially intriguing example of intertextuality.[3] The interpolation of the Vulgate *Queste del saint Graal*, at times almost verbatim, makes intertextuality one of the most easily recognizable techniques in this part of the Prose *Tristan*. Van Coolput likewise demonstrates the extent to which this mixture of Vulgate and non-Vulgate content changes the presentation of Galaad. At issue is therefore not *whether* intertextuality occurs in the *Tristan*, but rather what forms it takes and how it causes the secularization of Galaad that Van Coolput discussed.

Though at times the Prose *Tristan* seems merely derivative, its version of the Grail quest especially merits attention for the irony the author achieved by setting old against new. Much of the Vulgate material that appears in the Prose *Tristan* (either as overt borrowing or as inspiration for *Tristan* content) serves to elaborate Tristan's story and to establish him in the Arthurian world as the equal of Lancelot. But the presence of the Grail quest in the Prose *Tristan* functions differently. The *Tristan* borrows wholesale much of the Vulgate *Queste* and alternates this content with the freshly created adventures of Tristan and others. To the audience of the *Tristan*, which presumably knew both the verse Tristan romances and the Vulgate Cycle well, this intertextuality probably seemed perfectly normal. Furthermore, as D.H. Green emphasized, interlace (changes from the narrative present in one branch of the story line to a simultaneous point in another branch) generally carries with it the potential for irony, which the medieval audience would also have enjoyed.[4] By extension, intertextuality in which the simultaneous points are actually narrative strands from different works has perhaps even greater potential for irony. And in combining the mundane, chivalric adventures of Tristan and the mystical, allegorical Grail quest, the *Tristan* author fully exploits this potential. By juxtaposing these aesthetically different strata, the *Tristan* author creates irony, since the audience has insight that the characters can never have, and this irony accounts to a large degree for the changes that Van Coolput signaled in Galaad's role.

The following discussion will analyze two passages in which the Prose *Tristan* uses different forms of intertextuality to create the irony that recasts Galaad's presentation. The first segment retells the events of the Grail Pentecost and illustrates what I will call "vertical intertextuality," the layering together of narratives that derive from different sources but recount simultaneous events; the second includes a sequence of Galaad's adventures between his appearances at the Chateau des Pucelles and at the mystical Eucharist at Corbenic. Though this arrangement juxtaposes events from different sources, the narrative continues to move forward logically; it thus illustrates what I will call "horizontal intertextuality."

Vertical Intertextuality and the Grail Pentecost

The *Tristan*'s version of the Grail Pentecost retains all the important material of the Vulgate version but adds whole narrative units that introduce Tristan and show Arthur preoccupied with Tristan's arrival as well as that of the Grail and the Grail knight. By introducing Tristan into the Grail quest, the *Tristan* author renders this event much more complex: the narrative combines two different types of material (Vulgate and non-Vulgate) to recount the essentially concurrent thoughts and actions of three characters (Tristan, Arthur, and Galaad). And this vertical intertextuality significantly changes Galaad's portrayal.

The list below shows the key moments of Pentecost eve and Pentecost day (from the Vulgate *Queste*) as well as the additions made by the *Tristan* author (indented) in order to illustrate this layering of the new material with the Vulgate material:

Pentecost Eve
Arthur calls his court to assemble for Pentecost.
    Tristan decides to appear; he begins his voyage.
    Arthur admires his court; Bandemagu notes Tristan's absence.
Lancelot leaves court to dub Galaad.

Pentecost Day
Lancelot returns to court.
Stone bearing the marvelous sword appears.
    Messengers arrive with gloomy predictions for Arthur and court.
Galaad arrives at court and occupies the Perilous Seat.
    Arthur again examines his court; Bandemagu notes Tristan's absence.
Galaad draws the sword from the stone.
Arthur celebrates the marvels with a tourney, which Galaad dominates.
    Tristan arrives.
Grail appears at court.
Gauvain and others pledge themselves to the quest.
Arthur and his court lament the imminent departure of the knights.

Tristan's appearance at the Grail Pentecost is the logical consequence of adding him to the Round Table, but the *Tristan* author uses this change to divert attention from Galaad.[5] The *Tristan* account of Pentecost eve takes place in three parts, one each for Tristan, Arthur, and Galaad. Since the first segment focuses on Tristan and the second on Arthur, Galaad's preparations come last and appear only after Arthur has had time to consider the worldly splendor of his assembly.

In addition to displacing Galaad, the sections that focus on Tristan and Arthur also change the tone of the Pentecostal gathering. The presentation of Tristan concentrates on his decision to go to Camalot (four days before the gathering) and reveals his cavalier attitude toward the event. A latterday Erec, Tristan seriously considers not going to court because he does not want to be separated from Iseut: "Dame, fait-il, puis que vous n'i volés venir, or saciés que je n'irai mie" ("Lady, he says, since you do not want to go, I will not go," VI, 86:29–30).[6] Iseut insists that he go, however, fearing that otherwise the court will consider him a negligent knight and will criticize them both.[7] Tristan's ambivalence toward the Grail Pentecost (indeed his ignorance of the event's significance) contrasts with Galaad's holiness and purposefulness, retained from the Vulgate *Queste.*

As Tristan travels toward Camalot, the perspective shifts to Arthur, who presides over the court assembled for Pentecost eve and whose attitude is just as mundane as Tristan's. Arthur looks at the gathering, judges it the most impressive he has seen, and asks the venerable King Bandemagu what he thinks. Bandemagu's answer injects a note of caution into the atmosphere, however: the Maimed King had foretold that this event would mark the high point in earthly joy and chivalric honor as well as the beginning of Arthur's decline and the last joyful gathering of the court.[8] Arthur discounts the Maimed King's remarks, observing that they are not always true, in contrast to Merlin's, which are reliable: "Vous savés bien que des paroles que on vait disant en tele maniere, vous em poés plus trouver des fauses que des vraies, et ce me vait auques reconfortant. Entre nous ne devons pas croire les paroles du Roi Mehaingnié, ensi conme nous devons croire les paroles de Merlin, car li uns fu adés trouves voir disant en toutes paroles et li autres ne sot qu'il dist" ("You know quite well that such words are more often false than true, and that comforts me. We must not believe the Maimed King's words in the same way we must believe Merlin's, because the latter has proven to be ever truthful and the other does not know what he says," VI, 91:9–16). Bandemagu adds that the honor and joy of the Round Table cannot be complete until Tristan arrives: "se tout li compaignon de la Table Reonde ne sont a ceste court, l'ounour de la Table Reonde ne sera pas enterinement acomplie, puis que mesire Tristrans i falt . . . Diex voeille qu'il i viengne, fait li rois Bandemagu, si sera nostre joie entiere" ("if all the fellows of the Round Table are not at this court, the honor of the Round Table cannot be complete, since Tristan is missing . . . should God grant that he appear, our joy will be complete, said King Bandemagu," VI, 91:46–53). Arthur's lack of confidence in the Maimed King's prediction is ironic, given that the prediction is appropriate, and Bandemagu's remark shows how important Tristan is to this gathering, though Tristan's story actually has nothing to do with the quest story.

The third segment begins when the messenger from Pellés arrives to escort Lancelot to meet his son Galaad and preside at his dubbing. In contrast to the two other segments, this material (taken from the Vulgate *Queste*) presents its central figure, Galaad, exactly as in the Vulgate *Queste*. Galaad is a silent, obedient player in a predetermined script. We have no indication of his thoughts or character, except as the Vulgate text presents them.

These essentially concurrent layers of the Pentecost eve present basic information about Tristan, Arthur, and Galaad and prepare us for the events of Pentecost day. Tristan reacts to Arthur's summons by weighing the advantage of going to the king against the pleasure of staying with Iseut. Tristan finally maximizes both options: he deliberately stays as long as possible with Iseut and then rides at breakneck speed, almost killing his horse, to arrive at the last minute and astound Arthur's court: "Je demouerrai dusques a cel tans que je vous di, et si i venrai bien a tans a celui jour, car je n'irai mie armés, fors d'espee et de glaive, ne ne menrai avoeuc moi esquier nul. Je voeul venir entr'aus si soudainnement qu'il en soient merveillant tout et esbahi. Je voeul venir a cele feste conme cevaliers aventureus" ("I will remain here as long as I promised, and then I will arrive in good time on that day because I will ride unarmed except for sword and glaive, with no squire. I wish to appear among them so suddenly that they will all be astonished and wonderstruck. I want to arrive at this feast like a knight errant," VI, 86:70-76).[9] The contrast between the attitudes of Tristan and Galaad could hardly be more dramatic: the former wants to stay with his mistress, then arrive with dash as a "chevalier aventureux" (though he leaves his heavy armor behind in order to travel faster); Galaad spends Pentecost eve in silent prayer to prepare for initiation into knighthood and for the miracles set to occur the next day.

Arthur likewise considers how Pentecost eve affects his image. When he assembled the court, he knew the special purpose of the event: the knight destined to end the adventures of the Grail and to occupy the Perilous Seat was due to arrive.[10] Yet Arthur is clearly more interested in the splendor of the men and women assembled there and in Tristan's absence. As in the passage that presents Tristan's attitude, the scene depicting Arthur's admiration for his court clashes with the tone and events of the Vulgate *Queste*. Concurrent with Galaad's preparations for his vigil, we have Arthur's pride at the splendor of his court and his silly rejection of the Maimed King's words. The concerns of Tristan and Arthur provide an ironic foreground for the silent submissiveness of Galaad, whose character and destiny justify the assembly that preoccupies Tristan and Arthur. This imbalance in focus is easy to explain: the Vulgate *Queste* provides the material about Galaad; the rest is new.

Though Galaad's arrival actually motivates the events of Pentecost day, the *Tristan* filters the day through the mind of Arthur, who anticipates his arrival and that of Tristan. Before Galaad arrives, Arthur's attention turns to a strange mixture of marvelous events: the appearance of the floating stone bearing the inscribed sword, a Vulgate episode to which the Prose *Tristan* adds a series of three unambiguous messages that predict Arthur's decline. First, a weeping messenger predicts that all the knights rejoicing there will soon join him in sorrow. Second, he gives Arthur a letter that includes a restatement of Bandemagu's message to the king: "Et ta court qui tant est joieuse / Orendroit sera dolereuse, / Sour toutes autres et ploreuse: / Fortune t'iert contralieuse"[11] ("And your court that is so joyous/ Henceforth will be sorrowful, / And tear-

ful above all others: / Fortune will be against you," VI, 97). The messenger
states his point in yet a third form by singing for Arthur the lai "Riens n'est
qui ne viengne a sa fin" ("All things must end," VI, 99; Fotitch and Steiner,
97–101). This love complaint emphasizes that Love is responsible for the
messenger's death and that his life, like all things, must now end. This messenger then commits suicide. Though upset by the messages, Arthur feigns
disinterest. Not wanting the knight's death to delay his feast, he has the body
removed and immediately orders the tables to be set for the meal.[12]

The narrative returns to the Vulgate story line to recount Galaad's
arrival, yet the *Tristan* additions show that Arthur's attention strays from
this narrative thread and returns to the concern for his court. Galaad's arrival is one of the most important moments in the history of Arthur's court.
As the Chevalier Désiré, he closes the genealogical link between the prehistory and Arthur's reign; as the occupant of the Perilous Seat, he completes
the Round Table. Yet his arrival, so clothed in miracle, does not seem to
satisfy Arthur, who in the next scene (not from the Vulgate) again asks
Bandemagu to take attendance. Bandemagu reports that only Tristan is missing; otherwise the Round Table would be complete for the first time ever:
"mesire Tristans i faut. Se nous celui eüssom, la Table Reonde eüst toute sa
raison, ce que ele n'ot onques puis qu'ele fu premierement establie" ("Tristan
is missing. If we had him, the Round Table would be complete, which has
not happened since it was established," VI, 102:15–17). As Iseut feared,
Arthur (indeed the whole court) is angry with Iseut for keeping Tristan away:
"Ha, dame Yseut . . . vostre biauté fait cestui jor grant honte en mon ostel,
car ele nous taut la compaingnie du plus esprouvé cevalier du monde! Plus
fust mes osteus honerés seulement de celui avoir qu'il n'est de tels .C. cevaliers
i a il çaiens" ("Ah, Lady Iseut, . . . your beauty causes great shame this day
in my court, because it deprives us of the most worthy knight in the world!
My court was more honored by his presence alone than by 100 knights such
as are here," VI, 102:23–28). The emphasis on Galaad, essential to the
Vulgate *Queste*, is still present, but Arthur's interest in Tristan and his anger at Iseut greatly reduce the emotional impact of Galaad's imminent appearance.

By layering together borrowed material that focuses on the arrival of
Galaad and the Grail and new material that reveals the worldly preoccupations of Tristan and Arthur, the *Tristan* author ironically retells a familiar
story. In the Vulgate version of the Grail Pentecost, everything centers on
Galaad's arrival and the revelation of his identity. The date is right (454 years
after Christ's Passion), the sword appears that only the best knight can draw,
the Chevalier Désiré is brought to court, and the Perilous Seat suddenly bears

its master's name. Galaad steps into the messianic role defined for him, and everyone prepares for the conclusion of the Grail adventures.[13] But in the *Tristan*, competition with Tristan's arrival attenuates the marvel of Galaad's advent. As the Vulgate predictions are recalled and fulfilled, as each stage of Galaad's long-awaited arrival is completed, the audience is constantly aware of the other anticipated arrival. As Galaad approaches, so does Tristan. In the Vulgate *Queste*, once Galaad takes his place, the celebration begins. In the *Tristan*, when he is seated, Arthur's thoughts return to taking attendance, and Arthur's anger at Tristan's lateness clouds his joy at Galaad's coming. The point is clear: Galaad is not enough. He is the Chevalier Désiré, the person designated to occupy the last unclaimed seat at the Round Table, but Tristan is the knight whose presence completes the assembly.

Furthermore, the predictions of Arthur's decline (underscored in the *Tristan* additions) dampen the atmosphere of mystery and the anticipation of a marvelous new age that the Vulgate *Queste* creates. Instead of replacing the worldly preoccupations of Arthur's court, the quest story receives only divided attention, the rest going to Tristan. The Vulgate emphasizes that the Pentecost is the beginning of a grand new adventure, a sacred sequel to the worldly exploits of the Lancelot story. The *Tristan* additions, however, emphasize the impending loss: since the fictional world of Logres is held together by its identity as a place of marvelous adventures, the end of the marvels can only mean the decline of Arthur as leader of the Christian world and Logres as land of refinement and adventure. This message is so important to the Prose *Tristan* that it occurs in several versions (King Bandemagu's comments and those of the weeping messenger). As Arthur contemplates this juncture in his career, he clings to the possibility that the predictions of the Maimed King, the person so important to the Grail's history, might be less trustworthy than those of Merlin, the person so important to Arthur's history. Through vertical intertextuality the mystical and the mundane receive similar treatment in the *Tristan* account of the Grail Pentecost. Any audience familiar with the Vulgate emphasis on Galaad's marvelous arrival and on his holiness would notice the irony that the *Tristan* author creates by treating Galaad and Tristan with comparable importance. Galaad cannot be the sole focus of attention when Arthur and the court continue to regret Tristan's absence; this reduction of Galaad's stature is clearly subversive.

CORBENIC AND CAMALOT

The previous discussion revealed that by superimposing concurrent events from two very different inspirations, the *Tristan* author creates a narrative that reduces Galaad's importance by introducing Tristan to the Grail Pentecost. A second type of intertextuality—the sequencing of Vulgate and non-Vulgate episodes—causes an equally drastic change in Galaad's role: in the non-Vulgate episodes, Galaad increasingly resembles Tristan. This horizontal intertextuality characterizes the rest of the romance, but I wish to focus on two segments: Galaad's non-Vulgate adventures at Corbenic and Camalot.

In retelling the Grail quest, the *Tristan* author adds several non-Vulgate episodes for Galaad as well as for Tristan. In the Vulgate, Galaad appears in a relatively small number of important scenes, each of which adds essential elements to his portrayal:

Camalot	the quest begins
the white abbey	Galaad acquires his shield
Chateau des Pucelles	Galaad's messianic role is underscored
the Nef de la Joie	Galaad receives his sword and hears the story of his destiny
the leper's castle	God punishes the disobedient
Corbenic	Galaad participates in the Grail Eucharist and rejoins the parts of the Espee Brisiee
Sarras	Galaad receives his ultimate reward

The *Tristan* retains all of these episodes in their original order but adds adventures for Galaad that break the sequence at several points. Two insertions are especially interesting because they radically change the path Galaad follows in the Vulgate *Queste* and thereby alter his portrayal. Where the Vulgate itinerary takes Galaad in a "straight" line from Camalot to Corbenic to Sarras, the *Tristan* itinerary takes Galaad through two major detours: a non-Vulgate episode at Corbenic and a non-Vulgate visit to Camalot before he goes on to the Vulgate episode at Corbenic and to Sarras.

The new stop at Corbenic (V2542:457ff.) occurs between two well-known adventures in the Vulgate quest: the episodes at Chateau des Pucelles (*Queste*, 46–51) and on the Nef de la Joie (*Queste*, 119–228). Both passages emphasize Galaad's special identity, his Christ-like purity and sacred lineage. As the explanation of the Chateau des Pucelles episode makes clear (in both *Tristan* and *Queste*), this event is an allegory for Christ's harrowing of hell (*Queste*, 55) and thus restates Galaad's messianic function. The long passage concerning the Nef de la Joie presents Galaad's special nature in several ways: he demonstrates his faith and purity by boarding the boat (*Queste*, 201) and claiming the Sword of the Strange Belt; by retelling the history of the boat, the bed, and the sword, Perceval's sister reminds us of his link to the house of Solomon and his role as the person for whom all of these miracles were prepared.[14]

Between these two passages of the Vulgate *Queste* the *Tristan* inserts a new episode that takes Galaad to Corbenic. Galaad leaves Tristan at the conclusion of one adventure and wanders several days until he arrives at Corbenic for the annual celebration of King Pellés's coronation. Here an enchanter entertains the assembly with magic, but his powers mysteriously disappear when Galaad arrives. Intrigued, Pellés forces the magician to talk, and we learn that the enchanter acquired his powers from the devil and that Galaad's presence neutralizes them. Though Pellés doubts the story, it is powerfully demonstrated when the enchantor's body bursts into flames and is carried away by "li ministre d'infer" ("the servants of hell," V2542:457v°b).[15]

This new episode differs greatly in tone and content from the Vulgate material that frames it. First, the episode places elements appropriate to the quest story in a mundane context. Pellés celebrates the anniversary of his coronation on a beautiful April day; he has set his banquet in the meadow near the castle, and he has a magician entertain the guests. Elsewhere in the romance Arthur and Marc hold similar celebrations. But Pellés is not a king just like Arthur and Marc: he is the Grail guardian, and Corbenic is the Grail castle. Instead of being nourished in the Grail castle by the Holy Spirit, which the Grail symbolizes, Pellés is outside the castle—thus separated from the Grail—celebrating his worldly power by hosting a banquet. His guests are transfixed not by the Grail's mysterious passage but by the magic of the devil-inhabited sorcerer. The Grail is in the palace—it, at least, is still in its normal place, but it plays no role in the episode:

le rois Pellés seoit adont au disner et si cevalier entour lui et mengoient envoisiement, non mie de la grasse au Saint Vaissel, car li Sains Vaissiaus n'estoit nule fois aportés a Corbenic par main d'ome mortel. Tout cil sans faille qui demouroient el Palais Aventureus estoient repeu pour qu'il l'aourassent en sa venue. Li Rois Pellés qui celebroit sa feste u il avoit esté courounés seoit as tables ensi conme je vous di entre ses barons et avoit devant lui un encanteour qui faisoit par force d'yngremance si grans merveilles que tout chil qui ce veoient s'en esbahissoient. (V2542:457b-c)

[King Pelleas was sitting at dinner with his knights about him, and they were eating with great pleasure, not by the grace of the Holy Vessel, because it had never been born at Corbenic by mortal hand.

Those who remained in the Adventurous Palace stayed there so they could worship it when it appeared. King Pelleas, who was celebrating the anniversary of his coronation, was seated at the table as I said, among his barons, and had before him a sorcerer who was performing such marvels through his magic that all who watched were astonished.]

By placing the Grail guardian in a courtly festival, removed from the Grail's influence, the *Tristan* author parodies elements central to the Grail legend and causes the audience to suspect that Pellés is just another *seigneur*.

In addition to sabotaging Pellés's role, this new episode at Corbenic (non-Vulgate) undermines Galaad's identity, so carefully developed in the Vulgate episodes juxtaposed with it. For example Galaad comes to Corbenic quite by accident: "il cevaucha une eure avant et autre ariere, si conme fortune le menoit querant les aventures du roiaume de Logres" ("he rode here and there, where fortune led him seeking the adventures of Logres," V2542:457b). In the Vulgate *Queste*, "fortune" has nothing to do with his itinerary: he arrives where he is awaited, at the appropriate moment, to conclude the Grail adventures. In the *Tristan*, by contrast, Galaad wanders like any other knight errant seeking the adventures of Logres.

Furthermore, in the *Tristan*, Galaad must repeatedly prove his identity, the identity that the Vulgate so frequently acknowledges and celebrates. When he arrives Pellés's court treats him with the hospitality appropriate to any knight errant: he is welcomed, disarmed, and invited to join the feast. Pellés does not recognize him, nor does anyone else; for them he is no more than an Arthurian knight: "il connurent tantost que c'estoit des cevaliers aventureus de la maison le roi Artu" ("they knew right away that he was a knight errant of Arthur's court," V2542:457v°c). Perhaps Pellés does not know Galaad because they have not met for a long time and the latter is blackened from his armor (V2542:457c). The sorcerer, however, immediately realizes that this *sains hom*, this "holy man," has caused his powers to disappear. The sorcerer proves this to the doubtful Pellés by having Galaad leave to see if the magical powers return in his absence (V2542:457v°b). They do not; instead devils carry off the burning magician, who desperately crys "Ha, Galaad, saintismes cevaliers, se tu prioies pour moi encore quideroie je trover merci" ("Ah Galahad, most holy knight, if you prayed for me I think I could still find mercy," V2542:457v°b). In the Vulgate *Queste*, Pellés recognizes Galaad and his two companions the instant he sees them.[16] Not in the *Tristan*; the sorcerer's miraculous loss of power, his destruction, his appeal to Galaad by name—none of this convinces Pellés. Only Galaad's response,

"Je sui Galaad vostres nies" ("I am Galahad your nephew," V2542:457v°c), satisfies the king.

While Pellés's doubts might make him more realistic, they make him less suitable to the fantastic context of the Grail quest. Throughout the Vulgate material, total strangers recognize Galaad immediately as the Chevalier Désiré. They greet his arrival, knowing that his role is to conclude adventures: to heal Mordrain (*Queste*, 263), to free the soul of Symeon (*Queste*, 264), and to chase off the devil inhabiting a tomb (*Queste*, 36). In the *Tristan* additions, however, Galaad's uncle does not know him. His cousin even calls him "li plus orgueilleus cevaliers que je onques veïsse" ("the proudest knight I have ever seen," V2542:458b) and forces him to joust to reveal his name. The *Tristan*'s audience is already familiar with this pattern: it typifies the lives of knights errant like Tristan, but it is foreign to the Vulgate life of Galaad. This example of horizontal intertextuality trivializes Galaad's unique identity: by juxtaposing Vulgate passages with the new passage in which the Grail guardian does not recognize the Grail hero, the *Tristan* author demotes Galaad through irony.

Galaad's other major detour takes him to Camalot (V2542:469ff.) between the adventures at the leper's castle and the Grail Eucharist at Corbenic, and this detour, like the first, presents Galaad in a context foreign to the hero of the segments juxtaposed with it. In this episode, fortune does not govern Galaad's route. While Perceval's sister lies bleeding to death after curing the leperous woman, she gives Galaad two instructions: as in the Vulgate she tells the Grail triad (Galaad, Perceval, Boors) to separate until God reunites them to go to Corbenic (the Vulgate visit), but the *Tristan* author adds her request that Galaad go to Camalot to rescue Arthur from the attack by the Cornish and Saxon armies (V2542:469a). Thus in the Vulgate material, Perceval's sister "sends" Galaad into the *Tristan* material.

When Galaad leaves Perceval and Boors and goes to Camalot, he leaves a context that affirms his identity and enters one that not only rejects that identity but that also confuses him with other major knights. For the liberation of Camalot, he joins Palamède, Esclabor (Palamède's father), and Artus le Petit (Arthur's son).[17] This group is rather odd, certainly a drastic change from Galaad's company at the leper's castle (the Grail triad and Perceval's sister). Galaad knows none of his new companions, and only Palamède recognizes him. Since Artus is avidly interested in proving himself and acquiring prestige,[18] Palamède suggests that Artus challenge Galaad. Galaad defeats Artus easily and rides on to a bridge guarded by Guinglain, who quickly unhorses him because he is preoccupied with the mission to Camalot and pays no heed to Guinglain's challenge. Here the *Tristan* author effaces Galaad's uniqueness by using the motif of the great knight who appears incompetent. This scenario resembles the situation of Lancelot in the *Charrete* and other passages in the *Tristan*. In all cases a talented knight appears cowardly or unskilled because he is distracted.[19] When Galaad and the others stop for the night at the same castle, this motif reappears. Convinced of Galaad's mediocrity, Artus is surprised by his beauty when he removes his armor that night: "Certes ce seroit grans damages se nostres sires n'avoit fait cest cevalier plus preudomme que autre, car çou est sans faille li plus biaus cevaliers du monde et li mieus tailliés" ("Surely it would be a great shame if our Lord had not made this knight more worthy than others, because he is without doubt the most comely and well-formed knight in the world," V2542:472a).[20] This motif typically creates irony: the knight knows he does not merit the mockery he endures, and the audience shares this knowledge. But in this case the motif creates two-fold irony: Galaad's failure to defeat Guinglain suggests to Artus that the former does not deserve his physical beauty, though both Galaad and the audience know better; but by the same token, Galaad cannot see that his very appearance in this episode makes him *like* other major knights rather than special, as he is in the Vulgate passages that frame this one.

By rescuing Camalot from the Saxon and Cornish attack, Galaad also appears with Marc, a surprising combination for the Tristan legend as well as for the Grail story. After Galaad routs Marc's army, he finds lodging for the night and is soon joined by Farien le Noir, a knight of Loth's family, and King Marc himself. Galaad continues to guard his incognito, admitting only that he was at the battle of Camalot and that he is "cevaliers errans" ("knight errant," V2542:475a) and "compains de la Table Reonde" ("companion of the Round Table," V2542:475b). Marc, however, recognizes his shield (V2542:475c) and decides to kill him by giving him a deadly poison originally intended for Tristan. Fortunately divine intervention saves Galaad. After he rebukes Marc for his evil plot, the party disperses for other adventures, and the story of the siege of Camalot closes.

This episode contains virtually no mention of the quest, much less any progress toward its accomplishment. Galaad is essentially in a foreign narrative space—a world where he is only a knight errant and thus not the Chevalier Désiré. In contrast to the adventures of the Vulgate *Queste*, which present Galaad as a Messiah figure and repeatedly emphasize his identity and distinguishing traits, the *Tristan* adventures obscure or frankly reject his customary nature. Guinglain easily unhorses him, convincing Artus that Galaad is just an average knight errant. Of the group that Galaad joins to rescue Camalot, Palamède is the only non-Christian, the only one who has not joined the Round Table and who has not pledged himself to the quest (cf. V2542:360b). Why then is Palamède the only one to recognize Galaad by his customary white shield with the red cross?[21] In a strange parallel, Marc too recognizes the knight who shares his lodging, whereas Farien, the knight of the Round Table, does not. As in the case of Galaad's arrival at Corbenic, the person who most quickly recognizes him is the person most removed from Arthur's court. Galaad can hardly retain his special status when those who should recognize him do not.

By taking Galaad back to Camalot, the *Tristan* author transforms his holy itinerary into a heroic one and thus strips him of his unique identity. The knight errant's adventures follow a predictable trajectory: the knight leaves court to seek an adventure, often one that begins with some marvelous event at court; in the dark dangerous world he proves his valor by overcoming trials; and finally he returns to court to tell his story and claim the praise due him. This path is circular, beginning and ending at court, and it differs greatly from Galaad's traditional route. In the Vulgate, the path to Corbenic (and ultimately to Sarras) does not lead back to Camalot—the secular, courtly world from which Galaad departs and continually distances himself both physically and psychologically. As the ultimate *chevalier celestiel*, Galaad takes a direct path upward from the mundane court of Arthur toward the City of God. He never even looks back. He does not return to court to tell his adventures—that is left to Boors, his more worldly messenger. In the *Tristan*, by contrast, Galaad returns to Camalot. Thus when he tells Farien that he is a knight errant of Arthur's court, he does not simply protect his anonymity and exercise modesty—he announces to us that he is "un bon chevalier," rather than "le Bon Chevalier." By framing this episode between two from the Vulgate (the adventure at the leper's castle and the Grail Eucharist at Corbenic), the *Tristan* author portrays Galaad much differently than the Vulgate does.

As the discussion of vertical intertextuality revealed, the *Tristan* account of the Grail Pentecost reduces Galaad's importance by promoting Tristan to nearly equal status; similarly, in these examples of horizontal intertextuality, when Galaad leaves the Grail quest to return to the purely mundane world of Arthurian chivalry, his special nature is leveled to that of a fine Arthurian hero, certainly not the Grail hero.[22] The Camalot to which he returns is a shadow of the place at which the quest began. He finds a court emptied of the very people who justify its existence, his king wounded in body and ego, and the psychological heart of the Arthurian world surrounded by Marc and the Saxons, the symbols of all that Arthur's dream world rejects. When Galaad routs the enemies of the throne, he assumes the role of "best knight," the role that Tristan repeatedly plays for Marc and that Lancelot later plays for Arthur. Preoccupied with Camalot, Galaad forgets Corbenic. Afterward, he shares lodging with Marc, who gives him the poison originally intended for Tristan. Since Tristan is conspicuously absent from the whole episode, Galaad serves as stand-in for Tristan, even to the extent of becoming Marc's target. When Galaad rejoins Perceval and Boors soon afterwards to go to Corbenic for the Grail Eucharist, the reader must make an effort to remember that Galaad is again the Grail knight.

The thirteenth-century taste for cyclic romances perhaps made Tristan's entry into the Arthurian saga inevitable. And given the enormous popularity of the Prose *Tristan*, the medieval audience apparently enjoyed seeing the two great lover-knights, Tristan and Lancelot, together in one narrative. But I believe that the inclusion of Galaad and the Grail quest in the Prose *Tristan* reflects more than a simple interest in uniting all Arthurian heroes. Throughout the *Tristan*'s account of the Grail quest, the audience's appreciation of the narrative is colored by a detail from the prehistory that prepares the eventual joining of Galaad's story to Tristan's: the two knights are distant cousins.[23] Though these two branches of the Arthurian holy family diverge immediately, the *Tristan* seems designed to draw together the paragons of each family. Once Tristan joins the Round Table and becomes Lancelot's equal, the next logical step is for Tristan to enter the Grail story. He consequently joins Galaad and all the other Arthurian knights at the Grail Pentecost and quite naturally participates in the Grail quest, the ultimate Arthurian adventure. From this point in the romance, Tristan and Galaad remain together (not physically, but in the same psychological and narrative space), even dying at about the same time. Taking central characters and important events, as well as more general narrative patterns and atmosphere, the *Tristan* author created a work that at times seems more patchwork than whole cloth. But the use of the highly derivative passages reveals an intriguing technique at work—the setting together of blocks of material for ironic purposes. Tristan and Galaad actually enter each other's world, but with quite different results. Tristan drops out of the Grail quest as soon as he can and continues the type of life he previously led, utterly unchanged by his contact with Galaad and the Grail. The more lasting effect of the intertextuality we see in the Quest section of the *Tristan* is the "descent" of Galaad into Tristan's world. Introduced into a fictional world assembled to glorify Tristan, Galaad appears as a fairly impressive knight errant, perhaps as good as Tristan. But he is no longer "le Bon Chevalier," Tristan's moral superior.

NOTES

1. Intertextuality in the Prose *Tristan* is a topic far too complex to be exhausted in one brief discussion. The ideas of this paper (based on a conference presentation) are really only a portion of a much more extensive investigation, which began with a conference paper in 1988 and which will continue to occupy me for quite some time. For the earlier discussion, see Janina P. Traxler, "The Use and Abuse of the Grail Quest: Ironic Juxtaposition in the *Tristan en prose*," *Tristania*, 15 (1994), 23–32.

2. In this discussion I will refer to the *author* of the *Tristan*. The question of authorship is far from settled, but whether the *Tristan* is the product of one author or several, one compiler or several, or some other process is not pertinent to the present discussion.

3. Colette-Anne Van Coolput, *Aventures quérant et le sens du monde: Aspects de la réception productive des premiers romance du Graal cycliques dans le Tristan en prose* (Leuven: Leuven University Press, 1986).

4. Dennis Howard Green, *Irony in the Medieval Romance* (New York: Cambridge University Press, 1979) esp. pp. 132ff.

5. Similarly, Tristan's admission to the Round Table ultimately threatens Lancelot's status. By the end of the tourney at Louveserp, Tristan appears to be the equal of Lancelot, if not his superior. Eventually there are rumors that Tristan has surpassed Lancelot in prowess.

6. The citations of the Prose *Tristan* come from manuscript Vienna 2542 (=V2542), being edited under the supervision of Philippe Ménard. See *Le Roman de Tristan en prose*, vol. VI, ed. Emmanuèle Baumgartner and Michèle Szkilnik (Geneva: Droz, 1993) (VI). Since some of the passages discussed here are not yet available in edition, I have used my own transcriptions from the manuscript. Citations of the Vulgate *Queste* refer to the standard edition; see Albert Pauphilet, ed., *La Queste del Saint Graal* (Paris: Champion, 1975).

7. "il vous tenroient a mauvais et diroient tout plainnement que vous seriés recreans de bien faire pour les amours madame Yseut. Il diroient que vous ariés laissie toute cevalerie pour moi, vous en seriés ahontés et je en seroie deshouneree de l'autre part et il diroient tout mal de moi et diroient honte de vous" ("they would look down on you and say openly that you would be unworthy if you were governed by your love for Lady Iseut. They would say that you had given up knighthood for me, and you would be shamed just as I would be dishonored; they would consider me bad and you shameful," VI, 86:44–49).

8. "Ce est la cours aventureuse dont li Rois Mehaigniés nous dist ja, voiant moi, bien a .LX. ans u plus, que vous tenriés une cort qui seroit toute joie mortel et toute hounour de cevalerie et toute biauté de dames. Mais de cele joie naistroit un doeil si grant et une dolour si merveilleuse que tous li mondes en tourneroit em pleurs; et de cele feste avenroit la premiere acoison de ton deciement et de ta povreté, car, aprés icele court, iroient toutes cours apetichant plus et plus et plus, et d'illuec conmenceroit tes pooirs a apeticier et a descroistre, et aprés venroient dolours et plours et courous. E pour ceste [354a] court te clameras encore rois caitis et povres et eslongiés de toutes joies. Cele court metroit ton cuer en toutes dolours et en toutes angousses et cele seroit la deerrainne joie del roiaume de Logres" ("This is the adventurous court that forty or more years ago I heard the Maimed King describe, saying that you would hold a court which would feature all mortal joy and all chivalric honor and all womanly beauty, but from this joy would be born weeping so great and sorrow so marvelous that the whole world would be in tears; and from this feast would come the first moment of your decline and poverty, because after this court all courts would ever decline, and from that one forth your power would begin to decline, and afterwards sorrow and tears and anger would appear. And because of this court you will proclaim yourself a poor wretched king, whom joy has abandoned. This court will bring your heart total sorrow and anguish, and it will be Logres' final joy," VI, 90: 41–55).

9. The effect Tristan plans is important because it is expressed in the same words Merlin uses to describe how the Grail will appear: "Nostre sires l'envoiera entr'aux si soudainement que ce sera merveille" ("Our Lord shall send him among them so suddenly as to confound them all," *Queste*, 77; translation from *The Quest of the Holy Grail*, trans. P.M. Matarasso [Harmondsworth: Penguin, 1969], p. 99).

10. "Rois Artus, je te di pour voir et en confession que, au jour de la Pentecouste qui vient, sera cevaliers nouviaus cil qui les aventures du roiaume de Logres metra a fin, et venra celui jor acomplir sans faille le Siege Perilleus. Or gardes que tu semoignes tous tes homes, que il soient a Camaalot la veille de la Pentecouste pour veoir les mervelles qui le jour avenront" ("King Arthur, I tell you in truth that on the day of the upcoming Pentecost the one who will end the adventures of Logres will be dubbed knight and will accomplish the miracle of the Perilous Seat. Summon all your men to be at Camalot on Pentecost Eve to see marvels which will happen Pentecost day," VI, 84:36–42). The text in the Prose *Tristan* essentially repeats the Vulgate text. See *Lancelot*, ed. Alexandre Micha (Geneva: Droz, 1980), VI: CVIII, 16.

11. "A toi rois Artus"—text with music (VI, 97). For the edited version, see Tatiana Fotitch and Ruth Steiner, *Les Lais du Roman de Tristan en prose d'après le manuscrit de Vienne 2542* (Munich: Munchener Romantistiche Arbeiten 38, 1974), p. 95.

12. "Li rois, qui trop durement est esbahis de ceste aventure pour çou qu'il ne veut mie que la feste de son ostel remaingne pour l'acoison de la mort de chel cevalier, le fist il prendre et porter en la maistre eglyse de Camaaloth. Et pour donner essample a ciaus de son ostel de faire joie, conmence li rois a faire feste devant tous et dist c'on mete les tables huimais" ("The king, completely astonished at this adventure, does not want his court feast to be delayed by the death of this knight, so he orders the body to be taken to the church of Camalot. And to provide an example of joy for his household, the king begins to rejoice before them all and orders the tables to be set immediately," VI, 100:31–38).

13. The *Queste* details the importance of Galaad's place at the Round Table— the seat reserved for him has remained empty because only he could occupy it without being harmed (*Queste*, 9); it awaited its "mestre," due to arrive on this particular date ".cccc. anz et .liiii. sont acompli emprés la Passion Jhesucrist; et au jor de la Pentecouste doit cist sieges trover son mestre" ("four hundred and fifty years have passed since the passion of our Lord Jesus Christ: and on the day of Pentecost this seat shall find its master," *Queste*, 4; trans. Matarasso, p. 33), and the place even announces its master's name: "Ci est li sieges Galaad" ("This seat is Galahad's," *Queste*, 8; trans. Matarasso, p. 37).

14. For this analysis, I have looked especially at how the *Tristan* takes the material about Galaad from the *Queste* and adds Galaad material to that. Between Galaad's appearance at the Château des Pucelles and the Nef de la Joie, a good deal of other material also occurs in the Vulgate story, but it concerns other characters, especially Lancelot, Perceval, and Boors. During this intervening material—over *half* of the Grail quest—we hear nothing of Galaad. In the *Tristan*, however, Galaad reappears several times in new material: he has several adventures with Tristan, he is imprisoned by Brehus, and he fights Palamède, who thinks Galaad is Keux. All of these additional episodes weaken Galaad's identity as Grail quester because the quest is hardly mentioned and the adventures are purely chivalric.

15. "li encanterres conmencha a ardoir et enflamber ausi com feroit une buce bien sece et en fu portés en l'air si haut qu'il sambloit qu'il deust as nues toucier. Et la u li ministre d'infer l'emportoient en tel maniere, il crioit quanqu'il pooit si que cil du paveillon l'entendirent bien: Ha, Galaad, saintismes cevaliers, se tu prioies pour moi encore quideroie je trover merci" ("the sorcerer burst into flame and burned like a dry log, and was borne into the air so high that he seemed to touch the clouds. And as the servants of hell bore him off thus, he cried as loud as he could so those of the pavilion heard him well: 'Ah, Galahad, most holy knight, if you prayed for me I think I could still find mercy,'" V2542:457v°b).

16. "Et quant il furent laienz et le rois les conut . . . Et li rois Pellés plore sus Galaad son neveu, et ausi font li autre qui ja l'avoient veu petit enfant" ("When the king recognized his visitors . . . And King Pelleas wept over his grandson [sic] Galahad, as did all the others who had known him as a child," *Queste*, 266; trans. Matarasso, p. 272).

17. Here we have another example of how the Prose *Tristan* develops the "second generation" of Arthurian knights, the sons of the greats. Galaad is Lancelot's son; Palamède is Esclabor's son; they soon meet Guinglain, Gauvain's son. Elsewhere Galaad meets Claudas, son of Claudin, and Samaliel, son of Frolle. And in the episode at Corbenic just discussed, Galaad is challenged by his own cousin Elyezer, the son of Pellés.

18. "jentiex hom et jovenenciaus, je sui nouviaus cevaliers si ai mestier de los et de pris. Se je le puis conquerre, ne cevaliers ne doit refuser jouste d'autrui ne reposer" ("worthy young man, I am a new knight who seeks praise and fame. If I am to win such, I must neither refuse to joust with another knight nor rest," V2542:471c).

19. Similar events happen elsewhere in this romance. For example, when Brunor rides with the Demoisele Medisant toward the Destroit de Soreloys, he draws her scorn for refusing to fight a bridge guard. The lady does not know that Brunor promised the knight's father not to fight. Similarly Chrétien's Perceval appears unfit because he is lost in concentration on the drops of blood on the snow.

20. This incident is remarkably similar to another, which occurs immediately after this episode when Galaad is in the company of Agravain and several other Arthurian knights. Again Galaad refuses to fight a challenger, this time because he recognizes the other knight as a fellow of the Round Table. Despite the fact that Galaad is wearing his normal shield, which clearly announces his identity, the others seem not to know who he is. And already convinced of his cowardice, they do not believe him when he gives his name. Unable to accept the obvious—that the knight is Galaad—the others go to great lengths to explain how their confusion might have happened (476ff.). For a discussion of this passage, see my article "Use and Abuse" (see note 1).

21. "si tost conme il vit l'escu blanc a la crois vermeille il connut que c'estoit Galaad li tres boins cevaliers" ("as soon as he saw the white shield with the red cross he knew that it was Galahad the good knight," V2542:471a).

22. When Galahad and company actually leave Corbenic for Sarras, the *Tristan* inserts another little detail that again reminds us of the odd mix: they decide to return to Camalot to say goodbye to Arthur before going on to Sarras (V2542:496). Oddly enough, just as Galaad's added adventures constitute a pale version of the knight errant's trajectory, so also Tristan's death scene is an odd parody of Galaad's original path. For Tristan also does not ultimately go back to Arthur's court to tell his story. Instead he goes back to his place of origin, to Marc's court, where he dies in contemplation of the only being he has ever really worshipped: Iseut. As in the case of Galaad, Arthur's court hears of the final adventure through the report of the messenger, here Sagremors.

23. Throughout the quest section of the Prose *Tristan*, it is essential to recall that Tristan and Galaad are related. In the *Tristan* as in its source material (the Vulgate Cycle), Joseph of Arimathia takes charge of the fate of his twelve nephews, the sons of Bron. The youngest decides to remain virginal, which qualifies him to become the guardian of the Grail. The Prose *Tristan* author's innovation is to imagine what happens to another of Joseph's nephews, the next to youngest: Sador. Sador is the ancestor of both Marc and Tristan, a detail that establishes genealogical (though not moral) parity between the families of Tristan and Galaad. For the passage in the *Tristan*, see *Le Roman de Tristan en prose*, ed. Renée L. Curtis (Munich: Max Hueber, 1963), I, 40. For the other passage, see Robert de Boron, *Roman de l'Estoire dou Graal*, ed. William A. Nitze (Paris: Champion, 1971), p. 100.

LANCELOT IN THE MIDDLE DUTCH PLAY
LANSELOET VAN DENEMERKEN

AN EXAMPLE OF GENERIC INTERTEXTUALITY*

Bart Besamusca

In the Middle Dutch play to be discussed here, the main character, Lanseloet, is in love with Sanderijn, one of his mother's servants. Because his mother disapproves of a possible relationship between her son, the prince of Denmark, and a woman of inferior birth, she tries to undermine his love. When she offers Lanseloet the possibility of having sex with Sanderijn on the condition that he will thereupon renounce her by offending her in word and gesture, he readily accepts her proposal. After the rape Sanderijn leaves court and meets a knight whom she marries. After having looked for her for one year, one of Lanseloet's servants finds her and asks her to return to his lord. She refuses. Once Lanseloet realizes he has lost Sanderijn once and for all, he dies of grief.

This is a summary of *Lanseloet van Denemerken*, one of the four so-called *abele spelen*, usually translated as "noble or beautiful plays."[1] These are secular plays that, together with some two hundred other texts, have come down to us in the famous early-fifteenth-century Hulthem Manuscript, which probably served as an exemplar in a Brabantine scriptorium.[2] The *abele spelen*, all supposedly written around the middle of the fourteenth century, are of great importance, as they are among the oldest pieces of serious secular drama in Europe.

In 1979 the Dutch scholar and textual critic A.M. Duinhoven used the name Lanseloet as a point of departure in his search for the source of *Lanseloet van Denemerken*.[3] It is his view that in its present state the play contains all sorts of incongruities that cannot possibly have originated with the author. In his opinion the inconsistencies indicate that the play has a long textual history behind it in which a large number of scribes and adapters were involved. He argues that originally *Lanseloet van Denemerken* was a

* I would like to thank Frank Brandsma and Orlanda Lie for reading an earlier, Dutch version of this article, which was translated into English by Josephie Brefeld.

stage adaptation of an episode from the Prose *Lancelot*, specifically the story of the damsel of Escalot from the *Mort Artu*. This young girl is deeply in love with Lancelot du Lac and dies of grief when he refuses to respond to her love.[4] Duinhoven argues that the Middle Dutch stage adaptation in the course of time went through all sorts of changes. Lanseloet van Denemerken was actually "Lancelot van den Mere" (Lancelot of the Lake); at a certain moment a scribe misread, so the argument goes, "van den Mere" as "van Denemerken." Lanseloet's mother originally was his lover, the queen, and Sanderijn once was the damsel of Escalot.

Duinhoven's provocative hypothesis led another Dutch scholar, G. Kazemier, to react.[5] Kazemier believes that Duinhoven's reconstruction is strained. His criticism centers in particular on Duinhoven's interpretation of the play in its present shape. According to Kazemier the incongruities Duinhoven sees in the play rest on an incorrect interpretation of the text. I agree with Kazemier. On the basis of the similarities Duinhoven points out between the story about the damsel of Escalot and the Middle Dutch play, Kazemier is prepared to accept that the Middle Dutch author was influenced by the story from the *Mort Artu*, but even that, I feel, is not very probable. I think the parallels that are said to suggest a link between the *Mort Artu* and the play are weak and far-fetched. To offer a single example: the Sanderijn who level-headedly guards her virtue is a far cry from the damsel of Escalot who is desperately in love.

But if we cannot agree with Duinhoven, then how *should* we account for the name Lanseloet? There are reasons to assume that here we are dealing with a case of generic intertextuality. In the play's first scene Lanseloet is mentioned by name four times (ll. 100, 105, 124, 148). Upon hearing his name, Arthurian scholars attending a production of *Lanseloet van Denemerken* would no doubt be instantly reminded of Lancelot du Lac, Queen Guinevere's lover. But was this also true for a fourteenth-century Dutch audience?

In the medieval Low Countries, Lancelot was known through Chrétien de Troyes's *Chevalier de la charrete*. It is true that no Middle Dutch translation of this romance has come down to us, but allusions in other Arthurian romances, in the *Ridder metter mouwen* ("The Knight with the Sleeve") for example, indicate that the story was known.[6] Well known indeed this Lancelot must have been from the translations of the Prose *Lancelot*, a text that was rendered into Middle Dutch at least three times.[7] Furthermore it seems that after the end of the thirteenth century the literary influence of the prose romances surpassed the influence of the verse romances.[8] It is therefore to be suspected that by the time *Lanseloet van*

Denemerken was first performed, acquaintance with Arthurian matter rested chiefly on the Prose *Lancelot*.

The wide circulation of the story of Lancelot and its popularity make it very likely that spectators—in any case the most knowledgeable among them—were reminded of the Arthurian knight when they heard the name of Lanseloet mentioned on the stage. That this association must have been a favorable one is apparent from the fact that in the Low Countries, Lancelot was used as a first name in the fourteenth century.[9] Obviously this is possible only when the literary character was appreciated. Who wants to call his child Mordred?

The question that arises now is the following: was the association between Lanseloet of Denmark and Lancelot du Lac intended by the Dutch playwright? If we assume that this idea is not the fantasy of an Arthurian enthusiast, we must then conclude that by naming the protagonist of his play Lanseloet, the author expressly invited the spectators to compare the stage character with Guinevere's lover. Such a comparison could contribute to a better understanding of the story unrolling before their eyes. I would like to proceed from such an assumption.

The play is all about love. If Lanseloet's behavior is to be viewed against the background of Guinevere's lover, it is best to characterize the love of Arthur's most important knight first. Without a doubt Lancelot du Lac is a knight who is driven by love. His love for Guinevere is a source of inspiration, inciting him to great deeds. In Chrétien's *Chevalier de la charrete* as in the Prose *Lancelot*, it is the influence of love that enables Lancelot to cross the sword bridge, thus accomplishing something considered to be practically impossible. These two texts both show that he puts Guinevere first as he is prepared for the sake of her to get into a cart, even though by doing so he brings shame upon himself.[10]

Furthermore Lancelot is an absolutely loyal lover. He is always faithful to Guinevere and never does anything at all that could possibly cause his beloved harm. In the Prose *Lancelot*, this absolute loyalty enables him to free the prisoners in the Val sans Retour who *did* betray their ladyloves, either in reality or merely in mind. As a result of Morgain's spell they cannot leave this valley, which is also called the Val as Faus Amans. Only the knight who has always and in everything been true to his love will be able to lift the spell. Lancelot is that knight (Micha, *Lancelot*, I, § XXI–XXIV).

Yet the love of Lancelot and Guinevere has its less favorable side, too, as it is sinful and illicit. The *Queste del saint Graal* stresses the sinful character of Lancelot's love. Owing to his objectionable relationship with the adulterous Guinevere, Lancelot is no longer able to bring the Grail adventure to a favorable conclusion.[11] In the *Mort Artu*, Lancelot's love turns out to be destructive. Because it is an adulterous love, Lancelot is not presented as Arthur's benefactor, but rather as his betrayer. Here it is Lancelot's love for Guinevere that, together with Mordred's treachery and Gauvain's desire to avenge the death of his brothers, brings about the downfall of Arthur's realm (Kennedy, 303–8).

Although this characterization of Lancelot's love is an oversimplification, it is sufficient to permit us to interpret the behavior of his namesake in the Middle Dutch play. Lanseloet of Denmark is a passionate lover, just like the Arthurian knight. Both are motivated by their love.[12] Before Sanderijn, Lanseloet states: "Mijn herte dat es te male onstelt / Ende van uwer minnen ghequelt, / Dat mi costen sal mijn lijf." ("My heart is so shaken and so tormented with love for you that I fear lest it cost me my life," ll. 65–67).[13]

In a conversation with his mother he then once again stresses his love for the damsel who is in her service:

Sone wetic wijf int kersten rijc,
Die ic woude hebben voer Sanderijn.
Ic woude si mochte mijn eygen sijn,
Lieve moeder, bi uwen danc.
Al ware al die werelt an mi belanc,
Ic woude wel dat si ware mijn wijf. (ll. 200–05)

[There is no woman in all Christendom whom I would prefer before Sanderijn. If only she were mine! Dear mother, be content: if all the world were at my disposal, I would still wish her to be my wife.]

As noted, Lancelot's love for Guinevere has its less favorable aspects. Much the same holds true for the prince of Denmark's love: in both cases its destructiveness is stressed. By loving Arthur's wife, Lancelot du Lac brings about the fall of Arthur's kingdom. Lanseloet's love for Sanderijn leads to his *own* downfall. As I argued elsewhere Lanseloet is in the grip of lovesickness. Consistent with the clinical picture of this illness, *amor hereos*, he dies when he realizes that a reunion with Sanderijn is impossible.[14]

In Lancelot du Lac's case the negative aspects of his love are balanced by those that are more favorable. Guinevere inspires him to great exploits, and it is precisely his love for her that enables him to save Arthur's throne twice: in the fights against Galehot and against the Saxons (Micha, *Lancelot*, VIII,§ XLIXa–LIIa, LXVIa–LXXIa). It is here that Lanseloet of

Denmark's love for Sanderijn is different, as it is not ennobling. On the contrary: in contrast with his Arthurian namesake he is disloyal to his ladylove. Whereas Guinevere's lover under all circumstances seeks to protect the honor of his beloved, Lanseloet by raping and insulting Sanderijn causes her grief and brings dishonor on her (cf. also Kazemier, "Lanseloet," 233).

Lanseloet's mother is prepared to lure Sanderijn into her son's room on the condition that after the sexual act he will berate Sanderijn as follows: ". . . ic hebbe uus genoech, / Sanderijn, ic ben uus nu sat / Ende van herten alsoe mat, / Al haddic .vij. baken gheten" ("I have had enough, Sanderijn: I am sick of you and I have had my fill; and it is as if I had gorged myself on seven roast pigs," ll. 240–43). Lanseloet realizes that this is a horrible thing to say: "O lieve moeder, es dat u wille, / Dat ic spreke dese dorper woort? / Des ghelike en hebbic niet ghehoert" ("Oh mother, is this what you want, that I should say anything so coarse? I have never heard the like of it," ll. 250–52). Yet he agrees and submits to his mother's will. Where his namesake would be prepared to give his life for his beloved, Lanseloet of Denmark sacrifices Sanderijn for his lust. The poor girl is raped and, in her own eyes far worse, humiliated: "Nochtan deert mi boven al / Die woorde, die hi sprac, die ridder vri, / Ende keerde sijn anschijn omme van mi, / Al haddic gheweest een stinckende hont" ("And yet what torments me more than all is the words that that fine knight spoke to me as he turned his face from me as if I had been a stinking cur," ll. 332–35).

It will be clear by now that in their attitudes toward their lovers Lancelot du Lac and Lanseloet of Denmark are opposites. The Arthurian hero is a courtly lover through and through. For the spectators of *Lanseloet van Denemerken* his name must have functioned as a topos, it must have triggered an image of the excellent courtly lover.[15] One may expect someone who is called Lanseloet to put his beloved on a pedestal. In the course of the play, this expectation is frustrated: the lovesick Lanseloet who appears on stage hurts and abuses the object of his desire.[16]

The inevitable question is: what is the function of the contrast between the two lovers? The answer lies in the two different notions of love that can be distinguished in the play. Some years ago Orlanda Lie convincingly drew attention to this aspect of *Lanseloet van Denemerken*.[17] Lanseloet embodies one of the ways of thinking, one that we might label "traditionally courtly." He aims for a relationship with Sanderijn without the bonds of marriage. They both feel that a marriage between the two of them is out of the question because of class difference. Sanderijn tells Lanseloet:

Ghi sijt mi te mechtich ende te rike,
Edel ridder, te sine u wijf.
Daer omme soe moet sijn een blijf,
Al eest dat ic u met herten minne.
Ende oec en willic gheens mans vriendinne
Sijn, die leeft onder des hemels trone;
Al waer hi een coninc ende spien crone,
Soe en dadic mi niet te cleine. (ll. 76–83)

[You are too great and too rich for me to be your lady. So this must
now come to an end, for though I may love you with all my heart,
I will not be the love light of any man living under heaven, even
if he were a king and wore a crown: still I would not so abase
myself.]

This is what Lanseloet has to say on the subject:

Bi ridderscape, ic woude wael,
Dat si gheboren ware mijns gelijc.
Al en waer si niet van haven rijc,
Ic souder maken af mijn wijf,
Want si heeft een reine lijf
Ende haer herte es al vol eren. (ll. 170–75)

[By my knightly state, I wish indeed that she were born my equal;
however little she possessed, I would make her my wife, for her life
is pure and her heart is wholly honorable.]

With marriage out of the question, there is no impediment, however, to his
making love to her. It is here that he agrees with the Arthurian hero, whose
relationship with Guinevere is, after all, illicit. Yet in his behavior the stage
character is a rather uncourtly lover, and here he differs from Lancelot du
Lac. It is only fitting that he should show the symptoms of *amor hereos*. The
clinical picture adds to the condemnation of Lanseloet of Denmark's love
as a sick love.

It is Sanderijn who epitomizes the other notion of love. Wishing to
preserve her virginity for the man who will marry her, she connects love,
honor, and marriage. What she seeks is an honorable position as the lawful
wife of an important gentleman,[18] and the knight she runs into after having
been raped is a suitable candidate. He offers to marry her:

O scone wijf, inder minnen vier
Leght mijn herte te mael en blaect.
Ghi sijt hovesch ende wel gheraect.
Ghi selt bi ridderscape sijn mijn wijf.
Ghi hebt soe edelen scoenen lijf! (ll. 450–54)

[Lovely creature, my heart burns and consumes in the fire of love: you are so courtly and so beautiful that I swear on my honor as a knight that you shall be my wife for your beauty.]

The knight makes a favorable impression on Sanderijn, and when it appears that he does not take her loss of virginity as a hindrance to happiness, she agrees to marry him.

When, more than a year later, Lanseloet's servant Reinout discovers Sanderijn's whereabouts, it turns out that she is very happy. Her husband's forester sings her praise:

Hi heefter af ghemaect sijn vrouwe,
Want si es hem soe ghetrouwe
Ende ghehoersam ende onder daen;
Ende alle die minen here bestaen
Minnense om hare groter doeght;
Si sijnder al gader bi verhoeght,
Die den hove toe behoert. (ll. 673–79)

[My lord has made her his wife, for she is faithful to him and obedient and submissive; and everyone here who is of my lord's kin loves her for her great virtue. Every man living in this castle is full of joy on her account.]

Sanderijn confirms that she is a happy woman. She refuses to return to Lanseloet:

. . . ic ben eerlijc ende wale ghehout
Ende hebbe enen edelen man ghetrout,
Dien ic minne boven alle die leven.
Hem en willic niet begheven.
Al ware Lanseloet alsoe rike,
Dat hi ware Hectors van Troyen gelike,
Ende dat hi hadde van Gode te lone,

Dat hi droeghe die selve crone,
Die die coninc Alexander droech,
Soe en ware hi nochtan niet mijn ghevoech,
Ic en hebbe liever minen man,
Dien mi alder doeghden an.
Dien salic ewelijc sijn ghetrouwe. (ll. 745–57)

[I live here honorably and well, and I am married to a noble man, whom I love better than I love life itself. I would not leave him for anything. If Lancelot were as great as Hector of Troy, if it pleased God to endow him with the very crown that King Alexander once wore, still he would have nothing to offer to me. My husband alone is dear to me, who has shown me all courtesy, and I shall always be faithful to him.]

Thereupon she describes her husband in such terms that every spectator can identify with her:

. . . ic nie man op eerde en sach,
Dien ic meer doeghden an
Dan ic doe minen lieven man.
Hets recht, want hi eest wel weert:
Hi es een ridder wide vermeert,
Ende een vaelyant ridder van hogen moede,
Wael gheboren ende rijc van goede,
Ende gheradich ende vroet;
Oec es hi te wapene goet
Ende van groten doene bekint.
Want hem mijn herte met trouwen mint
Boven alle creaturen. (ll. 768–79)

[I never found so honorable a man on earth as is my husband. He well merits my love, for he is a knight of great repute, valiant, noble-hearted, well born and well endowed; prudent and wise, a famous warrior known for his great deeds. I love him with my whole heart, more than any other creature.]

Whereas Lanseloet's love for Sanderijn is destructive, she and her husband are a happy couple. In this way the implicit message of the entire play is made obvious: Sanderijn's view of love is to be preferred to Lanseloet's. According to Orlanda Lie (see n. 17), this message fits in an urban context in which the interaction between courtly and bourgeois ideals was still very much alive.

Seen against the background of the differing concepts of love in the Middle Dutch play, the function of the contrast between Lanseloet of Denmark and his Arthurian namesake becomes apparent. The association with Guinevere's lover backs up the intended interpretation of the play (see also Lie, 214). This makes it, in my opinion, very likely that the Dutch playwright planned the contrast.[19] In opposition to the Arthurian hero who adores Guinevere, we find the prince of Denmark who abuses and humiliates his beloved. The mere fact that this stage character bears a name that, when it comes to love, has favorable connotations makes his behavior all the more striking and despicable. And that is exactly what it was meant to do. A comparison of this negative Lanseloet of Denmark with his positive namesake adds another dimension to the former's bad behavior in matters of love. The spectators are made to understand that Lanseloet's love leads to trouble and that Sanderijn's ideas about love are the right ones. In this way the use of the name Lanseloet, a case of generic intertextuality, contributes to the implicit message of the play.

NOTES

1. *Een abel spel van Lanseloet van Denemerken*, ed. Rob Roemans and H. van Assche, 8th ed. (Antwerpen: Uitgeverij de Nederlandsche Boekhandel, 1982).

2. For this manuscript, see J. Deschamps, *Middelnederlandse handschriften uit Europese en Amerikaanse bibliotheken*, 2nd ed. (Leiden: Brill, 1972), pp. 131–36. For a description of the contents of the codex see *Klein kapitaal uit het handschrift-Van Hulthem*, ed. H. van Dijk et al. (Hilversum: Verloren, 1992), pp. 12–20.

3. A.M. Duinhoven, "De bron van *Lanseloet*," *Tijdschrift voor Nederlandse Taal- en Letterkunde*, 95 (1979), 262–87.

4. For an analysis, see Jean Frappier, *Etude sur la Mort le roi Artu*, 3rd ed. (Geneva: Droz, 1972), pp. 267–73.

5. G. Kazemier, "De bron van Lanseloet?" *Tijdschrift voor Nederlandse Taal- en Letterkunde*, 96 (1980), 1–11. See also Duinhoven's reaction (12–16) and Kazemier's response (16–17).

6. See Bart Besamusca, *Walewein, Moriaen en de Ridder metter mouwen. Intertekstualiteit in drie Middelnederlandse Arturromans* (Hilversum: Verloren, 1993), pp. 144–46.

7. See Bart Besamusca and Orlanda S.H. Lie, "The Prologue to *Arturs doet*, the Middle Dutch Translation of *La Mort le Roi Artu* in the *Lancelot Compilation*," in *Medieval Dutch Literature in Its European Context*, ed. Erik Kooper (Cambridge: Cambridge University Press, 1994), pp. 96–112.

8. See Beate Schmolke-Hasselmann, *Der arthurische Versroman von Chrestien bis Froissart: Zur Geschichte einer Gattung* (Tübingen: Niemeyer, 1980), p. 182.

9. See G.J. Boekenoogen, "Namen uit ridderromans als voornamen in gebruik," *Tijdschrift voor Nederlandse Taal- en Letterkunde*, 36 (1917), 77.

10. See Chrétien de Troyes, *Lancelot or The Knight of the Cart (Le Chevalier de la Charrete)*, ed. and trans. William W. Kibler (New York: Garland, 1984), ll. 320–94, 2999–3141; and *Lancelot: Roman en prose du XIIIe siècle*, ed. Alexandre Micha,

9 vols. (Geneva: Droz, 1978–83), I, § XXXVI, 23–27; XXXVIII, 44–50.

11. See Elspeth Kennedy, *Lancelot and the Grail: A Study of the Prose "Lancelot"* (Oxford: Clarendon, 1986), pp. 297–300.

12. See also G. Kazemier, "Lanseloet van Denemerken," in *Taal- en letterkundig gastenboek voor Prof. Dr. G.A. van Es: opstellen, de 70-jarige aangeboden ter gelegenheid van zijn afscheid als hoogleraar aan de Rijksuniversiteit te Groningen*, ed. G. Kazemier and P.P.J. van Caspel (Groningen: Archief voor de Nederlandse Syntaxis, 1975), p. 231.

13. For the translations, I make use of *Reynard the Fox and Other Mediaeval Netherlands Secular Literature*, ed. and intro. E. Colledge, trans. Adriaan J. Barnouw and E. Colledge (Leyden: Sijthoff, 1967), pp. 165–83.

14. See my "*Amor hereos* in Middle Dutch Literature: The Case of Lancelot of Denmark," in *Literary Aspects of Courtly Culture: Selected Papers from the 7th Triennial Congress of the International Courtly Literature Society*, ed. Donald Maddox and Sara Sturm-Maddox (Woodbridge: Boydell and Brewer, 1994), pp. 189–96.

15. See Douglas Kelly, *The Art of Medieval French Romance* (Madison: University of Wisconsin Press, 1992), pp. 198–200.

16. I would like to thank Lori Walters for drawing my attention to the fact that there are interesting parallels between *Lanseloet van Denemerken* and the Latin play *Pamphilus*, probably written in the first half of the twelfth century. In this play a bawd gives the main character the opportunity to be alone with his beloved, Galathea, an encounter leading to rape. See *Seven Medieval Latin Comedies*, trans. Alison Goddard Elliott (New York: Garland, 1984), pp. 1–25.

17. Orlanda S.H. Lie, "Het abel spel van Lanseloet van Denemerken in het handschrift-Van Hulthem: hoofse tekst of stadsliteratuur?" in Herman Pleij et al., *Op belofte van profijt. Stadsliteratuur en burgermoraal in de Nederlandse letterkunde van de middeleeuwen* (Amsterdam: Prometheus, 1991), pp. 200–16, 391–93.

18. See also Jeannette Koekman, "De stilte rond Sanderijn; over het abel spel *Lanseloet van Denemerken*," in *De canon onder vuur. Nederlandse literatuur tegendraads gelezen*, ed. Ernst van Alphen and Maaike Meijer (Amsterdam: Van Gennep, 1991), pp. 20–34, 229–30.

19. It is not impossible that the author thought of a second contrast as well, that is, between Lanseloet's mother and the Dame du Lac. My thanks to Douglas Kelly for this suggestion.

THE REPRESENTATION OF TIME AND ITS MODELS IN THE PROSE ROMANCE*

Katalin Halász

One day, in Morgain's prison, Lancelot, alone and idle, sees a man who is painting an "old story,"[1] that of Aeneas, and this gives him the idea of easing his own suffering by surrounding himself with images evoking the memory of his exploits, of his companions, and especially of the queen. He spends many days recounting and thus recreating his past. Two intertexts can be discerned in this passage: Aeneas and Tristan.[2] The former is evoked as an object of artistic representation only to be immediately supplanted by Lancelot, who has temporarily become an artist, eager to rescue from oblivion a past that he would like to be able to relive. The narrator attributes to the protagonist an activity implying a reflexive attitude toward his past and an effort to give it form by "assembling"[3] the different moments of his life. Similarly the reader/listener is invited to recollect the parts of the story that are already known; and since the peaks of Lancelot's career are juxtaposed by simple enumeration, the impression that we are witnessing the unfolding of an exceptional destiny becomes all the more intense. Here, of course, the text is speaking about time.

The other intertext, the *Tristan*'s Hall of Images, reinforces this impression. It emphasizes the analogous elements in the situations of the two lovers and underlines the motives for Lancelot's decision: unless he can find some solution, his future seems to be reduced to a succession of present moments, made intolerable by his awareness of the radical contrast between the privations of the present and a past radiant with grandeur, glory, and love. This empty and painful present, not unlike death—the hero feeling himself separated from life because he is far from the court and the queen—is related to an "elsewhere," a closed space dominated by an enchantment.

*This essay was translated from the French by Norris J. Lacy, who also provided translations of Old French quotations.

A single escape route is open to Lancelot: he can live in the past. But how to reach that past? At least as much as the comb in *La Charrete*[4] or the three drops of blood in *Le Conte du Graal*,[5] the painted images, representations of cherished beings, serve to mobilize memory while also causing forgetfulness of self, that is, an interior dislocation that is both temporal and spatial. But this transformation of the past into a livable present can succeed only partially. Thus we see Lancelot torn between two contradictory states of mind: the full awareness of his loss (*mescheance* in the text) and the euphoria provoked by the "*semblances*" of the past.[6] The presentation of his state of mind is therefore conveyed through antithesis, as are, in fact, most of the passages in which the characters (and the narrator with them) are grappling with temporal experience and its expression.[7]

But let us reexamine another, similarly crucial, episode, which tells how, after having been discovered in the bed of the daughter of King Pellés, Lancelot is banished by the queen. Here he takes a last look at the city and says,

> "Ha, Kamaalot, bonne cité et bele et bien garnie de toute chevalerie, beneuree de toute biauté de dames, en toi pris je conmancement de vie." Et ce disoit il pour sa dame par cui il li ert avis qu'il vivoit. "Et si ai pris en toi conmancement de mort et sanz faille je sui venuz au duel par quoi je morrai." (VI, 176)

> ["Oh, Camelot, great and beautiful city, endowed with all chivalry, blessed with all feminine beauty, in you did my life truly begin." And he said this on account of his lady, for it seemed to him that he was given life through her. "And I have also begun to die through you, and I have surely been afflicted by grief that will kill me."]

Before Lancelot lies Camelot, the city of his glory and his joy, a privileged place that, like a reliquary, contains the queen, a place that suddenly becomes an "elsewhere," a forbidden place. It is this spatial arrangement that predisposes our hero not only to conceive but also to express his experience of time in antithetical terms, and that experience is so overwhelming that he falls into madness. Now, madness is the flight from time, for Lancelot, out of his mind and no longer knowing what he is or was, is consequently unaware of his fall. Only those around him are able to realize his *mescheance*.

In these two examples the character's conscious mind is challenged by a complete and unexpected reversal of the situation, the stark opposition of past and present states. This reversal in fact seems to be an indispensable condition for the medieval mind to conceive of time. The sensibility of the period apparently responds less to the gradual accumulation of the effects of passing time than to spectacular changes that occur with suddenness. Reversals, disasters, diametrically opposed states (often represented by a spatial arrangement as well)—all these phenomena converge on a single point, the Fortune topos. Even before being introduced at the end of *La Mort Artu*,[8] this figure often makes furtive appearances in the *Lancelot*, where it, or more precisely the imaginative structure that animates it, dramatizes the basic experience of time's devastating effects and the precarious nature of all human effort. The narrator generally exploits this representational model to describe subjective reactions to time.

In support of this contention let us reread another episode of the romance, concerning Galehaut, a character who is particularly preoccupied with time: from the moment of his encounter with Lancelot, he will never cease to scan the future and to have presentiments of imminent misfortunes, all the while wanting at all cost to learn the precise hour of his death. In the episode in question[9] the two companions pass before Orgueilleuse Garde, Galehaut's favorite castle, a monument to his past ambitions. In nostalgic tones Galehaut, already uneasy because of a dream, recounts the castle's history to an amazed Lancelot, telling him, "Certes a cel point que je le commençai, baoie je a conquere la seignorie de tot le monde . . . " ("When I began it, my desire was to gain dominance over the whole world," I, 9). This plan to dominate the entire world is already a remnant of the past. Now his only ambition is to be able to keep Lancelot with him. His total self-sacrifice now contrasts strikingly with his former excessive ambitions.[10]

The dialogue of the two friends barely finished, a section of Orgueilleuse Garde collapses before their eyes, and with it, Galehaut's former being crumbles as well. We subsequently learn that all the castles of Sorelois have suffered the same fate. It might be said that a mysterious force attempts to make the change visible and irrevocable, as though, both metaphorically and metonymically, to offer on the one hand its own terrifying image, and on the other the spectacle of what would otherwise remain ineffable to man: the irresistible and irreversible march of human time. The primary witness of this scene is Galehaut, who is fundamentally a spectator, as was Lancelot when he was before his own paintings or the city of Camelot. Galehaut "correctly" interprets what he sees, and because he understands it, his first impulse is to flee: "'Ha, Diex, tant felenessement me conmence a *meschaoir!*' Lors retorne la resne de son frain et se met par mi les chans en travers, sor senestre" ("'Oh, God, how cruelly my downfall begins!' Then he pulled on the reins and set out across the fields, to the left," I, 11).

En travers, sor senestre ("across, to the left"): these terms perfectly express the disarray, the panicked flight—a flight that is however impossible. Galehaut will later regain control of himself, as we know, and will have the courage to look death in the face (*Lancelot*, I, 37–71).

If we consider the numerous passages where the characters' uneasiness about their future is expressed by their fear of a *mescheance*, we must acknowledge that our text is shaped by a mental structure that links to the experience of time a sudden vertical movement, a reversal that, although its source remains unknown, brings Fortune to mind. In our view, the medieval reader, accustomed to the fragility of earthly grandeur, must have made the same association as we.

This process is but one of the means by which the narrator can produce the effect that the reader of the *Lancelot* experiences so intensely. Time, in the prose romance in general and especially in the *Lancelot-Graal*, acquires a depth and importance that it does not have in verse romance. Although we cannot provide here a full inventory of the ways time is represented, we will point out, as in the case of the Fortune topos, the more or less original re-use of some other representational models. These models will bring us back ultimately to the Bible, which, in Paul Ricoeur's appealing formula, "est la grandiose intrigue de l'histoire du monde," each literary intrigue being "une sorte de miniature de la grande intrigue qui joint l'Apocalypse à la Genèse. . . . Ainsi le mythe eschatologique et le *muthos* aristotélicien se rejoignent-ils dans leur manière de lier un commencement à une fin et de proposer à l'imagination le triomphe de la concordance sur la discordance."[11]

This is the great narrative model informing most medieval stories, but as the model offers various possibilities for treating time, the stories themselves vary significantly. In historiographic narratives and in certain fictional forms, as R. Howard Bloch has shown,[12] the genealogical approach clearly prevails. Other temporal approaches implied in the model are adopted especially in Grail narratives, where the representation of time becomes more and more complex. Genealogical preoccupations do not by any means recede, however, as witness the plan of Robert de Boron's trilogy,[13] which was conceived as an attempt to elucidate the origins of both the Grail and the Arthurian world. The same could be said of the second stage of the formation of the great *Lancelot-Grail* cycle: the first two parts (preceded in internal chronology by *La Mort Artu*) were born out of a desire to elucidate. And in the intellectual context of the period, elucidation most often means a genealogical return to origins.

But beginning with Robert's verse romance of the Grail,[14] the eschatological perspective is also taken into account: the events that are recounted have a finality; human time is interpreted and relativized by the end (in both senses of the word) and what comes thereafter—*joie pardurable*.[15] First and last causes and the meaning to be attributed to things human now constitute the primary concern of the narrator. The time that characters have to spend in this world is of less import, and consequently the poignant experience of time is rarely expressed, except perhaps at the end of the trilogy, where Perceval's sadness at the disappearance of the Arthurian world echoes this theme (*Le Roman du Graal*, p. 301).

At first glance, *Le Haut Livre du Graal, Perlesvaus*[16] seems even more completely dominated by an eschatological vision, and yet passages dealing with the origins of places, families, and lineal conflicts are by no means lacking. However, as these passages are dispersed in flashbacks, the genealogical narrative must be reconstructed like a mosaic during reading. In this regard *Perlesvaus* is similar to the *Lancelot Proper*, as we will see presently. The awareness of the passage of time is communicated, sometimes strikingly, as Michel Zink's study has demonstrated so well.[17]

As for the *Lancelot-Graal* cycle, it is precisely the configuration of all the temporal aspects that, despite the large number of characters and the extraordinary diversity of the plot elements, ensures an exceptional coherence, with concordance predominating over dissonance. The principal unifying factor can be identified as the temporal framework for the three parts being considered here; it is a biographical framework, with the *Lancelot Proper* beginning with the events of Lancelot's earliest childhood and the *Mort Artu* ending with his burial. We should note parenthetically that the narrative presents its own genesis as a compilation of authentic biographies preserved at Arthur's court.[18] The length of a human life being a unit of time understandable by anyone, it is intimately linked to the fundamental everyday experience of all of us. In this frame, which is literally the "measure of a man," the story nevertheless puts us in contact with temporal dimensions that go beyond those of the individual but that nonetheless constitute unifying factors.

On the one hand, this is a question of what Ricoeur (199–203) calls monumental time or historical time, with the succession of generations and the representation of the *splendeurs et misères* of a kingdom whose disappearance Lancelot is witnessing after having unwittingly contributed to it. On the other hand, the narrative leads us to confront time's antithesis (that is, eternity), by bringing us, in the *Queste*, to the brink of that mystery beyond which representation is no longer possible.[19] It is true that, even in this dimension, events do occur, particularly those involving suffering, as if there were an intermediate zone between human time and the absence of time.

For the many inhabitants of the tomb, death has not brought an end to time: their suffering is lasting, just as the joy promised to those eventually able to escape this intermediate zone is *pardurable*. In either case eternity is not conceived as a total negation of time, but as a state that knows neither change nor death, and that endures nonetheless.[20] These various temporal perspectives develop and are elaborated, as we recall, within the span of a single life, that of Lancelot, in whom they are simultaneously maintained and affirmed, thereby reinforcing the temporal effect of the cycle.

We have seen that the appearance of Fortune at the end of the cycle is in a sense prepared in the *Lancelot Proper* by certain discourses and images that are antithetical in structure, conveying the simultaneous presence of discrete states of mind. The eschatological perspective, with all its implications, is similarly included in the *Lancelot*'s representation of time. The two faces of the End of Time (the final catastrophe of an earthly kingdom and the redemption reserved for an elite, each of these phenomena dominating that part of the cycle devoted to it) are eventually presented together, intermingled with the genealogical and the biographical perspectives. The End is present, indirectly, even in the narratives devoted to origins. If Eugene Vinaver could speak of *entrelacement* in regard to parallel intrigues,[21] we can do as much in regard to temporal perspectives, even about a single thread of the narrative: the story advances while making detours all the while, now toward the past, now toward the future.

Before reviewing the principal means by which the narrator manages to configure in his story a good number of the images, conceptions, and views that his period held about time, we should consider some of the givens on which our interpretation is based. In the *Lancelot* we can count 117 flashbacks. Ninety of them are in dialogue and thus constitute stories within the story; the remainder are the product of the narrator. The future is anticipated slightly less often—eighty-six times, more or less evenly divided between the narrator and the characters.

There is in addition a specific category, prophecies, whose origin is difficult to determine: in some twenty cases, premonitory dreams and letters engraved on tombs or crosses announce future events in veiled terms. Another characteristic should be mentioned at this point: more than once prediction is involved in a flashback, thus linking—if the predicted event has just been realized—past and present, or past, present, and future.[22]

A good many flashbacks stem from the protagonists' desire to understand the conflicts they encounter during their wandering. The narratives by which their curiosity is satisfied normally bring them into contact with a past that is comparatively close to the presentation of those narratives. In these cases the past of "secondary" characters is linked to that of their contemporaries, the protagonists, thereby conferring on the principal narrative thread of the romance a certain temporal density. The flashbacks of this type constitute the upper layer of the past, which rarely seems to revert farther than the beginning of the romance. Like a projector, the narrative within the narrative briefly illuminates parallel lives, especially those parallel to the protagonists'.

Another category of flashbacks, smaller but carrying considerable weight in the configuration of the different aspects of time, includes those that lead the protagonists, especially Lancelot, to discover the deeper layers of the past, a past that in this case extends well beyond the biographical framework of the romance. These flashbacks bring us back to the origins of lineages, of the Arthurian kingdom, of the Grail. "Au tens le roi Ban; au tans Uterpandragon; au tans Merlin le prophete; au tans Josep d'Arimacie; des le tans as paiens; au tans que li pueples Israel servoit Nostre Signor a foi" ("In the time of King Ban; in the time of Uther Pendragon; in the time of Merlin the prophet; in the time of Joseph of Arimathea; since the time of the pagans; in the time when the people of Israel served Our Lord faithfully")[23]—all are formulas that help us distinguish the superimposed layers of this venerable past, a past that is not yet completed, for its vestiges,[24] scattered through Lancelot's life and that of his companions, transmit messages to the protagonists and impose specific duties on them. Their presence is not a matter of chance: it is necessary, it has meaning.

Let us consider an example. Lancelot, in a dream, sees his grandfather, who announces to him the adventure that awaits him in the Perilous Forest (V, 114–15, 117–31). In fact, he will find in that forest a boiling fountain with the head of his murdered grandfather in it; the body lies in a tomb. Lancelot will also find there an old man who was a small child at the time of the murder. Having taken the head of his relative out of the fountain, he buries it properly. However, the mission given him by the past cannot be properly accomplished: the fountain cannot be calmed by Lancelot, burdened as he is by the sin of lust. The old man informs him that they must await the arrival of a knight who is pure and a virgin and thus better than Lancelot.

In order to illustrate the extent to which the narrator maintains the various temporal dimensions, we may point out that shortly after this adventure, Lancelot encounters Sarraz of Logres, who, giving news of the court, informs him of Galahad's birth (V, 139). Not only do these ancestors leave traces that preserve their memory, but they also leave work to be done, insults to avenge, sins to expiate; in this way, the ancestors program the lives of their descendants. The adultery of King Leodagan will provoke the crisis of the royal couple in the episode of the False Guenevere, just as the incest committed by Arthur (who was himself conceived in adultery) will lead to the final disaster. The broken sword that Joseph conveys to Galahad across time and generations emblematizes this point (II, 325–39). Through the interlace of temporal perspectives, such passages suggest that the course of time has a direction and that human time has finality.

As if by contrast, the representation of another perspective (or, rather, a false perspective) reinforces this suggestion. There is in this romance a charmed time that could be considered fairylike or magic and that displays some of the aspects of eternity. Ultimately, what we can learn from the episodes of the enchanted captives of the Valley of No Return or of the Lost Forest (I, 266–300; IV, 233–36, 286–95) or the scene of Lancelot's madness is, on the one hand, the dream of holding onto the present moment and, on the other hand, horror at the flight of time and at death. As a matter of fact, the prisoners of the Lost Valley or the dancers of the magic carol are in a sense removed from the normal course of human time, and Lancelot's madness can be interpreted as a flight from time.

But these are false solutions, traps set by eternity. The image that perfectly expresses that falsity to us is the *carol*: the dancers who turn in circles get nowhere, and nothing seems to change, but the knight who is responsible for the enchantment dies nonetheless. The circle that has neither beginning nor end stands in opposition to the rectilinear march of time, which has a meaning because it has a master. And the true remedy for the sufferings of the conscience in the face of death is to be sought in the promise of enduring joy (*joie pardurable*), which in this story is represented by and constantly embodied in the Grail. It is the Grail that cures Lancelot's madness (VI, 224), and he does not relapse into it.

The madness scene has its asymmetrical counterpart in *La Mort Artu* (161–63): Lancelot on the boat, exiled from the place where he had performed his exploits, separated from his youth, from the queen—in short, from his life—says farewell to Arthur's kingdom. Lancelot is perfectly aware that what once was is now definitively past, as witness his words and gestures: he sends his shield to the church of Saint Etienne at Camelot, where he had first received the order of chivalry. This time lucidity leads Lancelot, who wishes to confirm and safeguard his life's meaning, to overcome his grief and to accept death. The fact that the land of his glory and of his love has become enemy territory does not prevent him from asking God's blessings on all those who inhabit it. A certain pathos characterizes the actions of Lancelot, the vanquished man who faces his defeat with courage.

To return again to the genealogical dimension of the work, it should be pointed out that for Lancelot, the episode of the carol constitutes both a connection with the past and an act of liberation to be accomplished. This very past requires him to break the enchantment, instituted by one of his father's knights when his father committed the adultery that produced Hector. It is shortly before the adventure of the Lost Forest that Lancelot learns of his father's adultery (IV, 226–29); it should also be noted that this discovery and the flashback associated with the carol, as well as the one discussed above (note 24), occur in close proximity in the narrative. Thus it is that we see several genealogical narratives, if not an outline of history, inserted into the ensemble of biographical tales. But unlike the rectilinear composition that predominates in genealogical texts (e.g., the Bible, Robert de Boron's trilogy, etc.) and in biographical ones (e.g., saints' lives, many verse romances with a single hero, etc.), these stories are constructed of fragments, like a mosaic whose pieces are dispersed; as a result they are inextricably mingled with other temporal dimensions.

As Lancelot progresses along his path, the stratification of the past becomes increasingly complex, as if Lancelot (or conceivably another protagonist) were traveling in two different directions during a single journey. And to emphasize further the temporal effect, the dimension of the future is similarly stratified in the form of various anticipations or flashforwards related either to the future of a single character or to that of the kingdom. This dimension is in turn constructed out of dispersed details and of frequently enigmatic signs.

It is moreover present from the beginning of the romance. The young Lancelot, recently dubbed, suddenly finds himself at the castle of Douloureuse Garde, standing before his own empty tomb (VII, 331–32). If we compare the effect of this scene with that of its equivalent in Chrétien's romance (ll. 1855–1936), the difference is apparent only on the level of the overall structure: it seems to derive from the fact that the scene, which is not unique in the Prose *Lancelot*, is incorporated into a system of anticipations and flashbacks. Thanks both to the systematic use of some traditional narrative procedures and also to the conjoining of different models of writing, each with its own temporal dimensions, within a single work, the anonymous author of the *Lancelot* succeeds in creating original effects.

From one end of the story to the other, the narrator maintains or even intensifies the uneasiness generated by death threats, at first veiled and indistinct, then more and more specific—an effect that neither the verse romances nor the narratives attributed to Robert de Boron could produce. Striking images recurring quite regularly permit the creation of moments of terror that give the characters a presentiment of what time holds in store. These images, whose structure demonstrates a remarkable constancy in human imagination, are related to dreams or mysterious spectacles directed by someone whose identity can only be divined. Lost hair and fingers in Arthur's dream, to which Galehaut's dream corresponds with its image of a tree suddenly losing its flowers and leaves; a serpent first attacked by a leopard, then giving birth to young ones that kill it, in a scene that is precisely repeated in the Palace of Adventures; a serpent burning half of Galehaut's body in another dream; the leopard removing the boards of the bridge that Galehaut must cross, or the enormous arm unattached to any body, holding a sword that makes the months and years of the character's life vanish—all these are images of death, all are warnings sent on supreme authority.[25]

However, by continually evoking the eschatological dimension, the work also sends other messages as well, promising the advent of that one who will abolish nightmares and conquer death. At Corbenic, which is the secret center of the narrative and the source of its meaning, everything converges, everything can be encompassed within a single experience—serpents killing one another, a harpist martyred by snakes, and that healing light that is the Grail, which fortifies the soul, restores courage and confidence, and inspires hope for a victory over death.

NOTES

1. *Lancelot: Roman en prose du XIIIe siècle*, ed. Alexandre Micha, 9 vols. (Geneva: Droz, 1978–83), V, 52.

2. The intertext is both vague and rich. Evoked here are not only the story of Aeneas, but also all the passages from verse romances that present art objects representing illustrious stories (including that of Aeneas). For example, see Chrétien de Troyes, *Erec et Enide*, ed. Mario Roques (ll. 5290–98); *Floire et Blancheflor*, ed. J.-L. Leclanche (ll. 441–512); *Athis et Prophilias*, ed. A. Hilka (ll. 5581–6056); Jean Renart, *L'Escoufle*, ed. Franklin Sweetser (ll. 579–618).

3. See Paul Ricoeur, *Temps et récit*, 3 vols. (Paris: Seuil, 1986, 1991), especially the chapter "La mise en intrigue," I, 66–104.

4. *Lancelot*, II, 28. And see Chrétien de Troyes, *Le Chevalier de la Charrete*, ed. Mario Roques (Paris: Champion, 1970), ll. 1424–1442.

5. Chrétien de Troyes, *Le Roman de Perceval ou le Conte du Graal*, ed. William Roach (Geneva: Droz, 1959), ll. 4162–4461.

6. "Et quant il avoit grant piece dementé et plaint sa mescheance, si revenoit as ymages et les baisoit et lor faisoit la greignor honor que il pooit et ainsi se reconfortoit par lui meismes, et ce estoit la chose qui plus li avenoit" ("And when he had lamented his misfortune for some time, he returned to the images and kissed them and showed them full honor, and thus he comforted himself, and that was the thing that pleased him most," *Lancelot*, V, 61).

7. In this regard Galehaut's words are typical: "Certes, sire, mescheances ne me commencent ore mie, si sui je li chevaliers el monde a cui greignors cheances ont esté, et il est des ore mes bien raison que il me meschiece, qu'il ne me puet plus bien chaoir qu'il a fet: kar Diex fist ja un jor tant por moi qu'il me dona ce que je voloie;

et qui a quanque il velt, il ne puet plus gaaignier, mais il puet perdre: et je sui a la perte entrés" ("Certainly, sir, misfortune has not yet begun for me, and I am the most fortunate knight in the world, and it is reasonable that misfortune should now befall me; for God was once so good to me that he gave me what I wanted, and whoever has what he wants has nothing left to gain, but can only lose, and I have begun to lose," *Lancelot*, I, 6). For other examples, see *Lancelot*, VII, 11–12, 22–25; VII, 196; VII, 434; VIII, 13; II, 2; II, 99; V, 122; VI, 60–61; VI, 165; VI, 178; VI, 183–184.

8. *La Mort le Roi Artu: Roman du XIIIe siècle*, ed. Jean Frappier (Geneva: Droz, 1964), pp. 226–227.

9. The second voyage to Sorelois (*Lancelot*, I, 9ff.).

10. Here is how the narrator summarizes the consequences of what Galehaut experiences as a thunderbolt, a sudden reversal if ever there was one: "Mais nule dolor ne s'apareille a ce que Galehout sueffre, kar il avoit mis en l'amor Lancelot tot ce que hom i pooit metre, cuer et cors, et tote honor, qui miels valt. Il li avoit si doné son cors qu'il amast miels a veoir sa mort que la Lancelot; il li avoit si doné son cuer, la ou il ne pooit avoir joie sans lui. Et por lui fist il si grant amor qu'il cria merci le roi Artu, et si l'avoit il torné a desconfiture et approché d'estre deserités" ("But no sorrow can compare to the one Galehaut experienced, for he had given to Lancelot everything a man could give in love: his body and heart, and all his honor, which is worth even more. He had so given him his body that he would have preferred his own death to Lancelot's; he had so given him his heart that he could not experience any pleasure without Lancelot. And for him, he had such great love that he had begged King Arthur for mercy, even though he had overcome and almost disinherited him," *Lancelot*, I, 3). Not only does Galehaut feel this tension, but he also manages to communicate the gist of it to Lancelot: "Ha, Diex, fet il a soi meismes, tant me devroit cist hom haïr, que totes ces choses li ai je destornées a fere!" ("Oh, God," he said to himself, "this man ought to hate me, for I have stopped him from doing all these things," *Lancelot*, I, 10).

11. Ricoeur, II, 46–47. The Bible "is the grandiose plot [*intrigue*] of world history." Each literary plot is "a kind of miniature replica of the great intrigue that connects the Apocalypse to Genesis. . . . Thus the eschatological myth and the Aristotelian *muthos* are related by their way of linking a beginning to an end and of suggesting to the imagination the triumph of concord over discord."

12. R. Howard Bloch, *Etymologies and Genealogies: A Literary Anthropology of the French Middle Ages* (Chicago: University of Chicago Press, 1983).

13. Robert de Boron, *Le Roman du graal: Manuscrit de Modène*, ed. Bernard Cerquiglini (Paris: Union Générale d'Éditions, 1981).

14. *Le Roman de l'Estoire dou Graal*, ed. W.A. Nitze (Paris: Champion, 1927).

15. This is a promise made to Blaise by Merlin as a reward for his writing: "Je t'enseignerai quel loier tu en avras: a ta vie acomplissement de ton cuer et aprés la fin joie pardurable" ("I'll tell you what reward you will have: fulfillment in your heart at the end of your life and eternal joy thereafter," *Le Roman du Graal*, p. 119).

16. Ed. W.A. Nitze and T.A. Jenkins, 2 vols. (Chicago: University of Chicago Press, 1932–37).

17. *Vieillesse de Perceval: l'ombre du temps*, in *Le Nombre du temps, en hommage à Paul Zumthor* (Paris, 1988), pp. 285–94.

18. See *Lancelot*, I, p. 1; II, pp. 11, 255; IV, pp. 248, 393–398; VI, pp. 53–54, 192; *Queste*, pp. 279–280; *La Mort Artu*, pp. 1–2.

19. Albert Pauphilet, ed., *La Queste del Saint Graal* (Paris: Champion, 1923), pp. 277–78.

20. Among the definitions of eternity are *pardurable clarté* and *siecles pardurables*; see *Lancelot*, VII, 24 and VIII, 24.

21. *À la recherche d'une poétique médiévale* (Paris: Nizet, 1970).

22. For example, see *Lancelot*, VII, 336; I, 55, 57, 86; II, 212, 338, 376; IV, 274, 290; V, 114–20.

23. *Lancelot*, VI, 157; IV, 251; VII, 38; V, 82; VII, 11; VII, 255.

24. Most often, some material presence, some objective form of the past (tomb, chapel, crown, broken sword, etc.), occurs at the threshold of these returns through time. That object inevitably compresses the links between the past and the present of the character's experience, as does the fact that past and present often occur in the identical space. (This compression is further reinforced by the role of old people, living links who are witnesses and interpreters.) On this subject, we refer only to the episode in which Boort asks a hermit for hospitality. Near the hermitage is a chapel, whose history the hermit tells to Boort: ". . . je fui moult longuement sergent vostre pere et chevalier me fist il de sa main et ceste chapele et cest porpris fist il fere, si com vos le veez, a son vivant, et une grant coronne d'or que est çaianz i dona il por une grant honor que Nostre Sires li fist en ceste place meismes . . . " ("I was long your father's servant, and he himself knighted me, and during his life he had this chapel and its surroundings made, as you see it, and he donated a fine gold crown that is therein, in gratitude for a great honor that Our Lord did him in this very place"). In his narrative, the witness underlines yet again the identity of the space: "A l'andemain a ore de prime furent assamblé li .II. roi *en ceste place ou nos somes orandroit* . . . " ("The following day at the hour of prime, the two kings were *in this place where we are right now*" [emphasis added]). See *Lancelot*, IV, 273, 276.

25. See *Lancelot*, VII, 434–35; I, 358–59; II, 380–81 and V, 263–65; I, 7; I, 47–48; I, 65–70.

THE ARTHURIAN REFERENCES IN PIERRE DE LANGTOFT'S *CHRONICLE*

Thea Summerfield

In a famous article published in 1953, R.S. Loomis[1] draws attention to the frequent comparisons between King Edward I and King Arthur in medieval literature. In one work in particular, the Anglo-Norman verse *Chronicle* written by Pierre de Langtoft toward the end of Edward's reign, such comparisons are strikingly frequent. Loomis (125–26) lists the Arthurian references in this work to prove his point that contemporary, Edwardian authors were in the habit of associating Edward with King Arthur, an association that Edward himself had furthered by his well-known interest in Arthuriana. Curiously enough, however, not all the comparisons in Langtoft's *Chronicle* are flattering for Edward: some are used to point out that Edward falls short of his illustrious legendary ancestor in certain respects. Loomis concentrates in his article on the part of Langtoft's *Chronicle* that deals with the reign of Edward I; as a result the possible significance of a number of Arthurian references in the preceding part of the work has been not taken into account. Leaving aside the question of whether Edward I was exceptional in his interest in Arthurian matter, or whether such an interest was part of "the common currency of the knightly culture of the day,"[2] the references to King Arthur and his knights of the Round Table in Langtoft's *Chronicle* deserve closer scrutiny.[3]

Langtoft's *Chronicle* has generally been regarded as either an unattractive literary work or, as far as the section on the reign of Edward I is concerned, as a source of historical information. However, if the *Chronicle* is regarded as a work that both was generated by the political realities prevailing at the time of writing and was seeking to influence those realities, the work as a whole can be seen to be a coherent, well-designed construct.[4] In this article I shall show that the various references to Arthur in Langtoft's *Chronicle* are an integral part of the design and serve structural and thematic functions. More specifically they are used as markers or signposts to parts of the *Chronicle* that are especially significant with respect to the work's message and purpose. After analyzing Langtoft's use of Arthur to shape his historiographical narrative and, in doing so, to respond to and seek to influence the events of his own time, I will consider briefly Langtoft's use of Arthurian material in an earlier work and the possible connection between his career and his historical interests.

Langtoft's account of the reign of Edward I is often considered as a separate, independent part of his *Chronicle* on which modern scholarship has imposed a tripartite plan.[5] However, there is no justification for such a division. Langtoft himself divides the work into two parts. He marks the end of part I on British history by an *explicit* in which he refers to his Latin source, Geoffrey of Monmouth's *Historia regum Britanniae* (hereafter *HRB*). He then continues with a Latin *incipit* announcing that next he will deal with the "gesta quae sunt Anglis manifesta."[6] This second, or English, part recounts events from Cadwallader to the death of Edward I in 1307, for which a large number of Latin sources were used.[7] The large majority of Langtoft manuscripts show no division of any kind between the reign of Henry III and that of Edward I,[8] while the narrative also continues seamlessly from Edward's return from the Holy Land after his father's death to his coronation and reign. To impose an arbitrary division after the death of Henry III leads to a distorted view of what Langtoft has set out to do. I shall be concerned, therefore, with the whole *Chronicle*: dealing as it does with rulers and events from, roughly, 1300 B.C. to A.D. 1307, organized chronologically and compressed into about nine thousand lines of Anglo-Norman verse.

To focus attention on certain episodes in this mass of material, Langtoft employs a number of devices to highlight particular rulers or particular events. One might say that he uses several different spotlights to pick out, on the stage of history, those episodes to which he attaches a particular significance. Such a "spotlight" can take various forms: there is the simple structural device of the length at which an episode is recounted, as well as a number of thematic devices, such as recurring references throughout the *Chronicle* to the affairs of the bishops of Durham and to a particular triad of saints, references to Arthurian material, and changes of rhyme, metre, and even language. Let us have a closer look at what these "spotlights" consist of before investigating their function in the *Chronicle*.

First, a lack of correlation can be observed throughout Langtoft's *Chronicle* between the actual length of any given reign and the space allotted to it. The length at which the reign of a particular king is described is proportionate to his importance in the eyes of the chronicler rather than to the length of that king's actual reign. Thus, as in the *HRB*, Arthur's reign is described at length in the history of the Britons, whereas in the *gesta anglorum* part of the *Chronicle*, it is the reigns of William the Conqueror, Richard I, and Edward I that are treated extensively. By comparison the reigns of Henry II and particularly Henry III, both of whom reigned longer than any of the three kings just mentioned, are dealt with very briefly; the account of Henry III's reign of fifty-six years is devoted mostly to the exploits of his son, the future Edward I; Henry's own acts are discussed in a mere twenty-four lines. There is also considerable variation within a particular reign: in the reign of Edward I the years 1294–98 are dealt with in much more detail than the earlier or later years of the reign.[9] It is important to recognize the effect of the distribution of material in the *Chronicle*, as Langtoft has often been regarded as someone who recorded events dispassionately in his *Chronicle*, either as he found them in his sources or as they happened in his own time; in fact he can be seen to be no less manipulative than Geoffrey of Monmouth when the latter made Arthur his chief protagonist.

Second, references are found throughout the *Chronicle* to the affairs and the history of the bishops of Durham. It usually concerns gifts or privileges given by the king to the see of Durham, often in connection with the struggle against the Scots. William the Conqueror, Richard, and Edward are all associated explicitly with Durham; indeed, as we shall see, the bishop of Durham in Edward's reign is presented as playing an instrumental role in the fulfillment of the king's ambitions. Apart from the references to Durham, there are three saints who put in appearances regularly throughout the *Chronicle*: St. John of Beverley, St. Cuthbert, and St. Thomas Becket. They are much in evidence as a triad in the reign of Edward I.

Then there is another set of recurring references in the *Chronicle* concerning King Arthur, his knights, and his prophet Merlin. In the part on British history, these take the form of Merlin's prophecies and a few small but remarkable alterations in the description of Arthur as compared to the *HRB*, Langtoft's source. In the *gesta anglorum*, there are references to Arthur in connection with William the Conqueror and Richard I; moreover, as has been said, there are a large number of references of varying content in the part on Edward I, the last one of which has to do not with Edward I but with the later Edward II. A final spotlight is used exclusively in the years 1294–98 in the reign of Edward I, with which Langtoft seems particularly concerned; here the Anglo-Norman laisses of the *Chronicle* are interrupted frequently by tail-rhyme stanzas, also in Anglo-Norman, which occasionally merge with tail-rhyme stanzas in English that have all the appearance of having been picked up in the street or army camps.[10]

What we see, then, is that in this long *Chronicle*, which deals with well over a hundred kings, a number of reigns stand out by the length and detail in which they are depicted, while these same reigns are connected by a web of references: to Durham, to the saintly triad, to Arthur. In other words the spotlights tend to converge, picking out especially the reigns of William the Conqueror, Richard I, and Edward I. Having established the general principle at work, we must now examine the various references in detail to establish to what end they have been used. I shall show that they are vibrant with allusions to affairs that were of great concern to Langtoft's patron and the addressee of the work—contemporary concerns therefore. For this reason it will be best to begin with the part of the *Chronicle* that deals with nearly contemporary history: Edward's reign and, within that reign, the years 1294–98.

Langtoft describes in considerable detail the circumstances surrounding the loss of Gascony in 1294 and the delay in the reestablishment of English rule there caused by a rising in Wales. In 1296 John Balliol renounces his homage to Edward I, the terms of which Langtoft incorporated into his *Chronicle*,[11] and war breaks out between England and Scotland. The Scots are massacred at Berwick and at Dunbar; John Balliol and his son are imprisoned in the Tower of London on suspicion of conspiring with the King of France to invade England from two directions at once, and Edward assumes control of Scotland direct.

In this part of the *Chronicle*, Langtoft turns all the spotlights on the historical scene to reveal a setting in which he is clearly emotionally involved. There is a good deal of authorial comment here, some of it as part of the tail-rhyme songs. Violently opposed to both Welsh and Scots,[12] but especially the latter, Langtoft gloatingly wallows in the bloodshed of the battlefield, so long as it is the Scots whose corpses are pecked at by ravens and whose souls go straight to the devil (II, 250:1–10; Th.968–77). The audience is told emphatically that Gascony was lost because the crucial decision was taken in the bishop of Durham's absence (II, 198:21–22, II, 200:16–204:15; Th.349–50, 369–416); the establishment of English rule in Scotland, on the other hand, is due entirely to the indispensable efforts of the bishop of Durham:

> Le eveske de Dureme, ke molt fet à loer,
> En conqueraunt la terre fut tuz jurs le primer;
> Ne fussent ses emprises et hardiement de quer,
> Choses ore chevyes serraint à comencer
> (II, 260:17–20; Th 1115–18)

[The bishop of Durham, who did much to deserve praise, / In conquering the land was always the first; / Were it not his energy and boldness of heart, / Things now completed would be to begin.]

These lines are followed, first, by an Anglo-Norman tail-rhyme song justifying Edward's wars and the removal of the coronation stone from Scone to Westminster and, then, by a jubilant *laisse* in which Langtoft proceeds to tell his audience that now, at last, one realm has been made of two kingdoms, just as Merlin had prophesied, as a result of which Edward even exceeds King Arthur. He adds a program for the future: all Edward needs to do now is go to France to conquer his inheritance, i.e., Gascony, and then go on crusade:

> Ha, Deus! Ke Merlyn dist sovent veritez
> En ses prophecyes, [si]cum ws les lisez!
> Ore sunt les ij. ewes en un aryvez,
> Ke par graunz mountaynes ount esté severez;
> Et une realme fet de [deus] diverse regnez
> Ke solaint par deus rays estre governez.
> Ore sunt les insulanes trestuz assemblez,
> Et Albanye rejoynte à les regaltez
> Des quels li rays Eduuard est seygnur clamez.
> Cornewaylle et Wales sunt en ses poustez,
> Et Irelaunde la graunde à ses voluntez.
> Rays n'y ad ne prince de tuz les countrez
> Fors le ray Eduuard, ke ensi les ad joustez;
> Arthur ne avayt unkes si plainement les fez.
> Desore n'y ad ke fere for purver ses alez
> Sur li ray de Fraunce, conquere ses heritez,
> Et pus porter la croyce où Jhesu Cryst fu nez
> (II, 264:16–266:6; Th.1161–77)

> [Ah, God! how often Merlin said truth
> In his prophecies, if you read them!
> Now are the two waters united in one,
> Which have been separated by great mountains;
> And one realm made of two different kingdoms
> Which used to be governed by two kings.
> Now are the islanders all joined together,
> And Albany reunited to the royalties

Of which King Edward is proclaimed lord.
Cornwall and Wales are in his power,
And Ireland the great at his will.
There is neither king nor prince of all the countries
Except king Edward, who has thus united them;
Arthur had never the fiefs so fully.
Henceforward there is nothing to do but provide his expedition
Against the king of France, to conquer his inheritances
And then bear the cross where Jesus Christ was born.]

This *laisse* is in its turn followed by another tail-rhyme song, still in Anglo-Norman, which repeats that Edward has defeated his enemies; he should now cross the Channel to fight the king of France, "*li faus Phelippe de France*"; Saints John, Thomas, and Cuthbert will help him to unite the three regions under one king, just as Merlin prophesied. Thus to give weight to his justification of Edward's claim to Scotland, Langtoft brings to bear in this episode, which is remarkable not only for its length but also for the changes of rhyme and metre, the bishop of Durham, all three recurring saints, and King Arthur and Merlin. Edward, then, has fulfilled the prophecies; he has the whole island under his rule, and in doing so he has surpassed the ultimate historical model, King Arthur. But it should not be forgotten that the bishop of Durham was instrumental in bringing this about and that future success is assured because of the help of the three saints. The references to Durham, the saints, King Arthur, and the literary technicalities (length, change of rhyme, metre, and language) serve to highlight this episode in Edward's reign, while at the same time presenting events in such a way that they display a double orientation, a double perspective: it would seem that the author consciously aimed to please Durham and Westminster at the same time.

From the beginning Langtoft had prepared the audience for this justification of Edward's territorial ambitions. The reference to Merlin's prophecies at the beginning of the jubilant *laisse* refers back to the early part of the *Chronicle* where Langtoft states explicitly that Merlin's prophecies on the unification of England and Scotland have been appended as a separate entity in Latin and should be regarded as an integral part of the *Chronicle*: "Le Latyn est escriz de sa prophecye / En la fin del livre, ke l'em ne oblye" ("The Latin of his prophecy is written/ At the end of this book, that it may not be forgotten," I, 114: 18–19).[13] Merlin's prophecy is in fact already a reiteration of an earlier prophecy, also in Latin, by the goddess Diana. The recipient in that case was not Arthur but Brutus. The content of the two prophecies is the same: all Britain, that is, the island surrounded on all sides by the sea, will one day be united under one king. The use of Latin in the midst of the Anglo-Norman of the *Chronicle* not only draws attention to the prophecies but also enhances both the mystery surrounding prophecies and their prestige. By means of these prophecies, Edward's claim to Scotland is elaborately justified. The claim to Gascony, too, is made legitimate by an appeal to history: Langtoft's audience is reminded that Arthur gave this region to Sir Bedivere, his butler, after his coronation: "... le ray Phelippe et ... les xii. pers, / Ke à tort se deforcent la terre of les maners / Ke ly rays Arthur al duk sire Beduers / Donait en Aquitayne, cum à si botellers" ("... King Philip and ... the twelve peers / who wrongfully hold from him the land with the manors / which king Arthur to the duke sir Beduer / Gave in Aquitane, as to his butler," II, 278:25–280:2; Th.1342–45).[14]

A juxtaposition of references to Durham, Cuthbert, and Arthur is also found in Langtoft's description of William the Conqueror, resulting again in a double perspective. Much of the description of the reign of William I is designed to show that William had every right to the English crown, that he was a successor not by might but by right. To this end Langtoft describes in detail the relationship between Harold and William and their agreements prior to Edward the Confessor's death. It is also made quite plain that Harold, although brave and indefatigable, could not have won the Battle of Hastings, having broken his oath to William. As Langtoft shows elsewhere in the *Chronicle* a strong antipathy to everything coming from the continent, his tone here is often ambivalent, veering between regret, resignation, and justification. This changes with the coronation, when all doubts seem to be forgotten; the splendour of the occasion is emphasized and William is crowned with the crown that had once belonged to Arthur, the noble ancestor: "De Everwyk Aldrede, eveske et confessour, / Ly dona la coroune, ke fust à l'ancessour / Ly bon rays Arthur, de ly ne fu melliour" ("Aldred of York, bishop and confessor, / Gave him the crown which belonged to the ancestor / The good king Arthur, there was no better than he," I, 410:16–18).

Again the reader or listener has been prepared for this emphasis on the crown used. In his earlier account of Arthur's coronation, Langtoft had added to the description in the *HRB* that Arthur's crown was made of gold: "De or fu la corone ke porter beayt" ("Of gold was the crown which he desired to wear," I, 168:11).[15] This seemingly arbitrary, even commonplace addition gains significance by the later explicit statement that it is Arthur's crown that was used at William's coronation. Langtoft was probably referring here to the crown that was presented to Edward at Nefyn in Wales in 1284. It was said to be Arthur's crown and was a Welsh national treasure. Edward, recognizing "the preempting of Arthurian legend as politically expedient," carried it to Westminster as a token of Welsh subjugation in the same way that he later carried the Stone of Scone to Westminster (Loomis, 117).[16]

After the coronation William's swift and ruthless conquest is described by Langtoft. And again the bishop of Durham is presented in a striking manner: it is as a result of the bishop's timely warning that William is successful in quelling a rising in the North of disaffected Northerners and Scots. William's cruelty is deplored, but forgiven when he shows himself suitably repentant, not only by his generosity, but also by crying hot tears at St. Cuthbert's shrine (I, 424:18–426:3). As far as I know, both William's tearful repentance at Durham and the use of Arthur's crown for his coronation are unique to Langtoft.[17]

If Edward and William can be shown to have benefited from the assistance of different bishops of Durham, especially in the struggle against the Scots, this is not the case with Richard I; yet this king too is connected with both Arthur and Durham in a way that reveals both Langtoft's careful preparation and contemporary resonances of the references. Richard is described as being the possessor of Arthur's sword Excalibur, a sword that is mentioned frequently by name by Langtoft in interpolations to the *HRB*.[18] Richard is presented by Langtoft as an ideal king who goes to the Holy Land at his own expense. The *Chronicle* states explicitly that one possession that Richard sells to finance his expedition is the wapentake of Sadberge, which is bought by the bishop of Durham. We have again a reference to contemporary affairs here: Sadberge, an important possession still owned by the bishop of Durham in Edward's reign, was in danger of being seized by the Crown in the spring of 1307. The bishop's councilors argued in a petition that Sadberge was a "purchase from the king's ancestors" and separate, therefore, from the royal franchise of the bishopric, the administration of which Edward had taken into his own hands in 1305.[19] The reference of the sale of Sadberge to the bishop of Durham by Richard also served, therefore, as a legitimation of territorial ambitions—those of the bishop of Durham. Here, as elsewhere, Langtoft shows a double perspective, oriented toward both Westminster and Durham.

The Arthurian references investigated so far can be seen to form part of a pattern by which William I, Richard, and Edward are linked. Edward is placed in a continuous, unbroken chain of rulers stretching back beyond the exemplary crusader-king Richard I, to William I, emphatically presented as a legitimate successor, to King Arthur himself. Thus, as R. Howard Bloch puts it, is power "legitimated through recourse to origins."[20] The Arthurian references also serve to legitimize Edward's claim to Scotland and Gascony through prophecy and legendary history. Through the references to Durham, which are so closely bound up with the Arthurian references, history is made to provide examples of the successful cooperation between Durham and Westminster from a "national" perspective, especially in so far as the Scots are concerned. The references both to the distant past and to the more recent past of Edward's reign reverberate with allusions to contemporary affairs.

In the instances examined so far, the Arthurian references can still very well be interpreted as having been incorporated not only to refer implicitly to matters well-known to the intended audience, but also to please King Edward I. However, there remain a number of references that may not have pleased the King.

In an episode relating how in Gascony the English army is lured into an ambush by a spy, which results in the death of many noblemen, a list is given of great classical, biblical, British, and English rulers who have lost all they had as a result of sinful behavior. Arthur figures in this list as the king who lost all through treachery: "Et li rays Arthur surpris par tricherye, / Et Modred demaglé pur sa reverye" ("And King Arthur surprised through treachery, / And Modred slaughtered through his madness," II, 284:3–4; Th.1391–92). "Allas!" exclaims Langtoft, "ke nul homme par altre se chastye!" ("Alas! that no man corrects himself by the example of another!" II, 284:15; Th.1403). He then proceeds to apostrophize Edward, urging him to be reconciled with the church and the clergy, a course of action that will be rewarded by the continued and indispensable aid of the three saints; Thomas, John, and Cuthbert (II, 284:20–286:1; Th.1408–12).

After this, with a reference to *gestes anciens*, the conditions are outlined that for Arthur ensured continued support: by generously sharing out the profits of war, he was obeyed by one and all.[21] Edward, Langtoft points out immediately, has not been so generous, and it is owing to this fault that the earls and barons have refused to follow him to Flanders:

> Ly rays sir Eduuard ad doné trop petyt;
> Par quai à sun aler, quant en mer se myst
> Vers ly roys de Fraunce, fet ly fu despit,
> Ke nes un de ses countes of ly le aler emprist.
> (II, 296:19–22; Th.1540–43)

> [The king Sir Edward has given too little;
> Whereby at his departure, when he put to sea
> Against the king of France, the affront was shown him
> That not one of his earls undertook the expedition.]

To make matters worse, as Langtoft points out, the Scots, sensing the lack of unity in the opposite camp, attack: "La comune de Escoz la novele oyst . . . la route de raskaylle la guere renoue reprist" ("The commonalty of Scotland hears the news . . . the rabble of the lower people resumed war anew," II, 296:23–25; Th.1544–46). Such a direct cause-and-effect treatment of discord and resulting Scottish raids and of unity leading to the defeat of the Scots can be found everywhere in the *Chronicle*.[22]

These Arthurian references, then, are not meant to legitimize Edward's territorial claims, but serve as warnings: the illustrious ancestor was so successful because he behaved as kings should behave. Arthur is held up as a model—a model of which Edward falls short. When, finally, Langtoft laments Edward's death, it is as a king in the Arthurian tradition, but not as the king who surpassed Arthur: "De chevalerye, après ly reis Arthure, / Estait ly reis Edward des Cristiens la flure" (II, 380:7–8; Th.2561–62)—Edward was the flower of all Christians *after* Arthur. Whether *après* is taken as referring to rank or time (both are possible), a sentiment is expressed here that is quite different from the earlier exultation that, compared to Edward's achievements, Arthur's fall short: "Arthur ne avayt unkes si plainement les fez" (II, 266:3; Th.1174). Apart from the sudden critical note that enters the *Chronicle* here, the absence of any further reference to Bishop Bek—still alive and still a force to be reckoned with—is striking. The question that suggests itself is why this note of criticism has been introduced and whether the coincidental disappearance of the bishop from the pages of the *Chronicle* is significant. The answer is closely bound up with the question of patronage and with the relationship between Edward I, Anthony Bek, bishop of Durham, and Edward of Caernarvon, the later Edward II.

As I have argued elsewhere,[23] there is every reason to believe that Langtoft wrote his *Chronicle* at the request of Anthony Bek, the bishop of Durham in Edward's reign. The request probably reached him through John of Sheffield, who is named in one manuscript, B.L. Cotton Julius A.V. Sheffield was appointed sheriff of Northumberland in 1305. He was a staunch supporter of the bishop at a time when Anthony Bek and the king were involved in a lengthy, practically insoluble controversy after a friendship, both on a personal and an official level, of over thirty years.[24] From 1305 onward measures to curb the bishop's enormous power in the North increased in severity, culminating in Edward's preparations for the confiscation of the bishop's temporalities. Although Sheffield did all he could to shield the bishop from the king's wrath, incurring fines and the king's displeasure in the process,[25] he could not have delayed the measures indefinitely. Edward's death on 7 July 1307 gave Bek the reprieve he needed, as well as a second chance to play once again the prominent political role he had played in the past.

Anthony Bek had been closely associated all his life not only with Edward I, but also with Edward's son, Edward of Caernarvon. He had kept an eye on the young crown prince in the king's absence, later he had on occasion pleaded the young man's cause in the many disputes between him and his father. After the old king's death, Bek regained his old place—at the king's side—as well as his possessions and did all he could to stem the tide of discontent that threatened to flood the country within months of Edward's accession.[26] Bek maintained this position until his death in 1311.

If Sheffield was involved with the *Chronicle* from the start, writing is not likely to have started until his appointment as sheriff of Northumberland on 8 April 1305. By this time Bek and Edward were severely embroiled. As has been shown, a distinct double perspective can be detected in the *Chronicle*, an orientation toward Westminster and Durham at the same time. Yet where Westminster was concerned, some adaptation may have been necessary in the course of writing. The *Chronicle* was probably meant at the outset for Edward I; however, toward the end of the *Chronicle*, it would seem that the addressee was changed silently from Edward I to the future Edward II. Perhaps Bek despaired of ever finding Edward I favorably disposed enough to receive a chronicle, as he had earlier presented him with a luxurious Bible;[27] perhaps he sensed that Edward, who had been ill for some years, would not live; or perhaps the old king simply died before the work was completed. The change of addressee enabled Langtoft to be more openly critical. (There is, I should add, a good deal more criticism than is apparent from the Arthurian references alone.[28]) But major changes did not have to be made, for the political priorities remained exactly the same. France and Scotland had to be fought, and domestic discord had to be avoided in order to be able to do so.

In Langtoft's *Chronicle* the point is made that the king of England is justified in his territorial ambitions, that he is part of a long line of legitimate rulers, stretching beyond the Norman Conquest, but that his ambitions can be realized only by using generosity and reconciliation to avoid discord. In this way the *Chronicle* served the king's cause and preoccupations as well as the bishop's: not only was Bek passionately and sincerely concerned for the welfare and prestige of his country, which could be achieved only by solving existing conflicts, he was also faced with the threatened confiscation of his temporalities. The *Chronicle* also argues implicitly, by the sustained emphasis on the beneficial effects of the successful cooperation between the bishop of Durham and the king, both in the recent and in the distant past, that being reconciled with Bek would result in success in the struggle against the Scots for the English king, success that had so signally been wanting since the beginning of the conflict between the two great men, as the *Chronicle* showed: with the disappearance of the bishop from its pages, the once-established union between England and Scotland is lost.

Edward I was convinced of the need to gain God's approval and aid for his campaigns through the prayers of the clergy. From 1294 onward the King ordered prayers to be said on his behalf throughout the country whenever he went to Scotland or overseas. As the archbishop of York wrote in 1301 and 1303, "the king's affairs would have a more prosperous outcome when they were entrusted to God."[29] If Bishop Bek were reinstated, this might be expected to result also in the assistance of the three saints who are invoked all through the *Chronicle*. This triad of saints reflects accurately the double perspective of the *Chronicle* as well as its main preoccupation, consisting as it does of northerly Durham-based St. Cuthbert; southerly St. Thomas, closely associated with the English kings; and a saint specifically associated with victory over the Scots in battle, St. John of Beverley.[30] Langtoft points out explicitly that the king needs the bishop also where it concerns the saints' assistance, because ". . . si tu n'as de Deu ayde en longanye, / Pur kant ke tu fras ne doray un alye" ("if thou hast not aid of God in the struggle, / For all thou wilt do I would not give a garlic," II, 286:21–288:1; Th.1411–12).

If this message seems tailored to fit Edward I, it was just as relevant to the bishop's young friend, the Prince of Wales, who is never mentioned in the *Chronicle* without the addition of prayer being attached to his name. He too is drawn into the chain of Arthurian references, by having his knighting ceremony compared to the festivities after Arthur's coronation:

Unkes en Bretaygne puys qe Dieu fu nez
N'estoyt tel nobleye en viles n'en citez,
Forpris Karleoun en antiquitez,
Qaunt sire Arthur luy reis i fust corounez.
(II, 368:20–23; Th.2424–27)

[Never in Britain, since God was born,
was there such nobleness in towns nor in cities,
Except [in] Caerleon in ancient times
When sir Arthur the king was crowned there.]

In this way Edward of Caernarvon too is linked in the *Chronicle* with illustrious ancestors, all of whom are associated with Arthur: his father, who was at first so successful thanks to the bishop of Durham's efforts, but was so unwise as to alienate the bishop; Richard I, the king who like Edward and Bek had been to the Holy Land; William the Conqueror, a legitimate ruler, in whose wake Bek's ancestors had come to England, a matter on which, although false, the bishop's family prided itself,[31] and then, beyond, to Arthur and even Brutus, to both of whom the unification of Britain under one king had been prophesied.

The use of references to King Arthur in historical works was neither new nor unusual, of course, by the time Langtoft wrote his *Chronicle*. Such references were used for a number of purposes: to enhance the glamor of a particular occasion, as a tribute to Edward I,[32] or to support territorial claims.[33] Indeed Arthur and Merlin were freely used by opposing sides in such disputes.[34] References to Arthurian legends or prophecies uttered by Merlin were taken extremely seriously, and their use was not limited to historiographical or literary works: they are also featured in official documents, such as the exchange of letters between Pope Boniface VIII and Edward I on the subject of the overlordship of Scotland.[35] Whether Langtoft had anything to do with the original Latin correspondence cannot be ascertained; he did however make an Anglo-Norman rhymed version of this exchange of letters.[36]

In 1301 Edward replied to Boniface's bull *Scimus fili*, which had questioned his right to Scotland, by providing historical examples of English rule over Scotland. He based himself on the evidence accumulated in 1291, when a successor for Alexander III had to be chosen from more than a dozen candidates.[37] At that time a large number of religious houses, Langtoft's priory at Bridlington among them, had been asked to supply from their archives any records pertaining to the question of the succession, to be sent to Bishop Bek's castle at Norham, where the question was to be decided in a large conference.[38] This evidence went back to the reign of Edward the Elder. In Edward's letter to the pope this information was supplemented by historical evidence for the earlier years, derived from the *HRB*, and subtly reshaped to suit the king's purpose.[39] The letter also supplied emotive information on the destruction wrought by the Scots in the North as a further justification for Balliol's imprisonment.[40] A similar, much shorter letter was sent by a number of barons and earls. This letter also made an appeal to history, albeit a much more cursory one, and does not refer to Arthur.

Langtoft made a rhymed version of this correspondence, including the papal bull, the reply sent by Edward, and the barons' letter, staying on the whole very close to the original text. There are a number of additions, mainly assertions of veracity stating that a particular claim has been substantiated in true writing,[41] as well as the kind of violent anti-Scots coloring that is also such a typical trait of the *Chronicle*.[42] Nevertheless, the main argument remains unchanged: Edward's right to Scotland was established in the distant past when King Augusele carried Arthur's sword for the service of Scotland:

> Le rei Auguisele l'espeie Arthur porteit,
> Pur le service d'Escoce, qe à li deveit.
> Puis cel houre en sceà le reis de Albanie
> Unt touz esté suget au reis de Bretanie. (App. I, 406:4–7)

> [King Auguisele carried Arthur's sword,
> For the service of Scotland, which he owed to him.
> Since that time to the present the kings of Scotland
> Have all been subject to the king of Britain.]

It is not known where Langtoft first came into contact with legitimizing claims from Arthurian and later history; it may have been in his priory at Bridlington in response to Edward's request for documents; it is also possible that he picked up his interest in such matters when working in the royal chancery at Westminster. M.D. Legge, who put together some information from the archives concerning Langtoft, found that in 1293 he was absent without leave from Bridlington Priory, and "in Southern parts" (Legge, *Cloisters*, 70). If he did find work in the chancery in the 1290s, he may even have met John of Sheffield there.[43] Although this is largely speculative, a man of Langtoft's training and abilities would certainly not have been exceptional in exchanging a northern religious house, at least temporarily, for work in the chancery. In fact both Langtoft and Sheffield may well have formed part of a "remarkable inflow of Yorkshiremen and northerners in general" into the civil service in the capital.[44] Particularly between the royal chancery and the ecclesiastical court of the bishop of Durham there was a lively exchange and sharing of personnel, some receiving their training in Westminster and moving on later to Durham, others moving in the opposite direction.[45]

Langtoft's asides often suggest that information recorded in the *Chronicle* was picked up close to the governmental administrative center: "novel avoms oy, entre compaygnouns," he remarks, before divulging some details as to the way William Wallace was captured.[46] In general Langtoft's *Chronicle* has proved to be a well-informed source on the events of Edward's reign. It would be a mistake, however, to attribute this feature of the work automatically to a conscious desire on the part of the author to leave posterity an accurate, objective account of political events in the reign of Edward I, preceded by what the author believed to be the true history of the English and British kings from Brutus onward. If Langtoft proves to be a valuable and reliable source, this is probably due primarily to the author's position in life, which made him a witness to many of the political events of Edward's reign. Also, if the part of the work that precedes the account of Edward's reign is "not of much value to the historian today" as Gransden puts it,[47] it does not follow that it was of similarly negligible value to its author or audience.

Langtoft's *Chronicle* is in many ways a deceptive work. Its chronological organization and the frequent use of the present tense and of direct speech give, especially in the part dealing with coeval history, the impression that Langtoft recorded events year by year, as they occurred. It is tempting to regard statements like "Ore sunt les insulanes trestuz assemblez" ("Now are the islanders all joined together") as having been written in or shortly after 1296, the year when the events described took place. But phrases of this kind in Langtoft's account of Edward's reign ("Ore est tens à dire," II, 252:11, Th.1005; "Ore aidez, Auntoyne," II, 200:16, Th.369) no more indicate that writing kept step with events, proceeding year by year, than do similar phrases used profusely in the description of much earlier reigns when Langtoft cannot possibly have been a witness to the political events of the day.[48] The possibility that the author wrote with hindsight and with a particular purpose in mind must be taken into account when reading this *Chronicle*.

Pierre de Langtoft is a reliable recorder of historical facts and also displays what E.D. Kennedy has aptly called "a creative approach to writing history."[49] He displays a firm belief in the importance of historical precedents and considerable experience in their deployment. In his prologue to the rhymed correspondence between Edward I and the pope, he clearly expresses his attitude toward the past:

> Mult fu de grant reson le primer qe purvit
> Les overes des ancestres mettre en escrit,
> Du siecle les merveiles, des sages les dités,
> E les prophecies qe furent nunciez.
> Ne fust l'escripture qe home list e voit,
> Des gestes aunciens memorie perireit.
> Pur nostre rei Edward puit home vere coment
> Testmoigne d'escripture puit valer sovent. (App. I, 386:1–8)

> [He was a man of great judgment who first provided
> To put in writing the works of our ancestors,

The wonders of the age, the sayings of the wise men,
And the prophecies which were made public.
Were it not for the writing which man reads and sees,
The memory of the ancient history would perish.
In the case of our King Edward may be seen how
Testimony of writing may often be of worth.]

In his *Chronicle* Pierre de Langtoft skillfully used references to King Arthur, his feasts, prophet, and artifacts to draw attention to significant episodes in the history of the relationship between the bishop of Durham and the king of England. In a similar way references to saints associated with the two men and their cause are carefully placed in strategic places in the *Chronicle*. Thus a sophisticated grid was superimposed on the chronological record of events, by means of which attention was focused on those elements of the country's history that were central to the author's purpose: to make clear the benefits derived from the close cooperation between the bishop of Durham and the king of England in the past. As the support of the saints showed, such a program of cooperation had divine approval; indeed political results, as recorded in the *Chronicle*, bore this out: to be certain of success in establishing English rule in Scotland, such cooperation was a sine qua non. Langtoft's *Chronicle* voices a plea for reconciliation and reinstatement and, by means of historical precedents and examples, makes clear the benefits that will accrue to the crown and the country when the harmonious relations that once existed between the king of England and the bishop of Durham have been reestablished. This message becomes clear when the *Chronicle* is studied as a whole and the possibility of propaganda purposes is taken into account. Langtoft constructed his *Chronicle* with great care, using the Arthurian references in strategic places in the text to highlight those episodes that most effectively served his double perspective, oriented toward both Durham and Westminster, and his message that the successful resolution of the Scottish problem lay in the close cooperation between the bishop of Durham and the king of England. The Arthurian references are links in the chain by which this message is firmly anchored in history.[50]

Notes

1. Roger Sherman Loomis, "Edward I, Arthurian Enthusiast," *Speculum*, 28 (1953), 114–27.

2. See Michael Prestwich, *Edward I* (London: Methuen 1988), pp. 120–22, here p. 122.

3. References in this essay are to *The Chronicle of Pierre de Langtoft in French Verse, from the Earliest Period to the Death of King Edward I*, ed. Thomas Wright, 2 vols. (London: Longmans, 1866), by volume, page, and line number. Line numbers

have been added by me. This edition has the text of the complete *Chronicle*, plus a parallel translation into English. Translations quoted are Wright's, unless otherwise stated. A partial edition of Langtoft's *Chronicle*, dealing only with the reign of Edward I, was published in 1989: *Pierre de Langtoft: Le Règne d'Édouard Ier*, ed. Jean Claude Thiolier (Créteil: C.E.L.I.M.A., University of Paris, XII, 1989), vol. I (vol. II, containing notes and glossary, has not yet been published). This edition was based on all Langtoft manuscripts. Where possible I have added parallel references to Thiolier's edition. All such references are to what Thiolier calls Rédaction II; I am not convinced by Thiolier's argumentation that two partial and textually deviant manuscripts (printed in the edition as Rédaction I) represent a redaction of the text very close to Langtoft's autograph manuscript. On the deviant manuscripts see also T.M. Smallwood, "An Unpublished Early Account of Bruce's Murder of Comyn," *Scottish Historical Review*, 54, No. 157 (1975), 1–10, and "The Text of Langtoft's *Chronicle*," *Medium Ævum*, 46 (1977), pp. 219–30.

    4. See my article "Context and Genesis of Pierre de Langtoft's *Chronicle*," in *Literary Aspects of Courtly Culture: Selected Papers from the 7th Triennial Congress of the International Courtly Literature Society*, ed. Sara Sturm-Maddox and Donald Maddox (Woodbridge: Boydell and Brewer, 1994), pp. 321–32. For a survey of critical opinion of Langtoft's *Chronicle*, see p. 321, n. 4.

    5. The most recent adherent of this idea is Jean Claude Thiolier. See "Pierre de Langtoft: Historiographe d'Edouard Ier Plantagenet," *Anglo-Norman Anniversary Essays*, ed. Ian Short (London: Anglo-Norman Text Society, Occasional Publications Series, No. 2, 1993), pp. 379–94. The notion that the contemporary part of verse chronicles should be considered as a separate part originates with M.D. Legge, who imposed on all such chronicles a "tripartite plan—a History of the Britons, a History of the English, and a History of His Own Times" (M.D. Legge, *Anglo-Norman Literature and Its Background* [Oxford: Oxford University Press, 1963], p. 277). Here and elsewhere the so-called third part is even given a entirely spurious title: "*The Reign of Edward I*" (*A-N Lit*, 278), later used by Thiolier as the title of his edition, or "The *Life* of Edward I" (M.D. Legge, *Anglo-Norman in the Cloisters* [Edinburgh: Edinburgh University Publications, 1950], p. 73).

    6. The *explicit* to the story of the Britons reads: "Jekes à cel houre Cadwaldre perdist / Le honur de Brettayne, e nul Brettoun remyst, / Peres de Langetoft trove nent plus par dit / K'il n'ad complye e mys en cel escryt. / Les trofles ad lessé, à veritez se prist. / Nul autre trovera homme ke le lyst, / Si noun li latymers en sun Latyn mentist" ("Until the time when Cadwallader lost the honor of Britain, and no Briton remained, Pierre de Langtoft finds no more in record than he has completed and put in this writing. He has left the trifles, and stuck to the truth. Whoever reads it will find no other, unless the interpreter lied in his Latin," I, 264:1–8). For variations in the explicit see Wright, I, 264, n. 6. The Latin incipit to the subsequent history of the English runs as follows: "Incipiunt gesta quæ sunt Anglis manifesta, / Beda, pater, præsta Petro quod dicat honesta. / Lector narrabit id quod scriptura parabit, / Petrus dictabit quod sibi Beda dabit" ("Here begin the deeds which were brought about by the English; Father Bede, lead Peter so that he may tell the virtuous deeds; the narrator will recount that which shall appear written; Peter shall say that which Bede shall give him," my translation; I, 278:4). For variations in these Latin lines in the different manuscripts, see Thiolier, *Règne*, 112–13.

    7. Among them are William of Malmesbury, Henry of Huntingdon, Simeon of Durham, and Roger of Howden. For Langtoft's sources, see Wilhelm Tischbein, *Über Verfasser und Quellen des 2. Teiles der altfranzösischen Reimchronik Pierre de Langtofts* (Diss., Göttingen, 1913).

    8. Of the twenty extant Langtoft manuscripts, twelve contain either the whole *Chronicle* or a part in which the transition from the reign of Henry III to that of Edward I can be studied. The manuscripts have been extensively, if tendentiously, described by Jean Claude Thiolier (*Règne*, pp. 35–142). I have based myself on his de-

scriptions here, and I use the sigla assigned to the manuscripts by Thiolier. In three cases a short prologue, summing up what went before, has been interpolated between the death of Henry III and Edward's coronation (MSS. A, G, S; *Règne*, 37, 77, 122); in all the other cases (MSS. B, C, D, H, J, L, P1–2, U, Y) there is time and again, as Thiolier points out, no break of any kind; the *Chronicle* is continued "sans le *Prologue* ni aucune transition" (*Règne*, 51), or even "sans aucune transition ni espace, comme si le scribe refusait de le considérer comme un nouveau livre" (*Règne*, p. 87). See also *Règne*, 42, 57, 94, 99, 110, 120, 136.

9. The years up to 1294 average out at about twenty lines per year, the later years at seventy lines per year. By comparison 1294 alone numbers 438 lines.

10. The part of Langtoft's *Chronicle* containing these tail-rhyme "songs" was edited separately by Wright from a manuscript not used for his edition of the *Chronicle*. See Thomas Wright, *The Political Songs of England, from the Reign of John to that of Edward II* (London: The Camden Society, 1839). I am currently working on a reconsideration of these songs.

11. Langtoft records the terms of Balliol's homage in Anglo-Norman prose (II, 192:20–194:10). As is noted by Stones, although "many chronicles report the actual act of homage, none of them save Rishanger, Trevet and the versifier Langtoft give the very words used" (Lionel Stones, "English chroniclers and the affairs of Scotland, 1286–1296," in *The Writing of History in the Middle Ages: Essays Presented to R. W. Southern*, ed. R.H.C. Davis and J.M. Wallace-Hadrill [Oxford: Clarendon Press, 1981], p. 331).

12. See, for instance, II, 220:10–14 (Th.617–20): "Guales seit maudit de Dieu et de seint Simon! / Qar touz jours ad esté plein de tresoun. / Escoce sait maudite de la mere Dé, / Et parfound ad deable Gales enfoundré!" ("May Wales be accursed of God and St. Simon! For it has always been full of treason. May Scotland be accursed by the mother of God, And may Wales be sunk deep to the devil!").

13. Merlin's prophecies in Latin can be found inserted in Langtoft's *Chronicle* between the *historia brittonum* and *gesta anglorum* in one manuscript, B.L. Cotton Julius A.V, together with two illuminations of Merlin. It concerns the prophecies from Geoffrey of Monmouth's *Historia*, vii, 3–4. Langtoft's *Chronicle* is preceded in this manuscript by another Latin prophecy, in thirty lines of leonine verse, dealing with the future defeat and exile of John Balliol and further suffering for the Scots and the French (printed by Wright as part of Appendix III, pp. 450–51). As a whole this particular manuscript seems devoted to prophecies; Langtoft's *Chronicle* is also followed by two more prophecies. See H.C.D. Ward, *Catalogue of Romances in the Department of Manuscripts in the British Museum* (London: Longman, 1883), pp. 299–300 and Thiolier, *Règne*, 35–39. I should like to thank Professor Jean Blacker-Knight for her helpful comments on the prophecies. According to Thiolier, the prophecies occur in Anglo-Norman translations in five more Langtoft manuscripts: B.L. Royal 20 A.XI; B.L. Royal 20 A.II; B.N. (Paris) fonds français 12154, and Cambridge, Sidney Sussex College 43, all of which contain the complete *Chronicle*, and in MS. Cambridge, Univ. Library, Gg.I.1, which deals with the reign of Edward I up to 1296 (See Thiolier's description of MSS. B, C, P2, U, and G, respectively).

14. There is a curious little slip here: in the description of the festivities after Arthur's coronation, Langtoft has it that Arthur gives Bedivere, *son chef botillier*, Normandy, not Gascony: "As utaves de Paskes, Arthur, le gentil ber, / Volt ses gentils homes de terres avauncer. / Il doune Normondye à sir Roduer,* / Ke fu par drait de fé son chef botillier . . . " ("At the octaves of Easter, Arthur, the gentle baron, / Will reward his gentle men with lands. / He gives Normandy to sir Beduer, / Who was by right of fee his chief butler," I, 166:21–168:2). (* MS A; Normandie.à sire Beduer in B, C; Bedewere in D).

15. Cf. *HRB* Bk. ix.13; ed. A. Griscom and R.E. Jones (London: Longmans, 1929; rpt. Genève: Slatkine, 1977), p. 455: "Omnibus denique in urbe congregatis. sollempnitate instante archipresules ad palatium ducuntur ut regem diademate regali

coronent" ("Finally, when they had all assembled in the town and the time of the feast
had come, the Archbishops were led forward to the palace, so that they could place
the royal crown upon the King's head," trans. Lewis Thorpe, *The History of the Kings
of Britain* [Harmondsworth: Penguin Books, 1966], p. 228).

16. The crown used at William the Conqueror's coronation was long the subject of speculation, both in the Middle Ages and after. This was due to the unclear
circumstances in which William succeeded Edward the Confessor and to the fact that
Edward the Confessor's regalian ornaments, apparently bequeathed to Westminster
by the saintly king and mentioned as adorning the head of the dead saint in 1102,
were lost. (See Frank Barlow, *Vita Edwardi Regis qui apud Westmonasterium requiescit*
[London: Nelson, 1962], pp. 115–19). According to Wido of Amiens in *De bello
Hastingense carmen*, a contemporary of the Norman duke, William was not crowned
with Edward's crown, but had had a crown made for himself that was very like the
one worn by the Emperor Otto I. Like the Emperor's crown, it had an arc and was
decorated with twelve precious stones. This grand imperial copy was clearly intended
to impress. See P.E. Schramm, *Herrschaftszeichen und Staatssymbolik* (Stuttgart:
Hiersemann, 1955), II, 393–94; R. Leyser, "England and the Empire in the Early
Twelfth Century," *TRHS*, 5th Series, 10 (1960), 65; Krijnie Ciggaar, "Byzantine
Marginalia to the Norman Conquest," *Anglo-Norman Studies*, 9 (1986), 43–64.

17. Langtoft may have been inspired by the reference to King Arthur's tears
in the *HRB*. They were shed in response to the petitions of Scottish bishops to spare
the few men who remained after Arthur's destruction of the country. However, these
tears were prompted by the Scottish bishops' patriotism rather than repentance; in both
cases the church in the North benefited. (See *HRB* ix.6, Griscom, 442; Thorpe, 220.)

18. Cf. *HRB* Bk ix.4; Griscom p. 438: "Humeris quoque suis clipeum vocabulo
pridwen. in quo imago sancte marie dei genitricis inpicta ipsum in memoriam ipsius
sepissime reuocabat. Accinctus ergo caliburno gladio optimo. & in insula auallonis
fabricato. lancea dextram suam decorat. que homine vocabantur. Haec ardua erat.
lataque lancea. cladibus opta" ("a circular shield called Pridwen, on which there was
painted a likeness of the Blessed Mary, Mother of God, which forced him to be thinking
perpetually of her. He girded on his peerless sword, called Caliburn, which was forged
in the Isle of Avalon. A spear called Ron graced his right hand: long, broad in the blade,
and thirsty for slaughter," Thorpe, 217). In Langtoft's *Chronicle* this has been reduced
to four lines, in which only the sword is named: "Arthur prent l'esku, le ymage de la
Marie / Purtrait fu dedenz, ke Arthur ne l'oblye. / Se ceynt ke Caleburne, la meyllur
espeye / Ke unkes en Brettayne fu forgé ou furbye" ("Arthur takes the shield, the image of Mary / Was pourtrayed within it, that Arthur might not forget her. / He girds
himself with Caliburn, the best sword / That ever was forged or furbished in Britain,"
I, 152:10–13). Langtoft also refers to the sword by name in the following places: I
166:3, 190:2, 20; 192:1; 212:16. There is no corresponding use of the sword's name
in these places in *HRB*.

19. C.M. Fraser, *A History of Antony Bek* (Oxford: Oxford University Press,
1957), p. 207.

20. R. Howard Bloch, *Etymologies and Genealogies: A Literary Anthropology of the French Middle Ages* (Chicago: University of Chicago Press, 1983), p. 82.

21. "En gestes aunciens trovoums-nous escrit / Quels rays et quels realmes
ly rays Arthur conquist, / Et coment sun purchace largement partyst. / Roys suz ly
n'avoit ke ly countredist, / Counte, duc, e baron, qe unques li faillist,* / En guere
n'en bataille ke chescun ne suyst" ("In ancient histories we find written / What kings
and what kingdoms king Arthur conquered, / And how he shared largely his gain. /
There was not a king under him who contradicted him, / Earl, duke, or baron, who
ever failed him / In war or in battle, but each followed him"). * in MS A only (II,
296:13–19; Th.1534–39).

22. See Langtoft's depiction of the Battle of the Standard (I 232:16–17; 286:9–
10) and his comments on the effects of the quarrel between Henry II and Thomas

Becket, and Henry's subsequent generosity (II, 8:21–10:2; 10:10–14); in Edward's reign also II, 320:18–20, Th.1836–38 (see also Summerfield [note 4], p. 329).

23. In "Context and Genesis of Pierre de Langtoft's *Chronicle*," see above, n. 4. On the Sheffield connection, see p. 329, n. 30.

24. The quarrel was not of the bishop's making: he had inherited it from his predecessor. It concerned the bishop's visitation rights to the convent of Durham. For a detailed description see Fraser, 123–211. A contemporary eyewitness account of the early stages of the conflict can be found in *Gesta Dunelmensia A.D. MCCC*, ed. R.K. Richardson (Camden Miscellany XIII, 3rd series, 34, 1924). Sheffield was appointed by the Crown to act in the franchise of Durham, together with royal justices, even though the bishop still enjoyed his traditional regalian powers there (Fraser, 196).

25. It would seem that whoever appointed Sheffield seriously underestimated the charismatic powers of the bishop to win people for his cause. See Fraser, 201, for numerous examples of Sheffield's efforts on the bishop's behalf.

26. It has been suggested that the Boulogne agreement of 31 January 1308, a declaration of support of the king, was drawn up at Bek's instigation. It was probably intended to stem renewed and increasingly loud discontent by curbing royal abuses. The earls and barons present submitted themselves to Anthony Bek, giving him the power to excommunicate them if any should break the agreement to which each set his seal (J.R. Maddicott, *Thomas of Lancaster, 1307–1322, a Study in the Reign of Edward II* [Oxford: Oxford University Press, 1970], p. 73; J.R.S. Phillips, *Aymer de Valence, Earl of Pembroke, 1307–1324, Baronial Politics in the Reign of Edward II* [Oxford: Oxford University Press, 1972], pp. 26–29).

27. "A grand Bible of the late thirteenth and early fourteenth centuries [in which] Bek's shield is placed below the royal arms of England . . . may well have been intended for Edward I or II" (Adelaide Bennett, "Anthony Bek's Copy of *Statuta Angliae*," in *England in the Fourteenth Century: Proceedings of the 1985 Harlaxton Symposium*, ed. W.M. Ormrod [Woodbridge: Boydell, 1986], pp. 1–17; here p. 13. This Bible survives in Paris, Bibliothèque Mazarine MS. 34.

28. Such criticism concerns the intransigent attitude of the king, his habit of breaking promises, his tolerance in the treatment of the Scottish prisoners, and his credulity in the Thomas Turberville case. See for example II, 284:20, 256:14, 24–25; 264–5–6, 274:18–276:6, 350:4–8; 226:18.

29. On Edward I's spiritual need for prayers, the use made by the king for propaganda purposes of these requests for prayers, and the actual contents of these requests, see D.W. Burton, "Requests for Prayers and Royal Propaganda under Edward I," in *Thirteenth Century England III (Proceedings of the 1989 Newcastle upon Tyne Conference)*, ed. P.R. Coss and S.D. Lloyd (Woodbridge: Brewer, 1991), pp. 25–35; here p. 30).

30. King Athelstan successfully invoked St. John's intercession for victory against the Scots; King Henry V ascribed his victory at Agincourt to the fact that the battle was fought on the feast of the saint's translation (25th October) (*Oxford Dictionary of Saints*, ed. D.H. Farmer [Oxford: Oxford University Press, 1978], p. 216).

31. See Robert Kimball Richardson, "The Bishopric of Durham under Anthony Bek, 1283–1311," *Archaeologia Aeliana*, 3rd Series, IX, 1913, pp. 89–229, here p. 93.

32. Some chroniclers went so far as to describe events that had taken place in Edward I's reign in terms transcribed virtually *verbatim* from the Arthurian section of the *HRB*. See Laura Keeler, "The *Historia Regum Britanniae* and Four Mediaeval Chroniclers," *Speculum*, 21 (1946), 27–33; Keeler, *Geoffrey of Monmouth and the Latin Chroniclers 1300–1500* (Berkeley: University of California Press, 1946).

33. See Mary E. Giffin, "Cadwalader, Arthur, and Brutus in the Wigmore Manuscript," *Speculum*, 16 (1941), 109–20; Gordon Hall Gerould, "King Arthur and Politics," *Speculum*, 2 (1927), 33–51.

34. The Balliol family commissioned an Arthurian romance, *Fergus*, in which

its rise to power in Scotland was prophesied, in this way validating its claim to the throne of Scotland. See Beate Schmolke-Hasselmann, *Der arthurische Versroman von Chrestien bis Froissart* (Niemeyer: Tübingen, 1980), pp. 208–22. The author of the *Vita Edwardi Secundi* remarks that the Welsh rebel frequently because "from the sayings of the prophet Merlin, they still hope to recover England" (ed. N. Denholm-Young [London: Nelson, 1957], p. 69). Merlin's prophecies were also used against the English by the Scots and the French (see Rupert Taylor, *The Political Prophecy in England* [New York, 1911], pp. 91–92; P. Zumthor, *Merlin le Prophète: un thème de la littérature polemique, de l'historiographie et des romans* [Diss., Lausanne, 1943], pp. 66–72; J.R.S. Phillips, "Edward II and the Prophets," in *England in the Fourteenth Century: Proceedings of the 1985 Harlaxton Symposium*, ed. W.M. Ormrod [Woodbridge: Brewer, 1986], p. 191, n. 13).

35. Printed in *Anglo-Scottish Relations, 1174–1328: Some Selected Documents*, ed. E.L.G. Stones (London: Nelson, 1965), pp. 81–87, 96–109. The letter written by Edward to Boniface VIII survives in Latin as well as in a draft version in French. The draft has not been printed. My comparisons are based on the Latin text as printed by Stones and on Langtoft's translation as printed by Wright (see below, n. 36).

36. Printed by Wright as Appendix I of his edition of Langtoft's *Chronicle* (II, 386–425); also in Thiolier, *Règne*, 459–72. Quotations and translations are from Wright's edition.

37. This evidence was accumulated in the "Great Roll" drawn up by John of Caen, one of Edward's notaries. See E.L.G. Stones, "The Appeal to History in Anglo-Scottish Relations between 1291 and 1401: Part I," *Archives, Journal of the British Record Association*, 9 (1969), 11–21.

38. Lionel Stones refers to "scores of monasteries" (Stones, 329); Prestwich states that, apart from the abbot of Evesham, "probably some thirty other heads of monastic houses" were approached (Prestwich, *Edward*, 363). As Prestwich points out, Langtoft suggests that the collection of chronicles to decide the matter was the bishop of Durham's idea (Prestwich, *Edward*, 364, n. 32; cf. II, 190:10). According to Stubbs, the chronicle that was requested from Bridlington "may not improbably have been a copy of Hoveden's *Chronicle* annotated and continued in the *Gesta Regis Henrici*" (*Chronicles of the Reigns of Edward I and Edward II*, ed. W. Stubbs [London: Rolls Series no. 76, 1882], II, xxiv).

39. According to the *HRB*, Arthur is preceded in his coronation procession by "four kings . . . bearing before him four golden swords" (*HRB* ix.13, Griscom, p. 455; Thorpe, p. 228); in Edward's letter the sword is changed into a token of homage done for Scotland: "Anguselus rex Scocie servicium pro regno Scocie exhibens debitum gladium regis Arturi detulit ante ipsum et successive omnes reges Scocie omnibus regibus Britonum fuere subjecti" ("Angusel, king of Scotland, who manifested the service due for the realm of Scotland by bearing the sword of King Arthur before him; and in succession all the kings of Scotland have been subject to all the kings of the Britons," Stones, *Anglo-Scottish Relations*, 98).

40. See Stones, *Anglo-Scottish Relations*, 106–07.

41. See, for examples, Wright's Appendix I, 394:11, 412:26–27, 420:1, 6–7 (Thiolier, 462, l. 112; 479, ll. 197–98; 483, ll. 313, 318–19).

42. For example whereas the Bull states that the rule of the kingdom (Scotland) was given by Edward to a man ("illum cui prefati regni regimen," Stones, *Anglo-Scottish Relations*, 84), Langtoft has it that "La seignorie d'Escoce à un fous doneient" (App. I, 394:15); the followers of William of Scotland who wreak destruction in the North of England are "son fule sute" (his mad followers; App. I, 412:8), where Edward's letter states only "Willelmus rex Scotorum rebellare incipiens venit in Northumbriam cum exercitu magno" ("William, king of Scots, came into N. with a large army," Stones, *Anglo-Scottish Relations*, 101); the Scots are "fous e felouns" (App. I, 416:26), committing "fetz de felons" (App. I, 418:15). Both Edward's letter and Langtoft's translation describe the "slaying children in the cradle and women ly-

ing in childbed . . . , [burning of] small school-children of tender years learning their first letters and grammar . . . in the school where they were . . . by blocking the doors of the school and setting it on fire" (Stones, *Anglo-Scottish Relations*, 106–07, App. I, 418:1–9). Legge has called Langtoft "one of the most violent Scotophobe historians of all time" (*Cloisters*, 71).

43. Sheffeld was among the officers charged with the collection of debts on the king's behalf in July 1297. Sheffeld was appointed to Yorkshire. See *Documents Illustrating the Crisis of 1297–98 in England*, ed. Michael Prestwich, Camden Fourth Series, vol. 24 (London: Royal Historical Society 1980), p. 102, n. 1.

44. Gwyn A. Williams, *Medieval London: From Commune to Capital*, University of London Historical Studies, No. 11 (London: Athlone, 1963), p. 133; Elizabeth Salter, *Fourteenth-Century English Poetry: Contexts and Readings* (Oxford: Oxford University Press, 1983), pp. 53–55, 67, 75.

45. Fraser, 100–05, gives many examples.

46. See also II, 336:22–26, 352:1, 356:5, 358:4–5 (Th.2031–35, 2218, 2271, 2293–94).

47. Antonia Gransden, *Historical Writing in England, c. 550–c. 1307* (London: Routledge, 1974), p. 476–77.

48. For example, "Ore ad le rays Eduuard [the Confessor] chaungé volonté" (I, 390:21), "Ore est le ray William à Loundres rethorné" (I, 440:4), "Ore va le ray Richard . . . " (II, 64:15).

49. Edward Donald Kennedy, "John Hardyng and the Holy Grail," *Arthurian Literature*, 8 (1989), pp. 185–206, here p. 206.

50. This article is based on my work for a larger study of Langtoft's *Chronicle* and its translation into English by Robert Mannyng; the provisional title is *The Matter of Kings' Lives*.

The Atypical Grails, Or the Ravages of Intertextuality in the Thirteenth Century

Anne Berthelot

Chrétien de Troyes bequeathed a poisoned gift to the new romance genre being born in his time: the Grail is the very model of an explosive and dangerous literary object. Indeed, its power is considerable; the enigma that it presents assures the continuity of romance as a genre, but at the level of individual works it is instead an encumbrance. We could sum up the problem by saying that, at one and the same time, the Grail impedes romances from ending—provided there have not been answers to the constellation of questions related to it, questions on which the *Conte del Graal* itself only touches—and yet compels the romance material to end, despite efforts to the contrary, by a lethal parousia. It will take sixty thousand lines from four continuators[1] to resolve, in more or less satisfactory fashion, the initial problem of the Grail as an object; but thirty years later, after an enormous number of texts, the *Queste del saint Graal* will constitute an impassible *terminus ad quem*, a *memento mori* to which subsequent romances will have to find improbable parries.[2]

Overall, in fact, the *senefiance* of the Grail is fixed, so that, at least ideologically, it is virtually impossible to introduce changes. Esthetically the problem is more complex: there is an undeniable beauty in the choice made by the *Queste* in this sacred apotheosis, which parallels the profane apotheosis (or apocalypse, if you will) of the *Mort le roi Artu*, and it is difficult to imagine the text without it. In addition, it is a delicate structure, from which it is almost impossible to remove any single element without affecting the entire perspective. The best proof of that is the fact that all the great cyclic manuscripts, starting with those of the Prose *Tristan*, join the Vulgate account roughly with the Pentecost of the Grail and do not depart from it for the entire quest, even though through the remainder of it they manifest distinctly centrifugal tendencies and give evidence of an extraordinary imagination.[3] On the other hand, the Cistercian rigor that largely produced the

Queste achieved a vision that is indeed admirable, though very austere, and that does not entirely meet the demands of the more "flamboyant" taste gradually unfolding during the rest of the century.

This austere spirit, which seems to take great pleasure in showing the colors of courteous and chivalrous rhetoric in an unfavorable light, is nonetheless exhaustive: it effects a sort of "blockage" of fiction at the level of the Grail, essentially rendering the establishment of variants impossible, even in the form of pseudohistorical complements. The obvious meaning of the official Grail makes it an episode in salvation history and can become as boring as heaven can be made to sound in some representations. The *Lancelot-Graal* offers a complete *advisio mundi*, magnificently constructed and balanced but also desperately closed: that is, after the assumption of the Grail, there is nothing left—the age of marvels has drawn completely to a close—and even before this edifying disappearance, during which there occurred the triumph of the world's most boring knight, Galaad—the "robot-knight," as both Jean Cocteau and Jacques Roubaud suggested, each in his own way[4]—the "good" reading of the Grail precludes polysemy, efflorescence of meanings and branches. Now this layered structure, this ability to accommodate the coexistence of different "possible worlds,"[5] which so-called classical literature, under the influence of the Cartesian virus, will later prohibit, is consubstantial with thirteenth-century romance in prose (and in verse as well). The orthodoxy of the Grail can only be felt as an arbitrary restriction of the potentialities of fiction, and variant versions, which more or less efficiently rival the Arthurian Vulgate, rebel against this restriction.

Furthermore, the Vulgate, precisely because of the univocal choice that it effects, must put aside—out of the field of vision, as it were—some elements present in the initial hypothesis. The parallel versions, in order to redress the injustice committed against them, will therefore simply have to seize upon the rejected motif and to privilege not the Grail (assuming that it is accepted once and for all as the cup of the Last Supper, in which the blood of Christ on the Cross was collected) but instead some details that even the best exegetical intent could not assign to the liturgy, Byzantine or other. (And the best intent is not, after all, the most striking characteristic of the Cistercian establishment.)

In other words, if nothing really new can be done with the Grail, there remain the "accessories," the secondary elements of Chrétien's procession, on which the ferocious attention of Cistercian expurgation did not focus as radically as on the sacred object itself. Essentially, of course, these elements include the lance and also this curious sword that is to become the sword "aux Estranges Renges" ("with the strange hangings");[6] but we do not know if the sword is intrinsically associated with the constellation of the Grail or if its presence is an accident—assuming that there really are accidents in literature and especially in medieval literature. Seen from this angle the new romances offer enormous possibilities for exploration of questions that are peripheral to the Grail's linear development, even though this may now involve political investigation of the concept rather than of the object itself.

In fact, this potential is exploited very early, and it may be only the thirteenth-century preference for interminable "summas" that assures the unjustified and almost total victory of the Vulgate Grail over that of the real Robert de Boron. The third part of the trilogy that Bernard Cerquiglini published under the title of *Roman dou Graal*[7] approaches the problem from a political angle. In this text the Grail sinks its roots into the mythology of royalty in the Celtic manner,[8] and the important question is not the nature of the object, which goes entirely without saying, but the accession of Perceval to the throne of the Grail as substitute for, and successor to, Arthur, after a perilous seat directly adapted from the Irish "Lia Fail" has obligingly confirmed *a contrario* his election.

The *Roman dou Graal* contains a number of unsolved mysteries, focused in particular on Merlin, who has not yet been reclaimed by the system to the point of devoting himself simply to preaching the orthodox Grail. At very least it produces, in the form of a trilogy of modest if not excessively economical dimensions, a *compendium* of Arthurian and Grail material, offering an alternative to the huge weight of the Vulgate. This alternative, however, does not quite measure up to, and yet simultaneously fails to diverge sufficiently from, the Vulgate structure, which will eventually become dominant, to be able to compete seriously with it. Both the *Perlesvaus* and the *Merlin-Huth*, each in its own way, will prove to be much richer from this point of view and far more "solid."

The *Perlesvaus*[9] is in all respects a profoundly atypical romance, which creates a type of universe parallel to the usual Arthurian world: the reader moves through it with a feeling of disorientation, owing to the fact both that he can instinctively find his way in it and that everything is somehow subtly different. First off, the adventure of the Black Chapel, the hero of which, contrary to all tradition, is King Arthur himself, demonstrates how the text departs from a conception of the Grail that will later become typical: the "Terre Gaste" ("Waste Land") is the whole kingdom of Logres, and its lamentable state is due largely to Arthur's failure, without being irrevocably linked to the Grail.

Relatively little is said of the Grail;[10] indeed, Perlesvaus's task is to return to the castle and ask the appropriate questions, so as to succeed his uncle as Grail king. But this process of succession cannot be accomplished simply by the internal logic of selection by the Grail itself: it requires the quite opportune intervention of the "Roi del Chastel Mortel" ("King of the Death Castle"), the evil uncle, who by seizing the "Chastel des Armes" moves the struggle to a decidedly allegorical—or prosaic—level. Moreover, the name of the "Chastel des Armes," emphasized by Lancelot, underlines the theological, even eschatological, stakes of the conflict: it is Heaven against Hell, and the castle, which finds itself housing a Grail that is moreover elusive,[11] is primarily a sort of reproduction, more or less secularized, of the celestial Jerusalem.

The sequences devoted to Perlesvaus, and those among them that deal with the Grail iself, are apparently less numerous than all kinds of episodes that are only distantly—sometimes *very* distantly—related to it. For "Jehan," the so-called author of *Perlesvaus*, as later for the compilers of large manuscripts who basically hide behind the mask of a Luces de Gasse or a Helye (de Borron or not), the Grail is clearly something embarrassing, from which one tries to extricate oneself as best as one can, and about which few definitive statements can be made. To put it colloquially, the Grail in this text is a sort of "*schmilblic*," an obligatory "trick" that one cannot do without, but that is treated as succinctly as possible, because it is too dangerous and already too compromised.

How happily, on the other hand, does the writer give free rein to his imagination when it is a matter of constructing out of nothing the legend of the sword, which here will not be "aux Etranges Renges," but will instead, by a kind of exegetical hocus-pocus, be linked to the beheading of Saint John the Baptist![12] This is a significant choice, insofar as it goes back to the sources, to the time of the Precursor, by defiantly ignoring the actual time of the Passion, and its system of concordances bristles with incompatabilities. In addition, if the sequences devoted to this utensil occupy relatively little space, they are essential for the overall economy of the romance, since they include the unusually bloody and barbaric adventure of King Gurgaran and his anthropophagous conversion. This is a jubilant and resolutely heretical reading of Holy Scripture, and by this single stroke it escapes from the constraints of the Grail as it is being remade by tradition. Let us add to this that the hero taking charge of this "exterior" branch of the story is naturally Gauvain, the worldly alternative to Perceval/Perlesvaus, the counterpoise who, already (or still) with Chrétien, assures the balance of the work between excessive Christianization (conversion by the sword, so to speak!) and mythical appurtenance.

The *Perlesvaus* is a singular monument: it stands alone in the corpus of prose Grail romances, most of which are themselves made generally compatible with one another by certain manipulations. This singularity is the mark of its triumph but also of its failure: a romance too nearly perfect to be rewritten, as was the custom. Once and for all there is but one "Haut Livre du Graal," and it is sufficient unto itself, comprising paradoxically (if we consider its opening *in medias res*) the beginning and the end of the Arthurian universe. Not only does it not authorize "continuations," but it discourages the kind of counterfeiting that is the usual medieval form of homage. The accomplishment (in all senses of the word) of the work is the reason it stands alone and has no posterity; as a result the tangential and therefore elegant solution that it brings to the problem of the Grail will not be reused thereafter.

The case of the *Merlin-Huth*[13] is from the start quite different: according to the critics this text belongs to a rival cycle of the *Lancelot-Graal*, of more modest dimensions no doubt, but nonetheless conceived as a whole. Insofar as we can judge from the preserved parts, the tonality of this Pseudo-Vulgate was darker than that of the Vulgate and was based on a more pessimistic conception of the relationship between power and religion. The very fact that the figure of Merlin survived longer, before being put to death in a particularly tragic and unpleasant way, underlines this negative orientation of the work. The treatment reserved for the Grail is of the same kind: the emphasis is not on the *translatio* of the sacred object from the Orient (Jerusalem) to Great Britain[14]—a phenomenon whose close link with salvation history gives it, overall, a positive valance—but rather on autochthonous episodes, as it were, whose relationship to the Grail is moreover poorly defined.

In fact, despite Merlin's frequent allusions to the Grail itself and to the marvels associated with it, the text passes over this subject without comment. This silence can be explained in that the basic facts are supposedly known, and moreover because of discomfort with respect to explosive material. What is the Grail? No one knows. Everybody talks about it, beginning with Merlin, who uses it as a basis for his system of internal dating of the Arthurian era, but absolutely no detail is given regarding its nature. Who will be the chosen of the Grail? No clear response here either: it seems that the universe of the *Merlin-Huth* has no room for Galaad, except for passing mentions, and that Perceval, whose family plays an important role in the economy of the narrative, is still considered the Grail hero; nonetheless what his victory will be, or what his conquest will consist of, is never specified.[15]

On the other hand, the reader is given a great deal of information about a series of actions and events implicitly presented as belonging to the sphere of the Grail. This is first of all the story of a knight with the invisible lance, who kills his enemies without anyone seeing where the blow comes from. This is a curious way of reintroducing Chrétien's Bleeding Lance into fiction; *this* lance does not bleed, but it is invisible, which is certainly not insignificant. Second, there is the story's focus on the unfortunate "anti-hero" Balain, the Knight with Two Swords; one of these swords, which comes into his possession following a complicated and negatively charged sequence, structurally occupies the place given to the Sword "aux Estranges Renges" in the "classic" version. Finally, and above all, there is the sequence of the "Dolorous Stroke" ("le Coup douloureux"), dealt specifically by Balain to King Pellehan.

This is the stroke that triggers in his entire kingdom the phenomenon of instantaneous desertification traditionally known as the "Terre Gaste," the Waste Land. It should be noted that the kingdom in question is that of Listenois, identified here with the "Terre Foraine"; this is a fine effort at syncretism, which proves the advanced state of the Arthurian referential illusion but defines the limits of a work that tries, however intently, to organize onomastic and toponymic material. As if by chance, the lines in which the conclusion of the adventure should be presented are lacking in the manuscript, and we must consult late adaptations of texts like Malory's *Le Morte Darthur* to get an idea of the later development of the story.

Pellehan clearly is the new incarnation of the "Roi Méhaigné" (the "Maimed King");[16] no less clearly he is from the same family as Perceval, as his name suggests. Insofar as we can determine, he is doubtless a brother of King Pellinor of Listenois, father of the "chevalier nice" (the "naive knight"), and of some others, and he is the sworn enemy of the Gauvain lineage: the *Merlin-Huth* reconstructs here the bipolarity of Chrétien's original work. But this "Roi Méhaigné" does not appear in a relationship of internal necessity to the Grail. Nothing allows us to say that his castle is the one in which the Grail manifests itself (will manifest itself?). In addition, among other details, there is his brother, the traitor Garlan le Roux, who is a distant double of King Varlan of the *Queste del saint Graal*, and we cannot distinguish them clearly. But this phenomenon of reduplication seems to be a kind of unconscious reminiscence and is neither exploited nor, in reality, actually exploitable.

All in all, and as tragic as may be the story of the Dolorous Stroke, which illustrates in an exemplary way the "mescheance" of the knight, the victim of the original sin of hubris, it seems to be a secondary episode rather than the nucleus of a fiction. King Pellehan and his court, which includes Garlan, the famous knight of the invisible lance, do not occupy an essential place in the romance. It is a secondary court, doubtless a dependent of Arthur's, of the sort that we encounter by the dozens in the course of knights' adventures and that disappear after a few pages and are never mentioned again. That is in fact what happens, and the reader retains the disconcerting impression of having attended a "tragedy of errors," the founding events of which have taken place in an inappropriate framework, somehow out of context, in a desperate attempt to vulgarize the drama or to tame the eminently refractory material of the Grail.

On the route leading to the castle of Pellehan, Balain sees some landmarks that recall decisive stages of the Quest for the Holy Grail—the castle of the leprous woman, for example, about whom it is specified that she will later be healed by the blood of Perceval's sister. But if the scenarios strangely resemble each other, that is only to illustrate better their difference and their irreducibility at each step. Balain is not just a "dark" version of Perceval, nor is the adventure of the Dolorous Stroke a demythification of the sacred material of the Grail: all of it together provides an alternative solution to the Vulgate version and radically puts its ideology into question. Linked to Balain and Pellehan, the Grail is no longer the sacred object that serves as the foundation of an almost orthodox theology and soteriology.

We see in this text the repaganization of the Grail and the events connected with it, even though their mythical dimension, present in Chrétien's works, is not itself reactualized. The Grail of the *Merlin-Huth* is a Grail of human proportions and is for this very reason a very pessimistic one: without transcendence, the "estoire del Graal" ("history of the Grail") becomes a sordid series of settlements of account, each more sinister than the one before. In fact in this romance, whose action takes place early in the Arthurian cycle—like every "history of Merlin," this one recounts his coronation and his subsequent battles with unhappy barons—the predominant atmosphere is that of the "death of Arthur," the end of the world. The *Merlin-Huth* is haunted by the mortal anguish of a Merlin who is obsessed by the idea of his death and who prophesies the marvels of the Grail only through this tragic filter. In this work it is obvious that, if Merlin and the Grail are indissociable, they are also mutually exclusive: where the enchanter still presides over the destinies of King Arthur and of Arthurian fiction, the Grail is necessarily outside the temporal limits of the story, serving as a horizon of expectation. Scattered bits and pieces are all that remain of it. The structure of a "tale of vengeance," of which traces have been seen in the *Conte del Graal* by Chrétien, reappears here, undisguised and without ornamentation. The alternative Grail in this case is more fascinating than the real one, but also gloomier.

Now the Arthurian imagination has no desire to be gloomy; far from it. "Conter d'armes et d'amours" ("to tell a tale of arms and love"), as the programmatic statement of the *Roman de Perceforest* will indicate three-quarters of a century later,[17] means above all retelling heroic stories with exceptional characters, with adventures that are always the same and yet always renewed. But it is not the endless retelling of a tragic tale, threatening disaster and the complete annihilation of civilization. Even if we admit that the two parts of the Arthurian "twilight of the gods" are admirable, their atmosphere is somewhat oppressive, and the late compilations prefer to deal with less depressing material: during all the years of Arthur's reign, and in particular during the fifteen years that separate the conception of Galaad from the beginning of the quest, many things happened that can be pleasant and—according to the aesthetics of the period—necessary to relate. During these years, the Grail was there; earlier, there is some doubt that it was. But after Lancelot's visit to Corbenic, which quickly became one of the most frequented castles of Great Britain, it is obvious that the sacred object has been with the Fisher King for some time.

In compliance with the taste of these late texts for details and little-known episodes borrowed from the "matière de Bretagne" (even when those episodes are of a touching banality), some authors began to wonder what the Grail was doing all this time. Some aspire to write a kind of "daily life in Corbenic," and some daring people take the initiative, giving in effect original glimpses of the Grail's day-to-day behavior. So it is that one manuscript[18] describes an improbable picnic held by the inhabitants of Corbenic (the Fisher King, his daughter Amite, and the child Galaad) during which, as is appropriate, the Grail comes to feed his servants, as it will do at Arthur's court for the Pentecost of Galaad's arrival on the narrative scene. The difference is that the mood of solemnity and miracle that surrounds this unique scene in the *Queste* is replaced by a cheerful atmosphere, and the Grail loses much of its transcendence by traveling through the woods like a sophisticated catering service.

Similarly, another manuscript[19] describes a totally bewildering scene in which the Grail again leaves its castle; in this case it is not Corbenic but Camaalot, the Grail in this unorthodox variant having chosen to reside with Arthur. This time it returns to their magical river ("engingniée," "engineered," by Merlin) two fish that are presumably also magical and that an indelicate chef (or a chef who does not know much about magic) had simply fished from the river and put on to cook. The Grail resurrects them and returns them, half grilled, to the river, which quickly flows back toward the island of Avalon—without anyone who witnesses the scene having found it the least bit odd. Here is the last, inglorious avatar of one of the most noble and meaningful literary creations!

These episodes do not seem serious, and at least for the modern reader they provoke stupefaction mixed with hilarity. But in fact they constitute important evidence of an essential aesthetic and ideological evolution; the Grail, beginning in the second half of the thirteenth century, is a critical element of the literary material. But this very frequency cannot but create an impression of familiarity or habit: the more it is seen, the more it tends to be reduced to the role of a deus ex machina for all practical purposes;[20] the Grail becomes a narrative artifact that is useful for solving a momentary difficulty in the story or for renewing the waning interest of a sequence. Its mythical dimension is almost entirely concealed, as is its eschatological *senefiance*.

Of course this is a significant degradation: we cannot in any respect compare the scenes described above with the *Queste del saint Graal*. But this degradation permits the survival of the Grail as object and by the same token ensures the survival of the romance. A Grail in full possession of its capacities, as it were, leads to the apotheosis of Galaad and to the death of many lesser knights. An almost burlesque and parodic Grail creates a new tonality that enriches the proliferating branches of the great Arthurian summa of which second- or third-generation writers dream. That same Grail moreover permits the exponential growth of those works, a growth that is no longer—or not yet—threatened by the fatidic character of the Quest. The intertextuality that triumphs in the thirteenth century accomplishes in exemplary manner a task of alchemical transmutation: it manages to transform the Grail, a lethal threat that endangers the future of fiction, into a narrative artifact that is able to prolong it almost indefinitely. But can we say that it is still the *real* Grail of Chrétien de Troyes and Robert de Boron?

NOTES

1. Admirably edited by William Roach, *The Continuations of the Old French Perceval of Chrétien de Troyes* (Philadelphia: University of Pennsylvania Press/American Philosophical Society, 1949–83).

2. By attemping to situate themselves for example in the (presumably) happy period of the "fathers" of well-known knights. This is what is done by the two parts of the "Grand Palamède," *Guiron le Courtoys* (see the facsimile of the edition of 1516, ed. Cedric E. Pickford, London: Scolar, 1978) and *Meliadus de Leonnois* (see the facsimile of the edition of 1532, ed. Cedric E. Pickford, London: Scolar, 1980). Still another late romance, the *Roman de Perceforest*, the composition of which was undertaken about 1314, constitutes one of these attempts to impede the mortifying influence of the Grail.

3. For a nuanced analysis of insertion modes of the *Queste* in the cyclical manuscripts or those of the Prose *Tristan*, see Colette-Anne van Coolput, *Aventures querant et le sens du monde* (Leuven: Leuven University Press, 1986), pp. 131–90.

4. Jean Cocteau is particularly severe with Galaad (*Les Chevaliers de la Table Ronde, Théâtre I*, Paris: Gallimard, 1948); but Jacques Roubaud (*Graal Fiction*, Paris: Gallimard, 1978) is manifestly of the same opinion, that, by "botching the job," Galahad deprived the Arthurian adventure of all its charm.

5. Thus an episode that reappears within the same romance, and only at an interval of some fifty pages in two entirely incompatible forms (like those of Gauvain's love with the maiden from Lis in the *Continuation-Gauvain*), is inevitably excluded from the field of the romance by the principle of noncontradiction inherent in the system of the "official" Grail. The very notion of "branch," due to the pen of "Gautier Map" at strategic points in the *Lancelot-Graal*, becomes absolutely fundamental, according to (the so-called) Robert de Boron, in the *Merlin-Huth*.

6. Nobody, however, attempted to exploit the "taillior d'argent" (a silver carving tray) that follows the Grail in Chrétien's work (ll. 3168–69). Was this detail perhaps considered too trivial and thought to constitute an *anticlimax* after the appearance of the Grail itself?

7. *Le Roman dou Graal (Joseph, Merlin, Perceval)* (Paris: UGE 10/18, 1980).

8. See Jean Marx, *La Légende arthurienne et le Graal* (Paris: PUF, 1952; rpt. Geneva: Slatkine, 1981), pp. 120–23.

9. *Le Haut Livre du Graal: Perlesvaus*, ed. William A. Nitze and T.A. Jenkins, 2 vols. (Chicago: Chicago University Press, 1932–37; rpt. New York: Phaeton, 1972).

10. The "marvels" of the Grail are sometimes disconcerting in this romance; thus one of the *muances* under which it appears to the chosen is nothing more than a candle, "donc il n'ert gaires a icel tens" ("of which there were not many then," p. 119) as the text kindly comments!

11. The Grail in fact is not always in the castle, and the characters are not always able to give reasons for these absences. Perlesvaus himself has barely come into possession of what is considered to be his heritage when the Grail definitively disappears, to take refuge with its white monks on an "ille de mer."

12. Branches V and VI, pp. 86ff.

13. *Merlin-Huth*, or *Suite romanesque* of the Prose *Merlin*, ed. Gaston Paris and Jacob Ulrich, 2 vols. (Paris: Firmin Didot, 1886).

14. This is what the Prose *L'Estoire dou Graal*, a late prologue of the *Lancelot-Graal*, recounts in great detail starting from the founding text of Robert de Boron (*Le Roman de l'estoire dou Graal*).

15. It is not even possible to determine whether royalty is here linked to the Grail, as in Robert de Boron's works or in Wolfram von Eschenbach's German version, *Parzival*.

16. For reasons that, at least apparently, have nothing to do with the Grail but are related to the obscure sexualization of the basic material offered by the *Merlin-Huth*.

17. *Le Roman de Perceforest*, ed. Jane H.M. Taylor, Pt. I (Geneva: Droz, 1979).

18. Paris, B.N. 24400, unedited. It is in the same manuscript that we learn completely by accident that King Pellès maintains in his court a completely diabolic "enchanter," who, while prevented from doing his usual tricks because of Galaad's presence, coexists apparently without the least bit of difficulty with the Grail, which is reduced to its function of ambulatory catering service.

19. Bodmer 116, edited under the title *Les Prophesies de Merlin* by Anne Berthelot (Cologny-Geneva: Martin Bodmer Fondation, 1992). The episode is found on pp. 329–31.

20. Especially considering the culinary episodes mentioned above.

THE LONG AND THE SHORT OF LANCELOT'S DEPARTURE FROM LOGRES

ABBREVIATION AS REWRITING IN *LA MORT LE ROI ARTU*

Mary B. Speer

To observe that the writing of medieval romance, at the level of both composition and transmission, inevitably constitutes the rewriting of one or more pre-existing texts is to state a truism as profound as it is obvious. Many meticulous and imaginative text-based studies over the last thirty years have shown us in detail how the various forms of rewriting, whether due to design or misfortune, have reshaped the prototypes of works in a broad range of genres. As examples of the diversity and richness of these analyses, one might cite Jean Rychner's classic study of oral and written transmission in fabliau texts;[1] Brian Woledge's observations on the "champenization" of Wace's *Roman de Brut* by the scribe Guiot in Paris, B.N. fr. 794;[2] Peter Dembowski's remarks on the abridgment of early saints' lives to fit into compilation formats in the thirteenth century;[3] Emmanuèle Baumgartner's analysis of the progressive "aération" of the codicological paratext of prose Arthurian romances from the thirteenth to the fifteenth centuries;[4] and Sylvia Huot's exploration of *remaniement* and paratextual interpretation in manuscripts of the *Roman de la Rose*.[5]

As a contribution to the study of intertextuality in Arthurian romance, I shall in turn explore one particular form of rewriting—abbreviation, as internal intertextuality—and its consequences for *La Mort le roi Artu*, the moving conclusion to the *Lancelot-Grail* prose cycle. I shall first characterize the two redactions to be compared and comment briefly on what the techniques for *abbreviatio* outlined in medieval rhetorical treatises might have offered to the abbreviator who faced the awesome task of condensing that long, dense romance; then I shall focus on this abbreviator's work in two passages of *La Mort Artu*.

As Jean Frappier indicated in the introduction to his successive editions of *La Mort Artu*, the text survives in nearly fifty manuscripts, some offering a version of the entire romance, others containing only portions of it. By classifying the witnesses to that tradition, Frappier drew up a two-branch stemma that depicts a relatively straightforward transmission in Branch I; however, for Branch II, to which nearly all the extant manuscripts belong, he delineated a complex set of filiations and contaminations.[6] In his edition, first published in 1936 as the "thèse complémentaire" to his magisterial *Étude sur "La Mort le roi Artu"*[7] and revised only slightly in the 1950s, he took as base manuscript the only uncontaminated representative of Branch I (*A*: Paris, Arsenal 3347), which he controlled systematically with the texts of seven other manuscripts representing the principal families of Branch II.[8] The result is a true critical edition: a decidedly interventionist attempt not only to repair the numerous mechanical deficiencies of his base manuscript,[9] but also to reconstruct the archetype of both branches in its letter as well as in some of its forms. While performing "la toilette du texte," Frappier silently corrected *A*'s declensional lapses and attenuated the more extreme features of the scribe's dialectal and orthographic peculiarities. In a few cases where the text of the archetype seemed flawed, he took the liberty of modifying the manuscript readings with appropriate caution: "Je ne méconnais pas le danger des reconstitutions personnelles, mais il peut arriver aussi que respecter scrupuleusement le texte des scribes, ce soit trahir l'auteur" (lxvi).

Of the fifty-odd manuscripts containing *La Mort Artu*, seven offer what Frappier calls the "version abrégée": Bonn, University Library 526, a cyclical manuscript copied at Amiens in 1286 by a scribe named Arnulfus de Kayo (*B*), as well as two fourteenth-century manuscripts at the British Library in London (Royal 14.E.III [*S*] and Additional 10.294 [*S¹*]), and four manuscripts now at the Bibliothèque Nationale in Paris (fr. 110 [*P*] and 1424 [*Y*], from the late thirteenth century; fr. 112 [*Y¹*] and 116 [*N*], from the fifteenth century). According to Frappier, the immediate prototype of the abridged version is not the archetype but Paris, B.N. fr. 12.573 (*T*), a direct descendant of a group of manuscripts he named the zeta family.[10] For stemmatic purposes—that is, in order to establish the inauthenticity of the short redaction and its limited value in reconstructing the archetype—Frappier identifies the abridged version by listing eight passages that have been omitted or condensed in all its representatives and one chapter division found only in the short version. Beyond establishing separate categories for simple excisions of material and condensations of long passages into shorter ones, he does not explore either the process of abbreviation or its effect on the romance.[11]

Up to now the full text of the abridged version of *La Mort Artu* has not been easily accessible in print. Frappier's 1936 edition presents generous variants from the Bonn manuscript, which served as one of his controls, but the critical apparatus is greatly streamlined in the more compact later editions.[12] Much earlier, for his edition of the entire Vulgate Arthurian cycle, published before and during World War I, H. Oskar Sommer took as base a cyclical manuscript in three codices at the British Library (Additional 10.292–94), which offers the short version of *La Mort Artu*.[13] Because other manuscripts available to Sommer at what was then the British Museum offered different and seemingly more "complete" texts of all the romances, he inserted numerous passages from them into the single version that he had initially intended to reproduce exactly. The result was a set of composite texts that have long been read as the only edition of the whole cycle and valued for the wealth of textual information they supply. Despite their usefulness, however, Sommer's editions have long been roundly criticized—with reason—for the indiscriminate editorial method governing the establishment of the text. Because of its composite nature and unreliable use of square brackets to mark passages not found in the base manuscript, the Sommer text provides at best an unsatisfactory approximation of the short version of *La Mort Artu*, even when one takes the trouble to strip away the interpolations that come from other redactions.[14]

Now, however, a team of editors and translators, under the general editorship of Daniel Poirion, is preparing a new edition of the Vulgate *Lancelot-Grail* cycle for publication in the Pléiade series. This will be a semi-critical edition based on the elegant Bonn manuscript, with selected variants from the contemporary Paris manuscript *P*, which will also serve as the principal control.[15] Such an edition offers wonderful possibilities for studying a single scribe's rendition of the five romances that constitute this cycle; as a bonus, it provides, for *La Mort Artu*, the special opportunity to examine both the work of the scribe Arnulfus and that of the anonymous abbreviator. To the best of my knowledge, the Bonn manuscript offers the full Vulgate text for each of the first four romances, which are divided here into eight books. How Arnulfus happened to end his codex with an abridged Book IX is unknown, but his choice—if it was that—enables us to study abbreviation as a form of rewriting and, as a result, I think, to view with renewed appreciation the achievements of the author of the long version.

How might a medieval abbreviator have conceptualized his task? At first glance one would think that the sections devoted to *abbreviatio* in rhetorical treatises like the *Poetria Nova* and the *Documentum de modo et arte dictandi et versificandi* by Geoffrey of Vinsauf offered him relatively little practical guidance. Unlike amplification, which receives elaborate discussions illustrated by examples, abbreviation is itself treated briefly. A writer wishing to abbreviate is advised first to eschew all the techniques for amplification. Then he is enjoined to compress his material with the following procedures: *emphasis,* or "saying much in few words"; *articulus,* shortening a long account "with staccato speech"; reducing the number of clauses by employing ablative absolutes and omitting conjunctions or even verbs; implying more than is specifically stated; and, finally, compressing a whole narrative to a single memorable epigrammatic phrase. In the *Poetria Nova* Geoffrey provides examples only for the last, most reductive procedure, perhaps because it was considered the most difficult.[16] The *Documentum,* however, supplies more examples, including two illuminating ones for abbreviation by implication:

> Ponimus unam pro pluribus ita caute, scilicet quod indictis non dictam damus intelligi; ut dicturi "Iste ivit illuc et nunc reversus est", dicimus: "Inde reversus est". Similiter, dicturi "Ipse commodavit mihi et ego reddidi", dicimus: "Ego reddidi illi". In hoc enim intelligitur ipsum commodasse.[17]

> [The placing of one for many must be done cautiously, for in things stated we allow something to be understood which is not stated. Instead of saying, "He went to that place and now he has returned," one should say: "He returned from that place." Similarly, instead of saying, "He entrusted it to me and I returned it," one should say: "I returned it to him." For in this it is understood that he had entrusted it to me.[18]]

These examples suggest that reading an abridgment places new demands on its audience; textual consumers must be prepared to infer what is not stated in tightly compressed portions of the narrative.

The practical advantages of brief books over longer ones were also known to medieval writers. In the prologue to his French translation of *De excidio Troiae* by Dares the Phrygian, dated April 1262, Jean de Flixécourt insisted that his prose rendering was more accurate than the rhymed *Roman de Troie,* more convenient, and more accessible:

> Si que chil qui veulent oïr le [sic] batailles de Troies & ne pueent mie avoir le rommant qui est rimés, ou pour chou que il est trop grans ou pour chou que il en est peu, si porroit avoir chestui legierement car il est petis & porroit bien savoir par chestui le verité de l'estoire.[19]

[As for those who wish to hear the battles of Troy and cannot obtain the rhymed romance, either because it is too large or because there are few copies of it, such a person could easily obtain this version, for it is small, and he could certainly know the truth of the story from it.]

The truth of *l'estoire* does not depend on length.

Eighty years ago Edmond Faral judged the medieval theory of abbreviation largely irrelevant to vernacular texts: "Cette théorie ne paraît pas intéresser beaucoup la littérature en langue vulgaire, non seulement parce que tous les procédés qu'elle recommande n'y sont pas applicables, mais aussi parce que la brièveté n'y est pas souvent recherchée" ("This theory does not seem very pertinent to vernacular literature, not only because not all the procedures that it recommends are applicable to vernacular texts, but also because in them brevity is not often sought after," 85). More recently, Eugène Vinaver concurred, stating that of all the rhetorical techniques taught in the schools, amplification most fully embodied the poetics governing French vernacular romance in general, and the Arthurian prose romances in particular.[20] Ernst Robert Curtius and Douglas Kelly, however, have shown with great clarity that *abbreviatio* and *amplificatio* function as complementary procedures in both Latin and Romance literature.[21] Since the abbreviation procedures described by Geoffrey seem harder to categorize as neat rhetorical recipes than those for amplification, whose implementation we may readily observe in medieval compositions, it might be helpful to situate them on a continuum according to the nature and extent of intervention required in a pre-existing text. At one end we would place outright cutting—that is, major excisions—then the less drastic elimination of shorter passages deemed inessential as well as the pruning of amplifications and repetitions; toward the center, succinct rephrasing through implication and syntactic compression; at the far end, complete rewriting for maximum conciseness. Such procedures are not unknown to any scholar who has had to shorten a paper to accommodate a time-limit at a conference or a page-limit in a journal, and, despite Faral, our abbreviator, for whatever reasons, did seek brevity. Nonetheless, he intended at the same time to perpetuate the same *œuvre*, for in the prologue of the abridged version the work is still attributed to "maistre Gautier Map" and entitled "la Mort au roi Artu." Between this presumption of transparent textual fidelity and the distinctly different poetics that abbreviation imposes on text and reception alike lies a problematic area of textual tension that a critical edition of the short version will allow scholars to explore. This paper offers the results of a preliminary investigation of that space. I shall show how our abbreviator has radically rewritten portions of this romance by changing the psychology of certain characters, altering scenes, and obscuring themes considered important in the long version. As Gérard Genette commented in *Palimpsestes*, "on ne peut donc réduire un texte sans le diminuer" (264).[22]

If our abbreviator has mastered the techniques taught by the *arts poétiques*, he applies them very selectively—one might say with a certain degree of literary discrimination, though modern readers will not always endorse his decisions. For a dramatic example of his literary judgment in abbreviation, let us look first at the text of Lancelot's farewell to Arthur's realm of Logres as he sails away to his own kingdoms of Benoïc and Gaunes after restoring Guinevere to her husband for the last time:[23]

123. "Hé! douce terre

pleinne de toutes beneürtez, et en qui
mes esperis et ma vie remaint outreement,
beneoite soies tu de la bouche *de celui*
qu'en apele Jhesucrist, et beneoit soient
tuit cil qui *en toi* remanent, soient mi
ami ou mi ennemi. Pes aient il! Repos
aient il! Joie lor doinst Dex greignor que
je n'ai! Victoire et honor lor *doint* Dex
envers toz cels qui riens *li* voldront
forfaire! Et certes si avront il, car nus ne
pourroit estre en si dolz païs com cist est
qui ne fust plus bien eürez que nus autres;
por moi le di ge qui esprové l'ai, car
autant come g'i demorai m'i avint il toute
boneürté plus abandoneement que ele
ne feïst se je fuisse en une autre terre."

124. Itex paroles dist Lancelos
quant il parti del roiaume de
Logres; et tant comme il pot veoir le païs,
il le regarda,   *et quant il en ot*
perdue la veüe, il s'ala couchier en un lit.
Si commença a fere si grant duel et si
merveilleux que nus qui le veïst ne fust qui
pitié n'en preïst; et dura cist duelz jusqu'a
l'ariver. Et quant ce fu chose qu'il
vindrent a terre, il monta el cheval entre
lui et sa compaignie et alerent tant qu'il
aprochierent d'un bois. En cel bois
descendi Lancelos et commanda que si

214. "Ha! douce terre, *fait il, et*
delitable et debonaire et joiouse et envoisie
et plentieve de toutes boneürtés, et en qui
mes esperis et ma vie remaint outreement,
beneoite soies tu de la boche

Jhesu Crist, et beneoit soient
cil qui *aprés moi* i remaignent, soient mi
ami ou mi anemi. Pais aient il! Repos
aient il! Joie lor doinst Diex greignor que
je n'ai! Victoire et honour lor *envoit* Diex
vers tous ciaus qui riens *lor* voldroient
forfaire! Et certes si avront il, car nus ne
seroit en si dous païs conme cist est
qu'il ne fust plus bons eürés que nus autres.
Pour moi le dis je, qui esprové l'ai, car
entretant comme je i demorai m'avindrent
toutes boneürtés plus abandoneement qu'il
ne feïssent se je fuisse en une autre terre."

215. Tels paroles dist Lanselos
quant il s'en fu partis del roialme de
Logres; et tant com il pot veoir le païs,
il le regarda *volentiers.*

paveillon fussent illuec tendu, car il vouloit
la nuit remanoir; et cil le firent maintenant
qui de celui mestier devoient servir. Cele
nuit s'i herberja Lancelos et l'endemain
s'en parti, et   erra tant   Et ensi erra il tant par ses journees
qu'il vint en sa terre.   qu'il vint en la terre de Benuÿc.

In the first paragraph of the quotation—the speech itself—notice how faithfully the abbreviator has reproduced the text of this unforgettable valedictory. The amplification of *douce terre* to *douce terre et delitable et debonaire et joiouse et envoisie* is due to the zeta prototype, rather than our abbreviator, but what is remarkable is that he has kept the entire series of four additional adjectives instead of shortening it. He has also retained the near-doublet *mes esperis et ma vie* and the powerful sequence of syntactically parallel exclamations in the optative subjunctive that constitute the climax of the passage. Our abbreviator has left virtually nothing unstated here, an act of textual respect that occurs infrequently in his version of the romance. One is tempted to believe that he shared Frappier's admiration for this eloquent speech:

> Quant à l'adieu de Lancelot sur la nef qui l'éloigne de la terre de Logres, il décèle la profonde humanité du héros, la source cachée de tendresse et de générosité qui fait de lui un être d'élite; on ne peut comprendre son caractère sans tenir compte de cette sensibilité vive et discrète à la fois. Son adieu, rythmé par l'élan de son âme vers la charité—car il pardonne à ses ennemis et répond à la haine par l'amour—prend spontanément la forme d'une prière. (*Étude*, 315)

> [As for Lancelot's farewell on the ship that takes him away from the land of Logres, it reveals the hero's profound humanity, the hidden source of tenderness and of generosity that makes him a noble being; one cannot understand his character without taking into account this sensitivity, at once intense and restrained. His farewell, in which the soaring rhythm mirrors the ascent of his soul toward charity— for he pardons his enemies and answers hatred with love—spontaneously takes the form of a prayer.]

Some force of rhetorical integrity protected this speech from compression and excision; perhaps it was a passage that readers already knew by heart.

Our abbreviator has, however, excised two sequences in the paragraph that follows the adieu. First, and more important, he retains only one of the gestures that extend the pathos of the speech, which only Bohort overhears, and serve to communicate Lancelot's grief to other witnesses. The abbreviator keeps the highly visual image of the exiled knight as he stands on deck, apart from his retinue, staring back at the receding coast of Logres as long as it is visible on the horizon. In the archetype reconstructed by Frappier and perpetuated by the zeta family, when Lancelot can see Logres no more, he goes to bed and abandons all control in intense mourning until his ship reaches the Gallic shore. This is a nonverbal *planctus* that, as the narrator comments, with the imperfect subjunctive often used by omniscient narrators to invite audience empathy, would have moved anyone who saw him to pity. Psychologically both the prolonged public gaze on deck and the private grieving in bed are gestural amplifications of the emotions Lancelot expressed in his rhetorical farewell. The abbreviator has chosen to eliminate the more lachrymose amplification, the unrestrained outpouring of emotion that in the long version parallels the physical signs of sorrow that overwhelm Lancelot, in both versions, for a long time before he utters his adieu. Whether the redactor's choice stems from an attempt to downplay Lancelot's sentimentality is a question to be considered at a later stage in assessing his alterations throughout the romance; at this point we can observe that he has shortened the narrative by pruning an amplification, thereby implementing the fundamental technique advised by Geoffrey of Vinsauf. Perhaps our abbreviator believed that Lancelot's passionate grieving, described at his embarkment, can now be inferred from his speech and his gaze. And perhaps he overlooked the author's adroit use of framing and gradation to structure this departure scene into four powerfully moving stages. In the long version we see Lancelot in public consumed with grief, which he overcomes briefly to sum up aloud, for himself alone although Bohort overhears, what Logres has meant to him; he then stares silently at the disappearing coastline; and when Logres is out of sight, he succumbs again, this time in private, to a deep sorrow that the narrator means his audience to share. Instead of this heart-wrenching crescendo of pain and isolation, the abbreviator has settled for a simpler but symmetrical frame for the adieu, for gradation in three stages instead of four.

The second immediate excision following Lancelot's valedictory eliminates an account of the trip he and his party made from the coast to the kingdom of Benoïc. In the Vulgate this journey involves an overnight stop in the woods; Lancelot, apparently recovered from his mourning, behaves like a decisive leader, giving orders that his men readily obey. Our abbreviator might have had two motives for eliminating this trip: first, without the description of a Lancelot in bed, overcome by grief, the indication that he resumes his normal behavior is no longer necessary; second, in general the abbreviator tends frequently to shorten or cut accounts of travel from one point to another. Though they heighten the romance's sense of realism in time and space, they contribute little to moving the plot along.

Yet another excision—one that Frappier considered definitive for the abridged version—affects the thematic organization of the "chapter" containing Lancelot's farewell, whose boundaries are identical in the long and short redactions.[24] The long version of this transitional chapter is framed by transfers of power that link personal loyalties to feudal responsibilities. At the outset Lancelot, with Arthur's approval, entrusts Joyous Guard to a knight who has served him faithfully for years, stipulating that this unnamed vassal will henceforth receive all revenues from that fief; after crossing the Channel, Lancelot arranges to have Bohort crowned king of Benoïc and Lionel, king of Gaunes. The abbreviator has eliminated the passage relating the transfer of Joyous Guard but kept nearly everything about the coronation of Bohort and Lionel on All Saints' Day. Although such an excision hardly harms the plot, the characterization of Lancelot as a responsible suzerain, concerned to ensure seigneurial continuity for his holdings, is diminished, and the symmetrical thematic structure of the chapter is destroyed.[25]

Now that we begin to understand how our abbreviator operates and what the stylistic, thematic, and structural consequences of his interventions may be, let us examine some of the changes he introduces into an earlier passage in *La Mort Artu*, the memorable sequence that begins with the scene of the so-called "flagrant délit," where Agravain surprises Lancelot and the queen while they are making love in her chamber, and concludes with Guinevere's rescue at the stake in the skirmish during which Gauvain's three brothers are killed. In the long redaction this sequence of events constitutes a major climax; Frappier, for instance, considers the scene of the "flagrant délit" "une des parties les plus émouvantes de l'œuvre," leading to "le pivot du roman," Lancelot's unwitting slaughter of Gauvain's favorite brother, Gaheriet (*Étude*, 320). While our abbreviator seems to have shared Frappier's opinion about which scenes were indispensable, his changes express, or impose without necessarily intending to do so, an altered interpretation of these crucial scenes and characters. I shall focus here primarily on the local effects of his decisions and leave the full analysis of his probable overall intentions to a later study.[26]

Let us observe first that some of the abbreviator's excisions of brief phrases or clauses change the narrative very little. For example, omitting one of the adjectival doublets in Bohort's description of the secluded path he urges Lancelot to take in order to reach Guinevere's bedchamber unobserved merely eliminates a type of amplification favored by nearly all vernacular French writers:

89. "Si trouverez la plus coie voie
et la plus estrainge de gent que je saiche."

147. "Si i troverés la plus coie voie
del monde."

As with the excision of Lancelot's mourning in bed on board ship, abbreviation is the inverse of amplification and can no doubt be justified here also by the concept of implication. The relatively terse *la plus coie voie del monde* implies remoteness from other people, which the long version made explicit in *la plus estrainge de gent que je saiche*.

Similarly, in the passage below, the compression of the already brief account of Lancelot's single combat with Tanaguin at the door of Guinevere's room eliminates a near-doublet by reducing *li hiaumes ne la coife de fer* to *li hialmes*. Further, the abbreviator cuts the gory contact portion in the account of the swordstroke with which the unarmed Lancelot cleaves the skull of his fully armed opponent, also the triumphant twist that typically finishes off a fatal blow:

90. . . . et Lancelos, qui ot
l'espee hauciee, le fiert si
durement, a ce qu'il i mist toute sa force,
que li hiaumes *ne la coife de fer* nel
garantist qu'il nel *porfende jusqu'es
espaules; il estort son cop, si l'*abat mort a
terre.

149. . . . et Lanselos, qui tenoit
l'espee drecie contremont, le fiert si
durement, a ce qu'il i met toute sa force,
que li hialmes   nel
garantist qu'il ne
                    le rue mort en mi
la chambre.

Despite these cuts, the information necessary to appreciate the hero's extraordinary strength is retained: Lancelot raises his sword high, then kills Tanaguin, despite his armor, with one blow.

Other excisions of short passages and amplifications that seem operationally equivalent to the ones illustrated in those two instances signal a markedly different reading of the work, for they function, I think, as elements in a broader pattern.[27] Our abbreviator greatly diminishes the importance of the queen and Bohort in this sequence of episodes and systematically deletes nearly all passages in which the lovers reveal their intimacy and devotion to each other. As a brief example, compare the two accounts of Lancelot's leave-taking when Tanaguin's death causes Agravain's men to retreat:

90. Quant Lancelos vit ce, si
dist a la reïne: "Dame, ceste guerre est
finee; quant vos plera, ge m'en irai,
que ja por home qui ci soit nel lerai." La
reïne dist qu'ele voudroit qu'il fust a
sauveté, *que qu'il deüst de lui avenir.*

149. Et quant Lanselos voit ce, si
dist a la roïne: "Dame, ceste guerre est
afinee. Quant il vous plaira, je m'en irai."
                                        Et
ele respont qu'ele voldroit *ja* qu'il fust a
salveté, *"que que il, fait ele, deüst après
avenir de moi."*

Lors regarde Lancelos le chevalier qu'il avoit ocis, *qui estoit chaoiz a l'uis de la chambre par dedenz*; il le trest a soi et ferma l'uis; si le desarma et s'en arma au mieuz qu'il pot. Lors *dist a la reïne: "Dame, puis que ge sui armez, je m'en devroie bien huimés aler seürement, se il plaisoit a Damedieu."* Et ele dist que *bien s'en aut, se il puet. Il* vet a l'uis, si l'ueuvre	150. Lors prent Lanselos le chevalier qu'il avoit ocis et le sacha a lui et referme l'uis; puis li oste toutes ses armes et s'en arme moult bien. Lors vient a l'huis, si l'ovre . . . .

In both versions Lancelot, in direct discourse, asks the queen's permission to depart. The abbreviator has excised from that speech a clause that might be construed as amplification, but that also serves to express Lancelot's determination to escape his enemies. The abridged version of the remark seems abrupt, bordering on discourtesy. In reply, the Guinevere of the long version says, in indirect discourse, that she wants her lover to be safe, whatever might happen to her. Our abbreviator enhances the vividness of the queen's selfless declaration by putting the latter portion in direct discourse. Apparently, though, he considers that one exchange sufficient evidence—by implication, perhaps—of the lovers' mutual regard, for he completely eliminates Lancelot's parting salutation in direct discourse. In the short version, then, a preoccupied Lancelot leaves his lady in great danger without even saying a polite good-bye—hardly a farewell to enhance the reputation of a world-famous lover.

This cut in Lancelot's farewell exchanges with the queen is all the more significant because the one brief exchange that the abbreviator does retain in §149 functions in the long redaction as an echo of an important earlier conversation in direct discourse (ed. Frappier, § 90). There, as Guinevere informs Lancelot that she can find no armor for him to wear while confronting Agravain's party, she bravely acknowledges *la mescheance* that has brought them both near death; in her opinion Lancelot's death would be a greater misfortune than her own, and yet, if he should escape alive, she could be confident that he would save her. Following hard upon these remarks, Lancelot's victory over Tanaguin can be seen as a courtly triumph inspired by a lady. Our abbreviator, though, has excised this conversation completely, thereby removing the justification that the author provided for the rather surprising alacrity with which the best knight in the world leaves his beloved alone and unprotected in a palace full of enemies, including her own husband.

We recall that Ferdinand Lot judged it "impardonnable . . . de montrer Lancelot, surpris auprès de Guenièvre, échappant aux traîtres et laissant la reine exposée aux insultes et en danger de mort" ("unforgiveable . . . to show Lancelot, after he is caught by surprise with Guinevere, escaping from the traitors and leaving the queen exposed to insults and in mortal danger")[28] and that in the full version Bohort also reproaches Lancelot for his apparent lack of concern for the queen. Frappier, however, defended both the author and Lancelot: for the romancer, narrative necessity required Lancelot's speedy departure so that the plot could advance through Guinevere's trials to the real "pivot du roman," Gaheriet's death at Lancelot's hand; at the level of psychological realism, Guinevere herself authorizes his departure because, she declares, she may hope to be saved only if her lover-protector escapes first (*Étude*, 320). By excising the early conversation that looms so large in Frappier's defense and by compressing the two subsequent exchanges to a single brief one, our abbreviator has almost silenced Guinevere and obscured, from all but the most perceptive readers, both her generous impulse toward self-sacrifice on Lancelot's behalf and her optimistic willingness to bear short-term risks in order to gain eventual security. In the abridged version, incident takes priority over psychological motivation, and Lancelot figures as the most important character in this sequence of episodes; Guinevere's role is reduced to little more than a supporting one.

Our abbreviator's de-emphasis of the queen remains evident in his handling of the plans Lancelot and his cousin(s) make to save her immediately after Lancelot regains his lodgings:

90. Et il [Lancelos] li conte comment Agravains et si dui frere l'avoient espïé, qui le vouloient prendre prouvé avec la reïne et avoient avec els amenee grant chevalerie. "Si m'eüssent toutevoies pris a ce que ge ne m'en donoie garde, mes ge me sui deffenduz *forment*, et tant ai fet a l'aïde de Dieu que ge m'en sui eschapez. —*Ha!* sire, fet Boorz, *or vaut pis que devant, car ore est la chose descouverte que nos avions tant celee.* Or verroiz la guerre commencier qui jamés ne prendra fin *a nos vivans.* Car se li rois vos a jusques ci amé plus que nul home, de tant vos haïra il plus, *des qu'il savra que vos li meffesiez tant com de lui vergonder de sa fame.* Or couvient que vos esgardoiz comment nos le	150. Et il [Lanselos] li conte conment Agravains et Guerrehés et Mordrés l'avoient espïé et le voloient prendre *tout* prové avoc la roïne et avoient amené avoc aus grant chevalerie. "Si m'eüssent toutes voies ocis, *fait il*, a ce que *je estoie desarmés, ne* je ne m'en donoie garde; mais je m'en sui deffendus *moult durement*, et tant ai fait a l'aïde de Dieu que je en sui eschapés *mal gré aus tous*.—Sire, fait Boors, ore verrés vous la guerre conmencier qui jamais ne prendra fin *a vous ne a els.* 151. "Or vous harra plus mortelment li rois qu'il onques ne vous ama. Or covient que vous esgardés que nous

ferons entre nos, car ge sei bien
que li rois *nos* sera des ore mes ennemis
mortex; mes de madame la roïne qui por
vos sera livree a mort me poise trop, se
Dex m'aïst. Si voudroie bien, s'il
pooit estre, que l'en i meïst conseill en
tel maniere qu'ele fust delivree de cest
afere a sauveté de son cors."

91. *A cest conseill seurvint Hestor;
quant il sot que* la chose esta a ce venue, *il
en fu tant dolans que nus plus, si dist:* "Li
mieuz que ge i voie, si est que nos
partons de ceanz et alons en cele forest
la dehors en tel maniere que li rois, qui
orendroit i est, ne nos truist; et quant ce
sera chose que madame la reïne sera
jugiee, de ce vos asseür je bien qu'ele
sera la hors menee por destruire; *lors la
rescorrons, ou cil vueillent ou non qui a sa
mort la cuideront avoir amenee. Et quant
nos l'avrons avec nos, si nos en porrons
aler hors del païs, et irons el roiaume de
Benoïc ou en celui de Gaunes; et se nos
poions tant fere que nos l'eüssions la
conduite a sauveté, nos ne douterions riens
le roi Artu ne tot son pooir."* A cest
conseill s'acorde Lancelos et Boors.

Et puis que la chose est ensi alee,

li
miels que je i voie, si est que nous nous
departons de chaiens et alons en cele forest
la defors en tel lieu que li rois, qui
orendroit i est, ne nous truise **quant ce
sera chose que ma dame sera cha fors
menee pour destruire."**

A ceste
parole s'acorderent Lanselos et Boors.

In the short version Bohort's remarks in direct discourse do no more than
advance the plot by predicting "la guerre . . . qui jamais ne prendra fin." The
abbreviator has likewise eliminated the psychological justification for
Bohort's equally ominous prediction that Arthur's previous love for the man
who committed adultery with his wife will make his hatred all the more
powerful. More damaging to Bohort's character is the deletion of his regret
that he failed to shield Lancelot and the queen from discovery; in the short
version of this dialogue only a very astute reader could discern the affection-
ate loyalty to Guinevere that constitutes one of Bohort's most endearing traits
in the cycle. But however flattened he may be, Bohort is at least still present;
Hector, by contrast, has been completely removed from the conversation—
or rather, dialogue composed for him has been transferred, clumsily, to
Bohort. In the abridged version it is Bohort, not Hector, who comes up with
the scheme to save the queen's life. Whereas the long version contrasts
Bohort's impassioned plea to rescue Guinevere with Hector's sensible plan
of action, both cousins are flattened in the abbreviation, at some cost to

narrative coherence:[29] after pressing Lancelot to propose a plan ("Or covient que vous esgardés que nous porrons faire entre nous"), Bohort plows ahead, without a pause, to present his own strategy ("li miels que je i voie . . ."). Similarly, once the abbreviator has written Hector out of the scene, the conclusion, which he retains virtually unchanged, becomes awkward: where the original narrator had Lancelot and Bohort assent to Hector's proposal, the very same closure now signifies that Lancelot and Bohort agree mutually to implement Bohort's plan.

Further evidence of the de-emphasis of Guinevere and the dampening of Lancelot's intense emotions appears a few clauses later in a minor passage describing how a messenger goes to Camelot to inquire about the queen:

91. Lors prent Lancelos un suen escuier, si li dist: "Va t'en droit a Kamaalot et fai tant que tu saiches les noveles de madame la reïne et que l'en voldra fere de li; et se l'en l'a jugiee a mort, si le nos vien dire hastivement; car por peinne ne por travaill que nos doions avoir de lui rescorre, ne seroit il pas lessié qu'ele ne fust de mort guerie a nos pooirs." Lors se part li vallez de Lancelot et s'en va seur son roncin la plus droite voie qu'il pot vers Kamaalot, et fet tant qu'il vient a la cort le roi Artu.

151. Puis envoient .i. garçon a Kamaalot pour savoir que on voldra faire de la roïne.

In the long version, Lancelot sends his own squire. His instructions, given in direct discourse, anticipate the drama of Guinevere's harsh treatment at the hands of Agravain and Arthur, which will be recounted in the following chapter; they also end with a fervent vow to rescue Guinevere, however difficult that might prove. Our abbreviator, with an economical *emphasis* that Geoffrey of Vinsauf would approve, reduces the instructions and journey to a single bland sentence. The messenger, now sent anonymously by Lancelot's party as a group, has been downgraded to a *garçon*, and Lancelot's affirmation has vanished, along with the foreshadowing of upcoming scenes that appear only in the long version. Two paragraphs later, however, the abbreviator neglects to keep his version consistent, for he has Lancelot rush forward to hear the news from Camelot "si tost com il vit que *ses messages* retourna" (§ 158), a clause little different from the equivalent phrase in the long version.

So far we have seen how, by rewriting even apparently minor passages and introducing changes of various types into major scenes, our abbreviator is reshaping *La Mort Artu*. I now wish to describe briefly his revisions of the episodes following the *flagrant délit*, which are too long to quote here. The short version continues to de-emphasize Guinevere and cut psychological motivation by eliminating most references to Arthur's anguish and anger; it also favors action in the skirmish at the stake over deliberative dialogue, whether at Arthur's court or among Lancelot's companions. By backgrounding the royal couple, the abbreviator focuses his attention almost exclusively on setting up the tragic mishap that will touch off the war between the clans of Logres and Benoïc: the death of Gauvain's three brothers, especially his beloved Gaheriet, at the hands of Lancelot and his men.

The most striking evidence of Guinevere's lessened importance occurs in the account of what happens at Camelot after Lancelot leaves the queen in her chamber.[30] In a series of colorful scenes in the long version, Guinevere is seized by Agravain, reviled and threatened in shameful fashion, and then brought before Arthur, who orders Lancelot's arrest. When an extensive search fails to locate Lancelot, a frustrated Arthur determines to avenge himself doubly on the queen. He asks his barons to decide how she should die, but King Yon demurs, claiming that custom forbids issuing a death sentence after the hour of *none*. Having agreed to wait until morning, Arthur spends the night grieving so deeply that he neither eats nor drinks; he refuses to have the queen brought before him. Early the next day Agravain and two of his brothers, with Arthur's support, pressure the other barons to rule that the queen's adultery should be punished by death at the stake. Gauvain refuses to witness the death of the lady who has most honored him; to protest against *ceste desloiauté*, he renounces the fiefs he holds from Arthur and leaves the court, "si grant duel faisant com s'il veïst devant li mort tout le monde." Arthur, distracted by something else, makes no response to Gauvain, indeed does not even notice his departure. A huge fire is lit. As the queen is led forth, the people bewail her plight and accuse the king of *desloiauté* (ed. Frappier, §§ 92–93), a scene powerfully reminiscent of Iseut's condemnation in Béroul's *Tristan*, as Frappier indicated (*Étude*, 191–93).

Our abbreviator has condensed these vivid, emotionally charged scenes to a few sentences of dry narration, almost entirely in indirect discourse. He accelerates the judgment scene by cutting out the search for Lancelot: here the king orders *tantost* that Guinevere be sentenced, whereupon Mordret and Agravain, without consulting any other barons, recommend that she be burned; King Yon, that fiercely independent and compassionate jurist,[31] has been eliminated. While a brief account of Gauvain's surrender of his fiefs is maintained, it loses some of its psychological depth with the deletion of his moving declaration of loyalty to the queen; his withdrawal from Camelot is only implied, not described as occurring while his preoccupied uncle looks elsewhere. The elaborate crowd scene in which Guinevere is led before the sorrowful populace has been excised, too. Clearly, the abbreviator aims to move to the pivotal skirmish at the stake as fast as possible. As a result, his desire to maintain what he considers the indispensable elements of the plot, together with the need to cut significant amounts of dialogue, overrides the original author's interest in legal procedures and intertextual play.[32] Also sacrificed are a sensitive depiction of Arthur's ambivalence about Guinevere's guilt and a sympathetic portrayal of the queen as the victim of Arthur's traitorous nephews—all as a consequence of the psychological simplification that the abbreviator either favors or is constrained to impose on the romance. Guinevere is reduced to providing a pretext for conflict; neither she nor those who react to her plight are fully realized as characters in the condensed scenes. On the other hand, much of the dialogue that the abbreviator retains highlights Gaheriet: his reluctance to take part in Guinevere's punishment, Agravain's insistence that Arthur compel Gaheriet to join the escort that will oversee her execution, and the ensuing discussion between the two brothers as Gaheriet continues to refuse to fight Lancelot or to countenance Guinevere's death up to the moment when Lancelot's men ambush Agravain's party. The short version focuses, then, on the psychological conflict in Gaheriet and, to a lesser degree, in Gauvain, probably in preparation for the crucial skirmish at the stake.

By contrast, our abbreviator seldom intervenes in the relatively brief account of this battle; he keeps, with few reductions, the sequence and wording of the various combats through Lancelot's slaying of an unhelmeted and therefore unrecognizable Gaheriet. The only significant difference is that it is Lancelot, rather than Bohort, who kills Guerrehet. Although this change occurs in one zeta manuscript (R) as well as in the short version and may be due to a *bourdon*, its effect is to enhance Lancelot's offenses against Gauvain's family.

As in the aftermath of the *flagrant délit* scene, however, the dialogues that follow the skirmish are severely abridged; the abbreviator has employed similar procedures, with strikingly similar consequences. A conversation between Lancelot and Guinevere is greatly shortened, and throughout the rest of the scene the queen remains silent in the background. The recognition exchange, in which first Bohort, then Hector assures Lancelot that he has indeed killed Gaheriet, is compressed so that only Hector speaks those lines. Lancelot expresses no special grief nor love for Gaheriet—emotions emphasized in the long version by direct discourse and a narratorial aside; also, as before, he foresees the war to come only in terms of Gauvain's enmity, not Arthur's anger. Bohort, for his part, worries more about seeking refuge ("si prendons garde ou nous irons," §154) than protecting the queen. Once again we see Guinevere de-emphasized, Bohort flattened and made more interchangeable with Hector, and the politico-social tensions between Lancelot and Arthur's family simplified. Set against such significant modifications of the psychology and meaning of these dialogues, the abbreviator's relative respect for the integrity of the combat scene suggests either that that type of scene was particularly pleasing to him and his public or that he recognized its pivotal importance in the romance and chose to transmit the whole with few alterations, as he did with Lancelot's farewell to Logres.

Before concluding, I should like to mention briefly two stylistic traits that recur in the abridged redaction. One is a more frequent use of adverbs denoting speed than one finds in Frappier's text. *Tantost, maintenant,* and *tout droit* often serve in the short version to reinforce the acceleration in narrative tempo resulting from the abbreviation. A dense, rather slow-moving story is first shortened, then deliberately speeded up. By contrast, our abbreviator lengthens the narrative slightly as he almost compulsively inserts phrases in apposition to anchor proper names and substitutes proper names for common nouns indicating relationships, as if to remind his readers of the identity and lineage of even major characters. Thus, the simple title in the warning uttered by one of Agravain's spies, "Sire, par deça vient *messire Lancelos*" (ed. Frappier, §89), is lengthened in the short redaction to *mesire Lanselos del Lac* (§147).[33] An unqualified *Agravains* (ed. Frappier, §90) becomes, in the short version, *Agravains, li freres monsignour Gavain* (§148) when Lancelot explains to Guinevere, who surely needs no such identification, how they were betrayed. In the Vulgate *Boorz—tout court*—who urgently awaits Lancelot's return from his tryst with the queen, hears how *Agravains et si dui frere* have trapped his kinsman (ed. Frappier, §90), while in the abridgment Lancelot comes home to tell *Boort son cousin* that *Agravains et Guerrehés et Mordrés* have spied on him and Guinevere (§150). Similarly, when *la gent le roi Artu* flee in disarray after Gaheriet's death, their pursuers, characterized in the long version by a demonstrative pronoun with a relative clause as *cil qui les suivoient* (ed. Frappier, §95), are nominalized in the short version as *Lanselos et li sien* (§154).[34]

All these observations on abbreviation as rewriting raise a host of intriguing questions; indeed that was the goal of this preliminary analysis, so, in the absence of a complete critical edition of the abridged version, I shall end with questions instead of answers. For instance, with reference to the naming of characters, could our abbreviator have been writing for an audience that lacked the "infallible" memory Vinaver so eloquently postulated?[35] Or could the flattening of secondary characters and the acceleration of the narrative have made such tags necessary? More broadly, what is the overall effect of the more direct, accelerated narrative on the magnificent interlace Vinaver described? Does abbreviation produce a truly different type of prose romance operating under a radically new poetics? Or is the short version of *La Mort Artu* merely, or chiefly, what Rychner would have labeled a "dégradation"?

NOTES

1. *Contribution à l'étude des fabliaux: variantes, remaniements, dégradation*, 2 vols., Université de Neuchâtel, Recueil de travaux publiés par la Faculté des Lettres (Neuchâtel: Faculté des Lettres; Geneva: Droz, 1960).

2. "Un scribe champenois devant un texte normand: Guiot copiste de Wace," *Mélanges de langue et de littérature du moyen âge et de la Renaissance offerts à Jean Frappier*, Publications Romanes et Françaises (Geneva: Droz, 1970), II, 1139–54.

3. "Literary Problems of Hagiography in Old French," *Medievalia et Humanistica*, n.s. 6 (1976), 117–30.

4. "Espace du texte, espace du manuscrit: les manuscrits du *Lancelot-Graal*," *Ecritures*, 2 (Paris: Le Sycomore, 1985), 95–116.

5. *The Romance of the Rose and Its Medieval Readers: Interpretation, Reception, Manuscript Transmission* (Cambridge: Cambridge University Press, 1993).

6. The stemma and the most detailed descriptions of the manuscripts appear in Frappier's first edition of the romance, *La Mort le Roi Artu: roman du XIIIe siècle* (Paris: Droz, 1936), pp. ix–lviii. Frappier subsequently published a slightly revised text, with an abbreviated introduction and a greatly reduced selection of variants, in the Textes Littéraires Français (Geneva: Droz, 1954; 2d ed., 1956; 3rd ed., 1959). On manuscripts and studies of the *Lancelot-Grail* cycle, see also Brian Woledge, *Bibliographie des romans et nouvelles en prose française antérieurs à 1500*, Publications Romanes et Françaises (Geneva: Droz, 1954), pp. 71–79; *Supplément 1954–1973*, PRF (Geneva: Droz, 1975), pp. 50–59.

7. Paris: Droz, 1936.

8. Control manuscripts: Paris, B.N. fr. 342 (*D*), B.N. fr. 120 (*O*), B.N. fr. 344 (*R*), B.N. nouv. acq. fr. 1119 (*Z*); Rome, Vatican Library, Palatinus Latinus 1967 (*V*); Bonn, University Library 526 (*B*); London, British Library, Royal 19.C.XIII (*W*). Frappier explains his policy for using these controls in the 1936 introduction, pp. lxv–lxvi. Earlier James Douglas Bruce edited *D* very conservatively: *Mort Artu: An Old French Prose Romance of the XIIIth Century* (Halle: Niemeyer, 1910).

9. For Frappier's assessment of *A*'s proclivities, see his 1936 introduction, pp. lxiv–lxv. In his review of Frappier's edition, Ferdinand Lot criticized the scribe still more harshly: "le plus négligent, le plus paresseux des copistes." According to Lot, *A*'s only virtue is his inability to innovate: "[ce manuscrit] est incapable du plus simple enjolivement pour la simple raison qu'il est dû à un scribe plus que négligent, paresseux: il saute des mots, des phrases, des lignes entières, moins par distraction que pour épargner sa peine" (*Romania*, 64 [1938], 125, 129).

10. Manuscripts comprising the zeta family: Lyon, Palais des Arts 77 (*K*); Paris, B.N. fr. 344 (*R*) and fr. 1119 (*Z*); London, British Library, Additional 17.443 (*M¹*); Oxford, Bodleian Library, Rawlinson D.899 (*O²*). Frappier used two manuscripts from this family as controls (*R* and *Z*) and gives some variants from them.

11. Frappier's list of definitive alterations appears on pp. xlix–l. On the short version of the Prose *Lancelot*, see esp. Alexandre Micha's comments in the introduction to his edition, *Lancelot: Roman en prose du XIIIe siècle*, 9 vols. (Geneva: Droz, 1978–83), I, xii–xiv, and the texts in vol. 3. See also Micha, "Le Départ en Sorelois: Réflexions sur deux versions," *Mélanges de linguistique romane et de philologie médiévale offerts à M. Maurice Delbouille* (Gembloux: J. Duculot, 1964), II, 495–507; and Elspeth Kennedy, "The Two Versions of the False Guinevere Episode in the Old French Prose *Lancelot*," *Romania*, 77 (1956), 94–104.

12. The variants from *B* are neither complete nor totally reliable, even in the 1936 edition; occasionally they imply that *B* agrees with zeta manuscripts when *B*'s reading is distinct. In the passages under discussion here, for example, *B* is not accurately represented in variants at 89.15, 89.22, 90.2, 90.31–33, 96.8 (references to page and line number from the 1936 ed.). These are very minor flaws in an excellent edition, more than offset by Frappier's thoroughness in providing the full text of *B* in numerous passages where the abridged version diverges from both the zeta family and the Vulgate archetype; I have relied on the 1936 variants for readings in the zeta family and *T*. Note that Frappier also regarded *B* as a trustworthy witness to the author's precise observance of the two-case declension and used it to correct some of *A*'s morphological irregularities (lxviii); see, for instance, § 48, n. 23, where *B*'s *Morgue* supports the nominative form of a name that even *B* declines inconsistently elsewhere.

13. *The Vulgate Version of the Arthurian Romances Edited from Manuscripts in the British Museum*, 8 vols. (Washington, D.C.: Carnegie Institution, 1909–16; rpt. in 7 vols. New York: AMS, 1979).

14. On the defects of the Sommer edition, see Frappier, 1936, pp. lx–lxi, which reproduces much of Albert Pauphilet's critique from "Sur des manuscrits de la *Mort d'Artus*," *Mélanges de philologie et d'histoire offerts à M. Antoine Thomas* (Paris: Champion, 1927), pp. 342–43. See also E. Brugger's review, *Zeitschrift für Französische Sprache und Literatur*, 36, No. 2 (1910), 190–204, and Micha, *Lancelot*, I, xiii–xiv.

15. For *La Mort Artu*, S^1 will serve as secondary control because the *P* text is illegible on several folios and is marred by two long lacunae. The miniatures in the Bonn manuscript have been studied by Alison M. Stones: "The Illustration of the French Prose *Lancelot* in Belgium, Flanders, and Paris: 1250–1320," Diss. University of London, 1970–71.

16. The sample narrative for this reduction was the well-known story of the "Snow-Child"; see Edmond Faral, *Les Arts poétiques du XIIe et du XIIIe siècle: Recherches et documents sur la technique littéraire du moyen âge* (Paris: Champion, 1913; rpt. 1962), pp. 219–20; that same example is amplified in the *Documentum*, pp. 279–80. Note how closely this procedure of intense reduction corresponds to what Gérard Genette calls "*condensé, abrégé, résumé* ou *sommaire*"; see *Palimpsestes: La littérature au second degré* (Paris: Seuil, 1982), pp. 279–84.

17. *Documentum*, § 41, in Faral, p. 279.

18. Translation by Roger P. Parr, Geoffrey of Vinsauf, *Documentum de modo et arte dictandi et versificandi (Instruction in the Method of Speaking and Versifying)*, Mediaeval Philosophical Texts in Translation (Milwaukee: Marquette University Press, 1968), p. 54.

19. Françoise Vieillard, "La traduction du *De excidio Troiae* de Darès le Phrygien par Jofroi de Waterford," *Bien dire et bien aprandre*, no. 10: *Troie au moyen âge* (Lille: Centre d'études médiévales et dialectales de Lille III, 1992), p. 187. See also Vieillard, "La traduction du *De excidio Troiae* de Darès le Phrygien par Jean de Flixecourt," in *Medieval Codicology, Iconography, Literature, and Translation: Studies for Keith Val Sinclair*, ed. Peter Rolfe Monks and D.D.R. Owen (Leiden: Brill, 1994), pp. 284–95.

20. *The Rise of Romance* (New York: Oxford University Press, 1971), pp. 65–89.

21. Curtius, "Brevity as an Ideal of Style," *European Literature and the Latin*

Middle Ages, trans. Willard R. Trask (New York: Harper, 1963), pp. 487–94; Kelly, *The Art of Medieval French Romance* (Madison: University of Wisconsin Press, 1992), esp. pp. 58–61, 64, 178, 284. On abbreviation in rhetoric and romance, see also Karen Pratt, *Meister Otte's Eraclius As an Adaptation of Eracle by Gautier d'Arras*, Göppinger Arbeiten zur Germanistik (Göppingen: Kümmerle, 1987), pp. 448–56.

22. To a certain extent the overall result of the abbreviation in *La Mort Artu* corresponds in Genette's typology of textual reduction to "*la concision*, qui se donne pour règle d'abréger un texte sans en supprimer aucune partie thématiquement significative, mais en le récrivant dans un style plus concis, et donc en produisant à nouveaux frais un nouveau texte, qui peut à la limite ne plus conserver un seul mot du texte original. Aussi la concision jouit-elle, dans son produit, d'un statut *d'œuvre* que n'atteint pas l'excision: on parlera d'une version abrégée de *Robinson Crusoé*, sans toujours pouvoir nommer l'abréviateur" (271).

23. The Vulgate text, quoted from Frappier's third TLF edition, appears in the left column; on the right, that of the abridged version from my forthcoming edition. Text common to both the long and short redactions is printed in roman type; passages occurring in only one redaction, in italics; passages abridged in the short version, in boldface.

24. See n. 11 above. I use "chapter" for the major narrative divisions of the romance, whose boundaries are signaled by codicological and textual markers. Paratextually a miniature appears at the head of each chapter in the Bonn manuscript for example; in print Frappier uses three asterisks to set off chapters. Textually every chapter begins with a phrase like "Or dit li contes" and concludes with a sentence that both marks closure and announces the subject of the next segment of the narrative.

25. The disappearance of the unnamed knight who takes over Joyous Guard—admittedly a very minor character—is paralleled in the downgrading of another minor character, the Count of Kalet, at whose castle Lancelot, Guinevere, and their supporters spend the night on their way from Camelot to Joyous Guard. In the long version the count expresses such great love for Lancelot that "[il] li promist a aidier contre touz homes, neïs encontre le roi Artu" (§ 97). Our abbreviator not only shortens the description of the count's hospitality, but he also plays down the theme of the intense personal loyalty to Lancelot that overrides the count's feudal bonds. In the short version the count simply offers his guest a quid pro quo: forty knights from his household in exchange for a favor Lancelot once did for him. Arthur is not mentioned, nor does the count propose giving the very castle of Kalet to Lancelot and Guinevere. On the tension between feudal obligations and sentimental bonds in *La Mort Artu*, see Frappier, *Étude*, pp. 337–41, and R. Howard Bloch, "The Death of Arthur and the Waning of the Feudal Age (*La Mort le Roi Artu*)," *Orbis Litterarum*, 29 (1974), 291–305. Norris Lacy offers an illuminating discussion of both analogical composition and linear perspective in "Spatial Form in the *Mort Artu*," *Symposium*, 31 (1977), 337–45. The extent to which the abbreviator reconfigures the thematic and analogical patterning of the romance invites further study.

26. A more comprehensive study of the recasting of text and character must also reckon with the principal "variante-mère" that sets *A* against all the other manuscripts: the passage in which Gauvain tells Arthur and Guinevere that Lancelot has fallen in love with the damsel of Escalot. See the texts and analysis in Frappier, 1936, pp. xxxviii–xli.

27. Cf. Lot's suggestive remark: "le caractère de cette contraction du récit trahit un dessein systématique" (*Romania*, 64 [1938], 128). Although Lot probably meant systematically shortening the romance, our abbreviator may well have had other purposes as well.

28. *Étude sur le Lancelot en prose*, Bibliothèque de l'École des Hautes Études (Paris: Champion, 1918), p. 276, n. 2.

29. Frappier emphasizes the distinctly different characterizations of the five main protagonists (Lancelot, Bohort, Arthur, Gauvain, Guinevere) in the full version and argues for the individuality of even the secondary characters: "ils ne sont pas

interchangeables" (*Étude*, p. 333); see 324–33.

30. One of the major "condensations" signaled by Frappier occurs in this chapter: "les circonstances du jugement et de la condamnation de la reine sont rapidement résumées." Also distinctive in this section is a chapter break that occurs in all manuscripts of the abridged version and only in the abridged version (1936, p. xlix).

31. See Frappier, *Étude*, p. 334.

32. On the author's interest in legal procedure, see Frappier, *Étude*, pp. 337–42; on the juridical implications of the "capture in the act" in the *Mort Artu*, see Bloch, *Medieval French Literature and Law* (Berkeley: University of California Press, 1977), pp. 59–62.

33. The same expansion occurs in Gaheriet's question to Agravain: "cuidiez vos que g'i soie venuz por moi mesler a *Lancelot*, se il vouloit la reïne rescorre?" (ed. Frappier, §93); "quidiés vous que je i soie venus pour meller moi a *monsignour Lanselot del Lac* se aventure l'en aportoit pour rescourre la roïne?" (§153). Italics in all illustrative quotations are mine.

34. Counterexamples do exist, but they need to be examined with care. For instance Gaheriet and Agravain, after being named in immediately preceding sentences, become *li dui frere* in a summing up that introduces the abridged version of the skirmish but does not occur at the beginning of a paragraph (§153); in the long version, the recapitulation opens a new paragraph, so the brothers are formally named: "Tant alerent parlant *entre Agravain et Gaheriet*" (ed. Frappier, §94).

35. *The Rise of Romance*, p. 83.